Purchased for the
Lapp Children by
their Dad at Point
Loma, California on a
very special Day,
September 14, 1978.

SHIPS AND THE SEA

SHIPS AND THE SEA
A CHRONOLOGICAL REVIEW

By DUNCAN HAWS

Thomas Y. Crowell Company, Inc.

CONTENTS

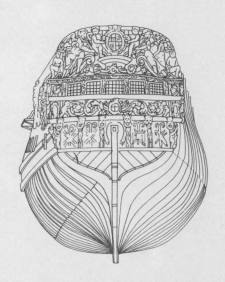
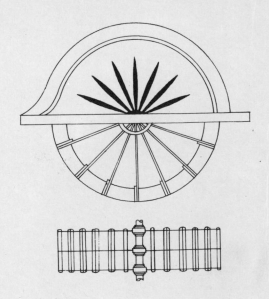

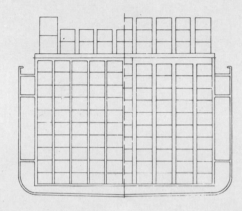

First published in the United States of America in 1975 by THOMAS Y. CROWELL COMPANY, INC., New York, New York.

Published simultaneously in Canada by Fitzhenry & White-head Limited, Toronto.

Manufactured in Spain.

Library of Congress Catalog Card Number: 75-13686

ISBN: 0-690-00968-2

1 2 3 4 5 6 7 8 9 10

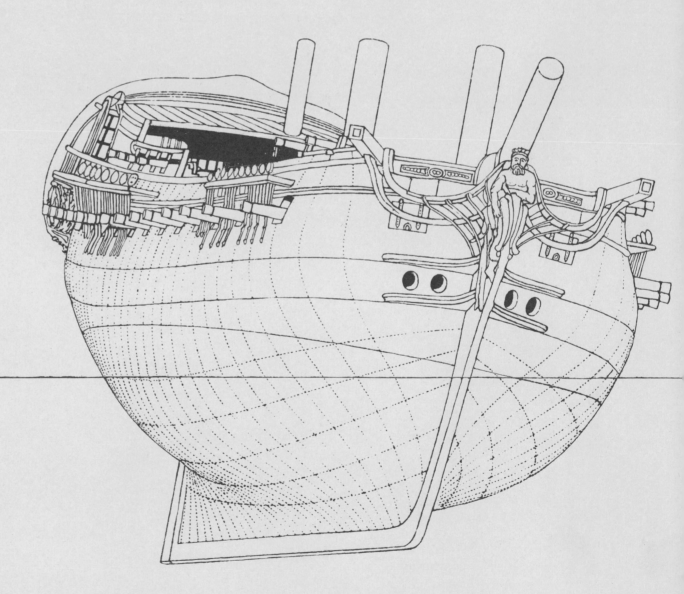

SHIPS AND THE SEA has been designed and produced by AB NORDBOK, Gothenburg, Sweden, in close cooperation with the author, Duncan Haws, and a number of nautical experts and institutions all over the world who have collaborated with the Nordbok art and editorial departments under the supervision of Einar Engelbrektson and Turlough Johnston.

Design: Tommy Berglund.

Other members of the Nordbok staff closely associated with the book were Kerstin M. Stålbrand, editor, and Syed Mumtaz Ahmad, artist.

Artwork: Syed Mumtaz Ahmad, Terry Allen, Leif Andersson, Toivo Andersson, Tommy Berglund, Bill Easter, Curt Edvardsson, Henry Forsell, Nils Hermansson, Bertil Karlsson, Hans Linder, David Penney, Holger Rosenblad, Spectron Artists, Tecknargården, Roland Thorbjörnsson, John Wood Associates.

The author and publishers would like to express their gratitude to those who have helped them with advice, information, and material, especially the following:

American Institute of Nautical Archaeology
George F. Bass
Charles Barren
British Museum
Compagnie Générale Transatlantique
The 'Cutty Sark' Society
Musée de la Marine, Paris
National Maritime Museum, Greenwich
Scheepvaartsmuseum, Amsterdam
Sjöfartsmuseum, Gothenburg
Sjöhistoriska Muséet, Wasavarvet, Stockholm
Tor Line

The illustrations on pages 25-28 are based on drawings by Richard Schlecht in *Archaeology Beneath the Sea* by George F. Bass (Walker and Co., New York, 1975).

The reproductions on pages 147 and 160 have been provided by the Mary Evans Photo Library.

The illustrations on pages 217–220 are reproduced by kind permission of the Exxon Corporation and *The Lamp*.

Certain of the illustrations in this book have been reproduced by kind permission of Tre Tryckare AB, whose copyright they are.

preface

Nothing has been more noble, more daring, and more demanding of man than his slow conquest of the vastness of the seas. The conquest of the air and of near-space may seem more spectacular, but the technology by which that conquest was made was founded when, in the early mists of time, primitive man first launched himself upon the waters. Without that first tentative step, that other small step in space might never have been taken.

Three quarters of the earth's surface are covered by salt water. The immense oceans are fed by the streams and rivers, small or mighty, slow or swift. It is not surprising, therefore, that the earliest records of most societies include references to waterborne vessels.

Among man's many achievements, the conquest of the sea, the ability to build, navigate, sail, and propel ships in all their multiplicity of design, stands as a monument to the ingenuity and rugged determination of mankind.

Yet, for almost seven thousand years, the story of the sea, and man's relationship with it, was the story of manpower alone: how muscle was needed to propel the raft or canoe in slack water, and how it was needed even when the sail ousted the oar.

The Romans added a bowsprit to their ships, and to this attached a small balancing spritsail—thereby emulating what the Chinese had done over five centuries earlier. The Vikings, a thousand years ago, used the single square sail that the Egyptians had used two thousand years previously.

The rigging and sails of Columbus's ship, SANTA MARIA, were virtually of the same pattern as those of the MAYFLOWER, used by the Pilgrim Fathers. After some moments of wonderment, and a few trial tugs at the braces, the crew of Drake's GOLDEN HIND could doubtlessly have sailed the CUTTY SARK. Only the clipper's size, and the fineness of her hull, would have astounded the sixteenth-century sea-dogs.

For thousands of years, sail had a single, limitless, unchanging task: that of catching the wayward breeze or the driving wind. Yet, from 1800 A.D. onwards, that is, in considerably less than two hundred years, mechanical means of propulsion have improved from an experimental infancy to a sophisticated maturity. In so doing, the face of seagoing vessels has been changed beyond recognition.

If the engineer of the SIRIUS of 1838 were put in the engine-room of any steamship of the 1920s, he would be lost. Move on but another brief fifty years, and the engineer of the 'twenties would be confounded—and perhaps dumbfounded—by the specialist range of today's ships.

It is the endeavour of this book to trace the splendid story of ships and the sea from its humble beginnings to its present-day significance.

chapter 1

Ecology, that science which, in part, examines the reaction of man in his environment, postulates two basic assertions:

Primitive man, confronted with the same necessities and having the same means available, will react in the same manner;

and:

When the means available do not change, the methods of achieving the necessities do not change.

Using these basic assertions, modern man can deduce that his earliest ancestors built and used craft similar in many ways to the simplest craft made today by primitive societies.

Thus, in the way that the shape of modern man has remained unchanged for thousands of years, so the form of the earliest types of single-manned craft has remained basically unchanged. Indeed, throughout the world, and not only in primitive societies, such single-manned craft are even now in common use. On many a reed and rush-edged African lake, bundles of papyrus, bound with strips of leather, carry man today as they have done since time immemorial. On the present-day shallow lakes of southern Sardinia, reed rafts, identical with their counterparts in Africa, are used by fishermen and bird-catchers. In South America,

the light balsa wood raft is still used, looking remarkably like its African relation.

These lake craft are a feature of still waters. Primitive man developed a different technique when braving flowing rivers or tidal estuaries. He built canoes.

On the rivers of the world, the split log, with its centre charred out by fire or chopped out by primitive chisels, was, and still is, used as a canoe. In northern latitudes, where sizeable softwood trees are scarce, ancient man lashed together a framework of brushwood spars, and covered the outside with panels of animal skin laced together with strips of hide.

In every instance, primitive man sought to construct the most simple effective waterborne transport. For example, he chose only two ways of propelling his craft when he moved from elemental hand work: that using some sort of pole, perhaps a convenient bamboo, and that using a paddle, perhaps half a large nut husk or a flat slice of wood. The oar does not occur in such simple craft.

The earliest use to which waterborne craft appear to have been put is for fishing or for crossing rivers and fairly narrow stretches of water. It is interesting to note that today's descendants of these primeval craft are still in

use, and for much the same purposes. An example is the bamboo raft of Malaysia, which, because of the simplicity of its design and the ready availability of the essential materials, cannot have changed radically over the centuries. The method of fishing there has certainly remained the same, despite the fact that the primitive plaited leaf-basket has now been replaced by a net.

A different design from that described above was used for craft sailing the Pacific Ocean. This was in order to counter the problem of the rolling surf around the thousands of small islands there. The tall, indigenous palm trees were too slender to be hollowed out and used as canoes. Rafts were far too cumbersome. So the outrigger craft was developed. This consisted of a main hull with either one or two outriggers lashed to the cross-beams. These outriggers provided the stability necessary in order to paddle through rolling waves.

The local environment, again, dictated the design of craft developed in the far northerly latitudes, where the waters are normally so cold that it means certain death to be immersed for more than a few seconds. Open boats and rafts were obviously useless. Man's solution was to design the kayak, a light, skin-covered canoe into which a fisherman could wedge himself through a small hole in the top. A long, double-ended paddle provided the necessary balance.

As the custom of barter became more and more widespread, the need to move goods and cattle as well as people was solved by the construction of bigger rafts. These were sometimes strengthened by the addition of inflated animal skins. Thus, the development of trade was from early times an influence on ship-building, a trend which can be noticed throughout history.

The years 5000 to 3200 B.C. are known to historians of Egypt as the Predynastic Period. This simply means the time before the Pharaohs ruled the land, a time, indeed, when 'Egypt' was not a single kingdom. Many other communities also lived around the shores of the Mediterranean and the Red Sea. There was no written word for the bulk of this period, for the use of hieroglyphics by the Egyptians did not commence until about 3500 B.C. Only oral communication from one generation to the next could be employed to give some idea of the continuity of the community, of its history and traditions, of its mythology, its folklore, its reservoir of story. Ancient history was spoken history. Story-tellers, then as now, had a natural tendency to bring their tales up to date, so that a story matured considerably in the telling. Indeed, at a time when a hundred years could span four or five generations, there was little point in trying to be precise about events that might have had origins perhaps one or even two thousand years before. Nevertheless, there is a point in recorded history where we suddenly become aware of ships. The chronicle of their story can begin at that point. This critical date is somewhere around the year 3500 B.C.

The earliest permanent record of ships occurs on the walls of tombs and on decorated urns and vases. The record takes the form of very crude illustrations. Sometimes they are found scratched on walls or on slabs of stone as though someone had passed an idle moment doodling. The impressions gained from these illustrations, which may be inspected in several museums, are somewhat hazy; for both the scale and the detail of the illustrations are as much distorted, or incomplete, as are the hesitant drawings of a child.

These early recordings of ships in Egypt undoubtedly prove the importance of the River Nile to Egyptian life, an importance that continues to this very day. The annual flooding of the Nile ensures that the land is watered and that it is also fertilized by silt and mud. The river has been a means of communication that has been of immense practical importance ever since man first settled in the Nile valley. Almost every day, for several hours, the wind blows directly from the north, and it is then possible to sail up river. Since the Nile flows in a northerly direction, boats can either drift or be paddled down river. This phenomenon has

led to the use of the Nile throughout recorded history, and probably before it, as the highway of Egypt. Indeed, in hieroglyphics, the ancient Egyptian sign for 'southwards' is a ship with a sail, whilst that for 'northwards' is a ship without a sail.

Egypt has never been well-forested. What trees it has are small, such as the acacia, the tamarisk, and the fig. In ancient Egypt, however, the green papyrus reed, *Cyperus papyrus*, grew profusely. It does not grow there now, but in those days its stems were made into paper, and its rushes were, for thousands of years, the chief material used in the building of river craft. To this day, in areas where papyrus still grows, the construction of the hull has remained unchanged. It consists of a central core of papyrus, along each side of which are bound several layers of long, thick tresses of papyrus, which give width without increasing the draught. There are no raised sides, and the top of the craft is more or less flat. In fact, the boat has no keel-stem or stern-post. It is a near relative of the pure raft. The deck shelter supports are held by being driven into the compressed rushes and lashed into position. These reed hulls last only one or two seasons before rot or waterlogging sets in. The balsa wood canoes of South America suffer from a similar characteristic.

Of course, Ancient Egypt was not alone in the use of ships. Similar papyrus craft were known on the Euphrates, in present-day Iraq, where the equally primitive cufa was also built.

According to Phoenician legend, the historian Sanchoniathon gives the credit for the idea of using wood in order to build ships to Onous. Unfortunately, it is not known when either of these Phoenicians lived.

Trading developed gradually over the next two thousand years. Many nations, notably Phoenicia, Greece, Rome, and Crete evolved their own seafaring traditions. During the summer months, their ships sailed the full length and breadth of the Mediterranean Sea, trading wherever they made landfall. Some intrepid mariners ventured even farther afield. It is recorded that, in 609 B.C., a Phoenician expedition left Suez with the intention of sailing with the land continuously to the starboard until it came to an end. Four years later, the expedition arrived back at Alexandria, having sailed right round Africa.

There is no record of the first use of a ship as a fighting vessel. However, the first pictorial evidence of a seagoing naval expedition is contained on an Egyptian bas-relief dating from about 2600 B.C. It shows the vessels in the service of the Pharaoh Sahure.

The rise of the Greek and the Roman empires led to the building of bigger and more effective warships and troop transports. Trade between the various outposts of the Roman Empire increased the demand for seaworthy merchant ships, under the control of captains skilled in the rules of navigation and seafaring. Recent

underwater archaeological finds have vastly increased our knowledge of the design of these ships, and also of the way of life of the men who sailed in them. It was from such an archaeological find that it is known that nails were used in shipbuilding as early as 300 B.C.

Progress in shipping received a marked impetus with the adoption of the *Lex Rhodia*. This was a set of laws governing conduct at sea, which was adopted by most of the maritime nations of the then known world. International affairs, both in shipping and in trade, acquired a new status with the adoption of the *Lex Rhodia*.

PRIMITIVE CRAFT

A *The eskimo's kayak is flimsy but watertight. The skin panels, which are stretched over the framework, must have enough 'give' in them to take a sharp knock against the ice without splitting.*

B *The American Indian's canoe has a wooden frame covered with hide or, in some cases, bark. A single-bladed paddle is used.*

C *The coracle is found in Ireland, Wales, and Scotland.*

D *The log canoe is found on rivers all over the world.*

E *A bark canoe from British Columbia. The bark is stitched onto the framework.*

F *A balsa canoe with a sail, from Lake Titicaca, South America.*

G *A West African canoe with sail and stabilizing outrigger.*

H *The papyrus boat is still used on Lake Tchad in Africa, where it usually lasts only one season before the reeds deteriorate.*

I *The cufa was described by Herodotus almost 2,500 years ago. It is still in use today on the rivers Tigris and Euphrates. It consists of a skin-covered wooden frame.*

J *The bamboo raft from the Malay Archipelago is used for fishing.*

A *A boat on an Egyptian vase of the fourth millenium B.C. An armed warrior stands on one of the two cabins. There are what appear to be numerous oars, as well as a leafy branch in the bow.*

B *A boat illustration, from a rock carving in the Wadi Hammamat, Egypt, fourth millenium B.C.*

C *A crescent-shaped boat, also from the Wadi Hammamat, fourth millenium B.C.*

D *The earliest ship-illustration known, Hierakonpolis, c. 5000 B.C.*

E *The Nubian Desert ship, c. 5000 B.C.*

F *Boat on a fourth-millenium Egyptian vase, with a design similar to that of illustration A.*

G *Fishing skiffs from the tomb of Tiyi, an official of the Fifth Dynasty, c. 2500 B.C.*

H *Binding a papyrus boat, c. 2800 B.C.*

I *Another ship from the carvings found in the Nubian Desert.*

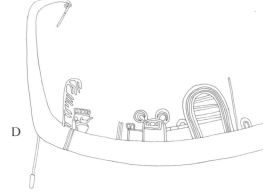

D

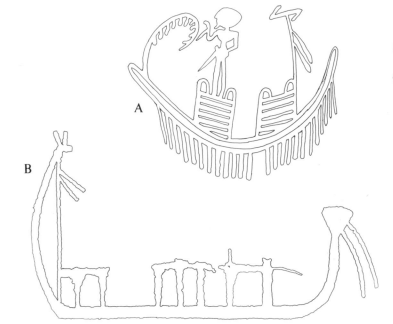

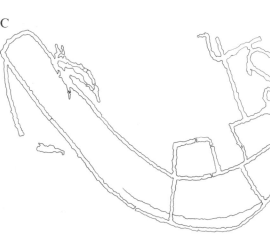

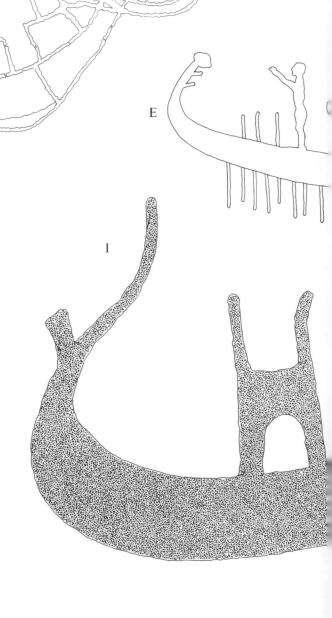

I

c. 5000 B.C.

The earliest known ship-illustration dates from this time. It is to be found at Hierakonpolis in Egypt. Patently, the ship is built from papyrus. It has the now-familiar 'scorpion's sting' type stern and the sloping bow. The steering-oar is worked from the port side, and in the normal position just forward of centre is a covered shelter. Two paddles are depicted.

c. 5000 B.C.

From approximately the same time comes the earliest illustration of a ship with a sail. This ship is painted on the outside of a funerary vase unearthed from near Luxor. The sail of the ship is fixed to a single mast. There is a shelter aft, and the high, ornate prow is decorated with what appears to be a bird, although it could well be a fish. Normally, the shelter would be sited forward of centre. And if this is true of the vase picture, then the ornate 'prow' could actually be the stern. The markings shown then become the steering platform, and the projection the steering-oar. In which case, why is the mast right aft? It should normally be as far forward as possible. Certainly, with the mast

as actually depicted on the vase, the craft would be hard to handle unless it is the type where the steersman adjusts the cut of the sail while steering. Perhaps the shelter is right forward because a passenger sat up front with the oarsman right aft, as with the gondolas of present-day Venice. If this is so, then we also have the earliest known illustration of a passenger ship!

c. 5000 B.C.

A rock carving of a ship also dates from this period. It is to be found in the Nubian Desert. Again, the ship has the typical 'scorpion's tail' or sting. The prow slopes upward and has a horned figurehead. This embellishment was common at the time. The skull and horns of a bull, for example, warned off evil spirits. They also acted as the 'eyes' of the ship. Lastly, they had a religious significance for the crew. The attitude of the man on the carving could be construed as supplicating a god. If so, the shelter might be an altar. The several projections on the carving are not thought to be oars. They could more likely be the artist's attempt to represent water.

The dimensions of the craft, calculated from the approximate height of the human figure, are about 20 foot (6.1 m) in length, and about 4 foot (1.2 m) in width. If one assumes the craft to have had a steering-oar, three paddles, and a couple of attendants, then it would have accommodated some six people.

3400 B.C.

Egyptian history under the rule of the Pharaohs commences with the first king, Narmerza, who united Upper and Lower Egypt to form what the historians call the 'Old Kingdom'. From this date onwards, it is possible to piece together a fair amount of accurate information about the way in which people lived and traded.

About this time, for instance, it is known that the Egyptians raided the coast of Syria in sea-going wooden ships. The vessels were planked, but did not have keel, prow, stern-post, or even ribs. Hulls were constructed by pegging together overlapping lengths of cedar wood with wooden egg-timer-shaped nails, which were driven into holes in the planks. When the wood swelled, the planks became firmly held together. Two ropes strengthened the construc-

tion. One rope was stretched fore-and-aft over the deck stanchions, the other was wrapped tightly round the hull to hold it rigid. The ships had bipod masts with one square sail on a yard-arm. This sail could only be used with a following wind. There is little or no indication of the ability to tack or to sail against the wind. The use of paired steering-oars, needing two or four men to handle them, indicated the weight and size of this type of ship.

There was a considerable number of paddlers, probably up to twenty-four. These took over when the sail was not in use. When that happened, the mast and sail of the craft were lowered into a cradle.

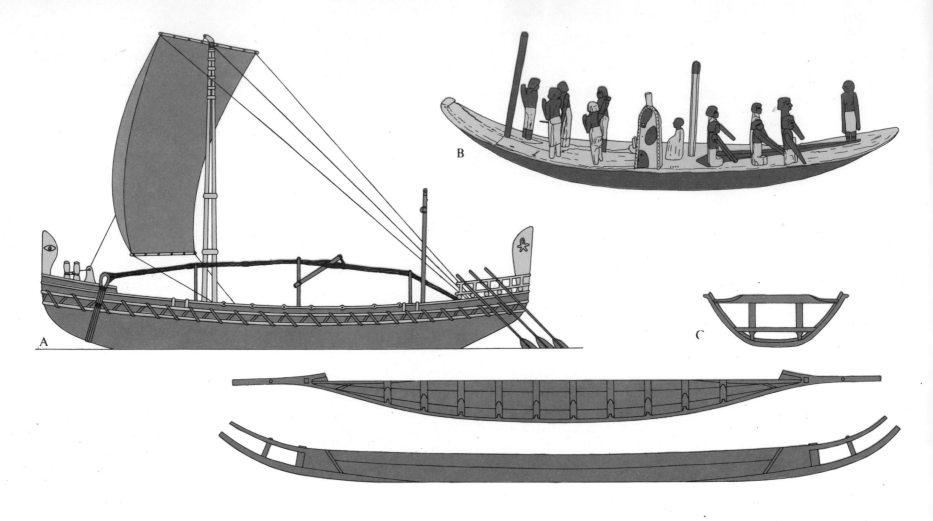

2613 B.C.
In Egypt, the Fourth Dynasty is founded with Sneferu as Pharaoh. He was a great shipbuilder. It is recorded that one of his achievements was the bringing of forty ships filled with cedar wood from Byblos in Phoenicia to Egypt. Indeed, an 'invoice' for cedar wood is the oldest 'shipping document' to survive—from this era! The cedar was used for various building projects, including shipbuilding.

Cheops was the next Pharaoh after Sneferu. He had the first Great Pyramid built. When he died, there were placed in his pyramid tomb the parts of a wooden boat, 160 foot (48.8 m) long and 20 foot (6.1 m) wide. The craft was to have been decked throughout, with paddles for twenty men, but without a mast.

c. 2600 B.C.
At about this time, the Chinese are credited with inventing the compass. It took the form of a piece of ironstone mounted on a bamboo splint floating in a bowl of oil. Ancient Chinese writings contain several references to the compass. Yet here is another mystery. Almost four thousand years after the Chinese invented the compass, Marco Polo visited China and method-

ically recorded all he saw. He was a commentator of repute, and yet nowhere in his stories and records does he mention the use of any instrument to show the direction of north. The sun and the pole-star were still the means for determining north, he records.

c. 2600 B.C.
Pharaoh Sahure sends eight Egyptian ships to raid the coast of Syria. They return carrying many prisoners. A detailed carved relief from Sahure's pyramid clearly depicts the appearance of these ships.

c. 2400 B.C.
The illustrations of this period introduce a new aspect of design, one that is to remain a feature of ship construction for centuries. As the ships became longer, so the tendency for the bow and stern to sag increased. To prevent this, several stout ropes, entwined like elastic, were run from bow to stern over a number of props protruding upright from the deck. The ropes could be tightened by twisting a spar in them, thus correcting any sag in the hull. Another rope—on the Sahure ship, two are shown—ran round the outside of the hull at

deck level. This indicates that ribs and athwartship beams were still not in use. Later, as ships continued to grow in size, the fore-and-aft braces were fastened to an equally stout series of ropes wrapped around the outer planking, fairly close to the extremities of the ship. This technique can be seen in the illustration of ships used in the expedition of Queen Hatshepsut to the Land of Punt.

These fore-and-aft strengtheners can be seen to this day on the shallow-draught Mississippi river boats.

2000-200 B.C.
Seagoing, sail-driven commercial and naval vessels are now commonplace in the Mediterranean. They were sizeable and, compared with the ships of the same time in use in northern Europe, they were also highly sophisticated.

In the far north of Norway, Stone Age rock carvings exist, depicting crude, canoe-like craft. Some experts believe the craft to be snow-sledges, but the drawings persist through the subsequent Bronze Age and into the Iron Age, culminating in the find of a 45-foot (13.7 m) long boat dating from 300 B.C. The site of the find is Hjortspring on the Danish isle of Als.

A *A ship from the fleet of Pharaoh Sahure, c. 2400 B.C.*
B *An Egyptian river boat, c. 2000 B.C.*
C *The Hjortspring boat, c. 300 B.C.*
D *The Chinese of the Hsia Dynasty are credited with the invention of the compass.*
E *An early Scandinavian ship, from a Bronze Age stone carving in Sweden.*
F *Odysseus's ship, from an Attic vase in the British Museum.*

F

D

E

It is clear that the earlier carvings illustrate ribbed canoes covered with hide. They are very similar to canoes still in use in Greenland. However, the Hjortspring boat is covered with wood, not hide, and the covering on the hull is stitched, not planked.

These early Scandinavian craft had a distinctive outline. The keel jutted out fore-and-aft so that the vessel could be carried by four men, two forward and two aft. The carvings and drawings, when they depict oarsmen, do, in fact, illustrate six or seven men.

None of the illustrations includes masts or sails. But in some of the carvings can be seen a mushroom-shaped outline amidships. This has not yet been identified. Björn Landström mentions that, as a child in Finland, he noticed that many sailors took a leafy branch with them in their rowing-boats. With a favourable wind, the leafy branch would be used as a sail. Perhaps that mushroom-shaped outline is the artist's impression of a bush.

1900 B.C.
A canal from Bubastis on the River Nile to Patumos on the Red Sea is constructed by Senusret. This is the early predecessor of the modern Suez Canal. It was built because Egyptian domination of commerce had led to the development and maintenance of fleets in both the Mediterranean and the Red Sea. By this time, Egypt possessed a war fleet also, and manned it with imperial troops. Thus the 45-mile (72.4 km) long "Suez" canal was a military as well as an economic necessity.

c. 1850 B.C.

The first rowing-boats are recorded on the River Nile during the reign of Pharaoh Sestoris III.

1530 B.C.

A thriving seagoing civilization exists in the Pacific Ocean region at this time. A migration eastward reaches Hawaii.

1500 B.C.

Queen Hatshepsut sends an expedition to try to find the legendary Land of Punt. Pictures of the ships used in this expedition can be seen on reliefs in the temple at Deir-el-Bahri. The ships were built at the port of Suez, and sailed in a southerly direction. There is no record of the countries that they visited, but it may be deduced from the cargo with which the expedition returned after a year's absence—gold, ivory, incense, myrrh, and spices—that India might have been reached. However, the route to India would have involved sailing directly into the Indian Ocean after having passed Aden and the island of Socotra, and the practice in those days was to keep land in sight unless sailing from known cape to cape or some other geographical feature. On the other hand, sailing southwards from Suez and keeping land in sight to the starboard would have meant that the expedition made for Ethiopia and East Africa. These, then, are more likely destinations than India.

At this time, too, the Phoenicians, who had their capital at Sidon, the present-day Saida, emerge as a powerful trading nation rather than a military power. They built their ships from the famous cedars of Lebanon, and used a form of construction different from that of the Egyptians. They also used planks of wood held together by wooden toggles, and gave their vessels greater strength than most contemporary boat-builders by including in the construction both bow and stern posts. Furthermore, Phoenician seamen depended mainly on sail for the means of propulsion. A typical crew of four working a merchantman would not include a single oarsman. Vessels were steered by the normal long oar, which was operated from the larboard (port) side. The rudder was not yet in use in the West although Chinese junks were by this time already equipped with the primitive form of rudder.

1200 B.C.

The fleet of Pharaoh Rameses III defeats the combined fleet of the Libyans, Syrians, and Philistines, at Pelusium. The Egyptian craft were a mixture of native and Phoenician ships, with ram-bows, crow's nests, and solid bulwarks, behind which the oarsmen sat secure from arrows and spears. The vessels lacked the fore-and-aft strengthening springer ropes, and, because of the bulwarks, were constructed with ribs. They were, however, flat-bottomed and keel-less.

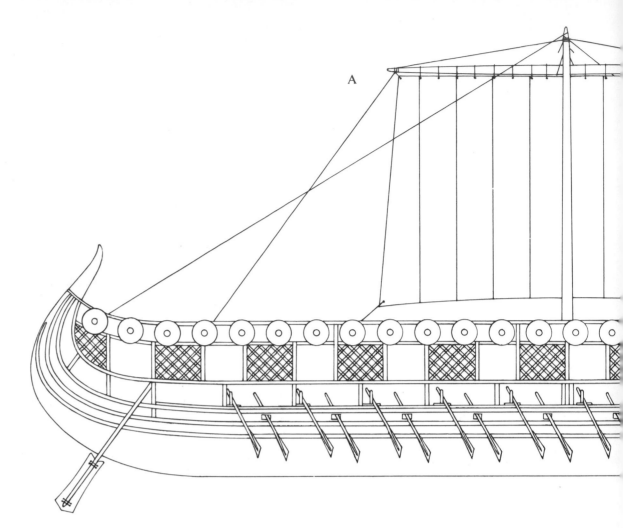

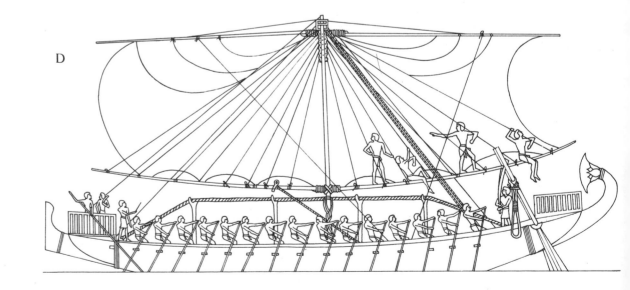

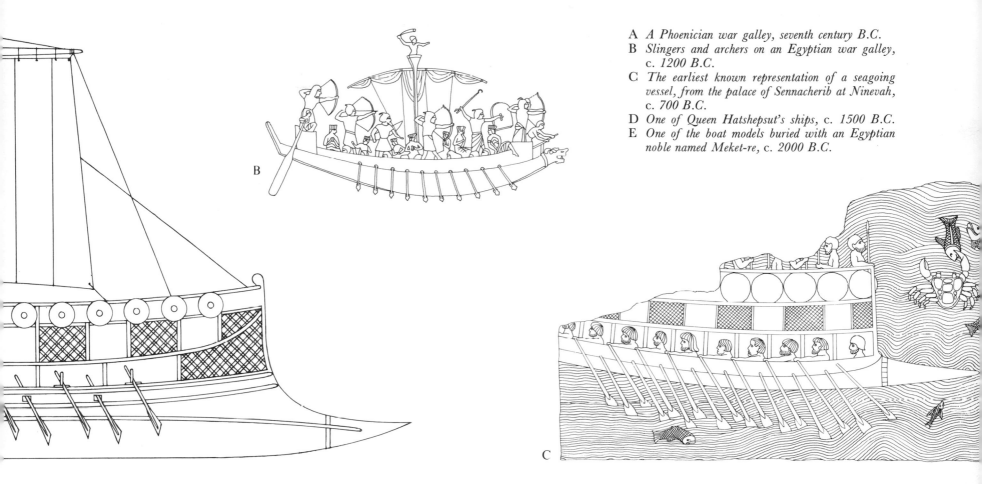

A *A Phoenician war galley, seventh century B.C.*
B *Slingers and archers on an Egyptian war galley, c. 1200 B.C.*
C *The earliest known representation of a seagoing vessel, from the palace of Sennacherib at Ninevah, c. 700 B.C.*
D *One of Queen Hatshepsut's ships, c. 1500 B.C.*
E *One of the boat models buried with an Egyptian noble named Meket-re, c. 2000 B.C.*

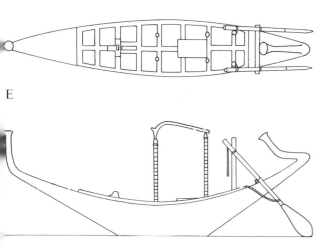

1180 B.C.
Homer tells how, as a result of the Trojan Wars, the Achaians opened up the Dardanelles for trading. Trojan war vessels had one bank of oars, and a single, square sail on one mast.

1000 B.C.
The Phoenicians are by now virtually masters of the Mediterranean. They are known to have traded as far afield as Cornwall, in England, where they bartered for tin. In order to trade with local tribes around the Mediterranean, they established colonies, where markets were built and banking facilities were developed. Such settlements were to be found in Tunisia, Algeria, Malta, Sardinia, and Italy.

The Phoenicians were not only efficient merchants; they were also accomplished seamen. Indeed, the navies of both Egypt and King Solomon were captained and officered by Phoenicians, despite the fact that originally the Phoenicians were not a warlike people. The crews of the navies consisted of slaves and other pressed men.

Generally, during the years under examination, seafaring was confined to the daylight hours. But the Phoenicians, through the study of stars, were able to draw astronomical maps. By using these, navigators were able to continue a voyage after nightfall, using the pole-star as the northerly bearing.

700 B.C.
In the ruins of Sennacherib's palace in Assyria, there are bas-reliefs which show a Phoenician ship with a detachable ram-bow. The ram-bow was designed to penetrate the hull of an enemy ship, and then, after inflicting damage, to snap off near the bow-post, thus leaving the Phoenician ship free and still watertight. This particular bas-relief is the first recorded illustration of a bireme, a ship with two banks of oars. It is interesting to observe, however, that the ship is still one-masted, and carries a single, square, sail. Additionally, there is a flat, open deck, ringed with shields above the oar-deck. Thus, the oarsmen were protected from falling arrows and, at the same time, the Phoenician soldiers who were carried in the ship had a platform upon which they could stand and fight.

609 B.C.
The first circumnavigation of Africa is ordered by Pharaoh Necho II, who commissions a Phoenician fleet, and instructs the captains to sail from Suez and to continue indefinitely with land always to the starboard. Many of the

GREEK SHIPS
A *A bireme warship, c. 500 B.C.*
  1 *The position of the oars*
B *A merchant ship with roped-in gang-plank,* c.
    600 B.C.

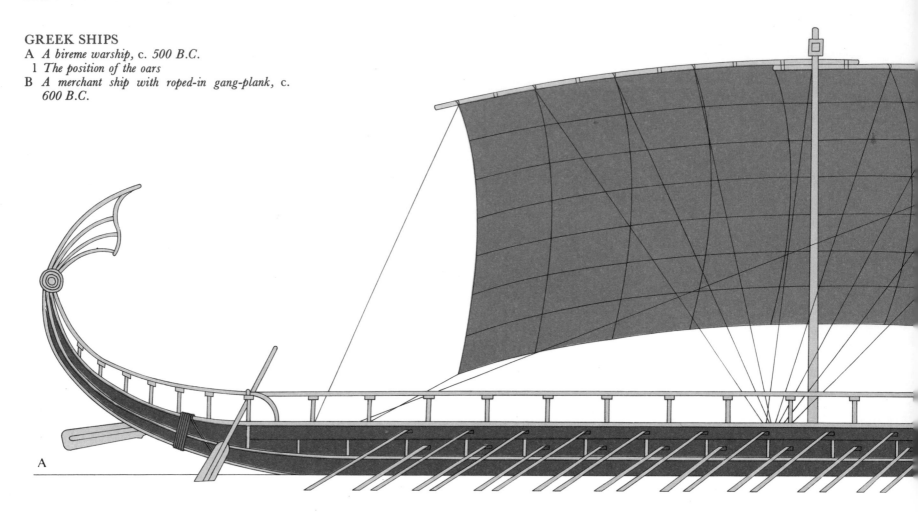

A

C

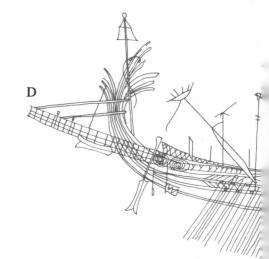

D

countries which lie to the south of Egypt were probably known, if not through trading expeditions, such as that of Queen Hatshepsut's fleet to the Land of Punt, then through legend. The Egyptians had already noticed that sails disappeared over the horizon, and had deduced from this that the earth was curved, but they had no reason to believe that it did not go on for ever. So, the expedition sailed forth, and four years later arrived back in Alexandria. The sailors told tales of green lands and jet-black people, darker by far than the known Nubians and Ethiopians. The adventurers had, of course, sailed right round the continent of Africa. It would be fascinating, had the Phoenician commander left some record of his impressions when he sailed through the Straits of Gibraltar and saw the familiar Mediterranean waters, and realised that he had circumnavigated Africa.

600 B.C.
The Greek merchant ship of this period is constructed with a spoon stern like a bireme, and has a similar rig. A long gang-plank was often carried on top of the cargo deck. This plank could be let down onto a beach or promontory. There were by this time many organized ports with piers or jetties, so from this it can be surmised that trading was so widespread

that ports without cargo-handling facilities were being regularly visited. These gang-planks had roped-in sides, and were of the type that could be used on a cattle-boat. It can be assumed, therefore, that a trade in livestock existed at this time.

Because of the spread of trading and colonization, the shipbuilding industry in different countries was beginning to influence each country in a marked way. An interesting example of this influence was found in the Etruscan cemetery at Cerveteri, which is near to modern Rome. There, a painting of an Etruscan bireme is recognizable as being very similar in construction to the Greek bireme of that time. It has an ornate ram-bow, a steering-oar, a single sail, and twin banks of oars. The vessel, however, is one deck lower than the bireme of contemporary Phoenician construction. Obviously, the Greek influence was far stronger in that part of the Mediterranean than was that of Phoenicia.

c. 500 B.C.
It is also at this time that the *Lex Rhodia,* of which mention has already been made, is introduced into the affairs of mariners. Indeed, all subsequent maritime jurisprudence, including that of modern times, is based in some

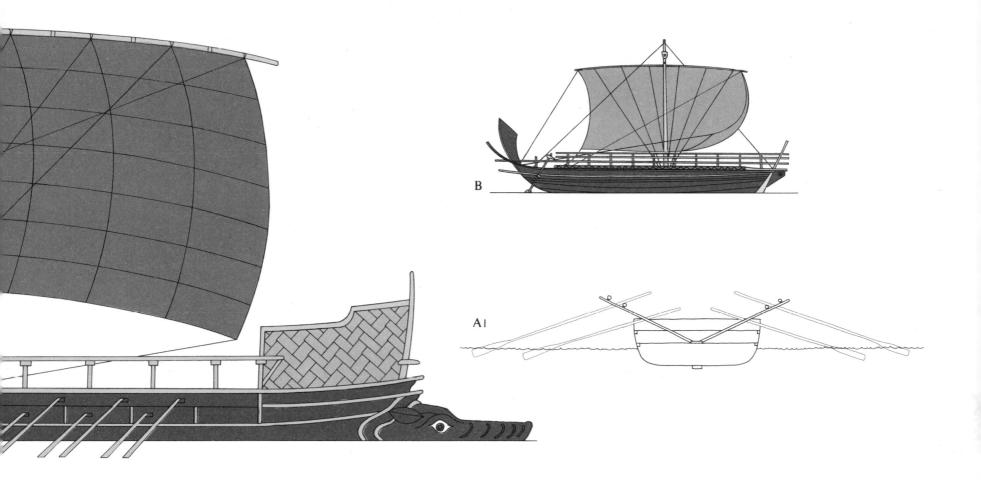

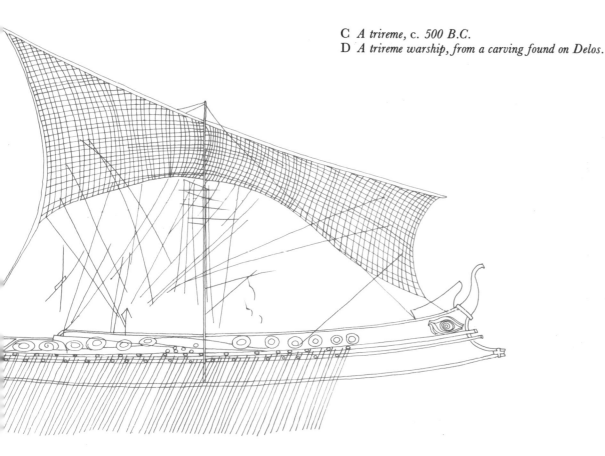

C *A trireme, c. 500 B.C.*
D *A trireme warship, from a carving found on Delos.*

way or other on this original statement of the laws governing the sea. The origins of this Rhodian set of sea laws are lost in antiquity. The laws are named for Rhodes, capital and island of the same name in the Mediterranean. The inhabitants of this ancient civilization, being islanders, were bred to a life of seagoing and trading, and they well understood the basic necessity to regulate their affairs in a well-publicized and orderly manner.

The importance of Rhodes lay in the fact that it was in a key position at the cross-roads of early Mediterranean trade. Almost every sailor of those times knew Rhodes and used it as a port of call.

Thus, when Rhodes laid down a code of behaviour for seafarers, it was readily accepted. It soon became common practice to settle maritime disputes by the *Lex Rhodia*. Indeed, two and a half thousand years later, at the end of the nineteenth century, it was referred to in the British High Court of Justice.

Before the codifying of the *Lex Rhodia*, maritime law was unclear. In fact, in most cases involving shipping, the law of the land prevailed. Nowhere did this land-based law, for example, state what should happen if, to save his ship, a captain jettisoned his cargo and cut down his mast and sails.

A *Casting anchor, from an Attic vase, c. 440 B.C.*
B *A carpenter working on a wooden anchor, from a Sardinian gem, c. 500 B.C.*
C *Boys fishing from a boat, from an Etruscan tomb, sixth century B.C.*
D *A hook anchor, from an Attic vase, sixth century B.C.*
E *Part of a marble eye, found at Piraeus, which probably decorated a ship's prow.*

F *Lead anchor-stock, Syracuse.*
G *Stone anchor-stock, Island of Aegina, near Piraeus.*
H *Wooden anchor, from a Greek coin, fourth century B.C.*
I *The earliest known anchor-stock, found at the site of an Etruscan wreck, early sixth century B.C.*
J *Weight anchors of stone found near Motya, Sicily.*

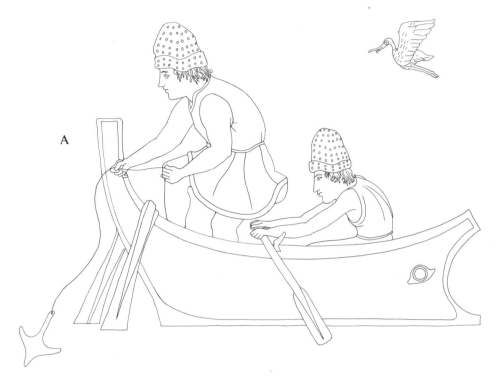

The reason was simple. Land law knew no such predicament as that which beset sailors. So the oldest references to sea law, applied long before the introduction of the *Lex Rhodia*, mention 'contribution'. This reference, which later was much more clearly defined by the Rhodian lawyers, deals with the rule whereby, if a person should lose equipment or goods in order to save others, then they must contribute to make good the loss.

The *Lex Rhodia* is in three parts. The first part is the preamble which, because of the innumerable times it has been copied, now no longer makes sense. However, a fairly accurate copy makes clear the point that the *Lex Rhodia* was important, and that the authority that supported the law was to be considered absolute. At the time that the copy under examination was made, the authority was Rome.

The second part of the *Lex Rhodia* has nineteen clauses, which set out basic rules; for example, that contracts should be written and not oral. The final part sets out forty-seven items concerning the law. It indicates, among other things, the penalties for stealing equipment, such as the anchor, which, by its loss, would imperil the ship at sea. It also made it mandatory for the crew to sleep aboard ship and not ashore when the craft was in harbour. This was a simple precaution against a sudden storm.

To this very day, one rule of the *Lex Rhodia* remains unchanged: 'Valuables to be declared to the captain, otherwise no claim for their loss to be admitted.'

c. 500 B.C.
The guild system emerges about this time in the city of Byzantium, later re-named Constantinople. Nowadays, it is called Istanbul.

The city was founded in 660 B.C. by the Greek Byzas, at the meeting point of Europe and Asia. The Greek, Roman, Egyptian, and Phoenician nations all variously struggled to dominate this key position overlooking the Bosphorus.

Guild members were shipowners, who joined together in order to rationalize the chartering of their ships, and to lay down codes of conduct governing sailors and others at sea and in port.

In those days, there was no precise demarcation between the ship-charterer, the passengers, and the crew. A group of merchants, meeting at a port, and needing a ship for a trading expedition, would charter a guild-recognized ship, and elect one of their number to be head

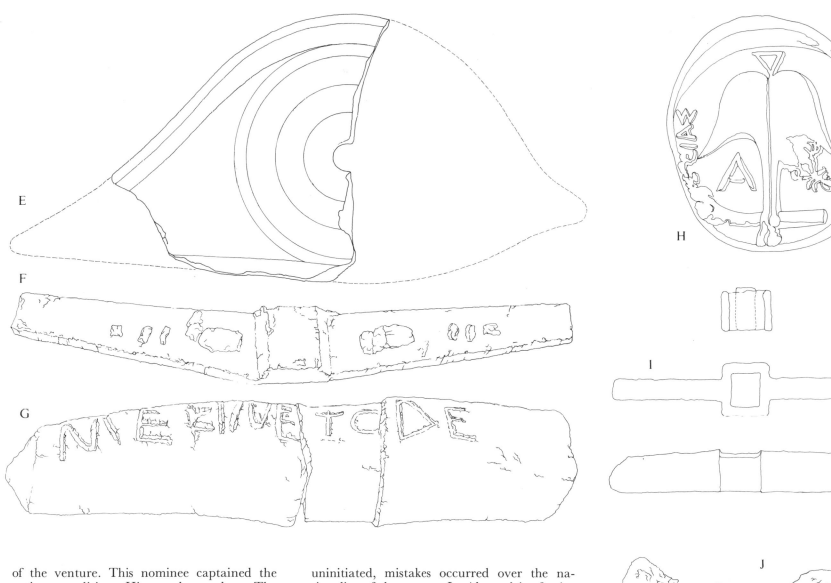

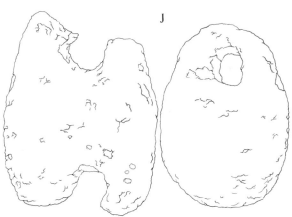

of the venture. This nominee captained the entire expedition. His word was law. The Head Seaman was in charge of the ship, its navigation, and its crew, which consisted of hired mariners who shared in the venture and its ultimate profits, if any. Crew members received their wages at the end of the trip, doubtless to guarantee their loyalty.

The port merchants became the first marine surveyors. In a large port, the inexperienced trader could hire the services of such an expert to check the cordage, wood, sails, and soundness of the hull. In order to fix an acceptable charter fee, the surveyor would obtain reports of satisfaction from previous charterers. Soon, lists of sound ships existed. Guild members would have their own vessels especially surveyed, so that they could be included in the list of vessels found sound for the sea.

At that time, coasts were uncharted. There were few lighthouses or other navigational aids. Merchants chartering a ship would also use the services of the surveyor to find a Head Seaman who had an intimate knowledge of the waters to be navigated. Many of these head seamen had the name of the area of which they had expert knowledge tagged on to their own proper name. Unfortunately, among the

uninitiated, mistakes occurred over the nationality of the expert. In Alexandria, for instance, Taran the Cretan would not be a native of Crete. The appellation would inform the knowledgeable that a Head Seaman named Taran had expert familiarity and experience of Cretan waters.

The cook was one of the most important of the various crew members. He not only cooked for the crew, he also victualled the ship and agreed with the leader of the expedition on the daily ration of food. A cook had to be able to bargain in every port of call, and had to know what was the best and cheapest food. Cooks were professionals in every sense of the word, especially in the art of preparing hot meals at sea.

Seagoing was a seasonal occupation. Between November 7 and March 7, all merchant shipping stopped. The Mediterranean in winter, with its severe gales and cold nights, was no place for the simple ships of two thousand years ago.

Suetonius, in his biography of Emperor Claudius (10 B.C.-54 A.D.) mentions a severe shortage of winter wheat in Rome. He describes how Claudius sent ships to Africa, under guarantee of compensation against loss or

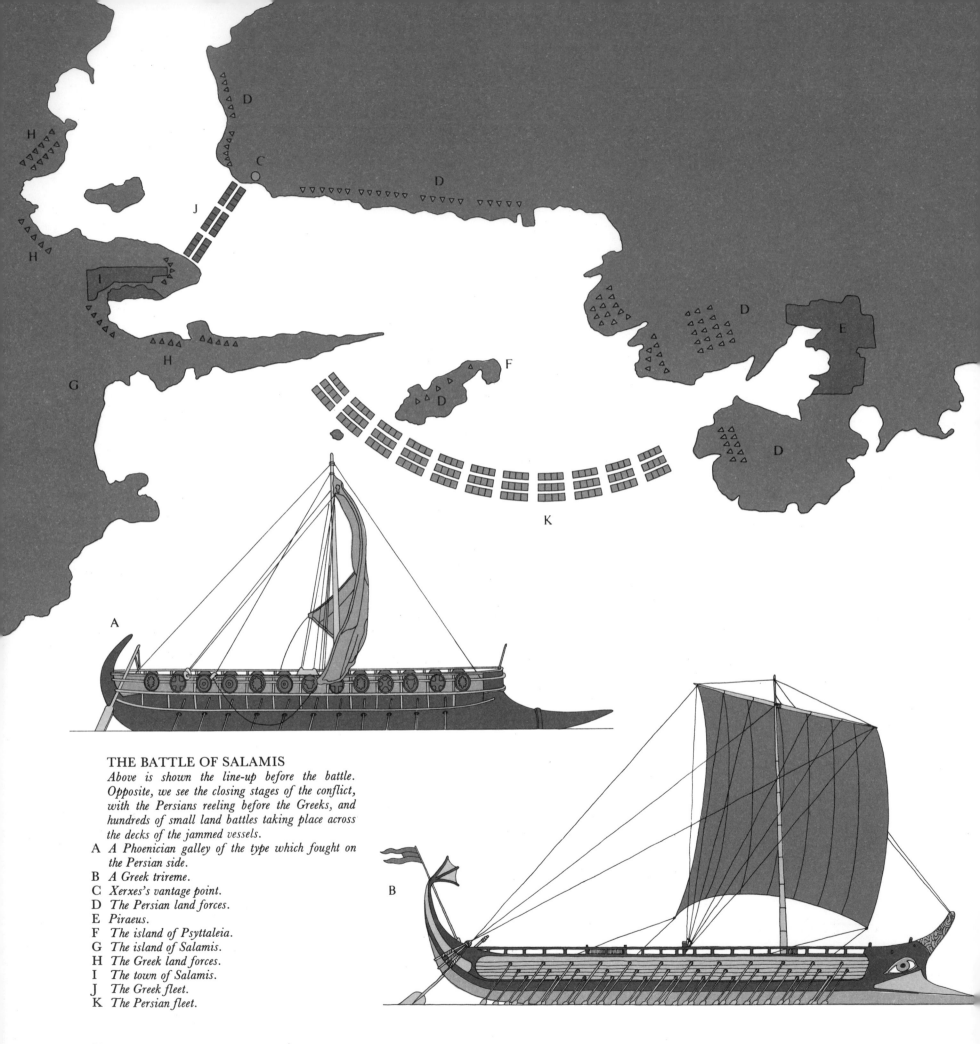

THE BATTLE OF SALAMIS

Above is shown the line-up before the battle. Opposite, we see the closing stages of the conflict, with the Persians reeling before the Greeks, and hundreds of small land battles taking place across the decks of the jammed vessels.

A *A Phoenician galley of the type which fought on the Persian side.*
B *A Greek trireme.*
C *Xerxes's vantage point.*
D *The Persian land forces.*
E *Piraeus.*
F *The island of Psyttaleia.*
G *The island of Salamis.*
H *The Greek land forces.*
I *The town of Salamis.*
J *The Greek fleet.*
K *The Persian fleet.*

damage, to bring extra wheat supplies back. Even in the Middle Ages, there were special penalties and prices in respect of winter voyages.

c. 500 B.C.
The Greek trireme, with its three banks of oars, is introduced around this time. Considerable numbers of this type of vessel are in use at the Battle of Salamis.

480 B.C.
A Carthaginian expedition under Hannon sails round Africa.

480 B.C.
One of the most critical battles of all history takes place: the Battle of Salamis, in which Greece defeats Persia.

The Persian fleet under King Xerxes consisted of 850 ships all told: 300 Phoenician, 200 Egyptian, 150 Cypriot, 100 Cilician, and 100 Ionic. Aeschylus records that only 200 of them were triremes. Actually, Xerxes's fleet was made up of 1,207 ships when it left Persia, but almost 400 were lost during the voyage to Greece.

The admiral of the Greek navy was Themistocles. He had 380 triremes under his command. Because Athens had already fallen to the Persians, and Sparta was the city state to be defended, overall command of the fleet was given to the Spartan general, Eurybiades. Eurybiades favoured a strategic withdrawal to the Gulf of Corinth, where the hinterland was held by loyal troops, whereas the Athenian shoreline was already in Persian hands.

Themistocles, however, wished to fight in the Gulf of Athens, using the island of Salamis to form a bottleneck which would prevent the superior Persian force from deploying line abreast. His plan was finally accepted. He allowed it to become known that the fleet would withdraw towards Corinth as soon as the portents were favourable. When Xerxes heard of this, as Themistocles knew he would, the Persian commander sent a third of his remaining eight hundred ships southwards to round the island of Salamis, thus cutting off the expected Greek retreat to the Peloponnese.

However, Queen Artemisia of Halicarnassus, an ally of the Persians, warned Xerxes that the Greeks were splendid sailors and renowned sea

fighters, and advised that a confrontation with them should be avoided. The Persian fleet, she suggested, should be used as a tactical rather than a fighting weapon. But Xerxes insisted upon a policy of attack. Thus, after the departure of the Persian Third Squadron, Themistocles found his 380 vessels matched against the 600 Persian men-of-war.

Themistocles drew up his fleet in the narrows between the island and the Greek mainland, in two parallel lines facing the anchored Persians who, because of the lack of space, could do no more than deploy in a similar fashion.

Themistocles then signalled his fleet that the Persian Third Squadron had cut off the line of retreat. The only choice was to fight for victory. Nevertheless, he had another tactic up his sleeve. Daily in September, the morning wind in those parts blows stiffly from the direction of Corinth. Thus, on the morning of the battle, it blew straight into the face of the Persian fleet. When the morning breeze was at its height, Themistocles attacked. The wind sped his ships towards the Persian vessels, and at the same time blew the enemy sails aback. The Persians were forced to break formation. In

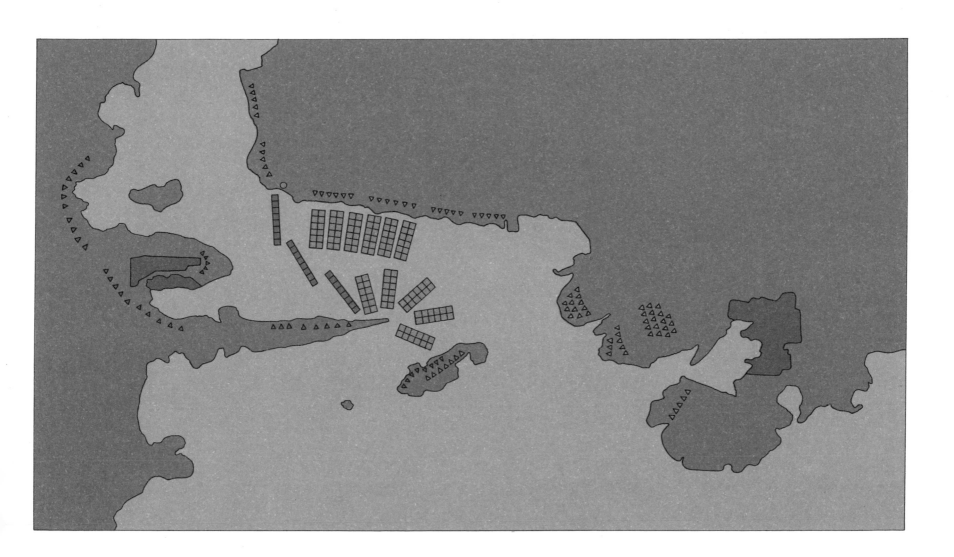

attempting to tack, their ships collided with each other.

The Persian triremes were now formed into a twin-headed column. Oars flayed at a tremendous rate. Xerxes gave the command to the column to plunge into the centre of the Greek fleet. Themistocles countered by ordering his ships to concentrate upon stopping the head of the column. This counter-thrust was successful. The ships following in the wake of the Persian twin-headed column had to veer in all directions in order to avoid collision among themselves. When the Persian might was in total disarray, Themistocles ordered a ship-to-ship engagement. Naturally, as the Greek ships were under full sail, they had the tactical advantage. The Persian vessels were wallowing in the rolling sea, sitting ducks for the Greeks. In the shambles that followed, the Persians lost more than two hundred ships, against the fifty lost by the Greeks.

Queen Artemisia herself commanded the Second Squadron of the Persian fleet. Obviously, she had been unimpressed with Xerxes's plan, because at the height of the battle the Greek colours were broken from her galley, and she engaged and sank one of the Persian flagships under King Clamasithymus, whom she hated. The Greeks, astonished at this change of heart, left her ship alone and she sailed unmolested from the scene of battle.

By evening, Xerxes, who had watched the battle from the safety of a throne especially erected on the shore, knew that the battle was lost. His piquant comment was that, 'The men behaved like women and the women like heroes.'

479 B.C.

The morale of the Persian navy was so shaken by the defeat at Salamis that, within a year, a further defeat was suffered at Mycale, which is in southern Ionia. This second defeat saw the eclipse of Persian power in this part of the world. Thereafter, Greece became the dominant Mediterranean power and also the leading commercial state; but her supremacy was short-lived. Weakened by intrigue, war, and internal strife, the ascendancy in this arena passed to Rome and Carthage, the former becoming the major land power, the latter the major sea power.

c. 400 B.C.

The 'ceres' type of ship makes its appearance in Greek waters. The characteristics of this type of ship were lightness, speed, and shallow draught. The hull was round-bottomed, but with a much broader beam than usual. The mast carried a large, square sail. This, aided by a single bank of usually twenty oars on each side of the vessel, made for speed and manoeuvrability.

The 'ceres' became the standard cargo carrier of the period, as well as being the naval maid-of-all-work. Thousands were built, and references to these sturdy little vessels are to be found in the earliest records of even the smallest of Mediterranean ports. The wording of these records indicates that the ships kept to regular scheduled trading routes.

324 B.C.

The first sea voyage to be recorded in detail is that of the Greek explorer Pytheas. He sailed from Massilia, modern Marseilles, through the Straits of Gibraltar, and, after visiting Brittany, continued up the English Channel to Kent and the Thames estuary. He then crossed the North Sea to Scandinavia, probably docking in Denmark, for he records the land as being 'similar to that which we had quitted'. Pytheas then goes on to describe a land which he names Thule, which was located some six days' sailing beyond Albion, the name by which England was then known. Thule, then, could have been Iceland, the Faroes, or even the Shetland Islands. He was astonished to find that the northern barbarians he encountered enjoyed a culture in no way inferior to that of his own country. Furthermore, he considered that the seafaring abilities of these peoples were the equal to those of the Phoenicians — no little praise indeed.

288 B.C.

In 1964, in the waters off Kyrenia, Cyprus, the wreck of a 60-foot (18.3 m) sailing-ship was found. The hull had been lined with lead, which was fixed to the timber by bronze tacks. Her cargo comprised almonds, and over four hundred wine amphorae. A cargo of twenty-nine stone grain-mills were used as ballast. They were neatly stowed along the axis of the keel. Aboard the ship were four wooden spoons, four oil jugs, four salt dishes, and four cups—indicating the size of the crew. Deck equipment included a heavy axe. By the mast, which was ornately carved, lay a pulley for hoisting the sail. A bronze cauldron, which had been used for cooking, was also found. Of the five bronze coins discovered, the earliest dated from 306 B.C. A Carbon 14 analysis of the almonds pinpointed the time of sinking to 288 B.C., but the same test on the planking dated the hull at 370 B.C. The Kyrenian ship was, therefore, more than eighty years old when she sank.

From the various items found on board, it has been deduced that she was trading southwards along the Turkish Anatolian coast, and had stopped at the islands of Samos, Kos, and Rhodes before she sank off her destination, Kyrenia.

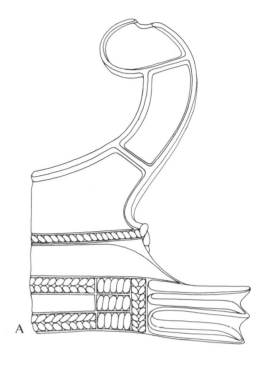

A *The prow of a Roman ship, from a bronze model.*

A

THE YASSI ADA SHIP
Seventh Century A.D.

An archaeological expedition from the University of Pennsylvania, led by Professor George Bass, has vastly increased our knowledge of the Byzantine merchant ship and of seaborne trade in seventh-century Byzantium. The expedition has thoroughly excavated a wreck which has been shown to be that of a small coastal freighter of some forty tons burden, just under 70 foot (21.3 m) long. She had foundered after striking a reef just off the island of Yassi Ada in the Aegean. We do not know the fate of the crew, but the ship's cargo of 900 amphorae of wine was a total loss. The owner of the ship was named Georgios. His name was found inscribed on a large steelyard found in the ship's galley. He was probably one of the many small, independent shipowners whose trading played such an important part in the economy of the Byzantine Empire.

Although less than ten per cent of the hull has survived, it has been possible to make a full set of plans, which are illustrated on the following two pages.

On this page we reconstruct the Yassi Ada ship in port undergoing repairs. On the quayside, carpenters are working on her mast. Unfortunately, no trace of the mast or rigging has been found, so it has not been possible to reconstruct these. It is probable, however, that the ship carried a square rig similar to that appearing in contemporary mosaics.

The deck plan on the following two pages illustrates how the ship's anchors were stowed. Four bower anchors were carried on the bulwarks in the forward quarter, two on each side, when the ship sank. Seven spare anchors lay piled nearby.

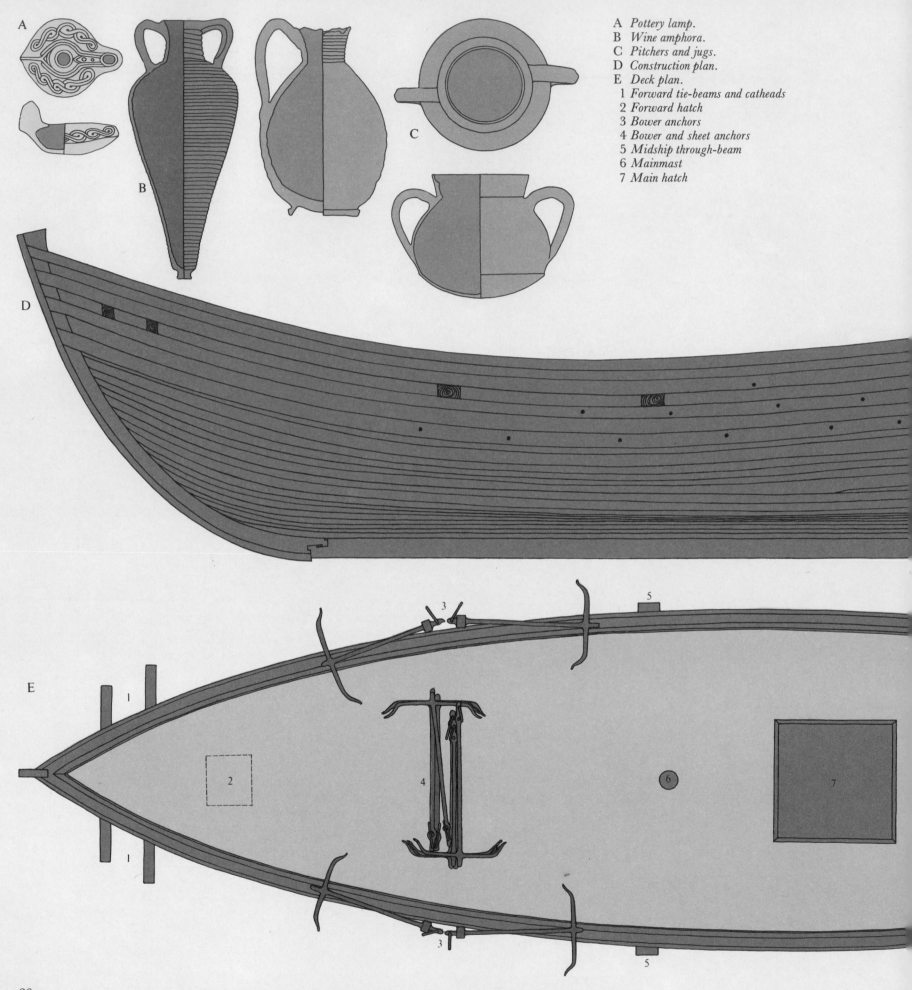

A *Pottery lamp.*
B *Wine amphora.*
C *Pitchers and jugs.*
D *Construction plan.*
E *Deck plan.*
1 *Forward tie-beams and catheads*
2 *Forward hatch*
3 *Bower anchors*
4 *Bower and sheet anchors*
5 *Midship through-beam*
6 *Mainmast*
7 *Main hatch*

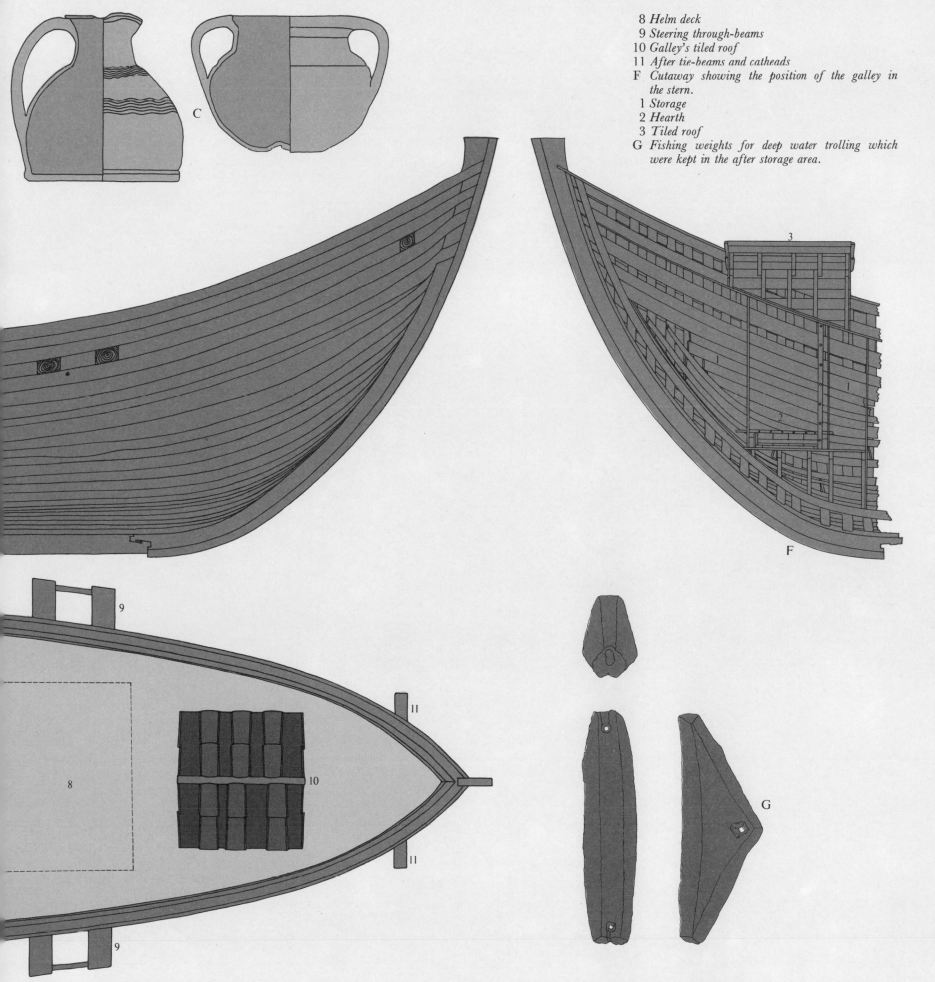

8 *Helm deck*
9 *Steering through-beams*
10 *Galley's tiled roof*
11 *After tie-beams and catheads*
F *Cutaway showing the position of the galley in the stern.*
1 *Storage*
2 *Hearth*
3 *Tiled roof*
G *Fishing weights for deep water trolling which were kept in the after storage area.*

A reconstruction of the galley as seen from the stern. The hearth (1) is a tiled firebox open at the front and erected on a bed of clay and fragments of thick tiles. Small iron bars form a grill. In the cupboard was kept the ship's tableware. As there were three settings discovered, we can assume that there was a crew of three.

280 B.C.

This is the date of the first recorded lighthouse, the famous Pharos of Alexandria, which became one of the Seven Wonders of the World. It was situated on an island of that name, about a mile (1.6 km) offshore. Alexander the Great planned the original city of Alexandria, to which Pharos was joined by a mole. Ptolemy II of Egypt had a 400-foot (121.9 m) marble tower erected on the site. On the top of this tower, a fire was kept burning to act as a leading mark for shipping.

c. 265 B.C.

From time to time in the annals of history, reference is made to enormous ships which could not possibly have been built under the existing technology. One gigantic ship that was built, however, was the SYRACUSA, owned by Gerone II of Syracuse. Achias is said to have built the ship at Corinth. She had twenty banks of oars, four masts, and mounted eight siege catapults on deck. If it is recalled that the massive quinqueremes had only five banks of oars, then some idea of the immense size of the SYRACUSA may be obtained. She was said to have been capable of carrying an entire army of four thousand troops.

It is indisputable that the vessel was completed, for it was presented to Ptolemy Philadelphis of Alexandria. The ship inspired his son, Ptolemy Philapatore, King of Egypt 285-247 B.C., to plan an even larger vessel. The historian Callixenus reports that this monster was to have forty banks of oars, a staggering four thousand oarsmen, and a literal palace on board for the king. The verb tenses used by Callixenus in his report suggest that, whilst the SYRACUSA was a reality, the new monster vessel remained a pipe-dream. It is of interest, however, that Callixenus counts oar banks in total, so that forty banks of oars means twenty banks on each side. Thus the SYRACUSA was a double quinquereme, a class of vessel that is named more than once in the annals of maritime affairs of the time, but one that is never mentioned in the chronicles of naval battles. Any naval vessels built of this type would merely have been prestige show-pieces.

264 B.C.

At the outbreak of the Punic Wars, the Roman fleet consisted of triremes, designed, built, and manned by Greeks. The Carthaginians fought from large quinqueremes, which gave them command of the sea. They regularly raided the Roman coasts, and met with little effective opposition. In order to redress the balance, the Romans built a fleet of one hundred quinqueremes and twenty large triremes. It took four years to complete this fleet. When it was ready for battle, it was placed under the command of Caius Duilius. Because the strength of Rome lay in her legions and their fighting skill, Caius Duilius devised the tactical ploy of converting each encounter into the nearest approximation to a land battle. Each vessel of the Roman fleet was equipped at the bow with a gangway, wide enough to take three men abreast. On the seaward end of the gangway a large, spiked, grappling claw, called a 'crow', was mounted. When the enemy was engaged, the Roman vessel was propelled bow first against the opposing ship. The gangway was dropped, and a hundred legionaries in the traditional army formation of long shields held around the sides by the outer ranks, and overhead by the centre rank, dashed aboard, spears at the ready.

260 B.C.

The first sea battle in the history of Rome takes place at Mylae, which corresponds to the present-day Milazzo. Hannibal's Carthaginian fleet of 125 galleys was sighted off the coast of Sicily at this point by no less than 130 Roman ships. Thirty Carthaginian galleys broke off from the main formation and bore down on the van of the Roman fleet. Unexpectedly, the Roman ships met those of Carthage bow to bow. The 'crows' were dropped, biting deep into the enemy decks and locking the ships together. The legionaries attacked across the gangways, slaughtering the Carthaginians. Nearly thirty of the Carthaginian galleys were captured. The rest of the Carthaginian fleet tried to manoeuvre so that the Roman ships could be rammed amidships. The Romans avoided this manoeuvre, which would have resulted in the traditional side-by-side fighting, and once more nosed the bows of their ships into position so that the 'crows' could smash into the enemy decks. When the battle was finally disengaged, the Romans had sunk fourteen enemy ships, captured thirty-one, and had killed over seven thousand Carthaginians. The Romans did not lose a single ship, and suffered only a few hundred casualties.

256 B.C.

The same tactics as those employed at Mylae cause the defeat of Hamilcar's Carthaginian fleet at the Battle of Ecnone. Two hundred and fifty Roman galleys under the command of Regulus and Naulius were attacked while they were escorting a convoy of troop transports and supply ships out of Messina.

249 B.C.

Not every battle became a Roman victory. In 249 B.C., Appius Claudius Pulcher tries to corner a Carthaginian fleet off Trapani (Drepaum) in Sicily by attacking from seaward using the 'crow' technique. The Carthaginians, now accustomed to Roman tactics, sailed in line astern keeping very close together. This manoeuvre caused the Roman ships to bunch. When they were almost too close to use oars, and the sails were masking each other, the Carthaginians turned and made the traditional side-by-side attack. Ninety-three Roman ships and twenty-two thousand men were lost.

SYRACUSA

She was a 'double quinquereme', with ten banks of oars on each side. Two thousand men rowed the 800 oars.

A *Three outriggers were needed for one row of ten oars.*

B *The ship had four masts, two guard towers, and a huge tent on board.*

C *One of the siege catapults. On the left, the firing mechanism. The arm of the catapult (1) is held by a 'trigger' (2), which in its turn is held down by (3), a deck fastening. The arm flies upwards when the point (4) is struck sharply to the left.*

D *The possible arrangement of the twenty-five oarsmen needed for the ten oars. Each group stood or sat a little behind and over the other.*

Oar 1: *One man sitting behind the hull, with a 20-foot (6.1 m) oar.*

Oar 2: *Two men sitting behind the hull, with a 32-foot (9.7 m) oar.*

Oar 3: *Two men standing, with a 40-foot (12.2 m) oar.*

Oar 4: *Two men sitting, with a 48-foot (14.6 m) oar.*

Oar 5: *Two men sitting, with a 52-foot (15.8 m) oar.*

Oar 6: *Two men standing, with a 60-foot (18.3 m) oar.*

Oar 7: *Three men standing, with a 64-foot (19.5 m) oar.*

Oar 8: *Three men sitting, with a 68-foot (20.7 m) oar.*

Oar 9: *Three men standing, with a 76-foot (23.2 m) oar.*

Oar 10: *Four men standing, with an 84-foot (25.6 m) oar.*

E *The rowlock of oar no 1 was in the hull, probably 4 foot (1.2 m) from the rower's end. That gave him a reach of 4 foot, and the sweep of the oar would then be 10 foot (3.1 m).*

F *The rowlock of oar no. 6 was in the outrigger, 12 foot (3.7 m) from the rower's end. An 8-lb (3.6 kg) weight would balance the 48-foot (14.6 m) length of the rest of the oar, if each foot weighed 2 lbs (0.9 kg).*

G *Siege catapult for firing grappling arrows.*

1 *Mast.*

2 *Ring for holding fasteners from the bowstring.*

3 *Chopping block.*

4 *Stanchion.*

5 *The trajectory of the arrow could be altered by changing the angle of the bow.*

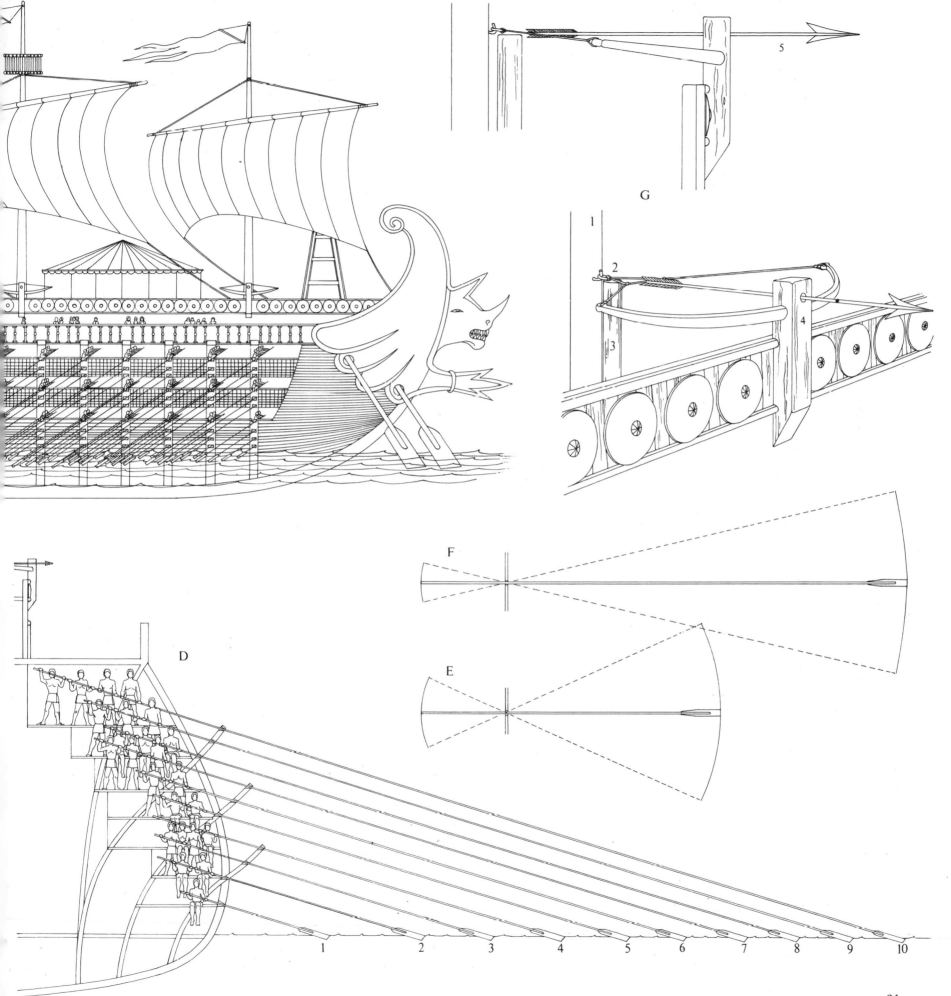

At this time, it becomes Roman policy to seek out and destroy the Carthaginian fleet wherever it might be. Command of the seas would give Rome command of the land. This policy was to become one of the outstanding strategic aims of every major war in history.

241 B.C.
The Battle of Egadian takes place. The Romans defeat the Carthaginians, sinking fifty ships and capturing another seventy. This defeat meant the end of Carthage as a sea power, and Rome became the undisputed master of the Mediterranean. Thirty-nine years later, Carthage was finally defeated by Rome, and the city was razed to the ground.

212 B.C.
The rebellion of Syracuse against Rome is of academic interest only. However, it is linked with the history of shipping because Syracuse was the home of Archimedes, the noted mathematician, whose major contribution to the three-year siege was to invent a parabolic mirror which, utilizing the rays of the sun, set fire to the sails of the Roman ships blockading the harbour. When Syracuse fell, Archimedes was killed by an impatient Roman legionary. The order to spare him arrived too late.

191 B.C.
A Roman fleet under Livius Salinator defeats a Syrian fleet under Polyxenidas, Admiral of Antioch, near Marmora on the Cilician coast. This victory reinforces Roman naval supremacy in the Mediterranean.

190 B.C.
The same Roman fleet, now under the command of Emilius, again defeats Polyxenidas and his re-grouped Syrian fleet. Thirteen Syrian ships are captured, and twenty-nine damaged and put to the flame. The Syrians dismantle their navy entirely. For the next hundred years, the Romans are undisturbed in the 'Roman Lake', the sobriquet for the Mediterranean.

100 B.C.
A drawing of a merchant ship of the period is to be found on a Phoenician sarcophagus unearthed at Sidon. The same type of ship as the one depicted is described by St. Paul, the only difference being a small angled foremast carrying a sail. The bowsprit and its studding sail will occur in sailing warships for the next eighteen hundred years.

70 B.C.
Trade flourishes in the Mediterranean under the peaceful conditions enjoyed because of the supremacy of the Roman navy. As trade increases, however, so does piracy. In the year under review, the Roman Consul Pompeius gathers five hundred ships to seek out and destroy all the pirate lairs along what is now the Algerian coast. The vessels were the tradi-

A ROMAN MERCHANTMAN, c. 200 A.D.

The merchant ship illustrated below is reconstructed from a relief in the harbour town of Ostia, Rome's ancient seaport. The vessel is carvel-built, and has two steering oars, one on each quarter. On the left is illustrated the arrangement of the steering oars on a similar vessel.

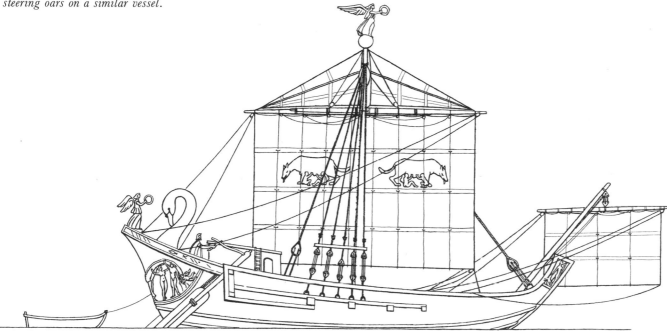

tional biremes, although they lacked mast and sail. The reason for discarding the auxiliary sail is not known; possibly it was a tactical decision so as to prevent sighting until the very last moment. These low-profile, canoe-like biremes were remarkably fast, and had little difficulty in catching the Barbary coast pirates.

55 B.C.

Julius Caesar invades Britain. One of the primary objectives of his expedition is to punish the Britons for sending aid, in the form of ships and of men, to the rebellious Veneti. Previous descriptions of British craft had referred only to skin-covered coracle type boats, but Caesar makes it clear that Scandinavian shipbuilding practices were employed in shipyards in southern England. He describes the Venetine warships which preyed on Roman shipping, including warships which had come from British ports, in the following terms:

Their bottoms were somewhat flatter than those of our vessels. Their prows were very high as likewise their sterns. The body of the vessel was built entirely of oak. The benches of the rowers were made of strong beams about a foot in breadth and fastened with iron spikes, the thickness of one's thumb. Instead of cables they secured their anchors with chains of iron and made use of skin

and a sort of pliant leather for sails. They had no canvas.

The attack of our fleet on these vessels had the advantage in swiftness only; all other things were more advantageous and favourable for them than for us, for our ships could not injure them with their beaks, such was their strength. Nor could we easily throw our darts because of the height above us which was also the reason that we found it extremely difficult to grapple the enemy and bring him to close fight.

40 B.C.

Pliny the Elder describes the quinquereme as having five banks of oars and four hundred oarsmen. Unfortunately, he omits to say how many oars there were, but it may be assumed that each bank consisted of about twenty oars. Pliny further reports that each porthole had paired oars only 2 foot (0.6 m) apart, and that they were joined inside and outside by leather thongs.

Quinqueremes have been mentioned earlier, but it is interesting to note that Pliny still refers to them as experimental vessels. They still have not been encountered as ships of war. The plain fact is that five banks of oars, even paired and thonged, are unwieldy and inefficient when compared, for example, with the pirate-hunting

biremes used by Pompeius some thirty years before Pliny was writing about the quinqueremes.

31 B.C.

The oft-repeated story of the love affair between Mark Antony and Cleopatra, immortalized in verse, prose, drama, and film, resulted in the splitting of the Roman Empire, and culminated in the Battle of Actium. On one side were grouped the forces of Octavian, great-nephew to Julius Caesar; on the other were those of Antony and Cleopatra. Numerical supremacy lay with Antony and Cleopatra. It is estimated that they mustered 500 Roman galleys, and 70 Egyptian, 200,000 foot soldiers, and 10,000 cavalry. Octavian commanded 80,000 soldiers and 12,000 cavalry; but he could scrape together less than 300 galleys. However, the combined fleet of Antony and Cleopatra was poorly equipped, untried in battle, and completely unreliable. On the other hand, Octavian's fleet was battle-proved, and ably commanded by Agrippa.

Mark Antony was in favour of a land battle, where he could deploy his three-to-one numerical superiority. Cleopatra, however, wanted to fight at sea, desiring to keep the army intact. She pointed out that all one had to do if

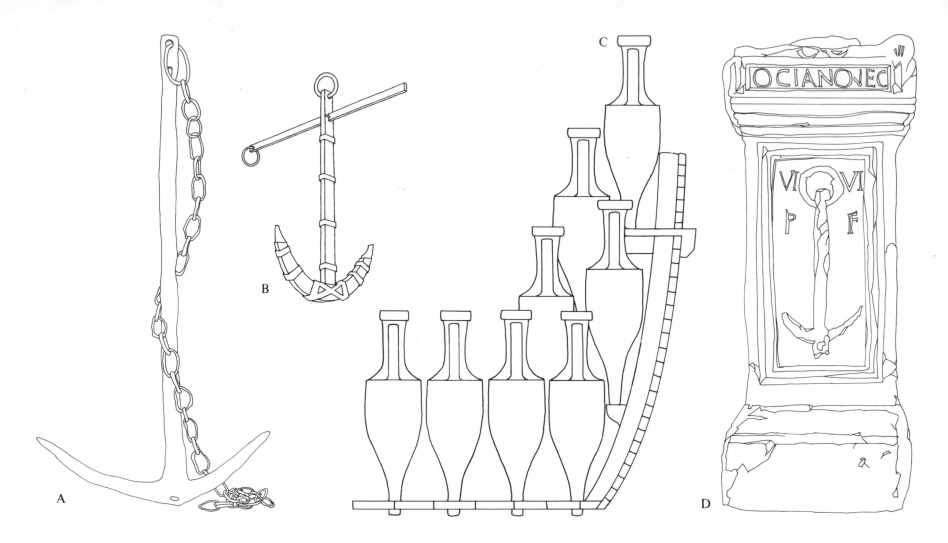

losing a battle at sea was to hoist sail and disappear over the horizon. Mark Antony, despite his misgivings, agreed with this argument. This suited Octavian perfectly, for he had faith in his fleet and greater faith in its commander, Agrippa.

At the Battle of Naulogue, 35 B.C., in which Agrippa had been victorious, a new weapon had supplemented the highly successful 'crow'. It was called a 'harpoon', and consisted of a smooth log with an iron tip. This weapon was fastened to a stout rope. The strategy was for two harpoons to be fired from crossbow type catapults into the fore-and-aft hull of the enemy craft. The two vessels were then pulled together so that the Roman seagoing legionaries could attack.

Despite continued warnings from his colleagues, who to a man preferred a land battle, Mark Antony went ahead with his preparations for a sea engagement, by which the fate of Rome was to be decided. It is doubtful if any sea battle, either before or after, has been watched by as many as the 300,000 troops who had a grand-stand view of the Battle of Actium.

The course of the battle is well authenticated. At its height, the sails of Cleopatra's flagship were unfurled. Others followed suit. Oars dipped into the water. Her seventy vessels moved in line abreast through Antony's fleet, which rode at anchor.

Octavian, who faced Cleopatra, hesitated. Her tactics were obvious. The sleek, speedy Egyptian galleys, mostly biremes, would dash through his lines, turn, and attack from the rear, whilst Antony unleashed a frontal assault. If he harpooned the enemy ships, then the ensuing confusion would enable Antony to attack practically unhindered.

Octavian had to let Cleopatra through, and waited anxiously. To his amazement, and also to the consternation of Mark Antony, the gallant queen did not turn. She sailed on and on, followed by the elements of her fleet. A low moan of incredulity arose from the shore, a moan that turned to shouts of rage when the watchers saw Antony jump into a fast scouting vessel, hoist his personal ensign, and speed after his errant love. Five of Octavian's ships gave chase, but Mark Antony reached and boarded Cleopatra's flagship.

Abandoned and leaderless, with a gale rising, the numerically superior fleet surrendered to Octavian at nightfall. Three hundred ships were captured by Agrippa and his force. Five thousand of Antony's followers died. Within the year, both Cleopatra and Mark Antony were dead, Octavian had become Augustus Caesar, and Egypt had become another province of Rome.

43 A.D.
Julius Caesar's punitive expedition to Britain in 55 B.C. had led to the establishment of trading posts there, but it was not until almost a hundred years later that, under the prompting of Emperor Claudius, a second and deliberate invasion of Britain was mounted. As a result of this invasion, Britain, or rather the part of the island group south of the River Tweed, became a province of Rome.

The historian Publius Cornelius Tacitus describes Londinium (London) as being a considerable port, and a chief residence of merchants. He also mentions that Clausentum (Southampton) was the chief centre of trade with France.

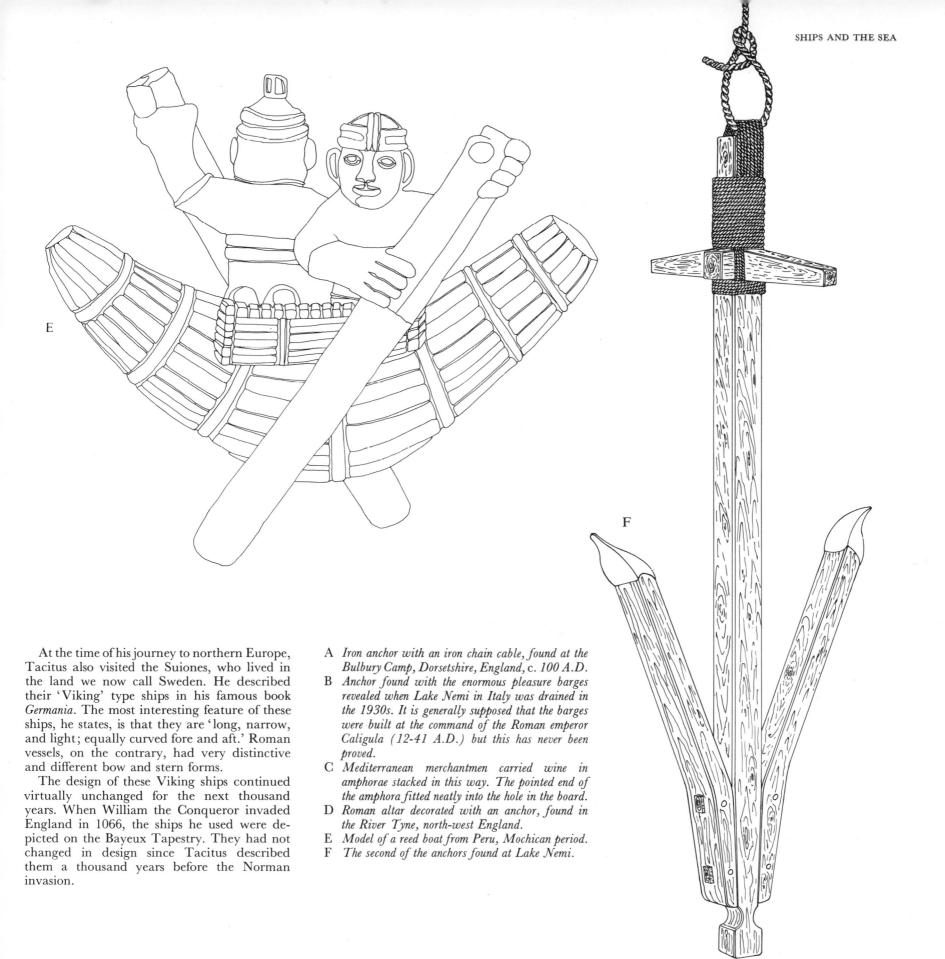

E

F

At the time of his journey to northern Europe, Tacitus also visited the Suiones, who lived in the land we now call Sweden. He described their 'Viking' type ships in his famous book *Germania*. The most interesting feature of these ships, he states, is that they are 'long, narrow, and light; equally curved fore and aft.' Roman vessels, on the contrary, had very distinctive and different bow and stern forms.

The design of these Viking ships continued virtually unchanged for the next thousand years. When William the Conqueror invaded England in 1066, the ships he used were depicted on the Bayeux Tapestry. They had not changed in design since Tacitus described them a thousand years before the Norman invasion.

A *Iron anchor with an iron chain cable, found at the Bulbury Camp, Dorsetshire, England, c. 100 A.D.*
B *Anchor found with the enormous pleasure barges revealed when Lake Nemi in Italy was drained in the 1930s. It is generally supposed that the barges were built at the command of the Roman emperor Caligula (12-41 A.D.) but this has never been proved.*
C *Mediterranean merchantmen carried wine in amphorae stacked in this way. The pointed end of the amphora fitted neatly into the hole in the board.*
D *Roman altar decorated with an anchor, found in the River Tyne, north-west England.*
E *Model of a reed boat from Peru, Mochican period.*
F *The second of the anchors found at Lake Nemi.*

A

A *Seventeenth- and eighteenth-century artists often
based their illustrations on fanciful reports of
the sizes of ancient ships.*
*The above illustration is one artist's impression
of a gigantic Phoenician galley. Its height above
the water line, its enormous steering-oar, and
masts on towers make it difficult to believe that
this design was ever built.*
B *This is a stern decoration from an ancient Roman
galley. In Latin, it was called* aplustre.
C *A highly ornamented prow figure from a galley.
This was almost definitely for decoration, as it
would have made a useless ram.*

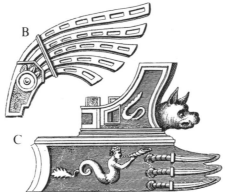

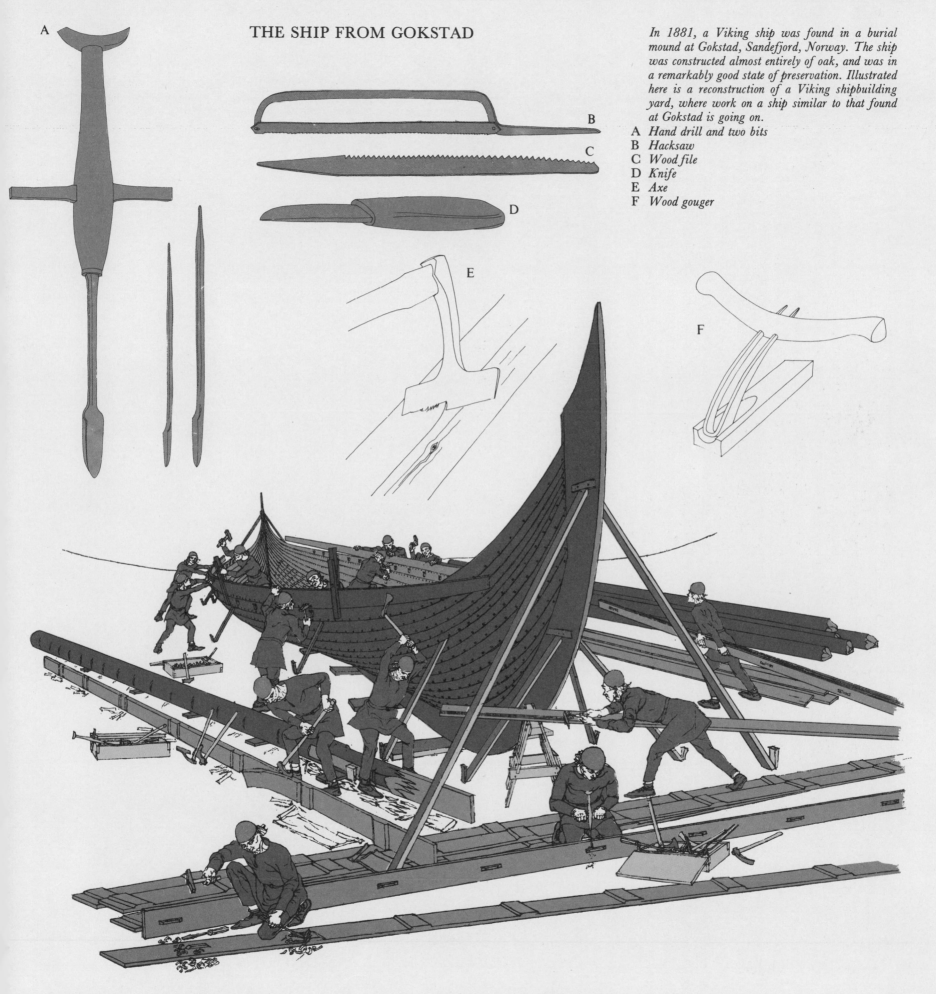

THE SHIP FROM GOKSTAD

In 1881, a Viking ship was found in a burial mound at Gokstad, Sandefjord, Norway. The ship was constructed almost entirely of oak, and was in a remarkably good state of preservation. Illustrated here is a reconstruction of a Viking shipbuilding yard, where work on a ship similar to that found at Gokstad is going on.

A Hand drill and two bits
B Hacksaw
C Wood file
D Knife
E Axe
F Wood gouger

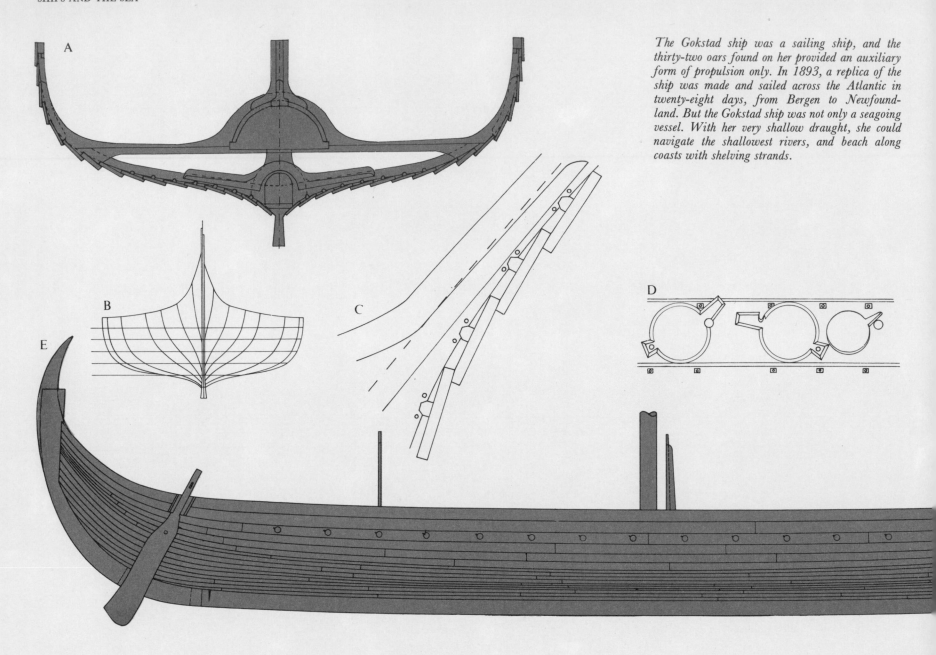

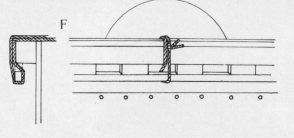

The Gokstad ship was a sailing ship, and the thirty-two oars found on her provided an auxiliary form of propulsion only. In 1893, a replica of the ship was made and sailed across the Atlantic in twenty-eight days, from Bergen to Newfoundland. But the Gokstad ship was not only a seagoing vessel. With her very shallow draught, she could navigate the shallowest rivers, and beach along coasts with shelving strands.

A *Midship section.*

B *Body plan.*

C *Cleats on the insides of the planks would take the ribs, and these were lashed with spruce roots through two holes in the cleats and two in the ribs.*

D *There were no rowlocks in the Gokstad ship. Instead they used holes in the fourteenth strake, which were closed when not in use by hinged wooden discs.*

E *The lines of the ship.*

F *The shields were fastened to the side of the ship by ropes through the shield grips and round a batten on the inside of the rail.*

G *When not in use, the mast could be lowered and neatly stowed away.*

H *The rigging used when the mast was raised or lowered also served as a support for the mast when it was lowered. It was then laid on the T-shaped upright.*

I *When the mast was raised, the slot in the mast partner was closed by the oak block on the deck.*

J *Raising the mast, which was made of pine and was quite heavy, must have been quite a job. In the oak block on the deck, there was a socket to take the foot of the mast. When in use, the mast would be pressed by the wind against the forward part of the mast partner.*

K *When sailing before the wind, the sail was possibly stretched by poles in the illustrated manner.*

G

H

I

J

K

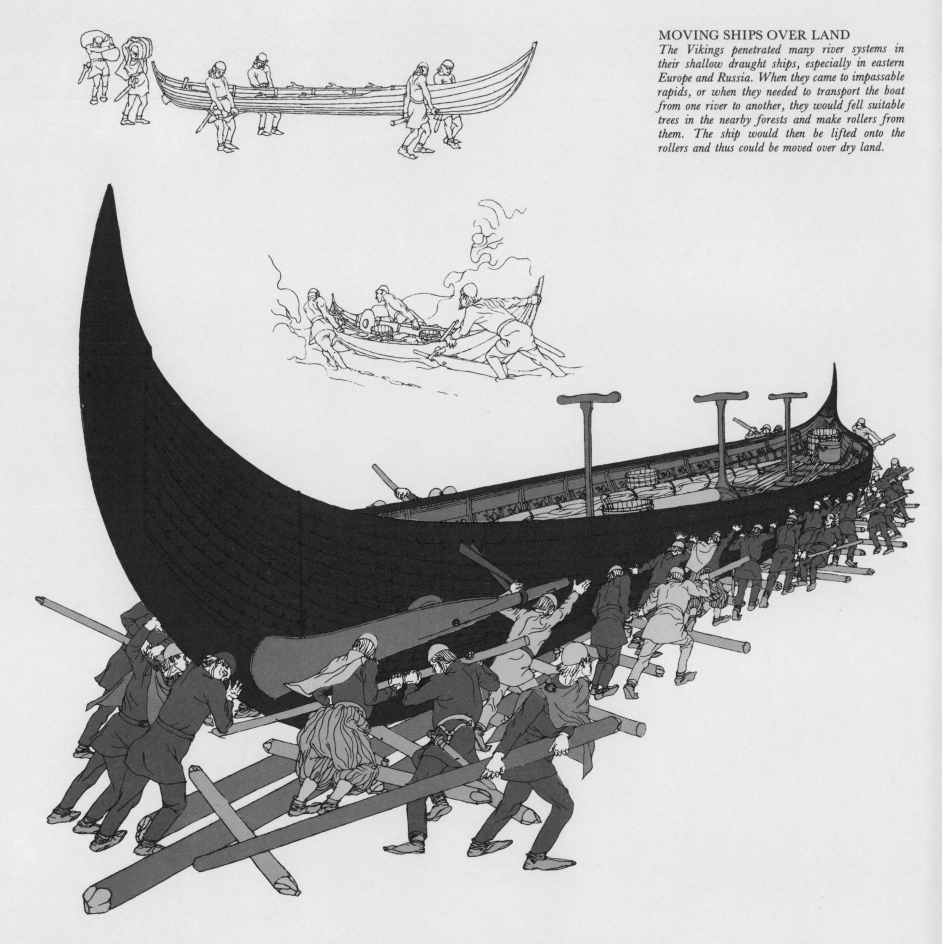

MOVING SHIPS OVER LAND

The Vikings penetrated many river systems in their shallow draught ships, especially in eastern Europe and Russia. When they came to impassable rapids, or when they needed to transport the boat from one river to another, they would fell suitable trees in the nearby forests and make rollers from them. The ship would then be lifted onto the rollers and thus could be moved over dry land.

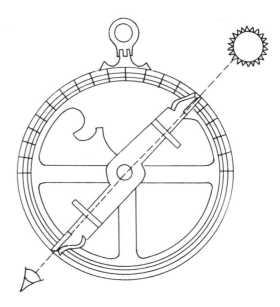

chapter 2

The following period is characterized by the attempts of law-makers and administrators to bring some sort of unity into the affairs of those who earned their living from the sea. There was, of course, a steady improvement in the design and capabilities of ships, despite the fact that, as we have seen already, the basic design of the vessels did not change for hundreds of years.

The single square sail of the Roman Mediterranean vessels of the second century A.D. was similar to that of the Viking ships, which came about five hundred years later. These same Viking ships were almost indistinguishable from the invasion vessels of Duke William of Normandy, when he crossed the Channel to invade England in 1066 A.D.

One important advance in rigging occurred: the lateen sail, said to have been introduced into the Mediterranean by the Arabs about the eighth century. This was used as a mizzen as well as a main sail.

At the end of the Viking era, an innovation in design was occasioned by the fact that sea warfare at the time consisted mainly of hand-to-hand fighting between the opposing crews. Higher vessels had, naturally, a tactical advantage over lower, and this led to the building of 'castles', which were fighting platforms placed at the bow and stern. Even the merchant ships were built in this way, for they very often had to be defended from pirates and hostile nations.

The final advance of note in this period was the development of the stern rudder, probably invented in Friesland during the twelfth century. This replaced the steering-oar, which had been in use from the very beginning. The oldest known illustration of a stern rudder is to be found on the christening font in Winchester Cathedral, and is considered to be from 1180 A.D.

In 127 A.D., Ptolemy published his *Guide to Geography* which contained a map of the world showing that India could be reached by sailing westward from Europe. America is not shown. For just over thirteen hundred years, this map remains the basis for man's knowledge of the geography of the sea. By 1415 A.D., the end of the period under discussion, little advance had been made on Ptolemy's writings. The influence of Henry the Navigator, whose encouragement of Portuguese voyages of discovery opened up the way to the Indies via Southern Africa, did not make itself felt until 1430.

The period starts with a powerful Roman Empire spread around the Mediterranean and dominating the known western world. This empire reached its maximum territorial extent by the second century A.D., but after that it weakened and decayed until, threatened by the Baltic Goths, the Huns, and the Vandals, the Romans were forced to evacuate Gaul and Britain. Into the vacuum thus created came first the followers of Mohammed and later the Vikings.

In 610 A.D., the Moslem religion was founded by Mohammed, and within fifty years this new faith was carried northwards by the Saracen Arab invaders. The African and Levantine coasts of the Mediterranean soon became strongholds of Islam, as they still are today. From 1071, Jerusalem became the focal point of conflict between the two religions of Christendom and Islam. In 1096, the 'People's Crusade' marched across Europe and was annihilated at Nicaea by the Seljuk Turks. The next crusade, now known as the First Crusade, was the first to involve whole nations and to use sea transport. The Crusades feature in this chapter because they demonstrate the importance of sea power and the necessity of improving the techniques of sea transportation.

Above all, this period will remain historic because of the Vikings, who brought a new dimension to the sea. Whether on commercial ventures, on voyages of exploration, or on military expeditions, the Vikings with their treasured longboats achieved a supremacy of the sea that was to last for hundreds of years, a supremacy that was virtually unchallenged in open waters and that ranks with the later supremacy of the Spanish, the Portuguese, and the British.

The Mediterranean arena eventually sapped the strength of all its protagonists, and, by the end of the thirteenth century, the exhausted city states of Genoa, Venice, Pisa, and Amalfi, which had contributed so much to the Crusades in the way of sea transport, foresook aggression for the far more profitable business of trading.

In 1337, the Hundred Years' War commenced, involving France and Scotland against England. In reality, the struggle was between the power of the Royal houses and their political ambitions. In sea terms, control of the English Channel was at issue, and the use of the blockade became frequent, occasioning the necessity of staying at sea for long periods. In 1348, the Black Death descended on Europe and brought the continent to a standstill. The fear of spreading the plague reduced international sea trade, and the shortage of seamen confined even coastal vessels to port.

By 1400, the scene was one of undeclared truce between England and France. Trading in the Baltic was expanding under conditions of relative stability. The 'Danzig' type of merchant ship increased cargo carrying capacity, and this, together with the experience of decades of sea warfare, placed man on the threshold of the next step forward; that of exploration and expansion.

This part of the story of the sea and shipping begins to be well documented. Artifacts, which today may be examined in museums all over the world, authenticate much of the written word. Conjecture gives way to proven fact. In retrospect, this period can be seen as a platform from which will eventually emerge modern ships, modern fleets, and modern navies.

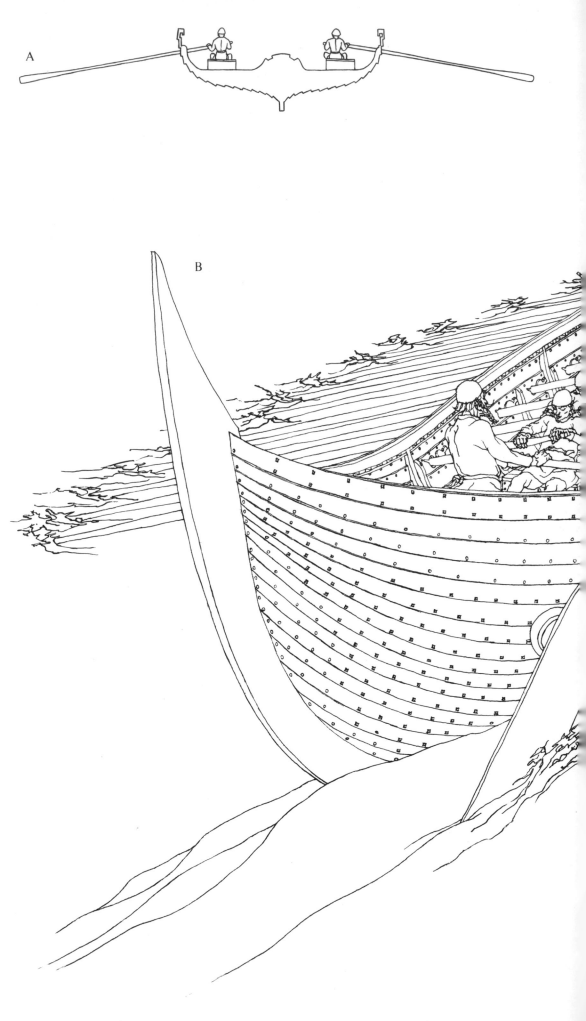

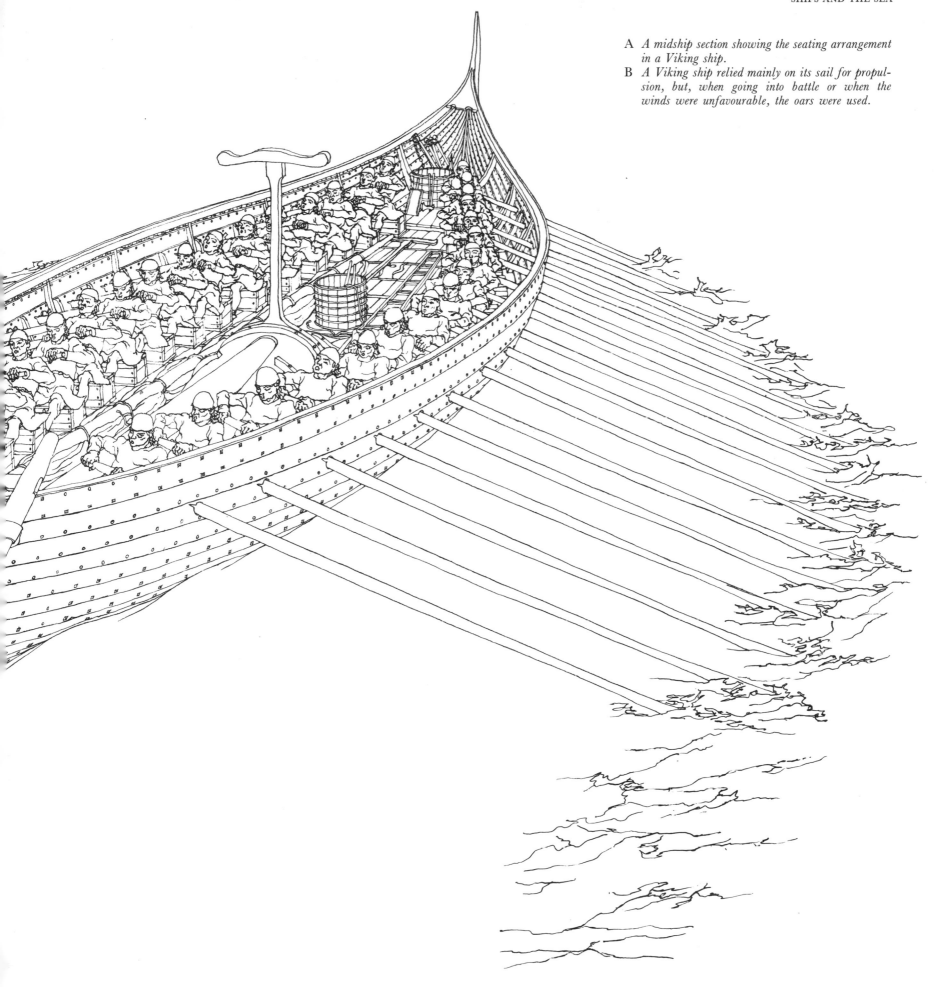

A *A midship section showing the seating arrangement in a Viking ship.*
B *A Viking ship relied mainly on its sail for propulsion, but, when going into battle or when the winds were unfavourable, the oars were used.*

127 A.D.
Ptolemy, the famous Greek astronomer and mathematician, was for some time a librarian at Alexandria. He wrote many books which influenced cultural development for centuries. He taught that the Earth was fixed in space, and that the Sun and the planets orbited around it. This concept was not really upset until the time of Copernicus, some fifteen hundred years after Ptolemy had enunciated his principles.

One of his major works was his *Guide to Geography*. This contained maps of Asia and Africa, and included notes on latitude and longitude. When suitable instruments had been invented, latitude and longitude became the navigator's chief method of plotting his position. Ptolemy's maps 'showed' that India could be reached by crossing the Atlantic, a cartographical mischance that, together with Marco Polo's account of China, would fire the imagination of Christopher Columbus to seek the western route to the East.

c. 350 A.D.
Nicholas, Bishop of Myra in southern Turkey, is executed on the orders of the Roman Emperor for adhering to his faith. He was beatified as Saint Nicholas, and sailors adopted him as their patron saint—as did the pawnbrokers, and little children under his other guise of Father Christmas.

484 A.D.
Saint Brendan is born at Tralee in Ireland. To this day, the Irish look upon him as the patron saint of sailors, rather than the more universally accepted Saint Nicholas. Travellers also claim him as their patron saint along with Saint Christopher. Brendan left an account of his voyage across the Atlantic to the 'Promised Land of the Saints'. He claimed that he had, in fact, reached the land that is now called America. This claim must fail for lack of corroborative evidence. However, it is indisputable that the Vikings found Irish monks already in residence when landing in Iceland, their own stepping-stone to America.

533 A.D.
For centuries, traders had used bills of exchange. Universal discount rates were also in operation. However, insurance was treated in a haphazard manner. In order to bring some sort of system into the Mediterranean area, a Justinian edict of 533 A.D. imposed a charge of six per cent as the legal rate for common usury. Double this rate, that is, twelve per cent, was allowed for maritime cover.

603 A.D.
This is a key date in the emergence of the Italian city states. In this year, Pisa becomes a city republic, building its own fleets of war and merchant ships. Other city republics soon proclaim their autonomy.

655 A.D.
Mohammedan, or Muslim, forces sweep out of Arabia and advance northwards. Mohammedanism, the religion founded by Mohammed (570-632 A.D.) had swept through parts of the Near East, challenging Christianity itself. It was part of the Mohammedan philosophy to spread the Muslim faith by the sword. At the Battle of Lycia, the Byzantine fleet was defeated by the Muslims. The way was open for Arab, and, therefore, Muslim penetration into the western world.

672 A.D.
A Syrian engineer named Callinias invents 'Greek Fire' for his Greek employer. Greek Fire probably was a mixture of naphtha, sulphur, and saltpetre. It was used by being packed into a large tube which had a set of bellows at the charging-end. When the mixture was ignited, it not only burnt furiously, it also floated whilst still aflame. This weapon was offered by the Greeks to the Byzantines, who were themselves of Greek origin. The Byzantines accepted the timely offer and utterly destroyed the invading Mohammedan fleet by fire which rained down on the unnerved Muslims.

8TH CENTURY A.D.
A revolutionary departure in the design of sails is to be noted at about this time, when the lateen or triangular sail becomes established in the Mediterranean. The Arabs were the pioneers of the triangular sail, but it was not given its definitive name—the lateen sail, derived from the very word 'Latin'—until it appeared in the Mediterranean.

Most experts consider the eighth century A.D. to be the correct date for the introduction of the lateen sail in the Mediterranean. However, a relief from a second-century tombstone, found in Piraeus and preserved in the National Archaeological Museum in Athens, showing what appears to be a triangular sail, would suggest that the lateen sail was known in the Mediterranean several centuries earlier.

LATE 8TH CENTURY A.D.
By this time, the Northmen, or Norsemen, as the inhabitants of southern Europe called the fierce raiders from the Scandinavian territories, had already spread terror both far and near. They were seafaring peoples, whose native lands were hard, forbidding, and often barren. In their distinctive craft, they pillaged the coasts of the tribes whose lands bordered the North Sea, the English Channel, and the northern part of the Bay of Biscay.

Soon, the Norsemen were given the name of 'Vikings'. Specifically, the term of Viking was given to the leader of a marauding expedition. The expression 'Viking' means 'the people of the creeks or bays', a reference to the many inlets that score the coastlines of Norway, Sweden, Denmark, and Iceland, the main areas from which the Vikings came. Some scholars suggest that the term was given to the raiding Norsemen because of their habit of lurking in bays until such time as it was considered propitious to launch an attack.

Viking ships were made of wood. Generally, they were long and narrow, and the bow and stern were of similar design. Merchant ships were shorter and wider in the beam than the dreaded longboats, the Viking war vessel.

The standard contemporary method of recording the size of Norse ships was by the 'room'. Thus, a twenty-roomed vessel had twenty pairs of oars. A longboat, which could be all of 130 foot (c. 39 m) long, could have thirty pairs of oars. Longboats had a single, upright mast which was placed dead amidships, and on which a single, square sail was hoisted. The homespun sail was brightly coloured, normally in stripes or in a chequer pattern. The windward surface of the sail was sewn onto rope reinforcements in order to hold the sail in the fierce, blustery winds encountered in northern waters.

Viking ships were given names according to their classification. The three main categories of vessels were merchant ships, war vessels, and craft for use on ceremonial occasions. The drakkars, or great dragon ships, had prows decorated with fiery dragons. Drakkars were the largest of Viking ships. Snekars, or serpent ships, had a snake-head bow. Ledung ships were those supplied as a levy by towns and provinces in times of emergency. They were regarded by the authorities as a strategic reserve of naval vessels.

The Vikings, above all, were explorers and adventurers. They moved south and established a colony that was to become the province of Normandy in France. They also looked westwards and undoubtedly reached North America. For centuries, they dominated the northern waters which became as much a Viking lake as the Mediterranean had been a Roman one.

716 A.D.
The Egyptians install the Nilometer at Cairo. This instrument was marked in cubits. (One cubit equals 22 inches or 55.8 cm.) The Nilometer was a stone pillar that stood in a well and measured the rise and fall of the waters of the Nile.

826-31 A.D.
Despite having suffered various reverses, the Arabs continue with their policy of conquest in Europe. A large seaborne force penetrates the Mediterranean and conquers the island of Sicily, which is held by Arab interests for the next 260 years.

844 A.D.
Vikings based in Norway mount major offensives as far south as Seville in Spain.

The Norsemen, who had travelled south by way of Walcheren in Holland and who ravaged

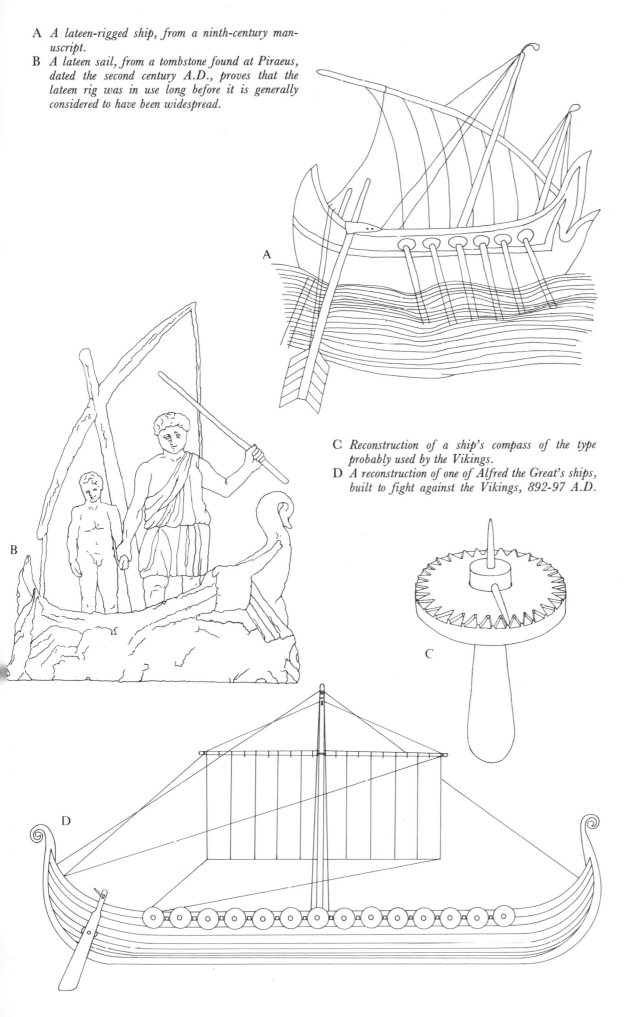

A *A lateen-rigged ship, from a ninth-century man-uscript.*
B *A lateen sail, from a tombstone found at Piraeus, dated the second century A.D., proves that the lateen rig was in use long before it is generally considered to have been widespread.*

C *Reconstruction of a ship's compass of the type probably used by the Vikings.*
D *A reconstruction of one of Alfred the Great's ships, built to fight against the Vikings, 892-97 A.D.*

parts of England, also establish a colony in Ireland. Dublin is one of the major Irish cities founded by the Vikings.

839 A.D.

Amalfi, a seaport of southern Italy near Naples, rebels against the Lombards and declares itself a city republic. Its navy wins a reputation for being one of the most fierce and barbaric in the entire Mediterranean theatre. It probably reached the peak of its influence at the beginning of the eleventh century. In 1010, the Amalfian Code was promulgated. The Code was a series of sixty-six articles regulating maritime law and custom. It had application over a wide spectrum of western commercial powers. Quarrels with more powerful neighbours, and the encroachemnt of the sea, eventually weakened Amalfi, which went into a decline from which it never recovered.

840 A.D.

The famous city of Venice, at the head of the Adriatic, was founded by refugees from Attila in the fifth century. It already had a long history of commercialism, good government, and cultural activities when it declared itself a city republic in 840 A.D. One of the prime tasks of the new government was to build innumerable ships, and Venice thus became one of the most important of the Mediterranean maritime powers. It was from Venice that Marco Polo began his famous journey to the East.

The city republic adopted the flag of the Lion of St. Mark in honour of its magnificent cathedral of St. Mark, one of the glories of the Romanesque-Byzantine style. It affirmed its dependence upon the sea and its maritime interests by instituting a ceremony in which each year the Doge, or leader of the City Fathers, symbolically marries the city to the sea by casting a ring of gold into the waters.

849 A.D.

The Saracens, an Islamic people from Palestine, continue the policy of bringing Mohammedanism to the western nations by the power of the sword. They attack Amalfi, but are beaten in a critical naval engagement at the Battle of Ostia.

MID-9TH CENTURY A.D.

About this time, reports appear in chronicles of the first use of the new compass perfected by Flavio Gioia. Basically, he merely improved the ancient Chinese compass by using water instead of oil to carry the float, and also by mounting a compass card, thus enabling actual sailing courses to be set accurately.

872 A.D.

Harald Haarfager (Fair-hair) succeeds in unifying Norway under his authority. He intensifies the incidence of Viking raids, and rarely remains in Norway for long periods, but leads

A

a large fleet of drakkars, which sails into the fjords of northern Europe, devastating the settlements that they encounter. However, he quarrelled with many of his erstwhile staunchest supporters, so that two years later, in 874 A.D., many deserted him. The defectors, most of whom were of noble birth and jarl status, threw in their lot with Ingolfur Arnarson, who led an expedition to Iceland. Here, they established a Viking settlement, which they named Reykjavik—Smoky Bay. It was from Reykjavik that Eric the Red left to settle in Greenland, and, according to some authorities, to discover America.

NOVEMBER 24, 885 A.D.
A combined force of Norsemen, Angles, and Saxons, under Sinric, attacks Paris. The force numbers some 30,000 warriors, carried in 700 longboats, which beach on the Seine opposite the French capital. After a siege lasting for a year, Charles the Fat, King of France, has to pay the raiders the sum of 700 gold livres to induce them to leave Paris and go and raid elsewhere. This they do.

892-897 A.D.
Alfred the Great, King of the West Saxons in England, creates a navy whose prime duty is to ward off the marauding Vikings. In this he had much success, although for some time the country was split into two parts, in one of which the Danes held power. In 897 A.D., Alfred captured all the Danish ships that were wintering at Benfleet, a small town near the mouth of the River Thames.

The Cottonian Manuscript, a Saxon record written during Alfred's lifetime, describes his new fleet. It was composed of galleys, twice the size of existing vessels, having forty or even sixty oars a side. They were deeper in draught than previous craft, and much steadier in sea lanes. They astonished the Danes by their power. The manuscript refers to an encounter off the Isle of Wight in 897 A.D., during which the Danes were routed. Incidentally, the deep-water sites where Danes landed were called 'hwearf' —the word that is now 'wharf'.

911 A.D.
Charles the Simple, King of the Franks, makes an arrangement with the Norsemen who, despite the bribes that had been paid by his predecessors, had persisted in raiding France and, in particular, Paris. He cedes a vast area at the mouth of the River Seine to them, and allows them to occupy it permanently. Charles was not so simple, for he appreciated that his new 'subjects' would not allow other raiders to harass the region. By the Treaty of St. Clair-sur-Epte, he created Rollo, leader of the Norsemen, Duke of Normandy. The area that the Norsemen occupied was renamed 'Normandy'.

c. 986 A.D.
Eric the Red leads a small expedition from Iceland to Greenland. A small Viking colony was soon thriving. It was the native Eskimos of Greenland who told the new arrivals about land to the south; land, moreover, that was beyond the ice-line, and which, presumably, would have a more equable climate. These Eskimo stories were confirmed by a Viking trader named Bjarni Herjulfsson who, whilst on a trading mission in his own vessel, was blown off course and brought up at a place called Markland, the modern Labrador. Bjarni Herjulfsson did not land, but sailed up and down the coast, noted the forests, and then came back and reported his discovery.

991 A.D.
Olaf Tryggvason leads a Viking fleet of 93

B

THE BAYEUX TAPESTRY
A *The Norman fleet sets sail for England.*
B *Harold returns to England after his visit to William.*

ships in an invasion of south-east England. Sandwich, in Kent, and Ipswich, in Suffolk, were destroyed before he sailed up the Blackwater estuary and landed at Maldon in Essex. Here, in a famous battle, he utterly defeated the army of King Ethelred. Three years later, another major Viking expedition under the command of Olaf Tryggvason and Swegen of Norway unsuccessfully attempted to capture London. King Ethelred was happy to pay protection money amounting to £16,000, the equivalent of £3,000,000 in present-day currency, in order to buy off the Viking invaders. This was one example of payment of the notorious Danegeld, most of which found its way back to the home lands of the Vikings.

c. 1001

This is one of the key dates in the story of sea exploration. About the summer of 1001, Leif Ericsson, son of Eric the Red, sails with a crew of thirty-five from Greenland, in an attempt to re-discover the legendary Markland of Bjarni Herjulfsson. Markland was duly reached, but the small band of Vikings continued in a southerly direction. Eventually, they reached a commodious bay, fringed with trees and masses of berries, very similar to the known wineberries of Europe. They landed at this spot, and named the land they had reached Vinland.

For many years argument has waxed over the exact location of the site of the landing of Leif Ericsson and his small band of Vikings. Runic stones have been discovered in Labrador. More recently, the site of two large houses, some 70 foot (21 m) long and 55 foot (16.8 m) wide, was discovered at L'Anse aux Meadows in northern Newfoundland. Turf walls and central fire-places were easily distinguishable. The C-14 test, which has a tolerance of plus or minus a hundred years, was applied to the charred remains that were discovered at the site. A date of 1000 A.D. was given to the remains. This accords well with the known date of Leif Ericsson's voyage. A Viking bronze pin was also found at the site.

Now, it is known that Leif Ericsson and his men built a large house near where they had landed. They probably spent the winter of 1001-1002 there before re-victualling their ship with fresh supplies, and returning home in the spring of 1002. On the face of it, this particular expedition of Leif Ericsson wintered at Newfoundland, and not on the mainland of America.

Over the next decade, further Viking expeditions travelled to the western lands. Almost certainly, the mainland of America was reached, as well as Newfoundland. But the Vikings never gained a serious foothold in these new territories, mainly because the native Red Indians, *Skraelings* as they were called by the men from the north, after an initial curiosity turned definitely hostile. In 1013, the Vikings abandoned their attempts to colonize these areas. Even the well-established settlements in Greenland were left to their fate when supply

A   *The oldest recovered ship with a stern-rudder, the Kalmar Ship No. 1, was found at Kalmar, Sweden, and is dated c. 1250.*

B   *Midship section of the Kalmar Ship No. 1, showing the capstan used to hoist the sail.*

C   *The earliest known illustration of a ship with a stern-rudder, from the font in Winchester Cathedral, England, c. 1180 A.D.*

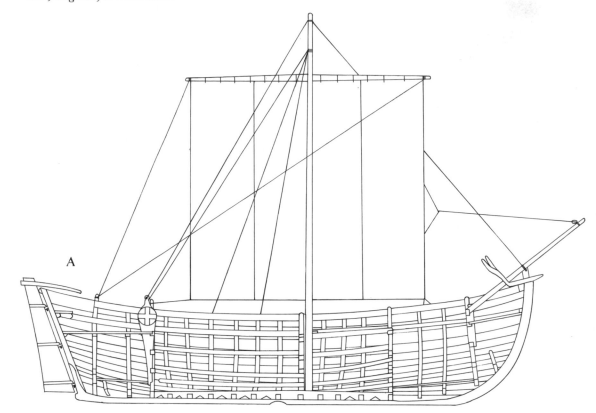

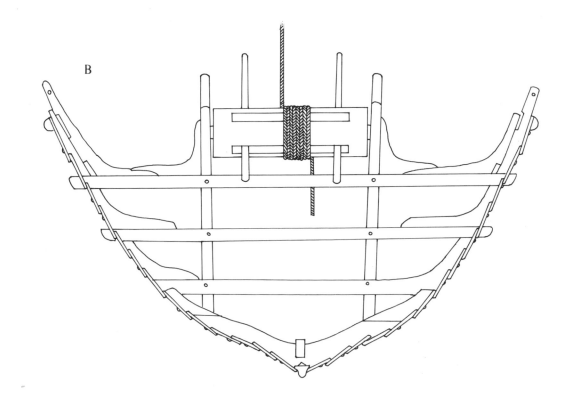

ships from the home countries failed to arrive. This was due to the increasing internecine struggles in the Scandinavian territories.

Time passed. In 1408, a ship, seeking refuge from a terrible storm, anchored in Greenland where the more easterly of the two settlements had been. Wild cattle bearing a distinct resemblance to Norwegian cattle were discovered. Five hundred years later, in the 1920s, another expedition discovered frozen bodies at the site of Eric the Red's settlement, where they had lain for nearly a thousand years.

All this evidence suggests that the Vikings discovered and colonized both the off-shore islands and the mainland of America some four hundred years before Columbus made his epic voyage in 1492.

1066

It is ironic that the two greatest amphibious invasions in history took place across the same stretch of water: the English Channel that separates France from England. On September 28, 1066, William, Duke of Normandy invaded and conquered England; on June 6, 1944, the Allied Powers returned to Normandy.

Traditionally, navies were 'bedded' down for the winter, which was rarely a campaigning season. In the spring of 1066, Harold of England had an excellent and totally adequate fleet that could have repelled any invader. The fleet, which assembled at Sandwich, would have proved too much of a stumbling-block to William. However, no Norman invasion occurred during the spring or the summer. Foolishly, because of faulty intelligence, Harold allowed the fleet to disperse when autumn gales suggested that no invasion was possible that year.

The cause of the non-event during the spring and summer of 1066 was the lack of an adequate Norman fleet to ferry William's army across the Channel. Energetically, he set about remedying this situation. He built ships in large quantities, and 'borrowed' many more from his allies and friends. Eventually, he had at his disposal about 400 big and 1,000 small craft, according to the historian Augustin Thierry. This vast armada assembled in the mouth of the River Dives, and then sailed the hundred miles (161 km) to St. Valery, where 65,000 troops had assembled by September 14.

For ten days, savage gales lashed the Channel. But on September 27, a sunny calm prevailed. William gave the order to embark, took to his own ship, the MORA, and arrived off a deserted Pevensey on the morning of September 28, 1066. The rest is history.

LATE 11TH CENTURY

It is during the reign of William that the Cinque Ports are first mentioned. In return for various trading privileges, the five towns of Dover, Sandwich, Romney, Winchelsea, and Rye, through the agency of the Warden of the Cinque Ports, had, in the event of a sudden invasion, to provide the English Crown with 'Fifty-seven ships, each ship to be furnished with twenty-one men, able, qualify'd, and well armed, and one boy. The master of each ship and the constables to receive a salary of sixpence a day, and each vulgar mariner to have three pence a day and thus to attend the King.' The Warden of the Cinque Ports kept this fleet available both for William the Conqueror and for his son, William II, better known as William Rufus. It is held by some historians that the interest shown by William Rufus in the fleet marks the origins of British sea power and supremacy for most of the next eight hundred years.

1097

The First Crusade takes place. Five city states provide the fleet. Venice and Genoa each contribute 200 galleys; Pisa donates 120, and Barcelona and Marseilles each provide large contingents. Philip I of France donates huge sums of money. Godfrey de Bouillon and Robert, Duke of Normandy command the force which occupies Jerusalem in July, 1099, and returns it to Christian government and worship until 1187.

1120

This is a tragic year for Henry I of England, one of the ten children of William the Conqueror. He had been to Normandy, accompanied by a large entourage, including his son, William, and his daughter, Mary. The return to England was scheduled for the November, a time notorious for Channel storms. Henry left Barfleur in the lead ship a little while before William, who was in the WHITE SHIP. Some of the prince's companions urged him to race it back to England, hoping to arrive there before his father, the King. William accepted the challenge. The WHITE SHIP had scarcely cleared Barfleur harbour before she foundered, her bottom ripped out on a hidden reef. William could have escaped in the ship's boat, into which he hastily descended; but he thought he heard his sister cry out from the stricken vessel, to which he returned, and was never seen again. It is reported that Henry I never smiled again after he had been told of the tragedy. Rahere, his private jester, made the pilgrimage to Rome to try to find solace for his master. On his return, he founded St. Bartholomew's Hospital, which has ministered to the sick of London ever since. As a direct result of the tragedy of the WHITE SHIP, when Henry I died, civil war tore the country asunder for nearly forty years.

1143

Portugal declares her independence from Spain. The first thing that an independent Portugal did was to commence a shipbuilding industry. From this beginning, she became one of the most powerful maritime powers of medieval times.

1147

For lack of a transport fleet, the Second Crusade, led by Louis VII of France, failed miserably.

1170-77

Attempts by Venice to dominate the eastern waters of the Mediterranean lead to war with Byzantium. Confrontations ranged from minor skirmishes between individual vessels to large-scale sea battles involving entire fleets. All the engagements proved inconclusive. Eventually, by tacit agreement, Venice and Byzantium followed a policy of trying to keep clear of each other whilst still retaining a naval presence in the area in order to preserve a balance of power.

Many Italian archives contain full descriptions of the Venetian ships of this period. The vessels appear to be of the same design throughout. They had an overall length of 117 foot (35.6 m), a beam of 12 foot (3.7 m), and a depth of 6.6 foot (2.0 m). The main propulsion came from the 108 oars that were provided, 54 on each side. The oars measured 26 foot (7.9 m), and were set on an outrigger a yard (0.9 m) away from the hull.

1180

Somewhere about this time, ships begin to acquire proper rudders. Hitherto, ships had used steering oars worked from the starboard side. Port, or larboard, was the side nearer the quay, and the tackle to unload cargo was fitted only to this side of a vessel. It is not known when a rudder was first used to replace a steering oar, but on the font of Winchester Cathedral, and on a wall of Fide Church in Gotland, Sweden, appear illustrations of a ship of this time with a rudder plainly visible instead of the

C

A *St. Louis of France's last crusade, 1270. This woodcut, dated 1518, shows the army disembarking at Carthage. St. Louis died shortly after this.*

B *The town seal of Sandwich, on the south-east coast of England, one of the Cinque Ports. Many European ports of the twelfth to the fourteenth centuries had their most common type of merchant ship depicted on their seals. However, as these seals were round, the illustrations are distorted, and cannot be regarded as accurate.*

customary steering oar. There does not appear to be any record of the inventor of the rudder, but Friesland probably first used the device.

1190

This is the time of the Third Crusade. Richard I of England, better known as Richard Lion Heart, was responsible for assembling the fleet that was to take the Crusaders to the Near East. In April, the Devonshire port of Dartmouth accommodated the largest fleet ever seen in an English port. It was a fleet of all nations. England made an enormous contribution, but the elements provided by Normandy, Brittany, Anjou, Poitou, and Aquitaine together outnumbered the English contingent.

The voyage was not propitious. The fleet of over 600 ships set sail in May, 1190, under the command of Robert de Sabloil and Gerard, Archbishop of Aix. It did not arrive off Acre, the port of disembarkation, until June 1, 1191. Richard, impatient with the slowness of the voyage, temporarily left the fleet, and proceeded on his way in hired, and speedier, Genoese craft.

Richard's sailing orders still exist. A triangular formation was adopted. In the van were three vessels transporting the ladies of the Court. Richard's fiancée, Berengaria, was in this party. Six ranks of ships followed the van. Each rank from the second to the seventh contained ten ships more than its immediate preceding rank: thirteen ships in the second rank (this allowed for the three ships in the van), twenty in the third, thirty in the fourth, and so on until the seventh rank, which contained sixty vessels. Finally, forming the rearguard, came Richard himself wearing his flag in the TRENCHE LE MER, with an escort of fifty galleys.

The blockade of Acre by elements of this vast fleet is remarkable for one of the most memorable engagements in the annals of the sea. A magnificent, three-masted Turkish vessel was encountered, taking over a thousand reinforcements to the Muslims besieged in Acre. Without even waiting to identify the ship—its name, in fact, was never known—Richard despatched a galley to reconnoitre. The reckless galley was driven off with a shower of arrows and a rain of Greek Fire. Piqued, Richard ordered an all-out attack. Wave after wave of Crusaders moved in, boarding the Turkish vessel at least a dozen times. Each time they were driven back into the sea. Richard now ordered ramming tactics. He also threatened to hang any captain who held back from the fight. Once again, the English attacked, successive galleys being driven hard into the Turkish transport.

These tactics prevailed. The Turkish vessel heeled over. The doomed reinforcements stood on her side, on her bottom, fighting in serried ranks until the vessel slipped beneath the waters. Even then, whilst drowning, the Muslims fought their would-be rescuers. Out of a complement of some 1,500 aboard that Turkish ship, only forty-two were saved.

It is an epic story of vain heroism—three days later, Acre fell.

1200

Richard, Coeur de Lion, is looked upon as a land warrior, a noble Crusader; but, as has already been shown, he was a sea-fighter as well. He long had the interests of the sea at heart. One of his major contributions to the story of the sea is the *Rules of Oleron*. The rules

B

attempted to regulate commercial ventures at sea, to up-date the *Lex Rhodia*, and to provide for the safety of both ships and seamen. The main clauses of the *Rules of Oleron* are:

§

All (legal) codes identify passengers as being part of the venture and community aboard ship.

§

They recognize the responsibilities of the Captain.

§

The obligations of the Captain, in case of danger and decision, are defined. He must consult his 'community' —especially the merchants whose cargo he carries.

§

The system of 'contributions' is defined. Today, 'contributions' bear the name of 'General Averaging'. By this system, everyone shares in the sacrifice or expenditure arising from the perils of the sea.

§

Owners, masters, and merchants are warned not to overload ships.

§

Valuables to be declared, or there can be no claim for loss.

§

The duties of seamen together with their responsibilities are listed. Chief among them is the instruction that, when anchored in port, a ship must have its crew sleeping aboard.

§

That any merchant left behind at a port because the safety of the ship demands that she puts to sea has no claim on the others.

§

That if a crew member be left behind, he is to receive no pay until he joins his ship at the next port.

§

Captains cannot ill-treat members of the crew. (A scale of fines was laid down, the fines increasing according to the severity of the ill-treatment.)

§

Bottomry—the borrowing of money to enable a voyage to continue—is legally recognized. The ship itself may be used as security for the loan.

§

A scale of fines to be laid down covering various contingencies.
　　N.B. The Lex Rhodia, *which also listed a scale of fines for similar contingencies, quoted its awards in gold. The* Rules of Oleron *quotes its awards in 'Tuns'.*
　　For some time, north European ships were measured by the number of wine casks they could carry. The casks in which the wine was carried were called 'tuns'. Today, ships are still measured in 'tons'. This is because the English authorities fixed the size of the tun at 252 gallons of wine, the weight of which was 2,240 pounds (1016.0 kg). This is still the weight of a ton, although the 'short' ton and the 'long' ton have been introduced.

§

Contracts should be in writing and not made verbally.

§

Penalties are exacted for the stealing of equipment which could imperil the ship at sea.

§

All participating in a voyage must stand together until the end of the voyage. An oath to this effect must be taken.

The *Rules of Oleron* remained effective for hundreds of years. It was not until 1494 that the city of Barcelona introduced its 'Consulate of the Sea' which reproduced much of the earlier codes. The Spanish code was translated into Italian and Dutch and was enforced in many waters. Richard's *Rules of Oleron* was also translated, for, as Edward I said of the code: 'They (the laws) were made by Lord Richard, formerly King of England, on his return from the Holy Land, corrected and declared and were published in the Island of Oleron and were named in the French tongue *La Ley Olyroun*'.

1202

The Fourth Crusade takes place; an event of little historic significance, but memorable in the history of the sea for the vast armada that a single city state—Venice—could muster for the transport of the combatants.

'The Queen of the Adriatic'—as Venice was to be called—provided and furnished, from its own resources, 1,200 ships, which embarked 4,500 horses, 9,000 horsemen and grooms, and 20,000 foot soldiers, with stores sufficient to feed the entire complement for a minimum of two months.

The mass movement of ships was usually under the supreme command of an Admiral of the Fleet. Enrico Dandolo was the Admiral for the Fourth Crusade. One can judge of the enormous wealth of Venice that it was able to supply such a fleet without bankrupting itself.

1229

Henry III of England issues a new law instructing the warden of the Cinque Ports to keep in instant readiness for the service of the Crown 57 ships, 1,140 men, and 57 boys.

1255

Venice decides to make its own sea laws. This was at a time of increasing rivalry among the city states of Venice, Genoa, and Pisa for the domination of the Italian seas, a struggle that Genoa won. However, all Venice's fleets came under the new Venetian laws. The Venetian council also fixed the size of ships, and the amount of port dues attracted by the craft. Two units of measurement date from this time: the amphora, which was equal to six gallons (27.3 l), and the modius—a word 'borrowed' from an old Roman measure—which was equal to two gallons (9.1 l). According to Venetian maritime law, a new ship was valued at fifty gold pieces for each thousand modii of size.

1263

Haakon Haakonsson, King of Norway, attempts to restore Norwegian rule in the Hebrides. His fleet of Viking galleys is dispersed by gales, and he is defeated at the Battle of Largs by King Alexander III of Scotland, who, under the terms of the Treaty of Perth in 1266, purchases the islands from money derived from sea tolls. In

A *A reconstruction of the ship on the seal of Dover.*
B *The Winchelsea seal, thirteenth century.*

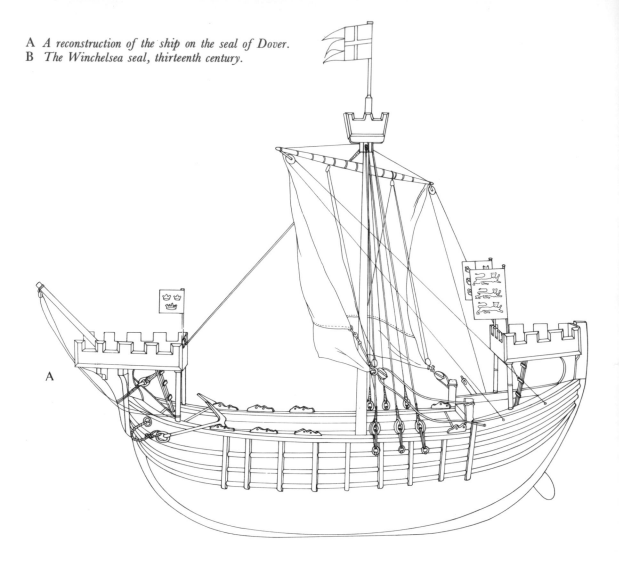

fact, so affluent was Alexander because of the tolls levied from sea traders, that he already had the purchase price available in cash and did not need to impose further taxes in order to meet the cost.

1266

Roger Bacon (1220-92), who is credited in the western world with the invention of gunpowder, declares that the earth is round and not flat. Not many people believed him. He also wrote, 'It is possible that great ships and seagoing vessels shall be made which can be guided by one man and will move with greater swiftness than if they were full of oarsmen.'

1270

An expedition to the Canary Islands by an Italian navigator, Malocello, is recorded. The Canary Islands were probably known by the ancients from the recorded circumnavigations of Africa, and had been known to the Vikings since 600 A.D. However, it was still an intrepid act of seamanship to navigate in those latitudes, for it was common belief that, because the waters were equatorial, then anybody sailing in them would be boiled alive. It was not until the time of Prince Henry the Navigator, whose life spanned roughly the first half of the fifteenth century, that this particular old-wive's tale was scotched.

1279

Fishing was one of the most important activities of those countries that had Atlantic coastlines. La Rochelle, a port in the west of France, was convenient for both French and Spanish interests for many years until the Basques, who had used the port, decided that it was too far south from the major fishing areas. Therefore, they erected a fish-drying plant in Brittany. This led to nearly twenty years of dispute and fighting among the various peoples who fished these waters. In 1292, Norman sailors attacked Bayonnese ships at harbour in St. Matthieu, a small sea port of Brittany. In retaliation, eighty Norman ships which were loading at Bordeaux, which at that time was an English possession, were attacked. This was the signal for a free-for-all in which something like 400 vessels of all nations engaged in general fighting and piracy.

1281

One of the first of many deliberate attempts to

C *The arrangement of the two steering oars on a thirteenth-century Mediterranean merchantman.*
D *The ship on the seal of Hastings, thirteenth century.*

B

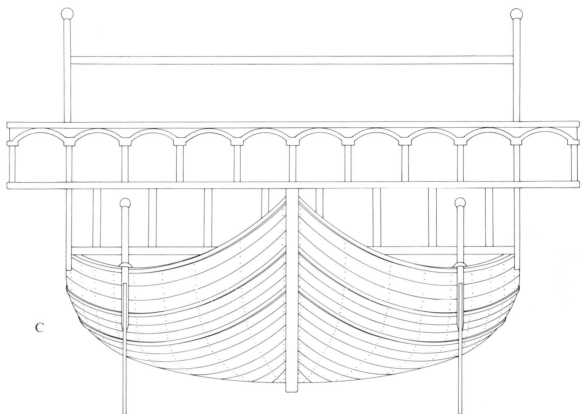

C

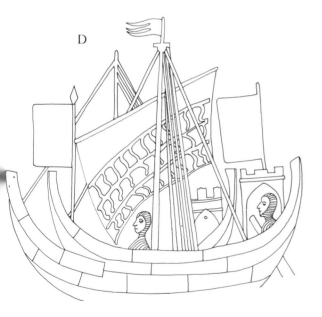

D

reach India by way of Africa and America is made. Two galleys under the command of Ugolino and Guido Vivaldi leave Genoa in an attempt to reach India by way of West Africa. They are never heard of again.

1284

Two significant changes in the design of ships occur about this time. Pictorial, rather than written, evidence has to be relied upon for proof of these changes.

The first change is registered on the seals of the Cinque Ports, whose vessels were now so integrated as a unit that they flew the same type of flag. The seals depict ships with forecastles, aftercastles, bowsprits, and reefed sails.

The second change involves ships that had adopted the lateen type of sail. Such vessels now are depicted with two wings projecting beyond the stern of the vessel. The size of the yards demanded a cradle for stowage. Where ships had two masts, then the stern cradle became a necessity to hold the stowed yard.

AUGUST 6, 1284

The Battle of Meloria occurs, by which the successful Genoese fleet under Admiral Oberto Doria and Admiral Benedetto Zaccaria not only defeats the Pisan fleet under Admiral Alberto Morosini but also captures the Admiral himself. Thus Genoa became the chief sea power in that part of the Mediterranean.

1292-94

Philip IV of France, nicknamed Philip the Handsome, issues instructions for ships to be built at Marseilles, and for others to be bought from Genoa, the leading naval power in the Mediterranean. He also gave instructions for a naval base to be built at Rouen to the design of the Genoese expert, Enrico Marchese. When finished, the base made a major contribution to the French naval organization. The Rouen base was a large walled area, with a moat and a central dock. The actual shipyard was entered by way of a lock. The repair yards and slipways were covered, thus assuring continuity of work. Seventeen ships at a time could be serviced at the base. From its slipways was launched a steady stream of vessels: galliots, which were speedy, galley-like craft native to the Mediterranean; nefs, which originated in Scandinavia; barjots, which were sailing barges; and flambarts, which were similar to barjots.

A

B

By 1295, Philip IV's Galley Yard at Rouen has turned out fifty ships, of which the RICHESSE became the fleet flagship.

1297

Now that Philip the Handsome had his fleet, he decided to blockade England. Aided by his allies, he mustered 200 galleys, 100 'great shippes', and 50,000 men under Admiral Michel du Mans, to whom he gave orders to sweep the English from the seas. Trade was, indeed, hampered to such an extent that the Flemings, who had enjoyed a thriving woollen industry with the English for many years, rebelled. Victories were won by both sides, with the French, whose navy was now commanded by Grimaldi, ultimately destroying the major part of the Flemish fleet at the Battle of Zieriksee on the Scheldt.

1300

The beginning of the century saw the beginning of one of the first and one of the most famous of the commercial 'leagues' that abound in history: the Hanseatic League. The cities of Hamburg, Bremen, and Danzig, which were later joined by Lübeck, banded themselves together for protection and for the furtherance of their trading interests. Eventually, they even rationalized the design of their ships, which were built primarily in order to engage in the northern trade. These ships relied solely upon sail for propulsion, without even supplementary oars. The hull design incorporated a straight stem with a fitted rudder.

Apart from its main functions of building ships and engaging in trade, the Hanseatic League also introduced various banking practices. This it did by opening four 'counting

A *The seal of the Flanders port of Damme, 1309.*
B *As evidenced in this early fourteenth-century manuscript, sea battles were very much an extension of land battles. The ships illustrated are cogs, fitted with fore- and stern-castles, which were used as fighting platforms. Cogs were normally merchant ships.*
C *The ship on the seal of Poole, 1325.*

D

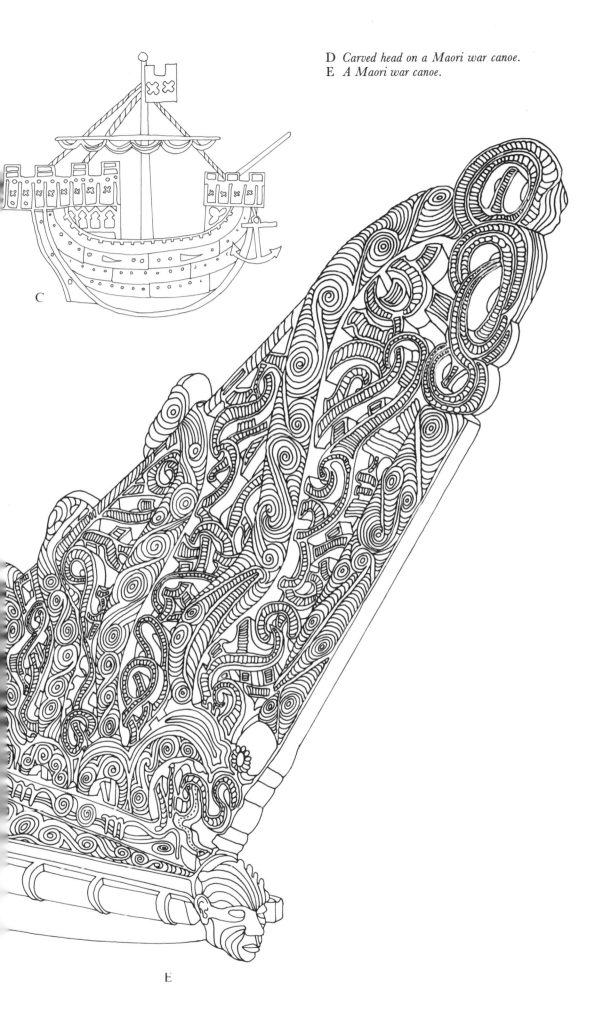

D *Carved head on a Maori war canoe.*
E *A Maori war canoe.*

C

E

houses' at Novgorod, Bergen, Bruges, and London respectively. These counting houses were, in fact, Exchanges where merchants and owners, who were often represented by agents, could deal in most currencies. Shipping documents were also rationalized by the League.

The influence of the Hanseatic League waxed as that of the Viking 'empire' waned. In 1349, Norway surrendered her seaborne trade to the League. In 1370, by the Treaty of Stralsund, Denmark ceded her Baltic fish exporting interests to the League. Eventually, the Hanseatic League claimed that all northern European waters and the Baltic Sea were her sphere of influence.

The League undoubtedly did a vast amount of good. It introduced a system of standard weights and measures, introduced mercantile law, maintained a maritime intelligence service, constructed canals, and made—and unmade—kings. The League remained a major power until the middle of the seventeenth century. It still existed, if in name only, until well into the twentieth century.

1319
The use of cannon mounted on suitable ships is reported in this year. The Genoese are credited with introducing this type of warfare.

JUNE 24, 1340
The Hundred Years' War between France and England had already dragged on for three years when the Battle of Ecluse, perhaps better known as the Battle of Sluys, is fought. As a result of the English victory, Edward III, whose vessel actually sank underneath him, was given the title of 'King of the Sea'. The name of Edward's flagship was THOMAS, a cog, with Richard Fylle in command. Six years later, Edward reinforced the victory at Sluys with another at Calais, in which 738 small sailing-ships came under his command.

Edward III also greatly encouraged English trade with the Continent, for which he was given the nickname of 'The Father of English Commerce'.

1350
The Maori Great Fleet leaves Tahiti and crosses to the land now known as New Zealand, there to establish a flourishing colony. The islands forming New Zealand had, in fact, been invaded in the twelfth century, when Toi-kai-rakan, a Polynesian adventurer, founded a settlement there. The Maoris overcame the tribes that had established themselves, mainly of Tangata Whenua stock, and introduced a system of policing the waters and rivers near their settlements, using their large and speedy war canoes for the purpose.

AUGUST 29, 1350
A Spanish 'pirate' fleet under a notorious freebooter, Don Carlos de la Cerda, harasses Channel shipping and invests the port of

A *A hulk of the Hanseatic League, loaded with a cargo of dried fish, perhaps on her way from Bergen to Lübeck. The hulk was the most important type of ship used by the Hanseatic League in the fifteenth century.*

B *Three types of medieval tops.*

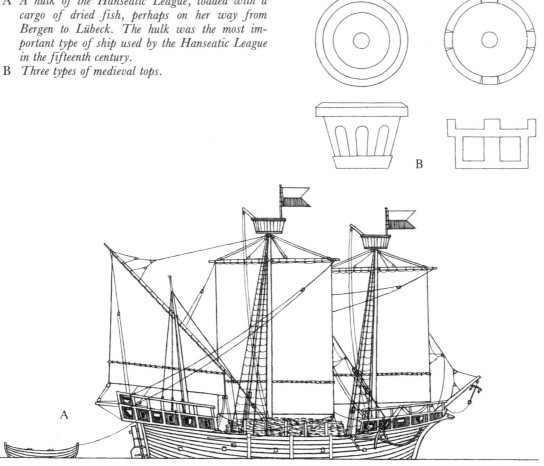

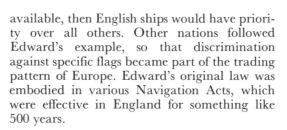

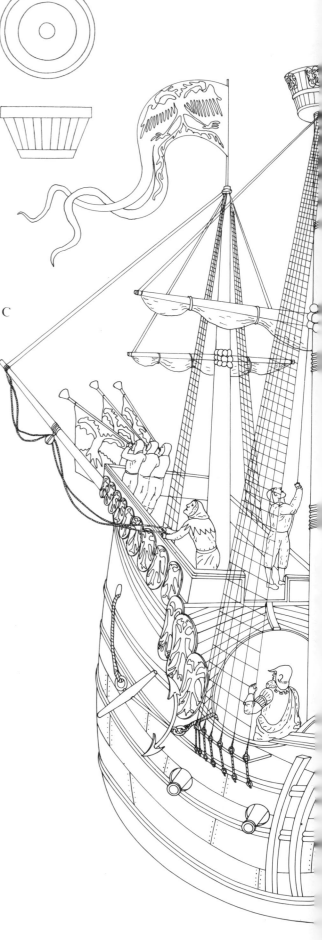

Winchelsea. Edward himself and his son, the Black Prince, were in the squadron that defeated the Spanish, twenty-six of whose ships out of a total of forty were taken as prizes.

1364

Charles V of France, Charles the Wise, disbands the French Mediterranean Fleet under the command of Etienne de Brandin, and concentrates French naval power, in alliance with Castile, in the Bay of Biscay and the English Channel. The strategy was highly successful, for by 1375 he had driven the English out of Europe, except for their holdings in Bayonne, Bordeaux, and Calais.

1368

Edward III of England commences the practice of discrimination against foreign vessels. At this time, Edward ruled not only England but also Guienne and Gascony in France. These French possessions were large-scale exporters of wine, mainly to England. In the year under review, Edward passed a law which stated, 'Only ships owned in Guienne and Gascony may carry wine to England.' The law also contained a clause that if no Guienne or Gascoigne ships were

available, then English ships would have priority over all others. Other nations followed Edward's example, so that discrimination against specific flags became part of the trading pattern of Europe. Edward's original law was embodied in various Navigation Acts, which were effective in England for something like 500 years.

c. 1370

A radical advance is made in the sail pattern of ships. Specifications and drawings of some ships from this time show both lateen and square sails. In the Mediterranean, such ships are carvel-built and are given the name of 'carracks'. In northern waters, they are clinker-built and are called 'hulks'.

JUNE 22, 1372

England suffers one of her worst defeats when the attempt by the Earl of Pembroke to relieve the besieged town of La Rochelle fails. Pembroke's squadron is completely destroyed, and he himself is captured by Admiral Bocanegra and his Castilian fleet. As a result of this crushing defeat, Guienne returns to French sovereignty.

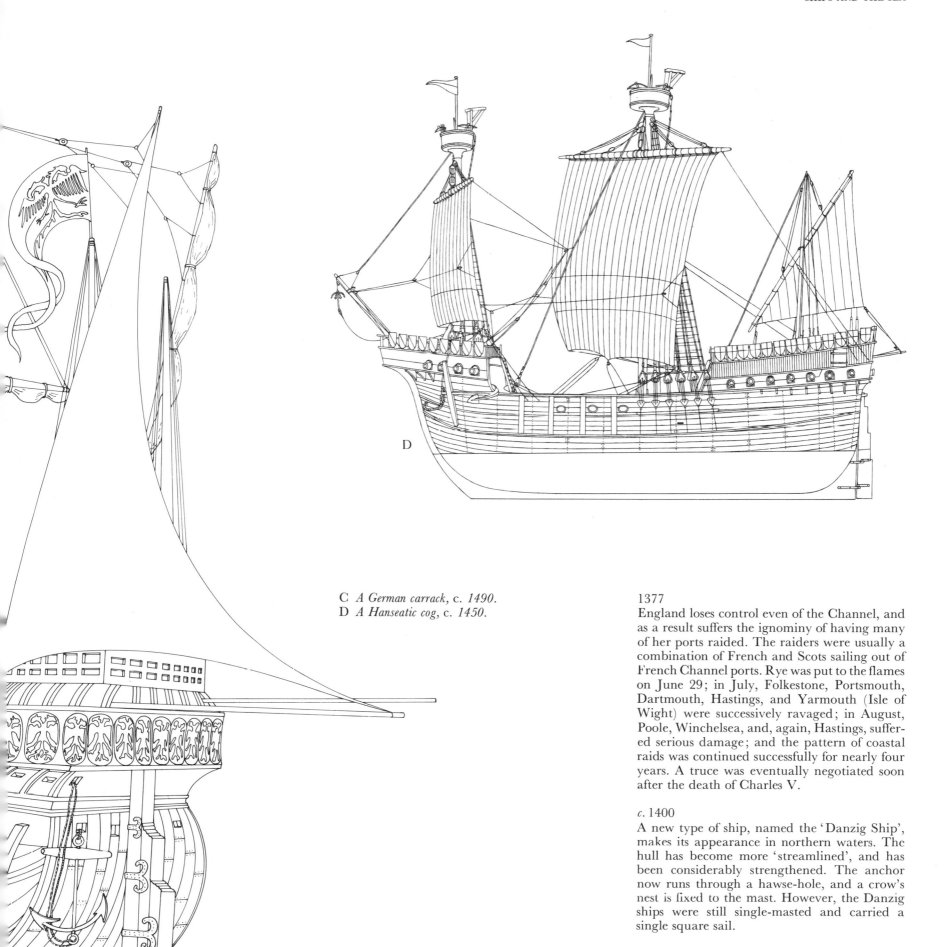

C *A German carrack, c. 1490.*
D *A Hanseatic cog, c. 1450.*

1377

England loses control even of the Channel, and as a result suffers the ignominy of having many of her ports raided. The raiders were usually a combination of French and Scots sailing out of French Channel ports. Rye was put to the flames on June 29; in July, Folkestone, Portsmouth, Dartmouth, Hastings, and Yarmouth (Isle of Wight) were successively ravaged; in August, Poole, Winchelsea, and, again, Hastings, suffered serious damage; and the pattern of coastal raids was continued successfully for nearly four years. A truce was eventually negotiated soon after the death of Charles V.

c. 1400

A new type of ship, named the 'Danzig Ship', makes its appearance in northern waters. The hull has become more 'streamlined', and has been considerably strengthened. The anchor now runs through a hawse-hole, and a crow's nest is fixed to the mast. However, the Danzig ships were still single-masted and carried a single square sail.

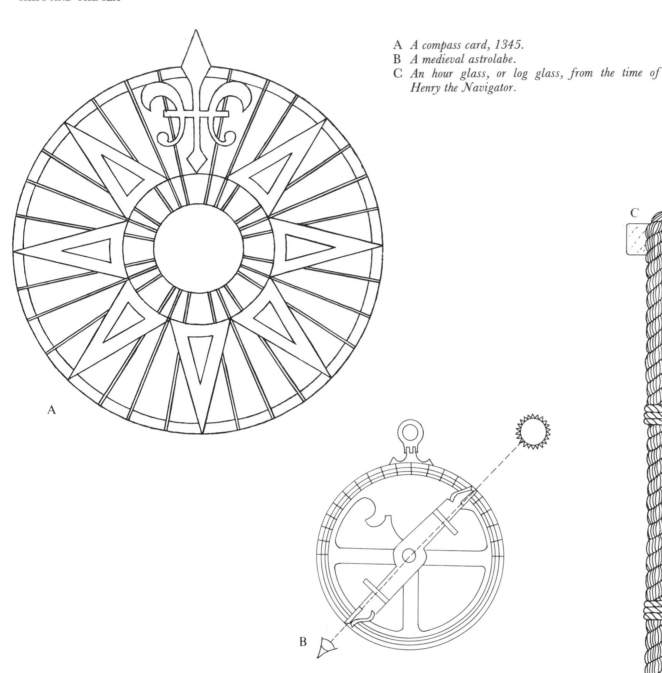

A *A compass card, 1345.*
B *A medieval astrolabe.*
C *An hour glass, or log glass, from the time of Henry the Navigator.*

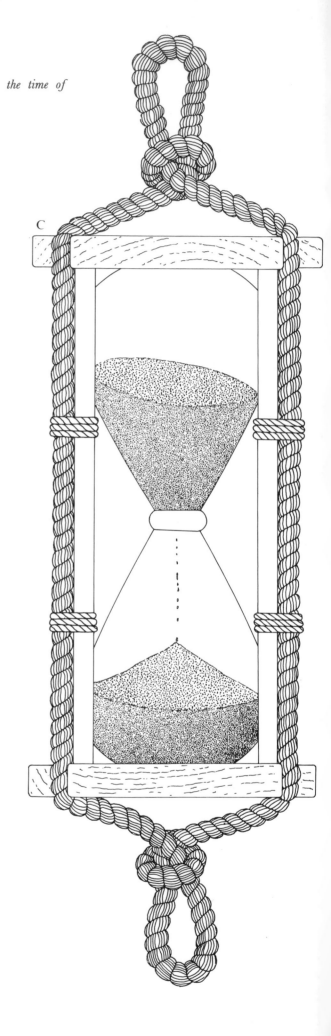

The Venetians were also improving their ship-design. Two-masted vessels were by now commonplace in the Mediterranean. These always had the lateen rather than the square rig.

1406
The office of Lord Admiral of England is created. John Beaufort, son of John of Gaunt, is the first holder of the title.

1410
Henry IV of England records the ship CHRISTOPHER OF THE TOWER as having three iron guns, each with a separate firing chamber. These guns are the first known examples of breech-loaders.

1415
The Portuguese commence extensive trade with the Arabs of Ceuta in North Africa. Four years later, the Portuguese colonize the uninhabited Madeira Islands.

SEPTEMBER 23, 1415
The English regain naval supremacy. Henry V, with a fleet of 1,400 vessels and a force of 30,000 men, takes Harfleur. Later, he wins the Battle of Agincourt, and, by the terms of the Treaty of Troyes, in 1420, becomes heir to the title of King of France. Mont St. Michel, an off-shore island, resists for thirty years the efforts of the English to capture it. The sailors of St. Malo win undying fame for their defence of it.

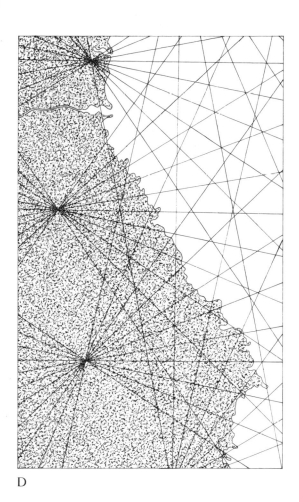

D

D *Part of a Portuguese map of the west coast of Africa, 1490.*

E *Henry the Navigator, Prince of Portugal (1394-1460).*

F *A pocket sun-dial, dated 1453. The indicator, which cast the shadow of the sun on the figures, is under the lid in the middle.*

E

F

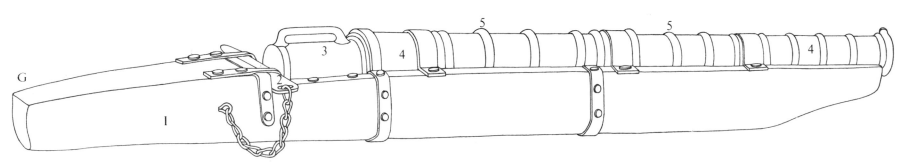

G

G *A fifteenth-century breech-loading gun.*
  1 *Stock*
  2 *Lock wedge*
  3 *Chambered breech block*
  4 *Barrel*
  5 *Iron hoops*

1430

Portugal becomes a great maritime power, mainly through the voyages sponsored by Prince Henry the Navigator (1394-1460). He devoted the whole of his life to the study of navigation, and founded the Observatory at Sagres, near Cape St. Vincent, in southern Portugal, where he gathered the greatest geographers of his day. These men's experience and skill were then passed on to Henry's captains.

Henry believed in the legend of Prester John, the white Christian king supposed to rule somewhere in Central Africa. Many of his sponsored voyages sought information about Prester John. One of the earliest maps brought back from the voyages contained an oblique reference to the legendary white king of a black people.

During the seventeenth century, Holland became an increasingly important maritime nation, with a strong navy and a large mercantile fleet. Many Dutch books were published on the subject of navigation in this period, and the above illustration is made after the frontispiece in The Light of Navigation, *originally published by Blaeu at Amsterdam in 1620. Behind the cartographers and* seamen, who are gathered about their instruments, we can see the Dutch fleet at sea. The cartographers are exchanging information with the seamen, who can be picked out as those wearing conical, brimless hats.

The Light of Navigation *was an anthology of the best authors on navigation, such as Waghenaer and Barents.*

WASA 1627

This magnificently preserved ship, which sank in Stockholm's harbour in 1628, gives us a unique opportunity to study the shipbuilding methods of the early seventeenth century as well as the everyday life of the seamen of the period. Clothing, food, drink, tableware, furniture, personal possessions, even the preserved parts of bodies of some of her crew and their wives, have all been recovered.

A *The wood carving of a lion's head is found on each of the gun-port lids.*
B *One of the* WASA'S *cannon.*
C *Section showing the position of the cannon on the gun-decks.*
D *Rammer and sponge.*
E *Gun ladle.*
F *Hand spike.*
G *Flexible rammer and sponge.*

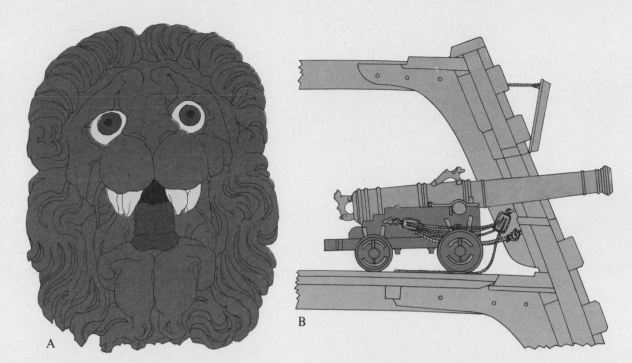

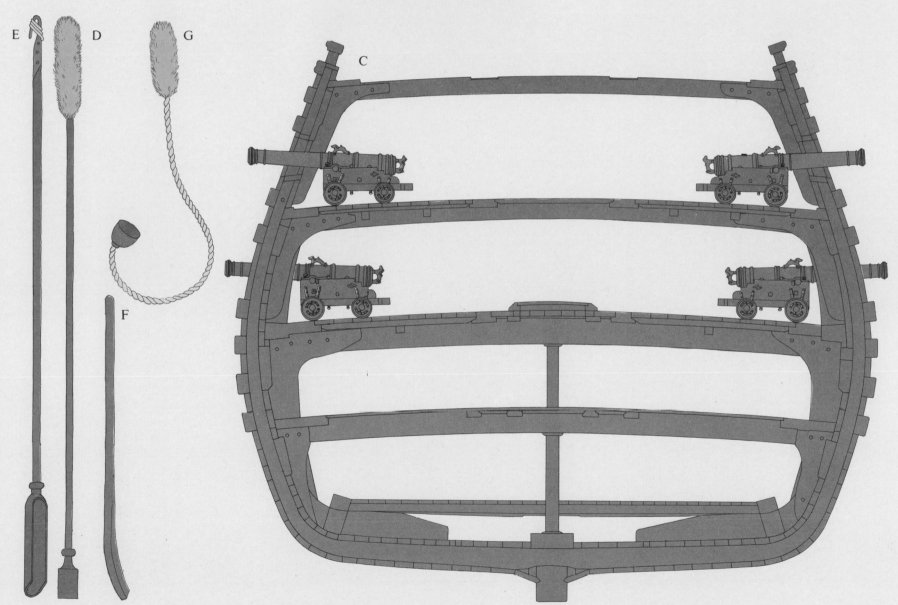

Wasa

In 1956, the WASA was located and five years later was raised to the surface in a salvage operation of great technical difficulty. Now she is on display at Wasavarvet in Stockholm for all to inspect.

The WASA carried sixty-four bronze cannon. They consisted of forty-eight 24-pounders, eight 2-pounders, two 1-pounders, and six mortars. The size of her crew is estimated to have been 133 sailors and 300 soldiers. She had a displacement of about 1,350 tons at a draught of about 16 foot (4.9 m).

Research work on this ship still continues, and new facts are constantly being brought to light.

A A reconstruction of the captain's table. It is laid
   with a pewter bottle (1) which, when found, still
   contained an alcoholic beverage which was similar
   to rum, a measuring glass (2), a glazed earthenware dish from Holland (3), a bronze chafing-dish
   (4), and various other articles of tableware.
B A wooden lidded jug in which the spout is a
   natural part of the rest of the wood.
C The brick fireplace from the galley. There was no
   chimney, so the smoke had to find its own way out.
D The pattern on the glazed earthenware dish marked
   (3) on the table.
E A fine pewter tankard, made in Germany.
F The bronze chafing-dish.
G A pestle and mortar.
H A wooden ladle.
I A wooden spoon.

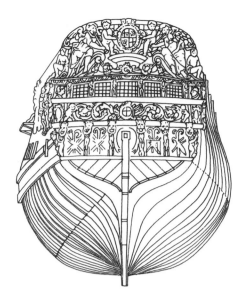

chapter 3

It was Henry the Navigator who, through his sponsorship of many voyages of exploration and his life-long interest in navigation, began to fill in the map of the world during the first half of the fifteenth century. It was Christopher Columbus, the Cabots, and other explorers who pushed back the frontiers of known geographical knowledge so extensively in the second half of the fifteenth century. More, they proved to some timid souls that disaster did not inevitably follow the sailing into the unknown. Their pioneering led to an increasing number of expeditions deliberately geared to the discovery of new lands.

New lands brought new colonies, new areas for trading in. These large-scale operations demanded changing techniques in ships and seamanship. Above all, the improved science of navigation meant that much longer voyages could be attempted with more than a hint of success at the end of them.

This maritime expansion also meant the growth of national and political rivalries. European countries sought power and influence, wealth and status in the new territories that were being discovered.

The rivalries led to many unseemly squabbles between Christian princes, so much so that the Pope, Alexander VI, was forced to intervene. By a papal edict dated 1494, he drew a line on the map of the world and awarded all new lands on the one side to Portugal and all new lands on the other side to Castile, or Spain.

This unilateral action engendered a great deal of activity among other maritime nations, especially the northern European countries. Meantime, Spain concentrated her efforts and resources in the arena of Central America. Portugal dominated South America, particularly that part which is now called Brazil, and also moved into eastern waters with her colonization of the Spice Islands of Indonesia.

At first, England chose to be active in North America. Her first American settlement was Newfoundland, which the Cabots re-discovered in 1497. The Cabots, father and son, were Venetians in the service of Henry VII of England. Incidentally, despite their maritime rivalry, Portugal and England entered into a treaty of alliance that has lasted for something like 500 years.

Friction between England and Spain turned to deep hostility when Henry VIII (1509-47) took England out of the Catholic family of nations by assuming the role of Head of the Church in England at the expense of the Pope. Hostility to England was intensified when Edward VI, and later Queen Elizabeth I, took England out of the Catholic fold entirely and introduced Protestantism as the state religion.

There were two decisive sea battles about this time, both motivated by religious causes. The first was the Battle of Lepanto, in 1571, when the invading Turkish fleet was defeated by the fleet of the Holy League, a loose confederation of the Vatican under Pius V, Venice, Genoa, Savoy, and Spain. The allied fleet was under the supreme command of Don John of Austria. As the result of the defeat of the Turkish fleet, the spread of the Islamic religion into the western world was halted.

The second decisive naval battle was the defeat of the Spanish Armada in 1588. This is one of the epics of all time. One hundred and thirty-one ships, under the overall command of the Duke of Medina-Sidonia, bore down in a huge crescent, seven miles (11.3 km) in width from horn to horn, intent upon crushing the

English. Eight thousand seamen, 30,000 soldiers, and 85 doctors manned this fleet. They were to be joined by another 30,000 soldiers and 1,800 cavalrymen who had mustered in the Spanish Netherlands. For good measure, 180 Catholic priests accompanied the fighting men in order to re-convert the lapsed Catholic country.

Lord Howard of Effingham, the supreme commander of the English naval forces because of his position as Lord High Admiral of England, together with such as Drake, Frobisher, Sheffield, Southwell, Grenville, Raleigh, Hawkins, and Seymour, apprised of the coming of the Armada by the Scottish privateer FLEMING, defeated the Armada. Those elements of the invading force that escaped the English fleet were savaged by the force of the elements, and less than 10,000 Spaniards returned to their homeland, where many soon died as a result of their experience. The medal that Elizabeth ordered struck to mark this victory contained the now-famous words, in Latin, 'God blew with His breath, and they were scattered.' Spain was broken, and England remained a Protestant nation.

The seventeenth century saw the world shrunk by endless voyages of exploration. The blank places on the maps had been fairly accurately filled in, except for the Arctic, Antarctica, Australia, and the central Pacific. Of course, individual territories had not been fully explored, but they were known and earmarked for further investigation. Trade, too, was vastly expanded. Many of the trade routes crossed the Indian Ocean, for ships maintained a constant traffic with the erstwhile Spice Islands, which came under Dutch control. The Dutch East Indies were a prize worth fighting for, and sea engagements underlined the rivalry between England and the Dutch, which replaced the earlier rivalry that existed between Portugal and Holland.

By this time, too, ships had shed their medieval look. Typically, the square-rigged, three-masted ships, with their lines of threatening gun-ports and ornately galleried sterns, had a squat grandeur about them that was lacking in the castellated sail-heavy ships of the previous century.

A unique feature of the seventeenth century was the development of the great trading companies. The Dutch East India Company and the English East India Company both governed vast trading empires that were, in fact, real empires virtually above the law of the land in which the companies were registered or operated.

During all these years, sail was supreme. Almost every ship of the line resembled all others of similar size and rating. Cannon were muzzle-loaded. Indeed, there was little new that was added to ships during all this long period.

A *Black pepper*, Piper nigrum, *was the most important of the spices which lured explorers and merchants to the fabled Spice Islands.*

A

B

B *The 'kraeck' painted by the Dutch artist W.A.*
C *Jacques Coeur (1395-1456).*
D *One of the ships of Jacques Coeur's fleet.*

C

D

1440

The years of the second quarter of the fifteenth century really belong to Jacques Coeur (1395-1456), one of the most famous and influential merchant princes of all times. His 'capital' was Montpellier in the south of France, where his shipyards turned out merchant ships that were to transport every class of merchandise. Such was his enormous wealth that it represented no less than one fifth of the total revenues of the King of France.

His fleets were 'permitted ships' to the Arabs, who allowed them to come and go without let or hindrance. He controlled thirty residences and warehouses scattered around the Mediterranean. Unfortunately, he became embroiled in politics, and was accused of lending vast sums of money to opposing politicians, thus making enemies everywhere. Conspirators had the ear of King Charles VII and, in 1451, Coeur was imprisoned on various counts, one of them being the attempted murder of Agnes Sorel, Charles's mistress. He escaped from imprisonment in 1453, and died at Chios in 1456. Almost single-handed, he had turned Marseilles into the leading Mediterranean port.

1445

At this time, the Portuguese extend their trade with Senegal and other lands of West Africa. The chief commodity in which they dealt was pepper, the local name for which was 'manguette'. The Portuguese were intrigued to discover that maniguette was the Norman-French for 'pepper'—proof that there had been some trade in that area with European traders two or three hundred years before, a trade that had been completely forgotten.

1466

Three-masted ships are depicted on the seals of Louis de Bourbon. It is clear, however, that the fore and mizzen masts were steering auxiliaries only and not wind-bearing masts.

1470

The Dutch artist W.A. painted pictures about this time of a craft named a 'kraeck'. This was either a carvel or a carrack with three masts. There is no reason to think that the ship he illustrated was not based on reality. The vessel also carries a cannon on deck, and, as far as is known, W.A. was the first artist to indicate this type of weapon aboard a vessel.

1487

SOVEREIGN and REGENT were the names of two mighty naval vessels built for the navy of Henry VII of England, who had but two years before established the Tudor dynasty in England when he defeated Richard III at the Battle of Bosworth. Henry VII, for political reasons, wished to upgrade the navy. The REGENT boasted four masts, and is the first known English ship with this number of masts. The ships mounted 141 small cannon apiece, carried

200 long bows, and stocked 800 sheaves of arrows each.

1487

Bartolomeo Diaz leaves Lisbon and makes for the mouth of the Congo in Central Africa. From there he continues to Natal on the east coast of Central Africa, rounding the Cape on the way. He actually named the Cape the 'Cape of Storms', but King John II of Portugal renamed it the 'Cape of Good Hope'.

1492

The most publicized of all voyages takes place. Christopher Columbus, on August 3, leaves the Andalusian port of Palos, near to Huelva, on a trip ostensibly undertaken to discover the direct route to the Indies. By this time, despite historic evidence, many people were convinced that the world was round; they knew, too, that there was a large land mass on the other side of the Atlantic, although it had not been visited for hundreds of years—not at all by western people, according to the sceptical. What was lacking was any definitive map that would be of use to the explorers. Therefore, Ferdinand and Isabella of Spain financed Columbus in his attempt to discover the westerly route to the Indies, which were known to be in the east.

Columbus was in command of a fleet of three. His flagship was the SANTA MARIA, which he himself called *la Nao*—the ship. The other two ships were the NIÑA and the PINTA, and these Columbus referred to as *las Carabelas*—the caravels. Las Casas, the priest who accompanied the expedition as its chronicler, says that the SANTA MARIA was rather larger than the other two vessels. The PINTA was the first to sight land, on October 12, nearly two months after the voyage had commenced. Columbus set foot on the island of San Salvador in the Bahamas. He later visited Cuba and Haiti, where the SANTA MARIA was wrecked. On November 19, in that same year, Columbus landed at Puerto Rico. He still had not reached any mainland territory.

By March 15, 1493, Columbus was back in Palos. He had named the islands he had visited the 'West Indies', because he was convinced that he had reached some islands that lay to the west of his objective, a conviction that he retained to his dying day. It was not until 1498 that he set foot on the mainland of what is now called South America, a year before Amerigo Vespucci, after whom 'America' is named, began his explorations in Central and South America.

Columbus made other voyages to the West Indies, as the islands must be called. On May 3, 1494, he discovered Jamaica, and landed at Discovery Bay. Jamaica had a Spanish governor by 1509, and remained part of the Spanish Empire until it was annexed in the middle of the seventeenth century by the English as part of Cromwell's Grand Design. Bartholomew Columbus, the less famous brother of Christopher, founded Santo Dominigo de Guzman,

A

A *Christopher Columbus (1446-1506).*
B *A reconstruction of the* SANTA MARIA, *1492.*
C NIÑA, *the 'Small One', 1492.*

B

D PINTA, *the 'Painted One', 1492.*
E *Measuring the height of the sun with a fore staff.*

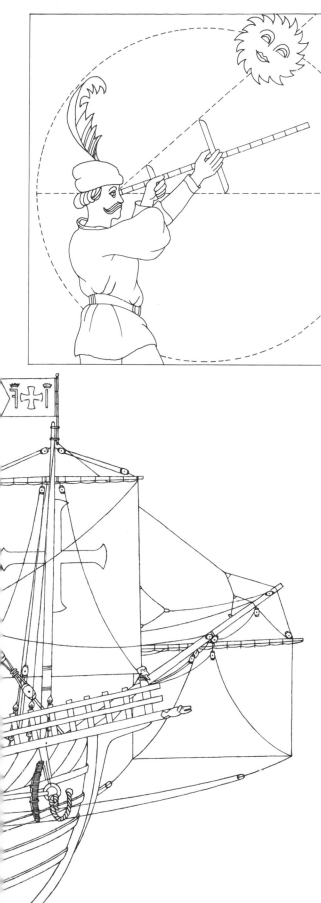

capital of the present-day Republic of Dominica in 1496. In the cathedral of that city, Christopher Columbus was finally interred after his death in 1506 at Valladolid, Spain.

1497

The voyage of the Cabots was overshadowed by that of Columbus five years before, but it was of far more importance to England than the voyage of 1492 was to Spain. Henry VII of England, who revitalized English commerce and who commenced the rebuilding of the navy, awarded a Royal Charter to the Venetian father and son. There is some doubt if the Cabots did come from Venice. Some authorities claim that they came from Genoa. Sebastian Cabot, the son, was born in Bristol, undertook voyages for Henry VII, but then went into the service of Spain. However, he returned to England and was finally granted a life pension by Edward VI, in recognition of his own voy-

ages, his organizing various voyages to Russia and to the North West Passage, and also for his work in connection with the variation of the compass.

On May 2, 1497, the Cabots left Bristol in the MATTHEW, a cockle-shell of a ship with a crew of only eighteen. They sailed in a north-westerly direction, and on June 24, 1497, which was St. John's Day, reached land. The new-found land was named 'Newfoundland', and the landing site was named St. John's. These names remain to this very day. Labrador was visited after leaving Newfoundland, and the expedition sailed as far south as Florida before returning to Bristol.

Under the terms of the Royal Charter, the Crown received one fifth of all that the Cabots discovered. Goods imported were to be free of customs duty. Lastly, Bristol was given the monopoly to import and trade in all cargoes shipped by the Cabots.

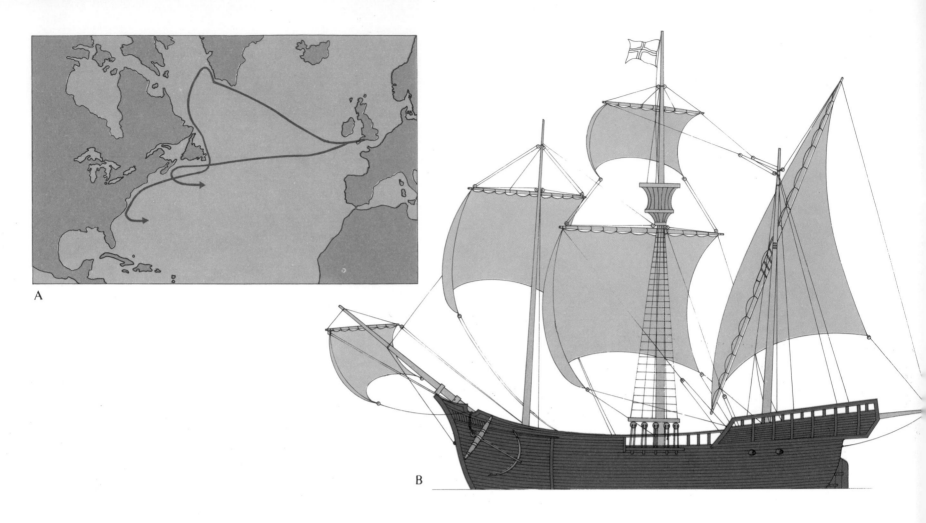

A

B

C

1497

Also in this year, we have the voyage of Vasco da Gama (1460-1524), as epoch-making a voyage as any of these times. His small fleet, also of three vessels, was built at Lisbon in the spring of 1497. They were named the ST. RAPHAEL, ST. MICHAEL, and ST. GABRIEL respectively. Vasco da Gama took his fleet round the Cape, encountering such stormy weather that the ships were damaged and repairs had to be effected in Natal. He then visited Mozambique and M'Lindi before making the still hazardous crossing of the Indian Ocean to the Malabar coast of south-west India. He berthed at Calicut before sailing north and docking at Goa, which became his headquarters. Da Gama returned to Lisbon in July, 1499. In honour of this exploit, he was awarded the title of 'Dom', given a life pension and the chance to make a fortune from certain trading privileges in the Indies, after which he took his title of 'The Admiral of the Indies'. Some authorities state that four ships went on the expedition, but three is the generally accepted number.

1499

Amerigo Vespucci, a Florentine cartographer, borrows a ship, LA DAUPHINE, from France, and sets sail in a westerly direction. Eventually, he lands at the place now called Surinam. He made several voyages to the New World, serving both the King of Portugal and, later, the King of Spain, receiving the title of 'Chief Pilot and Hydrographer' from these two monarchs. His maps helped to fill the gaps in geographical knowledge, but his handwriting was not too good. When a German cartographer tried to copy the name 'Vespucci' in an area discovered by the explorer, he found that he could not read the name. So he put in the name 'Ameriga'—which he could read! The name stuck, and that vast land has been called America ever since.

1499

In the same year, another place is named almost by accident. A Spaniard, Alonso de Ojeda, sails up the little-known Orinoco River. He discovers an Indian village built entirely on piles and intersected by narrow waterways. Jokingly, he calls the place 'Little Venice'— Venezuela, and the country retains that name today.

1500

Brazil is discovered by the explorer Pedro

A *The route followed by John Cabot when he discovered Newfoundland, 1497.*
B *John Cabot's ship* MATTHEW, *1497.*

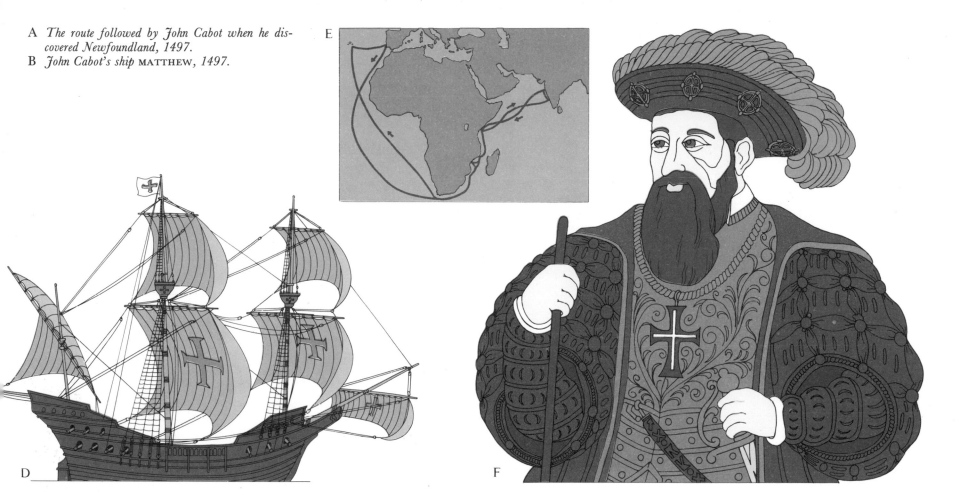

Cabral. Unfortunately, the imaginary line drawn to divide the new-found lands in the western regions between Portugal and Spain left the 'bulge' of Brazil on the Portuguese side, effectively cutting what might have been a united country into two. At first, Cabral named the land he had discovered 'The Island of the True Cross'. Later, it was renamed 'Brazil', after the red brazil tree indigenous to that area. Two years later, he took another expedition into a wide estuary, which he named 'Rio de Janeiro'—the River of January, on the banks of which a town was subsequently founded in 1565.

1501

A Brest shipbuilder named Descharges is the first man to cut holes in the hulls of the vessels that he built in order to accommodate the guns that were mounted on the ships.

1503

Admiral Tristan da Cunha, a Portuguese sailor, discovers a group of four islands in the South Atlantic, some 1,800 miles (2,900 km) from the nearest land. He named the islands after himself. They are said to be the loneliest islands in the world.

C *In 1489, Martellus Germanus printed this map of the world as it was then understood. No mention is made of America, but the west coast of Africa is mapped in some detail.*
D *Vasco da Gama's* ST. GABRIEL, *1497.*
E *The route taken by da Gama on his epic voyage to India, 1497-99.*
F *Vasco da Gama (1460-1524).*

1510-33

These years mark a frenzy of building in the shipyards of Europe. Much of the building is sparked off by the rivalry among various monarchs. The HENRY GRÂCE À DIEU is built for Henry VIII of England soon after he succeeds his father to the throne. France builds the GRAND FRANÇOIS, and the Knights of Malta launch the SANTA ANNA. Portugal builds the SAO JOAO, James IV of Scotland the GREAT ST. MICHAEL, and Sweden contributes the STORA KRAFVER. The GRAND FRANÇOIS, which was a carrack built at Le Havre, suffered an ignominious fate. She stuck on the launchways when she should have been launched, and nothing could budge her. She remained in this position for six mocking years until a violent storm made her keel over. There she remained until time and vandals eventually broke her up.

1512

This date is a watershed in the history of naval battles. For the first time, at the Battle of Brest, which was fought on August 12, ship fought against ship with cannon fire that was intended to sink the vessel rather than to kill the crew.

Small cannon had been used at sea since 1319. However, these had been anti-personnel weapons. Over the years, the size and effectiveness of the cannon developed to such an extent that it became a weapon of utter destruction. Fighting ships now had cannon mounted within their hulls so that they could be fired through unlidded ports.

In August, 1512, an English fleet of forty-five ships, among them fire-ships, under Sir Edward Howard arrived off Brest. The French fleet of thirty-nine vessels under the command of Sieur Porsmoguer—he was a Welshman whose real name was Sir Piers Morgan—came out to engage the raiders. Both fleets were armed with destructive cannon, and broadsides were fired in an attempt to blow each other out of the water. Sir Thomas Knivett in the REGENT grappled with Porsmoguer in the CORDELIER, while both ships continued firing. CORDELIER blew up, taking REGENT with her. Sixteen hundred men, the complements of the two ships, were blown to smithereens.

The watchers were so stunned at the occurrence that the engagement was broken off by mutual consent. The battle, although inconclusive, had proved once and for all the superiority of this type of sea warfare. Henceforth, ships tried to knock out each other rather than to knock out the crews only.

1513

A famous Spanish explorer, Vasco Núñes de Balboa (1475-1517), had established a Spanish colony at Darien in Panama. He heard rumours of a great sea beyond the mountains from a friendly Indian chief. He determined to find this sea, and so, with a band of 190 men, he cut his way through the jungle to the top of the

mountains that backboned the isthmus of Panama. From this vantage point, they were able to see the great waters on the far side of the divide. They were, in fact, the first white men to gaze upon the Pacific having approached it overland from the Atlantic seaboard.

Balboa was created Admiral of the Pacific by a delighted King of Spain. The new admiral set about building a large fleet of small ships, hoping to open up new commercial ventures. However, he ran foul of the new governor of Panama, Don Pedro Arias de Avila, who arraigned him for treason, found him guilty, and had him executed.

1514

Henry VIII of England, combining piety with shrewdness, gives a charter to a religious order based at Deptford, one of the shipbuilding areas on the Thames, just outside the old City of London. Its title is 'The Brotherhood of the Most Glorious and Undivided Trinity of Deptford-Stronde', and its royal charter gives the brotherhood charge of all sea-marks, and makes it advisor to the navy. After various vicissitudes, Trinity House, as it now is, has control over

A GREAT ST. MICHAEL, *1511.*

B HENRY GRÂCE A DIEU, *also known as the* GREAT HARRY, *1514.*

C *Transporting horses by sea was quite a problem, as rough weather could frighten them and drive them wild. Illustrated is one of the ways used to secure horses in the hold of sixteenth-century ships.*

D GRAND FRANÇOIS, *1533.*

B

C

D

A

A *An early woodcut which is supposed to show Magellan with his navigation instruments.*
B *Ferdinand Magellan's* VICTORIA, *the only ship of his fleet to complete the first round-the-world trip, 1519-22.*
C *The Straits of Magellan, after a map in Antonio Pigafetta's book.*
D *Jacques Cartier landing in Canada, 1534. From a map dated 1546.*

B

C

lighthouses, lightships, and various buoys in English waters. It works in close association with the Royal Navy, especially with the hydrographic department. It has an unbroken record of nearly five centuries of service.

1519

This year marks the beginning of the first known successful circumnavigation of this globe.

Ferdinand Magellan (1480-1521) was a man who spent his entire life at sea. His first major assignment was with the fleet of Francisco de Almeida, the first Portuguese Viceroy of the East, who in 1505 set sail in an attempt to curb the growing sea-power of the Muslim world. From this and other voyages, Magellan gained invaluable experience, which the King of Spain was happy to command when Magellan, having quarrelled over the question of his promotion with his then employer, King Manuel of Portugal, left that monarch's service and proceeded to Madrid, where he changed allegiance and became Spanish by adoption.

It will be recalled that by the terms of a Papal Bull, issued by Pope Alexander VI in 1494, Spain and Portugal had their zones of overseas influence set by a line of longitude, specifically that line 370 leagues west of the Cape Verde Islands. Now, the precise position of the wealthy Spice Islands—modern Indonesia—was disputed. Magellan offered to prove that they came within the jurisdiction of Spain under the terms of the Papal Bull of 1494. He also offered to continue to sail round the world annexing all territories in the Spanish zone for Spain. The offer was accepted, and on September 20, 1519, Magellan left Cadiz with a squadron of five ships manned by 265 sailors. He wore his flag in the TRINIDAD. The remainder of the squadron comprised the SAN ANTONIO, the CONCEPCIÓN, the VICTORIA, and the SANTIAGO. On the way southward, early in 1520, the TRINIDAD sailed into the broad estuary of the River Plate in South America. Flat land stretched as far as the eye could see. Suddenly, as the ship sailed deeper into the estuary, Magellan cried out, 'Monte vide eu!'—I see a mountain! The modern city of Montevideo marks the rising ground that Magellan spotted.

Tierra del Fuego, the land of the fires, appeared so bleak and inhospitable that many officers thought that any farther progress south was impossible. Many of the crews also thought this, and some of the men mutinied. Magellan decided to stop the voyage in order to carry out essential repairs. The place where he stopped is now Port St. Julian. When the voyage recommenced, Juan de Catagena, the captain of the SAN ANTONIO, was left behind. Two officers implicated in the mutiny were executed.

Further trouble occurred during the passage of the straits that now bear Magellan's name—the Magellan Straits, off the extreme south of South America. Captain Gomez, who had taken over the command of the SAN ANTONIO, refused to go any farther, turned about, and returned to Spain.

Despite these misfortunes, despite outbreaks of scurvy, despite conditions of near-starvation, Magellan carried on. He reached the Philippines on April 27, 1521, and was killed in a fight with the natives of Mactan Island.

The leadership of the expedition fell to Captain Juan Sebastian de Elcano of the VICTORIA. He decided to carry on with the voyage, the success of which was almost assured by reaching the Philippines. The Spice Islands were reached, and, in the fulness of time, the

D

expedition returned to Spain without having had to turn round. The voyage proved that the world was round and that it could be circumnavigated. The knowledge was dearly bought; for out of the original complement of 265 men, only 19 returned to Spain to tell their story.

Thus, although Magellan thought of the idea, it was, in fact, one of his captains, Elcano, who actually accomplished the feat of being the first known man to circumnavigate the globe.

1534
Jacques Cartier (1491-1557), one of the most distinguished of French explorers, leaves St. Malo, crosses the Atlantic, and explores the coast of modern New Brunswick. He discovers many of the off-shore islands, and eventually begins opening up inland Canada by way of the River St. Lawrence. He so set the seal of France on the territories that he visited that a long rivalry developed between France and England in that part of the world—as it did in other parts for similar reasons. The rivalry in Canada was not even ended with the victory of the English under Wolfe over the French led by Montcalm at the Battle of Quebec, 1759. Today, large parts of Canada are still French-speaking.

1536
Determined efforts are made during the next few years by the Spaniards to colonize many of their recently discovered lands. One of the first settlements in this phase was built 125 miles (201 km) up the wide estuary of the River Plate, on the site where present-day Buenos Aires stands. The attempt to make a permanent settlement failed, mainly because of the hostility of the local Indians and the chronic shortage of suitable food. Pedro de Mendoza, the leader, was forced to abandon the settlement, and the Spaniards did not return there until 1580.

1541
Another Spanish expedition under Francisco de Orellana roams the coastal waters of the new-found Americas looking for suitable sites for Spanish settlements. He came across a mighty river, with crowded, tree-lined banks, and had sailed up this river for a distance of some 200 miles (322 km) when he was confronted by a 10-foot (3 m) high tidal wave. The local Indians called this phenomenon 'Amasonas'—the boat destroyer; for they had long suffered its destructive power. Thus Orellana discovered and most suitably named the River Amazon.

JULY 19, 1545
The English warship MARY ROSE is lost. This vessel had been built in 1509, and was a galleon of Henry VIII's new navy. She was still in active service in 1545 when a French fleet appeared in the Solent. An English fleet was sent to engage the intruder, but before the battle was joined, a severe gust of wind caught the MARY ROSE, and she keeled over. Her lower gun ports were open. Before anything could be done to help the stricken vessel, she went to the bottom. Four hundred and fifteen of the 700 men aboard her were lost.

The MARY ROSE, which carried ninety-one muzzle and breech-loading cannon, was the first warship to carry siege artillery on her main deck.

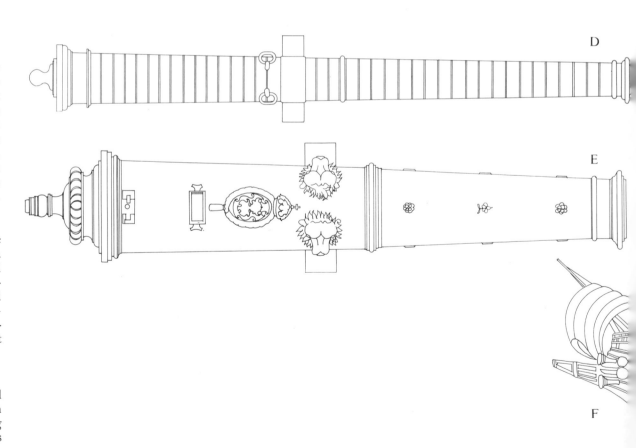

1553

The Muscovy Company is formed by a group of English merchants. The prime object of the company was to trade with China, which it was thought could be reached by sailing the northern seas. Sir Hugh Willoughby and Richard Chancellor led the first expedition to set sail on this venture. China was not reached, but Willoughby and Chancellor succeeded in making a trade agreement with the then Duke of Moscow, the nominal head of the Russias.

1562

John Hawkins (1532-95) is the first white man to ship a cargo of slaves from Sierra Leone to the West Indies. He thus inaugurated a trade that was to last until well into the nineteenth century, a trade that was formalized into the infamous triangular run, West Africa— the Americas—Liverpool—West Africa. Hawkins was later knighted for his part in the defeat of the Spanish Armada.

1565

The Spanish, although preoccupied in Central and South America, also have interests in eastern waters. In this year, a Spanish trading colony is founded near Manila in the Philippines

A *The Battle of Lepanto.*
B *Don John of Austria.*
C *Andrea Doria, the great Genoese admiral (1468-1560).*
D *A wrought-iron serpent, c. 1450.*
E *Brass cannon royal from the MARY ROSE, sunk in 1545.*
F *A great galley, from a sixteenth-century manuscript in the Biblioteca Marciana, Venice.*

by Miguel Lopez de Legazpi. Spanish influence in the Philippines lasted until 1898.

1565

A Turkish fleet, composed largely of galleys, besieges the Knights of St. John in Malta. The siege, which lasted four months, failed; but in order to discourage the Turks, the Grand Master of the Knights of St. John, Jean de la Vallette, built the fortified port of Valletta. Valletta, with its famous Grand Harbour, eventually became one of the major British naval bases in the Mediterranean.

1569

Gerard Mercator, a Flemish cartographer, perfects his system of drawing maps using the projection which to this day bears his name. Mercator's Projection represents the globe as a cylinder. There is, consequently, a gross exaggeration of maps using this projection beyond the sixtieth parallel north and south of the Equator.

OCTOBER 7, 1571

The greatest galley battle ever fought takes place in this year. This is the famous Battle of Lepanto in which the fleet of the Holy League defeats that of the Turks. Many historians claim that this victory by Don John of Austria saved Europe for Christianity.

The circumstances preceding the battle are well known. Pope Pius V, worried about the spread of the Muslim faith into former Christian countries, appealed to Christian Europe to form a Holy League against the Turks, the main upholders of Mohammedanism. Initially, the response to the appeal was lukewarm. The Turks, however, precipitated a crisis by claiming Cyprus as part of their Ottoman Empire. Mustapha Pasha, one of their great leaders, laid siege to Famagusta in furtherance of this claim. In June, 1571, the city capitulated. Despite promises of clemency, the Turks executed all the defenders, and flayed alive their Venetian commander, General Bragadino. It was this last act that persuaded Christian Europe—including Venice—to form the Holy League.

It is worthwhile examining the tactics of the Battle of Lepanto. Don John of Austria, a young man of twenty-five, was appointed the supreme commander because of his position of Admiral of Spain. The Allied Fleet assembled at Messina on August 25, 1571. Admiral Ali Pasha, the Turkish commander, knew that something was brewing. He sent two galleys under Kara Khodja to report. Black sails were hoisted at night, white by day. The oarsmen were picked Muslims, not captured slaves. They had the reputation of being the fastest rowers in the entire Turkish fleet. Soon, Ali Pasha, who was waiting in the Gulf of Lepanto, received a full intelligence report.

The Allied Fleet left Messina on September 16. It was drawn up by nationality in five squadrons. Don John, in his flagship REALE, led the fleet, which consisted of 200 galleys and 6 galleasses. A further 100 sailing-ships with no auxiliary oars brought up the rear. The fleet anchored off Corfu in order that Gil d'Andrada with 4 galleys could reconnoitre the Turkish fleet, and also in order to allow the sailing-ships to catch up with the bulk of the Allied Fleet.

Kara Khodja, who had watched the Allied Fleet anchor off Corfu, sent a further despatch to Ali Pasha reporting the arrival of 200 Christian ships. There were actually 202 in the formation. He missed the 100 sailing-ships toiling well in the rear. D'Andrada for his part reported to Don John that there were 200 ships in the enemy fleet, when, in fact, there were 250.

Ali Pasha, thinking that he had numerical superiority, decided to attack. He deployed his fleet in line abreast, right across the mouth of the gulf. Mohommed Scirocco, Pasha of Alexandria, commanded the right flank; Ouloudj Ali, Dey of Algiers, commanded the left; Ali Pasha himself was in the centre.

The Allied Fleet approached the Gulf of Lepanto. Don John transferred to a small galley, and, holding aloft a large crucifix, passed slowly along the line of his fleet, being acclaimed by all his men. When he returned to REALE, a signal-gun sounded the attack.

The wind dropped. Sails were useless. Oars flashed. Six great Venetian galleasses, followed by 150 galleys, line abreast, charged towards the Turkish lines.

The opening broadsides from the giant galleasses caused havoc in the Turkish ships which, however, did not break formation but sought to grapple. The left flank of the Allied Fleet under the command of Agostino Barbarigo faced Mohommed Scirocco's right flank formation. The pasha almost turned the Christian flank, but in a counter-attack, he himself was killed and his flagship was captured.

Meanwhile, in the centre, Ali Pasha had managed to board the REALE. Don John led a fierce close-quarter attack to try to repel the boarders. Ali Pasha withdrew to the fore-quarters, where Don John found it difficult to dislodge him. Fortunately, Prince Antonio Colonna in his galley came to the rescue of the REALE. Ali Pasha was cornered amidships. Rather than fall into Christian hands, he committed suicide. His head was promptly struck from his shoulders, exhibited, and was then thrown overboard.

Ouloudj Ali also tried to outflank Andrea Doria, who commanded the Allied Fleet's right flank. At the last moment, the Turkish commander wheeled and went to the support of Ali Pasha and the centre. Ten of his galleys singled out the squadron of the Knights of Malta, who supported Don John in the centre. A great roar went up when the banner of the Knights of Malta was seen to fall.

The situation was critical. The Christian centre was in confusion. Luckily, the Marquis of

Santa Cruz arrived with the rearguard reserves, of which the Turks knew nothing until he bore down upon them. Andrea Doria now moved in, and a classic pincer movement ensued with Ouloudj Ali being well and truly nipped. Abruptly, he disengaged those elements of his command that had escaped the carnage and fled the scene of battle.

Lepanto ended in a massacre. More than 30,000 Turks were killed. Over 200 ships, mostly Turkish, were sunk or beached. More than 12,000 Christian galley slaves in the Turkish craft were freed. As the sun set on that momentous day, Don John gave thanks to God for the victory that had preserved Europe for Christendom.

Reference has already been made to some of the types of ships that fought the Battle of Lepanto. The major ship types of the period were:

Galleons: *These were the 'battleships' of the period. They were specifically designed for war purposes. They were longer in proportion to their beam than were the 'great ships'. Galleons had three decks and three masts. There were both bow and stern-castles. They were armed with grape-shot cannon mounted on the two castles. These cannon were trained so as to clear the 'waist' of enemy ships of soldiers. In these times, soldiers still fought sea-battles, boarding enemy ships and engaging in hand-to-hand fighting until they were either victorious or vanquished.*

Galleys: *These were long, slim craft of shallow draught. They usually had ram bows. They were propelled by oars manned by captive slaves. Galleys were built both with and without masts.*

Galleasses: *Galleasses were masted galleys which combined the speed and manoeuvrability of the galley with the wind-assisted speed of the galleon. In a following wind, the galleass was the fastest vessel afloat.*

Great Ships: *These were heavy, armed merchantmen which doubled as commerce raiders and more orthodox warships in time of need.*

1576

The North West Passage is the name given to the supposed route to the Far East by way of the waters off the coast of northern Canada. Sir Martin Frobisher was one of the first explorers to attempt the passage. In so doing, he

A *Sir Francis Drake (1540-96).*
B *When Drake returned from his epic voyage, he brought news of a strange weed called tobacco. Columbus had seen natives on Cuba smoking cigars.*
C GOLDEN HIND. *A reconstruction based on the only known illustration of this ship.*
D *Ship's lantern on the* GOLDEN HIND.

E

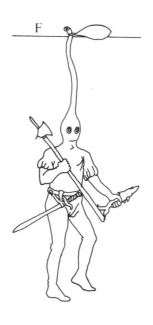

F

G

discovered Baffin Island. It was he who brought back the first authentic accounts of the Eskimos and their kayaks.

NOVEMBER 15, 1577-SEPTEMBER 26, 1580

The voyage of the GOLDEN HIND ranks as one of the finest achievements of man in the realm of exploration. The GOLDEN HIND, which was originally called the PELICAN, was the flagship of Francis Drake, a Devon sea-dog, who commanded a small flotilla of five vessels on this momentous circumnavigation of the globe.

On November 15, 1577, Drake slipped into the grey Channel. He was accompanied by Captain Winter on the ELIZABETH, 100 tons, originally out of London, some 20 tons smaller than the GOLDEN HIND. Two sloops, the MARIGOLD and the CHRISTOPHER, of 50 tons and 40 tons respectively, together with the 20-ton pinnace, BENEDICT, completed the flotilla. The crews numbered 164.

South of the River Plate, one of the sloops deserted. She was recaptured by the MARIGOLD. Tom Doughty, the defecting captain, was tried, found guilty, and was executed at Port Julian, where, some fifty years earlier, Magellan had dealt with his own mutineers. The MARIGOLD was lost near Cape Horn. The other ships in the flotilla scattered before the storms.

Drake had fixed upon Valparaiso as the rendezvous in just such circumstances. However, Captain Winter in the ELIZABETH decided

E *A nocturna, c. 1580. It was used to tell the time from the stars.*
F *An early diver, from the 1511 edition of Vegetius.*
G *An example of the traverse board, which was used to record the direction and distance made on different tacks during a watch.*

SECOTAN

WEAPEMEOC

Dasamonquepeuc

Roanoak

Trinety harbor

Hatorasck

A

B

to return, just as Gomez had decided to do in Magellan's expedition. Drake, therefore, changed his plans slightly and ranged along the Pacific coast of South America, capturing Spanish ships and 'confiscating' their cargoes —often of bullion. One of the captured Spanish ships was OUR LADY OF THE CONCEPTION. This ship, Drake was delighted to discover, carried ballast of bars of silver, a cargo of gold, and had deck chests studded with emeralds and rubies.

Drake sailed north looking for a passage that would take him into the Atlantic and back into home waters. He reached California, anchoring in Drake's Bay. It was July, but the weather turned cheerless. Therefore, he decided to return to England by way of the East Indies and the Cape of Good Hope.

The details of this part of the voyage are rather humdrum. He careened the GOLDEN HIND at the island of Celebes, watered at Freetown, Sierra Leone, and berthed at Plymouth Sound on September 26, 1580.

The Spaniards were furious at the rapturous welcome given Drake and his men, more so when Queen Elizabeth I knighted him. Such

blatant privateering as Drake indulged in un- doubtedly added to the bad blood between Spain and England at this time, especially when it became common knowledge that Elizabeth herself knowingly shared in the spoils.

A year after Drake commenced his epic voyage, Sir Humphrey Gilbert (1539-83) wrote a best-seller entitled 'To Prove a Passage by the North West to Cathaia—China—and the East Indies'. Gilbert tried to find the passage himself, but never succeeded.

1585
Determined efforts are made by Sir Walter Raleigh (1552-1618) to colonize Virginia. He sponsored two major expeditions, the second of which was commanded by his cousin, Sir Richard Grenville. A colony was founded on the Roanoke River, but the venture failed. The few starving survivors were brought back to England by Sir Francis Drake. They arrived on July 28, 1586, bringing with them tobacco for the first time. It was Raleigh who introduced the potato into Ireland where he resided during 1588 and 1599.

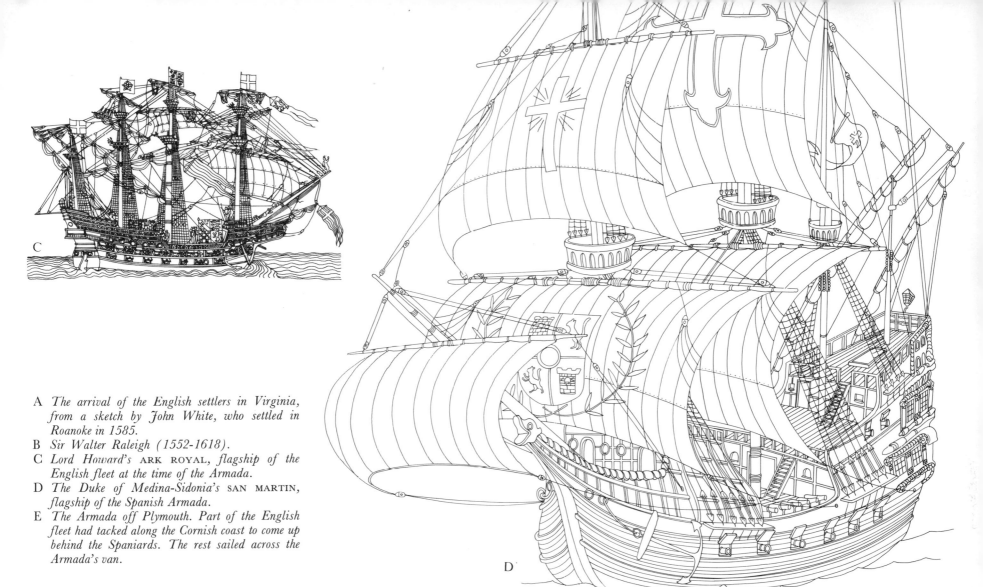

A *The arrival of the English settlers in Virginia, from a sketch by John White, who settled in Roanoke in 1585.*
B *Sir Walter Raleigh (1552-1618).*
C *Lord Howard's* ARK ROYAL, *flagship of the English fleet at the time of the Armada.*
D *The Duke of Medina-Sidonia's* SAN MARTIN, *flagship of the Spanish Armada.*
E *The Armada off Plymouth. Part of the English fleet had tacked along the Cornish coast to come up behind the Spaniards. The rest sailed across the Armada's van.*

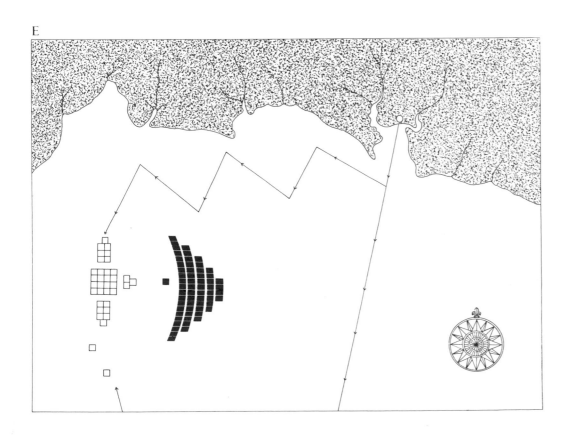

favour, mainly because of the pressure that the Spaniards put upon the incoming King, James I. He spent thirteen years in the Tower of London on a trumped-up charge of treason, eliciting from the sympathetic Prince Charles the remark, 'Why do they cage this innocent bird?' Raleigh was released from the Tower in When Elizabeth died, in 1603, Raleigh fell from 1616 in order to lead an expedition to South America to search for gold. He failed to find any, returned to London heartbroken at the death of his son, Walter, killed by the Spaniards, and was himself executed on October 29, 1618, in Old Palace Yard, Westminster, a victim of the classic misplaced trust in princes.

1587
Two years after the Virginian misadventure, Drake, in a state galleon of 550 tons named BONAVENTURE, with LION, one of Lord Howard's ships, together with eighteen other vessels, sails into Cadiz Harbour. Elizabeth's instructions to preserve the peace failed to arrive. Drake attacked, and sank some thirty Spanish ships. On his way back to England, Drake captured the Portuguese vessel, SAN FELIPE, worth

A

C *The engagements off Portland Bill and the Isle of Wight. Frobisher's squadron is inshore of the English fleet, engaging four Spanish galleasses. Howard and Hawkins are in the centre, and Drake is on the right. The Armada, in its crescent-shaped formation, then moved off towards the Isle of Wight, pursued by the English, who had regrouped into four squadrons.*

D *Philip II (1527-98).*

C

A *The Armada under attack by the English. Reproduced by courtesy of the National Maritime Museum, Greenwich.*
B *Queen Elizabeth I (1533-1603).*

B

D

£140,000 in total. He gave Elizabeth her share of £40,000, and also reported that he had singed the King of Spain's beard, his classic reference to the Cadiz exploit. He did more than singe the King of Spain's beard; he bought precious time for England to look to her defences before Philip was able to give the command for the Armada to sail.

1588

A closer look can now be taken at the Armada story. Philip II of Spain had married Queen Mary of England, although he himself kept to his own country. When Queen Mary died, her half-sister Elizabeth, a practising Protestant, unlike Mary who was a practising Catholic, ascended the throne. Philip proposed marriage to her so that the loose alliance between the two countries might be preserved. Elizabeth finally rebuffed the offer of marriage. Conditions between England and Spain were further worsened when Elizabeth reluctantly agreed to the execution of the tragic Mary, Queen of Scots. This took place on February 18, 1587. Catholic Europe looked to Philip for reprisals against England; for the Scots queen had also been a Catholic. After some little hesitation, the 'Empresa'—Enterprise—against England was proclaimed.

Don Alvaro de Bazan, Marquis of Santa Cruz, the hero of Lepanto, Lord High Admiral of Spain, advised a massive sea invasion, while Alexander Farnese, Duke of Parma, Commander-in-Chief of the Spanish forces in the Netherlands, favoured a cross-Channel invasion. Philip compromised, and an army assembled in the Netherlands ready to link up with the sea-borne forces.

Santa Cruz died on March 31, 1587, and was succeeded in the command by Alonzo, Duke of Medina-Sidonia, an organizer rather than a naval commander. Prudently, he appointed a War Council, which consisted of his Second-in-Command, Juan de Recalde, Pedro de Valdes, Miguel de Oquendo, and Alonso de Leyra, the last-named being appointed commander of the army.

Religious services were conducted in Lisbon Cathedral, after which, on May 30, 1588, the Armada moved out of the River Tagus. It must be remembered that, at this time, Spain and Portugal were united under the one sovereign. The Armada of 131 ships, instead of the 550 originally planned, carried 8,776 sailors, 2,088 galley slaves, 21,855 soldiers, the 85 doctors and 180 Catholic priests previously referred to, and 150 gunners. Fire power was provided by 3,165 pieces of ordnance, of which 2,431 pieces were cannon of one sort or another. Once at sea, the Armada formed into squadrons named after the regions of Spain. The headquarters of the army were located on the RATA CORONADA, commanded by Martin de Bertendona.

On Sunday, July 21, 1588, fifty-four English ships warped and kedged out of Plymouth

Sound, and encountered the Armada, now sailing in that famous crescent formation. The store ships and lesser craft were in the centre. Recalde was to port, Bertendona to starboard. Valdez and Oquendo were stationed on either side of the store-ships. England was clearly visible to port.

The single, opening cannon-shot was fired from a tiny eighty-ton English pinnace, the DISDAIN, which flounced its way in front of the Armada and roared Lord Howard's defiance.

The English squadrons were led by Lord Howard in the ARK ROYAL, Drake in the REVENGE, Hawkins in the VICTORY, and Frobisher in the TRIUMPH. The morning engagement was significant, for the opening broadsides caused the Armada to bunch towards the centre, reducing its ability to deploy against the English. Retaliatory gunnery was almost impossible.

A running battle ensued, lasting for several days. Various actions were fought, involving small elements of the fleets. On July 23, with the Armada mauled but still more or less intact, the English fleet divided into four separate squadrons. The following day the Armada was off the Isle of Wight. The following English squadrons harried the invaders from the rear. The Spanish were forced towards the shallow waters of the Ower Bank.

Medina-Sidonia realized his danger. He changed course, and stood out towards the Channel making for Calais. The English shadowers followed one culverin-shot away. That was the real end of the promised invasion. The Armada anchored two miles off Calais and awaited the Duke of Parma's army. The Duke refused to expose his shallow-draught barges and defenceless troops to the gunfire of the English fleet which was lurking, waiting to pounce.

Eighty ships in the two squadrons of Lord Seymour and Lord Winter, who had been keeping a watchful eye on the Duke of Parma and his army, now arrived to join the shadowing four English squadrons. Their help was not needed. Soon after midnight on July 29, eight fire-ships were let loose on the Armada. The English fire-ships, under Captains Young and Prowse, were normal in every respect except that their cannons were double-loaded in order to make very loud bangs. Spanish pinnaces grappled two of the fire-ships away, but the other six wreaked havoc among the tightly-packed Armada. Once more the Spanish were thrown into utter confusion as the flaming hulks barged against them amidst the din of exploding cannon.

The end of the story of the Armada has already been told. There is, perhaps, a sequel to it. That same REVENGE which had been Drake's flagship at the time of the invasion passed into the command of Sir Richard Grenville. On August 31, 1591, she was part of an English squadron of twenty ships anchored at Flores in the Azores. Unexpectedly, fifty-three Spanish

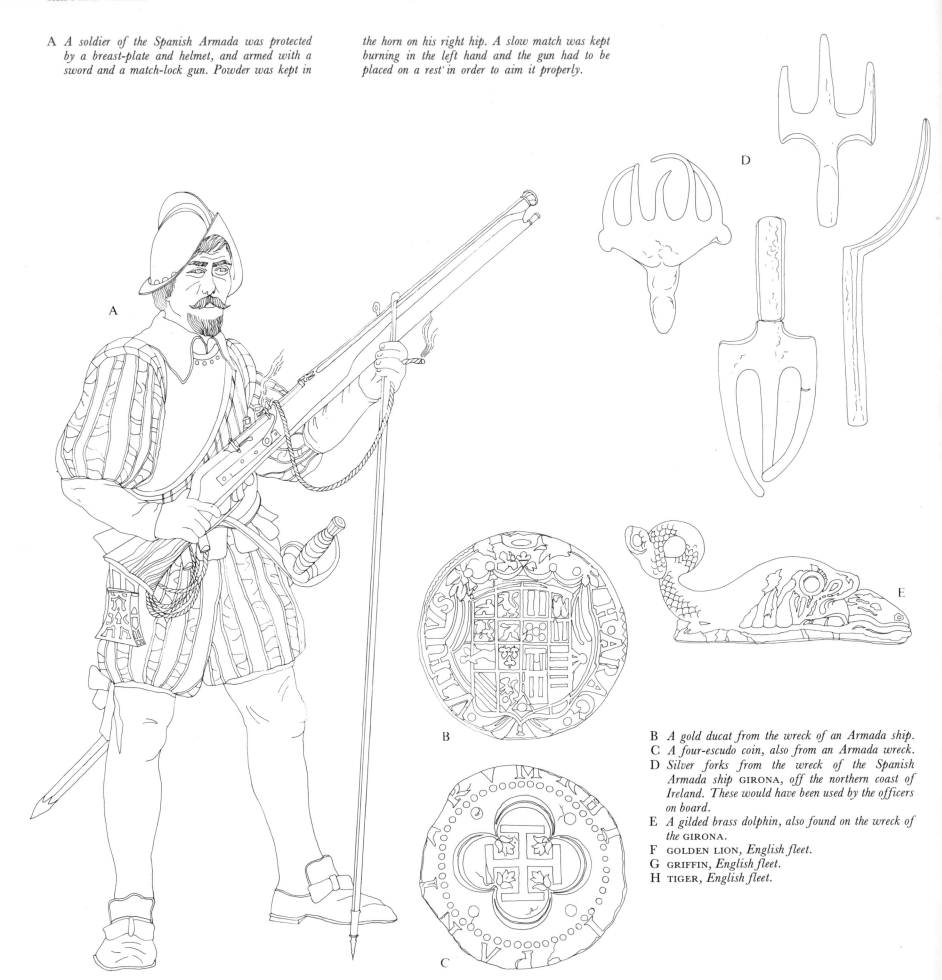

A *A soldier of the Spanish Armada was protected by a breast-plate and helmet, and armed with a sword and a match-lock gun. Powder was kept in the horn on his right hip. A slow match was kept burning in the left hand and the gun had to be placed on a rest' in order to aim it properly.*

B *A gold ducat from the wreck of an Armada ship.*

C *A four-escudo coin, also from an Armada wreck.*

D *Silver forks from the wreck of the Spanish Armada ship* GIRONA, *off the northern coast of Ireland. These would have been used by the officers on board.*

E *A gilded brass dolphin, also found on the wreck of the* GIRONA.

F GOLDEN LION, *English fleet.*

G GRIFFIN, *English fleet.*

H TIGER, *English fleet.*

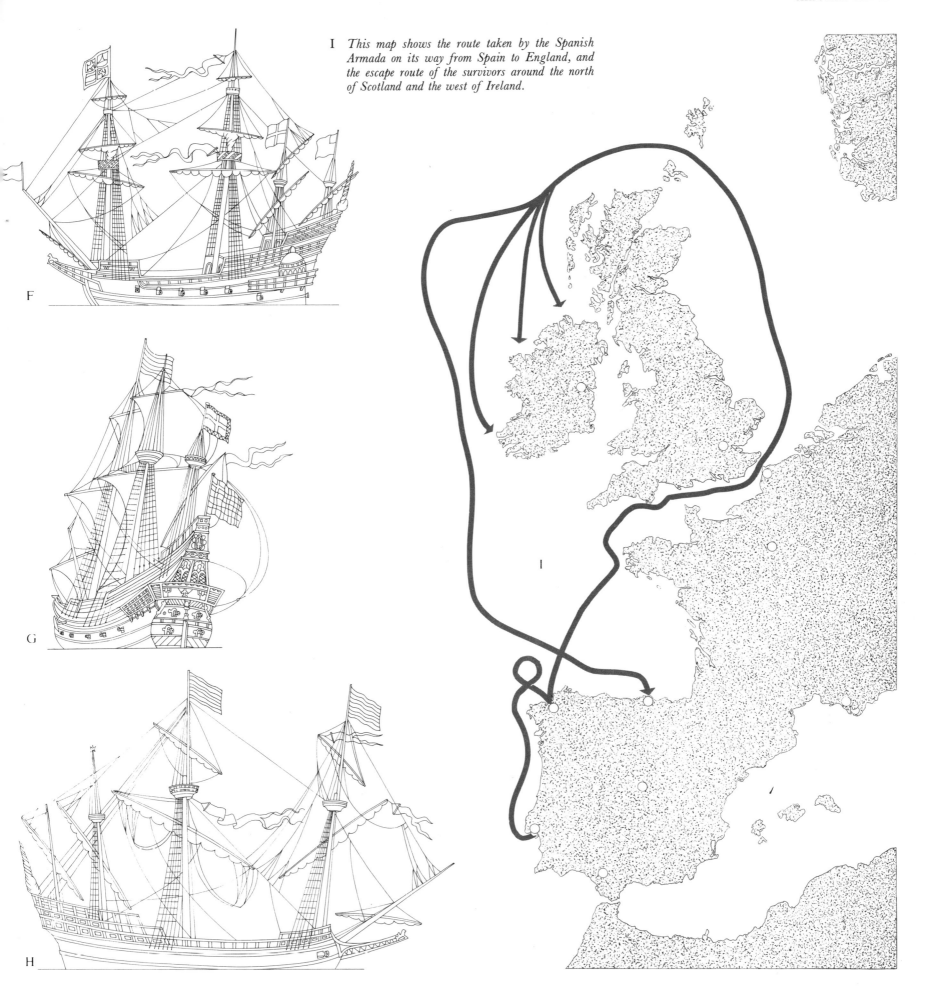

I *This map shows the route taken by the Spanish Armada on its way from Spain to England, and the escape route of the survivors around the north of Scotland and the west of Ireland.*

F

G

H

warships converged on the island in order to cut off the squadron. All the English ships except the REVENGE managed to scatter. Grenville's only way of escape was to turn tail and flee. This he stoutly refused to do, a decision in which he was supported by his entire crew.

The brave REVENGE fought until her ammunition was gone. Every mast and spar on her was levelled. She was boarded several times. Each time, the enemy was thrown off. She sank two Spanish galleons. The remainder of the Spanish fleet formed a circle round the stricken REVENGE, waiting for the inevitable end. The mortally wounded Grenville ordered the master-gunner to blow the ship up, taking all down with her. The master-gunner turned a deaf ear for love of his captain. When the handful of survivors finally surrendered, they were treated with typical Spanish honour and chivalry. Sir Richard died aboard a Spanish ship two days after the engagement. The REVENGE sank in a storm.

1589-1600

The last years of the sixteenth century saw the pattern of the previous half century continued, except that there were no critical sea-battles fought during the period. Nor was there any fundamental change in the design of ships or in the way that they were handled. Voyages of exploration still attracted the adventurous and the greedy, but no major discoveries were recorded during this period. The English charted the desolate Falkland Islands in 1592 during a passage round Cape Horn, but the islands remained unsettled for a further 200 years and never really came to life until a military garrison was installed in 1834.

EARLY 17TH CENTURY

The first two decades of the seventeenth century are full of naval activity. The century opens with the unification of Japan under the rule of the Tokugawa Shogunate. For the first time, trade with Europeans was officially permitted. The Dutch were favoured. Indeed, by 1641, they became the only foreigners allowed to live in Japan.

DECEMBER 31, 1600

The East India Company is founded. It remained in business, often the business of government, until 1858.

The company was nicknamed 'John Company', and received its charter from Queen Elizabeth I. The charter members were London merchants, who financed an inaugural voyage to the Spice Islands of Java, Sumatra, and the Moluccas. In 1613, John Company extended its interests to India, where a trading post was established at the port of Surat. The Portuguese had been active in the area for a hundred years.

The Mogul Emperor, the titular head of India, allowed trade with the interior, and in 1616 the first cargo from India was despatched to England by way of the Cape of Good Hope in a vessel named, appropriately enough, HOPE.

A

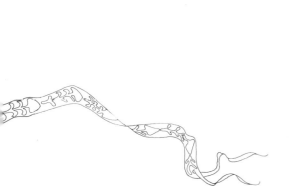

B

A *A large Spanish galleon.*
B *An English galleon, from the 1586 manuscript*
Fragment of Ancient English Shipwrightry.
C *A Spanish carabela.*

C

The Dutch were not at all happy with the turn of events. They knew from bitter experience that when the English came, they came to stay. The Dutch, therefore, opposed the English in the East Indies. Politics bedevilled commerce. In 1623, ten English merchants were executed, allegedly for plotting a native uprising. This is the so-called 'Massacre of Amboyna'. The incident led to a great deal of bad feeling, and to a company decision to concentrate its efforts in India. This was a wise decision, for in that very same year, the Japanese authorities turned anti-British and forced the English factory at Hirado to be closed.

John Company acted like a semi-sovereign state. It had its own army, navy, mercantile marine, and civil service. It even minted its own money, and dispensed justice through its Court of Directors. It organized three Presidencies in India: Fort St. George at Madras, Fort William, which was later renamed Calcutta, and Bombay. Its great dock in London, the East India Dock, became world famous, and continued in business until recent years.

Time and custom led to a despotism within John Company, which strengthened its political involvement at the expense of its commercial interests. The Indian Mutiny of 1857 led to the dissolution of the company and to the incorporation of India into the British Empire.

1602

The Dutch East India Company is founded. The main rivals to the Dutch were the Portuguese, who were, in fact, driven out of the Moluccas as early as 1605. Spain moved in to fill the vacuum, but it was the Dutch who exercised a major influence in the area, an influence that extended beyond the winding up of the company on December 31, 1795.

1606

This is a year of intense activity. Exploratory probes are being made southwards into the unknown waters of the South Pacific. Luis de Torres, an intrepid Spaniard, in the sole surviving ship of his expedition, sailed between Australia and New Guinea by way of the stretch of water named after him: the Torres Strait.

MARCH 1606

A Dutchman, Willem Janszoon, becomes the first authenticated discoverer of Australia, when he sails into the Gulf of Carpentaria and discovers the Australian coast at the mouth of the Pennefather River, on the Cape York Peninsula. The name of the ship he sailed on was the DUYFKEN. A landfall was made near the stream which is now known as the Wenlock River, on the west of the Cape York Peninsula.

1607

The explorer Henry Hudson leaves London in a small ship, taking with him his ten-year-old son, and a crew of ten. The object of the voyage was to reach Japan via Greenland and the North Pole. The voyage was a failure, although Hudson penetrated far beyond Spitsbergen. The following year, that is, in 1608, Hudson tried once more to reach the Far East by way of the northerly passage. On this occasion, he sailed round Norway, reached the northern shores of Russia, calling at Novaya Zemlya before pack-ice made him abandon the voyage.

Still undaunted, Hudson continued with his voyages of exploration. In 1609, he crossed the Atlantic in the HALF MOON, reached America and sailed southwards along the eastern coast-line of present-day Canada. He sailed up a river, now called the Hudson River in his honour, and claimed an extensive area for his new employers, the Dutch Government. He named this site Nieuw Amsterdam, which the English later made more famous under its present name of New York.

Hudson made his fourth and last voyage in 1610-11. This time, he was again in the service of the English. His brief was to attempt to discover the fabled North West Passage. He was able to sail along the northern coast of Canada, naming the Hudson Straits and Hudson Bay

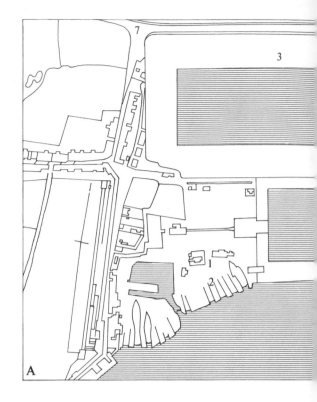

A *Map of the East India Docks in what were then the outskirts of London.*
1 *Dockyard*
2 *Slips*
3 *Unloading dock*
4 *Loading dock*
5 *Entry basin*
6 *River Lee*
7 *The road to London*
B *A company ship, early seventeenth century.*
C *Henry Hudson (c. 1550-1611).*

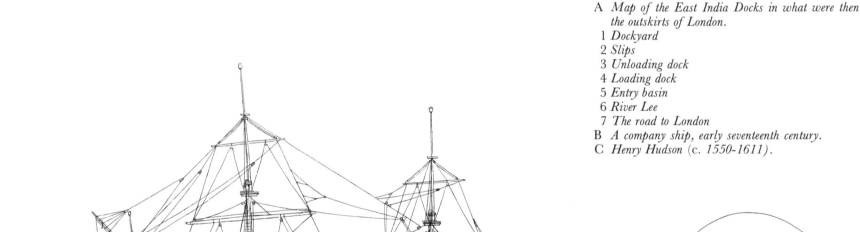

B

C

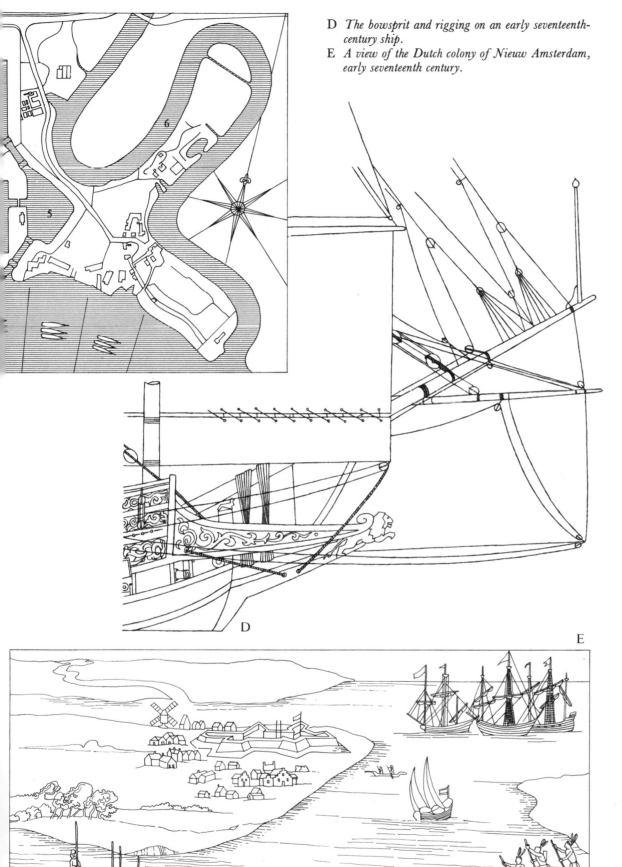

D *The bowsprit and rigging on an early seventeenth-century ship.*

E *A view of the Dutch colony of Nieuw Amsterdam, early seventeenth century.*

D

E

as he did so. The winter was a bitter one. His ship became ice-bound. Food was short. In the spring, his crew mutinied. Hudson and his fourteen-year-old son were seized, bundled into a ship's boat with seven loyal members of the crew, and were then set adrift. They have never been heard of since.

MAY 13, 1607
One hundred and forty-four English colonists disembark at the mouth of the James River in Chesapeake Bay. Jamestown is about to be put on the map.

Three small ships had ferried the colonists across the Atlantic. They were the SUSAN CONSTANT, of 100 tons burthen, some 110 foot (33.5 m) long: the DISCOVERY, 20 tons burthen and 49 foot (15 m) long: and the GODSPEED, 40 tons burthen and 61 foot (18.6 m) long.

By 1612, the group had become reasonably established. More, it had learnt the art of growing and curing tobacco from the Indians. Soon, the demand for tobacco was so great that the settlers were even putting public streets under the crop. From this small beginning, the vast tobacco industry developed. Virginia, the hinterland of Jamestown, became one of the most prosperous of the New World colonies. It is doubtful if the white settlers could have provided sufficient labour to cultivate all the tobacco that was demanded. However, in 1619, a Dutch ship arrived at the colony. The captain was short of provisions, so he bartered twenty Negro slaves for essential supplies. These slaves were put to work on the many tobacco plantations that were being carved out of the virgin territory. The slave trade had come to North America, and the long association of the Negroes with the tobacco trade had begun.

1608
A Dutch spectacle-maker living in Middelburg, Hans Lippershey, puts two lenses together in a specific relationship, inventing the telescope.

1609
Sir George Somers leads an expedition to reinforce the infant colonies in Virginia. On the way, his flagship is wrecked. He and the survivors reached Bermuda, an uninhabited island that had been named after its discoverer, Juan de Bermudez. The admiral organized the building of a fleet of small boats, and the survivors managed to reach Virginia. Here, there were many settlers ready to listen to the glowing tales that were told of the island paradise. Eventually, in 1612, sixty of the settlers arrived at Bermuda to start a new life.

1615-16
William Baffin and Robert Bylot, still in search of that elusive North West Passage to the Far East, probe the waters between Greenland and Canada. Again, they were as unsuccessful as their predecessors. However, they did dis-

cover a summer-time open sea passage through Baffin Bay, the large stretch of water that separates Greenland from Baffin Island, a major off-shore island of the North West Territories of Canada.

1616

Willem Barents leads a Dutch expedition that attempts to reach China by way of Northern Russia. He is unsuccessful. However, he spent the winter on the island of Novaya Zemlya in a house built mainly of timbers from his ship. This house was discovered in a fair state of preservation in 1871.

SEPTEMBER 6, 1620

The MAYFLOWER leaves Plymouth. Aboard were the Pilgrim Fathers, a group of seventy-three men and twenty-nine women, mainly of the Puritan faith, who were leaving England to set up an overseas colony where they could practise their faith without let or hindrance. Two months later, they landed near Cape Cod, Massachusetts, well to the north of the existing colony in Virginia. At the end of a hard winter, only half the original number remained. Yet they declined to return to England when the MAYFLOWER left for 'home' in the spring of 1621. With the coming of the Pilgrim Fathers, colonization in the New World entered a new phase, that by which the persecuted and poor of all nations were to be welcomed. That policy lasted until modern times.

1628

The second quarter of the seventeenth century is marked by the growing importance of Sweden as a major European power. This increase in her international stature is accompanied by the growing might of her navy. A very experienced Dutch shipwright, Henrik Hybertsson, was engaged by King Gustavus II Adolphus, who for some time led the allied forces in their opposition to the Emperor during the Thirty Years' War. In 1625, the Swedish Government ordered four vessels which were to be the first ships in the new navy. Of these four, one was the WASA, and on Sunday, August 10, 1628, the newly completed WASA left the quayside of Logården below the Royal Castle, Stockholm.

The WASA was a magnificent ship of 1,350 tons displacement, with a crew of 433 men under the command of Captain Söfring Hansson. Her length, excluding the bowsprit, was 200 foot (60.9 m), and from keel to truck she was 175 foot (52.0 m). Her beam was 38.4 foot (11.7 m). She had an armament of 64 bronze cannon.

She was a splendid sight in gold leaf and brilliant colours as she kedged out into the roads. Four large sails were set, the foresail, foretop, maintop, and mizzen.

Suddenly, a powerful gust of wind filled her sails. The WASA heeled to port. For a few brief seconds, the wind dropped. The WASA righted herself. A second fierce gust embraced her.

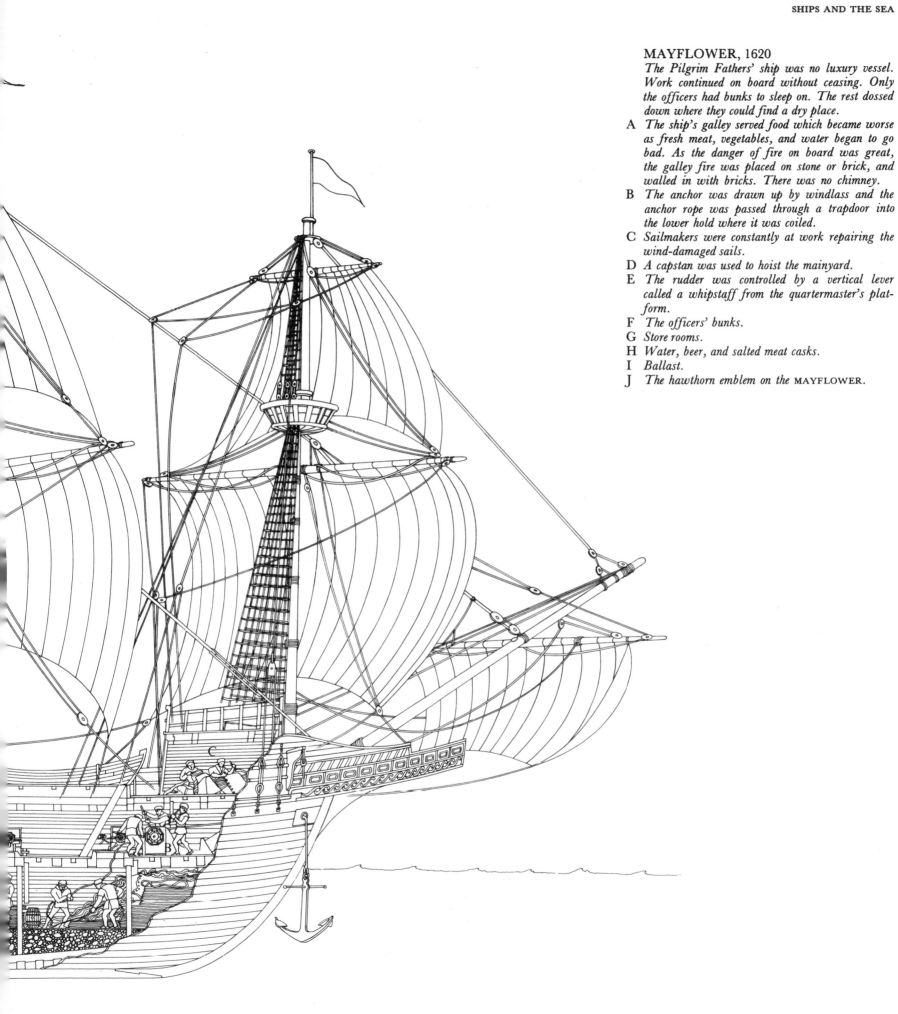

MAYFLOWER, 1620

The Pilgrim Fathers' ship was no luxury vessel. Work continued on board without ceasing. Only the officers had bunks to sleep on. The rest dossed down where they could find a dry place.

A *The ship's galley served food which became worse as fresh meat, vegetables, and water began to go bad. As the danger of fire on board was great, the galley fire was placed on stone or brick, and walled in with bricks. There was no chimney.*

B *The anchor was drawn up by windlass and the anchor rope was passed through a trapdoor into the lower hold where it was coiled.*

C *Sailmakers were constantly at work repairing the wind-damaged sails.*

D *A capstan was used to hoist the mainyard.*

E *The rudder was controlled by a vertical lever called a whipstaff from the quartermaster's platform.*

F *The officers' bunks.*

G *Store rooms.*

H *Water, beer, and salted meat casks.*

I *Ballast.*

J *The hawthorn emblem on the* MAYFLOWER.

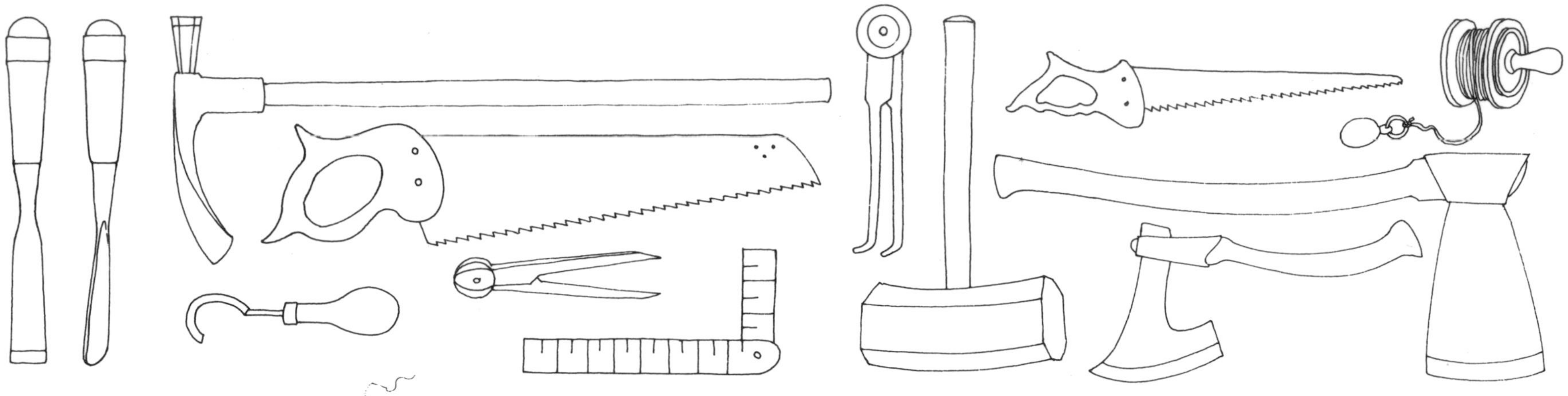

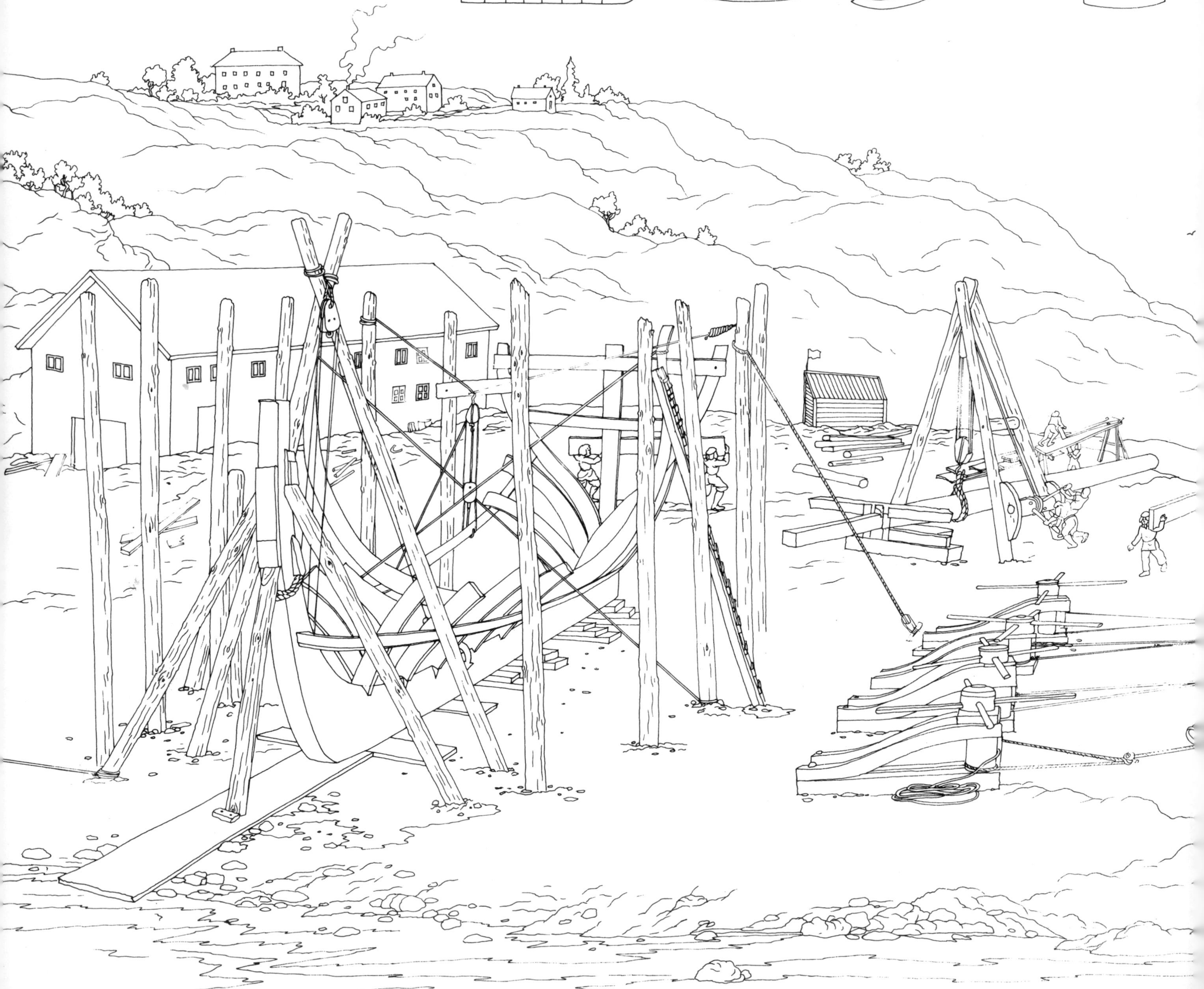

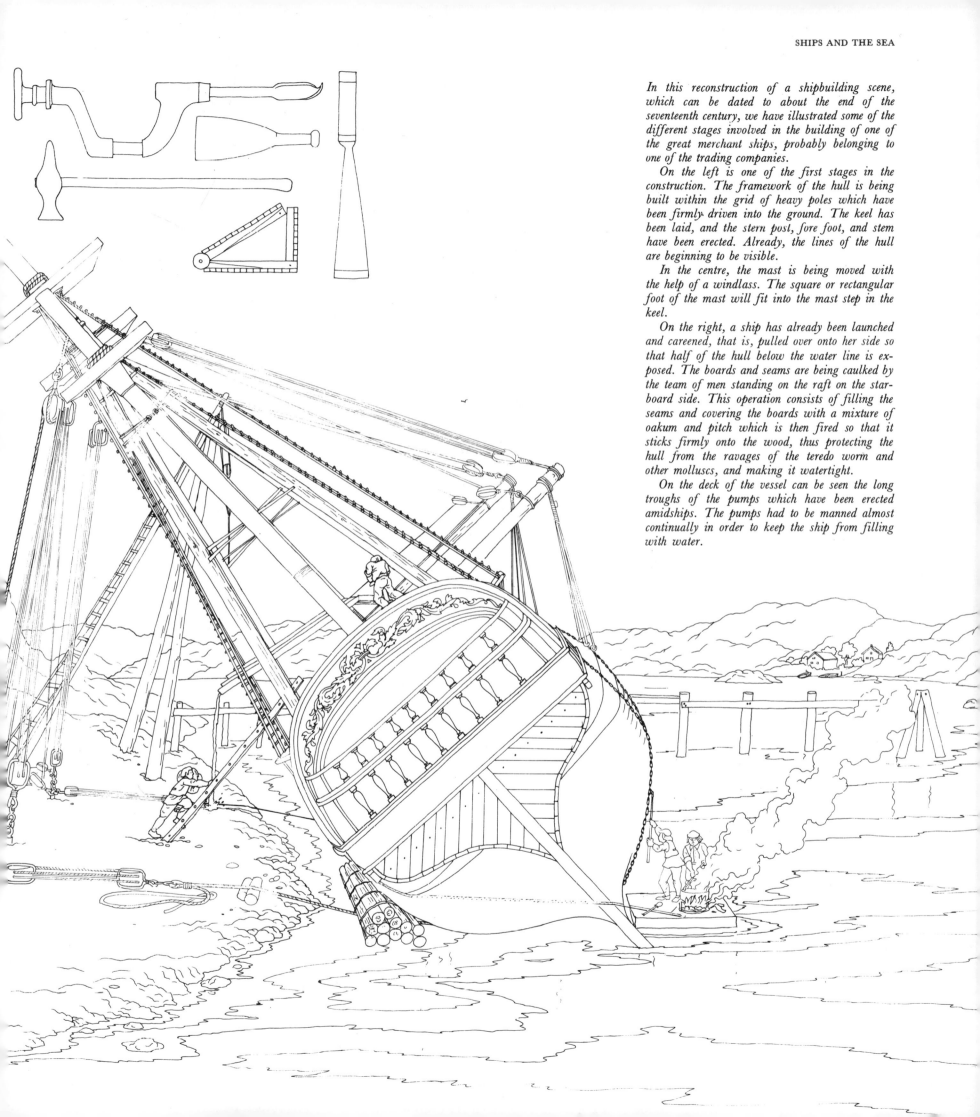

In this reconstruction of a shipbuilding scene, which can be dated to about the end of the seventeenth century, we have illustrated some of the different stages involved in the building of one of the great merchant ships, probably belonging to one of the trading companies.

On the left is one of the first stages in the construction. The framework of the hull is being built within the grid of heavy poles which have been firmly driven into the ground. The keel has been laid, and the stern post, fore foot, and stem have been erected. Already, the lines of the hull are beginning to be visible.

In the centre, the mast is being moved with the help of a windlass. The square or rectangular foot of the mast will fit into the mast step in the keel.

On the right, a ship has already been launched and careened, that is, pulled over onto her side so that half of the hull below the water line is exposed. The boards and seams are being caulked by the team of men standing on the raft on the starboard side. This operation consists of filling the seams and covering the boards with a mixture of oakum and pitch which is then fired so that it sticks firmly onto the wood, thus protecting the hull from the ravages of the teredo worm and other molluscs, and making it watertight.

On the deck of the vessel can be seen the long troughs of the pumps which have been erected amidships. The pumps had to be manned almost continually in order to keep the ship from filling with water.

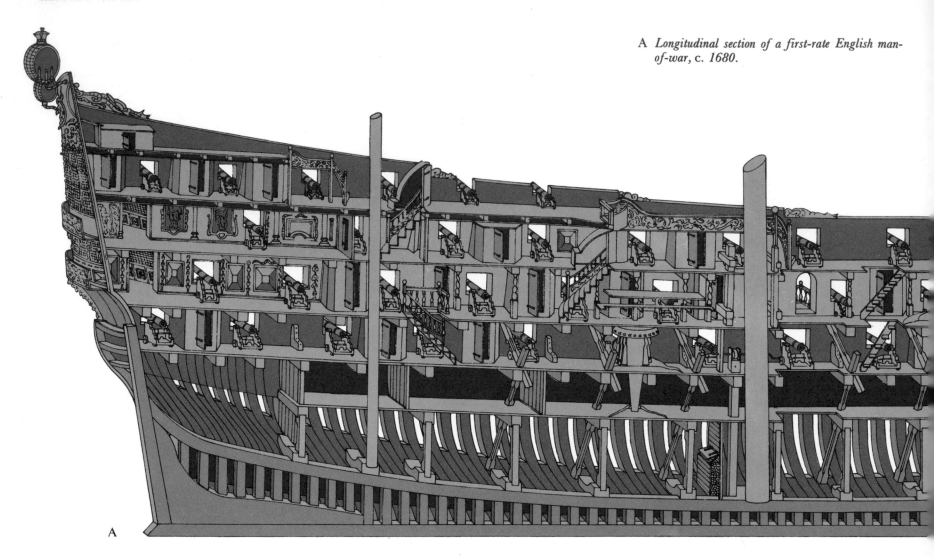

A *Longitudinal section of a first-rate English man-of-war, c. 1680.*

A

She heeled to port even more alarmingly. Her gun ports were open. Water rushed through them. The WASA sank like a stone in 110 foot (33.5 m) of water, 'under sail, pennants, and all', according to an eyewitness of the tragedy.

An investigating tribunal that was convened soon after the loss of the WASA held that no one was to blame for the foundering of the vessel. However, Admiral Klas Fleming, the chief investigating officer, disclosed that a stability test had been carried out on the WASA by thirty men running from side to side. Already after the third run, the vessel had been in real danger of capsizing!

In 1663-64, fifty-three of the WASA's bronze guns were salvaged. Then all trace of the wreck seems to have vanished until 1956, when it was rediscovered by Anders Franzén. The WASA was finally salvaged on April 24, 1961, was refurbished, and can now be seen in her home port of Stockholm.

1637
The SOVEREIGN OF THE SEAS, a British naval vessel, is the first ship to mount 100 guns.

1638
The Emperor of Japan formulates two decrees, the one closing all ports to foreigners, and the other banning international trade. As has already been mentioned, the Dutch were the only exception to this.

OCTOBER 21, 1639
The Dutch admiral, Maarten Tromp, defeats a Spanish fleet of seventy vessels under Admiral Antonio Oquendo. Thus the grip of Spain on the Netherlands was loosened. Nine years later, by the Treaty of Westphalia, the seven Dutch provinces received their independence.

1642
At this time, a man named Anthony van Diemen was the Governor-General of the Dutch East Indies. He sent a competent navigator, Abel Tasman, to explore the southern seas. Tasman discovered a large island which he promptly named 'Van Diemen's Land'. Today, that island is called Tasmania. Later on the same voyage he sighted land. He thought he had stumbled across the tip of South America, so he named the territory 'Staten Landt' after the Dutch homeland's Staten Island. Later,

B

B *The ship's galley.*
C SOVEREIGN OF THE SEAS, *1637.*

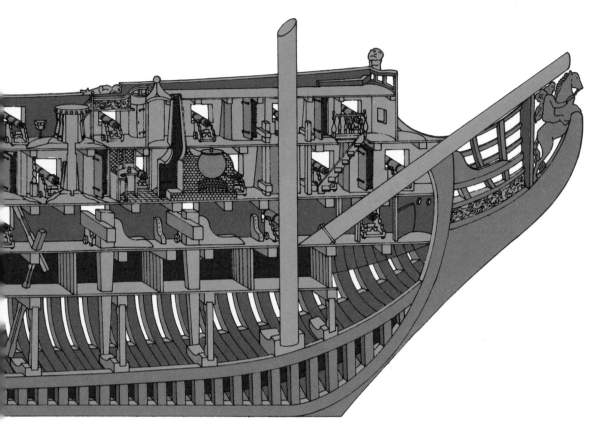

C

when the mistake was rectified, the name was changed to New Zealand, also after metropolitan Dutch territory.

1652

War breaks out between Holland and England. It is inconclusive.

One of the sea battles of the war was fought off Portland in 1653. It lasted for three days, and was unique in so far as the English employed new tactics. The admiral in command of the English fleet happened to be a general, Robert Blake. He conducted a three-day battle against Admiral Maarten Tromp, whose fleet was protecting a large convoy of merchant ships proceeding down the Channel. The English moves in the battle were processed through General Blake who, in his flagship, acted as the co-ordinator of a pre-planned attack. This was highly successful. The Dutch lost a great number of merchant ships and nine naval vessels. Seven years later, in 1660, the British Navy 'lost' all its Generals-at-Sea, when the rank was abolished, to be replaced by 'Admiral'. Henceforth, the commander had to excel in seamanship, not in military tactics. Four years later, the Duke of York founded a maritime regiment on foot to serve with the fleet. By 1672, this maritime regiment had become the 'Marines'. Much later, in 1802, they were renamed the 'Royal Marines'. The organization is still effective.

1652

The voyage from Dutch ports to Celebes, Sumatra, Java, and the other former Spice Islands was so long that scurvy frequently broke out among the crews and passengers making the journey. Scurvy is caused by a dietary deficiency. Even in these early days it was known that a diet of fresh vegetables would help to keep scurvy at bay. The Dutch East India Company, therefore, sent one of its doctors, Jan van Riebeeck, to establish a settlement at Cape Town. The settlers were to grow fresh vegetables which Dutch ships, calling at the port, could take aboard for the second leg of the journey.

The incidence of scurvy diminished. Van Riebeeck stayed at Cape Town for ten years. When he left, the Dutch colony had a population of 260. His statue may be seen in Cape Town to this day.

LATE 17TH CENTURY

An interesting phenomenon of the second half of the seventeenth century is the buccaneer. The word 'buccaneer' comes from the French word 'boucanier', which means 'to cure meat on a boucan'; a boucan being a barbecue. Pirates used this method of cooking, and thus acquired the name of buccaneers. Strictly speaking, the word was limited to those pirates who operated in the Caribbean area. Tortuga was one of their original lairs, but it was Port Royal in Jamaica which became the buccaneers' capital. When Port Royal was obliterated by the terrible earthquake of 1692, many said that it was God's justice on the most sinful town in the West Indies.

One of the most 'successful' of the buccaneers was a Welshman, Henry Morgan (1635-88). He amassed a fortune in a comparatively short life, and, rare amongst that pirate breed, managed to hold on to it. Indeed, his exploits, which included the sacking of the Spanish city of Panama in 1671, attracted the attention of no less a personage than Charles II of England, his ostensible sovereign. An arrangement was made between the king and the buccaneer by which the one-time pirate chief gave up his dishonest practices, accepted a knighthood and eventually became the Governor of Jamaica, which had been wrested from the Spanish by Admiral Penn, one of Cromwell's favourite admirals, in 1655, although it was not formally annexed to the British Crown until 1670.

Another notorious pirate who was employed by the British Government was Captain William Kidd (1645-1701). Put delicately, he was a privateer. Technically, a privateer was a ship which was privately owned, but which had government permission to act as a warship. Letters of Marque were issued to Captain Kidd and to many another privateer. Kidd's Letters of Marque gave him permission to attack any French ship. He was also, on the concept of setting a thief to catch a thief, required to put down the pirates in the Indian Ocean. Of course, what most privateers did was to play the pirate themselves and thus get a triple reward: immunity for their actions from the government issuing the Letters of Marque; the proceeds of their own piratical acts; and a share in the spoils that were handed over to the government.

Captain Kidd himself enjoyed all these three rewards for helping the British Government. He did not enjoy so much that self-same British Government hanging him for murder at Execution Dock, Wapping—a famous London Thames-side landmark—on May 23, 1701.

A *Design for a frogman's suit, by Borelli, 1680.*
B SOPHIA AMALIA, *Denmark's first partial three-decker, 1650.*
C *Anchors from the end of the seventeenth century.*
D *A cannon belonging to the Dutch East India Company, seventeenth century. Beside it, the crest on the barrel.*
E *The first Eddystone lighthouse, 1698.*

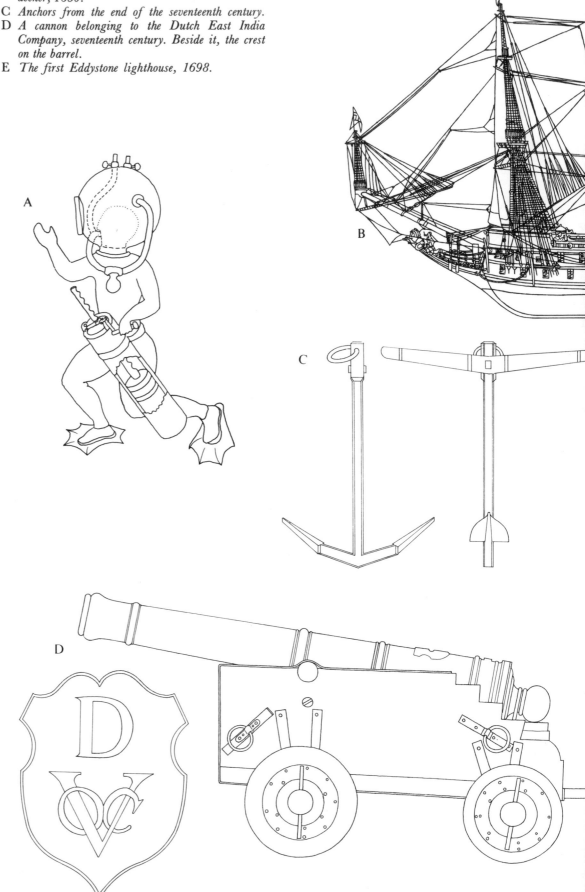

1680

The GRIFFIN is launched on Lake Ontario, Canada. She was the brain-child of Robert la Salle (1643-87), the notable French explorer who opened up the Mississippi and Ohio rivers to white infiltration. More, he opened up the Great Lakes when he and his men built the GRIFFIN, the first ship of any size to by launched on the five great lakes that straddle the border country between the United States and Canada.

1688

William Dampier (1652-1715) was another English buccaneer and explorer who struck out on his own and, in 1688, reached Australia. He explored part of its coastline, then came home and wrote a book entitled 'A Voyage Round the World'. His poor reports of Australia reinforced the reports made by the Dutch on that territory at the beginning of the seventeenth century. These adverse reports resulted in Australia being left severely alone for almost another hundred years, until, indeed, the time of Captain Cook.

On one of his subsequent privateering expeditions, which sailed in May, 1703, William Dampier had with him, as sailing master on board the CINQUE PORTS, one Alexander Selkirk, or Selcraig (1676-1721). Selkirk was the son of a Scottish shoemaker from Largo, Fifeshire, and was an experienced seaman. In October, 1704, he was stranded on the uninhabited island known as Más a Tierra, one of the Juan Fernandez group of islands. There are conflicting stories as to why he was left there. One story alleges that Dampier deliberately abandoned the young man there because of the latter's mutiny. Another story reports that Selkirk was shipwrecked on the island. The most probable version is that, after quarrelling with his captain, Thomas Stradling, Selkirk was marooned at his own request. He remained there for over four years, and was then rescued by the DUKE, a ship from an expedition led by Captain Woodes Rogers, later famous for his ruthless campaign against the pirates in the Bahamas, after he had been made Governor there.

But the real reason that Alexander Selkirk is remembered today is that he was Daniel Defoe's model for Robinson Crusoe in the famous book of that name.

1698

The first Eddystone Lighthouse is built. It is designed by Henry Winstanley, and constructed of wood. The lighthouse lasted for four years before it was destroyed in a violent storm. However, Winstanley's structure proved that it was possible to mark the dangerous submerged reef some 14 miles (22.5 km) southwest of Plymouth.

1698

It is about this time that Peter the Great, Czar of Russia, busied himself with the creation of the new Russian navy. For two years he toured European dockyards, finding out for himself how ships were built. He even worked for a time in the Dutch yards, gaining experience. His visit to the Deptford yard has been well publicized throughout the ages. Eventually, he returned to Russia taking with him a great army of skilled workers who helped in the construction of his new navy.

END OF THE 17TH CENTURY

Perhaps of even more significance to the story of the sea is the work of Cornelius van Bynkershoek (1673-1743), an eminent Dutch jurist who specialized in naval cases. Among other matters, he was concerned about the sovereignty of a nation's coastal waters. Eventually, he prevailed upon the Dutch Government to introduce a three-mile (5.6 km) limit to local territorial waters. The distance of three miles was fixed as that which could be covered by the fire from the most powerful known cannon. Most countries adopted the Three Mile Limit as the extent of their sovereignty over coastal waters. This international law remained in force for over two hundred years until various countries, usually by unilateral action, advanced their territorial boundaries to include coastal waters up to fifty miles (92.6 km) on the pretext of safeguarding national fishing and mineral 'rights'.

The century ends, then, with Britain, Holland, France, Sweden, and Russia emerging as the major maritime powers. Spain and Portugal have already fallen behind in the scramble for supremacy. The centre of the power struggle, too, has shifted from the Mediterranean to the Atlantic. Ships have undergone a radical change in design. The sail has ousted the oar except in small boats. Tactical and strategical dispositions have been given a fresh look. European governments, many of which are busy carving out vast empires, realize more than ever that he who rules the waves rules the world.

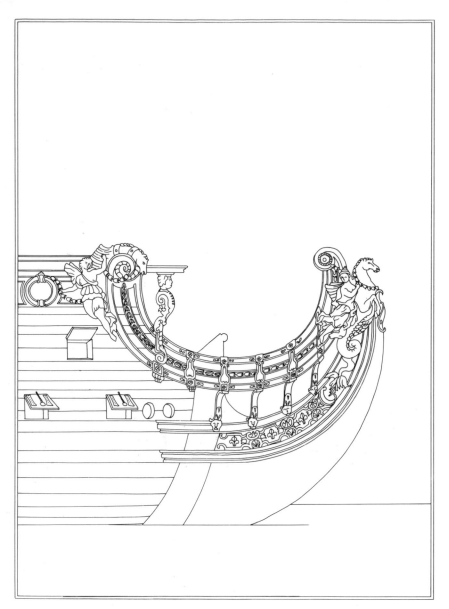

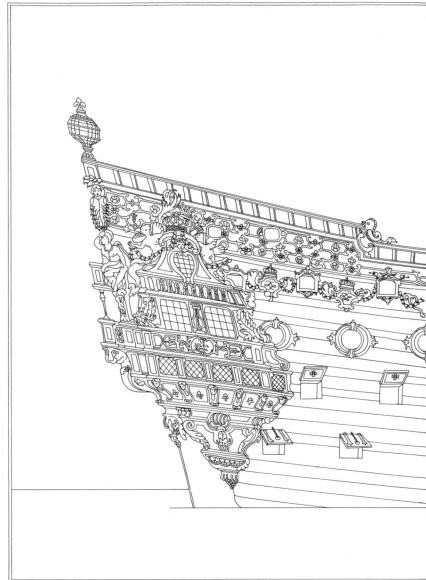

The prow and stern of the French ship LE SOLEIL
ROYAL, *1669.*

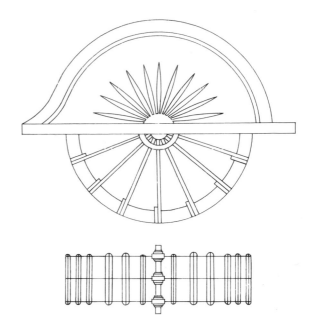

chapter 4

The next one and a quarter centuries fall into a convenient unit of development, in which the beginning and end are marked by critical naval battles. That at the beginning is the Battle of Vigo Bay, in 1702, as a result of which French power was seriously weakened; and that at the end is the Battle of Navarino Bay, in 1827, which was the last major fleet action conducted by sailing-ships.

But this period is not just notable for its sea battles. The eighteenth century saw significant advances in all the sciences, and many of these had a direct influence on seafaring.

Although the first scientifically conducted and recorded hull resistance experiments took place in England as early as the 1670s, it was not until 1746 that the first stability treatise was published. This was in France, where some valuable experiments were conducted in this field. However, ship designers were very slow to benefit from this information, and there was little improvement in the form of ships during this century. Indeed, it was difficult to spot the difference between merchant ships and medium-sized warships from their forms. It was almost impossible to construct long wooden ships due to the elasticity of the structure. This problem was solved later with the introduction of iron knees and strapping, but, at that time, warships had to have full lines at the ends to support

the armament carried there, and, as naval architecture led the way and set the pattern, merchant ships followed suit.

Accuracy in navigation had been seriously hampered by the lack of a really accurate timing instrument that could be used at sea. The method of determining latitude had long been known, and it was possible to work it out with a fairly acceptable degree of accuracy. But the correct degree of longitude could not be calculated at sea without a chronometer. On land, it was possible to work it out by a very complicated and time-consuming system, but this was too difficult for use aboard ship. In 1714, the British government offered a prize of £20,000 to the inventor of a reliable chronometer. The prize was won in 1773 by the Englishman John Harrison, who spent his life working on his invention until it was perfected.

Then, in 1731, John Hadley invented the Hadley octant, which brought the art of measuring altitudes at sea to theoretical perfection. The Hadley octant was a forerunner of the sextant, which was invented in 1757 by the British naval officer Campbell. When used, the sextant is held in the hand, which is essential on board ships at sea. In 1755, further progress was made in the systematization of navigation when Tobias Mayer, a German scientist living in Göttingen, edited the tables

necessary for finding Greenwich mean time in celestial navigation. Then, in 1767, the British Nautical Almanac, that invaluable aid to navigators at sea, was first published.

As trade by sea increased, covering insurance on both ship and cargo became a necessity. Lloyd's, the greatest marine insurance company in the world, began its business in the informal atmosphere of a London coffee house. In 1688, Edward Lloyd kept a coffee house in Tower Street in the City of London, which was frequented by bankers, merchants, shipowners, and sea captains, who would meet to transact business whilst drinking their coffee. Marine insurance followed the sixteenth-century Florentine pattern, in that risks were shared by subscription, each taking as large a portion as he wished, or dared. Merchants willing to take portions of a marine risk would write their names, one under another, on the insurance policy. They were, therefore, called 'underwriters'.

From the beginning, Lloyd's flourished. Edward Lloyd organized an information service for his customers, based on all kinds of sources and on a system of runners to the docks, who would bring back the latest news of arrivals and departures. In 1696, he brought out *Lloyd's News*, which contained details of shipping movements and also covered other matters of business. This became *Lloyd's List* in 1734. Thirty years later, a group of underwriters formalized the company, which published *Lloyd's Register,* a guide to all available vessels. The earliest surviving copy of this is the biennial issue of 1764-66. In it, the ships available are awarded gradings according to their seaworthiness. 'A1', the symbol for the highest class of ship, was introduced in 1775, and has since passed into many languages.

The accuracy of John Harrison's chronometer was established beyond doubt by Captain James Cook, who used it on the last two of his three much-chronicled voyages to the southern hemisphere. Cook, arguably Britain's greatest seaman, was the man who greatly increased the knowledge of that part of the world by exploring and mapping the Pacific and Antarctic Oceans, demonstrating that the fabled southern continent was a myth, and putting Australia and New Zealand on the world atlas. Cook was a true scientist, who contributed to many fields of knowledge. Among his important achievements, the elimination of scurvy must rank high. The crews on the expeditions were fed with fresh fruit, especially limes, so that they did not suffer from the vitamin deficiency which had proved fatal to so many of their predecessors.

As the period under discussion drew to a close, the clouds of war loomed on the horizon. From its very beginning, the American War of Independence (1775-83) was as much a sea war as a land war. At the onset of hostilities, the colonies were without any organized navy. However, there was a large maritime population, and many merchant ships which traded in coastal and foreign waters. These merchant ships and their crews were not new to war, as many of them had taken part as privateers in the recent French war. Furthermore, they were constantly armed, even in peace-time, as a protection against pirates. In 1775, therefore, it was possible to recruit these ships as privateers with legal authorization from individual colonies or the continental congress. It is estimated that over 2,000 privateers fought on the American side during the war, operating out of French as well as American ports, and preying on hostile commerce. Individual states organized navies, and these two forces exerted a sustained offensive against British merchant ships throughout the war, which in turn influenced the British people to thoughts of peace. Furthermore, merchant shipping losses were so great that Lloyd's, by now more important and influential than ever, brought pressure to bear on the British government to encourage a system of protecting shipping against enemy warship action. This was the later renowned convoy system.

By the end of the American War of Independence, the British government had understood the importance of a powerful, mobile navy to back up a land army during a campaign. This lesson was well learned, and the results of it

are to be seen during the Napoleonic Wars. In 1803, for instance, the French had twenty-three ships of the line and twenty-five frigates, while Britain had thirty-four ships of the line and eighty-five frigates in service, with seventy-seven ships of the line and forty-nine frigates in reserve. In 1816, Britain had twice as many ships of the line and almost six times as many frigates as France. The Battle of Trafalgar, in which Nelson was killed, was the decisive sea battle of the war and established British mastery of the seas for more than a hundred years.

The most revolutionary development of all during the years under discussion was, undoubtedly, the emergence of the steam-powered ship as an alternative to the sailing-ship. The theory of steam propulsion had been known for many years. The Frenchman Denis Papin experimented with steam engines at the beginning of the eighteenth century. He never tried to apply his engine to a boat, but his many experiments with a steam-operated water-pumping device were followed up in England by Thomas Newcomen, whose 'atmospheric' engine was soon widely used for pumping water out of mine shafts. A Dr. John Allen proposed using Newcomen engines to propel a boat by pumping a jet of water at pressure through the stern. However, it was not until July 15, 1783, that steam power was successfully used to propel a boat. On that day, Marquis Claude de Jouffroy d'Abbans's PYROSCAPHE moved against the current of the River Saône in France for fifteen minutes. Unfortunately, Jouffroy d'Abbans failed to get financial support for his scheme. On the other side of the Atlantic, the American engineer John Fitch successfully tried out his steamboat EXPERIMENT on the River Delaware in August, 1787. In the summer of 1790, Fitch inaugurated a passenger service with the boat between Philadelphia and Trenton. Fourteen return trips were made in all, and a total distance of over 2,000 miles (3,220 km) was covered. Unfortunately, the service operated at a loss, and Fitch went out of business.

In Britain, Thomas, Lord Dundas of Kerse, a director of the Forth and Clyde Canal, commissioned William Symington to build the CHARLOTTE DUNDAS, in 1801, and this is considered to be the first practical steamboat. From this time on, development proceeded apace. By 1812, Henry Bell, a Scot, had introduced commercial steam navigation in European waters with his COMET. In 1819, the SAVANNAH crossed the Atlantic from America to Europe, partially assisted by her auxiliary steam engine. Steam power was becoming a force to be reckoned with. Sailing-ship owners, however, ignored these happenings and continued to invest in faster and bigger sailing-ships, little aware that the successors of these little steamboats would come to banish the sail from commercial navigation within less than a hundred years.

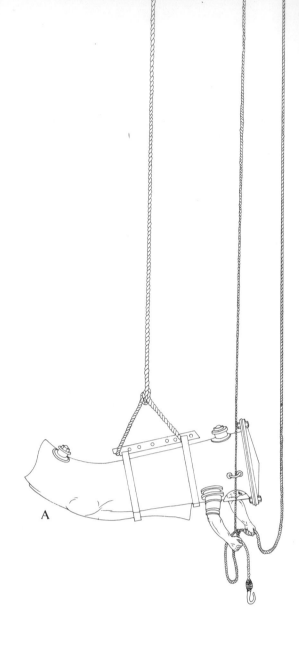

A

1702

The Battle of Vigo Bay marked the beginning of hostilities in the War of the Spanish Succession, in which Britain sided with Holland and Austria against France and Spain. Incidentally, the battle was a watershed in armaments; it was the first battle in which pikes were not used, for by an order issued on June 20, 1702, the last twelve pikemen in each company of the British army were relieved of their medieval weapons.

A combined fleet of English and Dutch vessels numbering 203 sail under Vice-Admiral Sir George Rooke, carrying the Union flag at the mainmast head of the ROYAL SOVEREIGN, defeated a French and Spanish fleet which was protected by a floating boom, and several batteries of shore guns.

1703

The worst storm ever recorded in the English Channel occurs. The English lost about 150 merchantmen and 13 warships in the space of twenty-four hours. Many of the ships were wrecked on the Goodwin Sands, a notorious graveyard for shipping.

1707

The ASSOCIATION, with Admiral Sir Cloudesley Shovel aboard, grounds on the Scilly Isles. Of the fifteen ships in his fleet, four were lost, together with 800 men. Even now, salvage is being obtained from the wreck of the ASSOCIATION.

1718

In the West Indies, the buccaneers had shifted their headquarters to the Bahamas. Fortunately, they met their match in Captain Woodes Rogers, who about this time became the Governor of the Bahamas. He ordered an all-out campaign against the pirates. Eight leaders were captured, and publicly hanged.

1728

Peter the Great sends a Danish explorer, Vitus Bering, to find the spot where Russia joins America. Bering started his search from Kamchatka in Siberia, but although he reached the strait which now bears his name, he did not succeed in landing in Alaska. Thirteen years later, Bering again explored the strait, and actually crossed the 56 miles (90.1 km) to reach Alaska. Unfortunately, he died when his ship was wrecked.

1732

Britain introduces the lightship to the world. This was the Nore lightship, which was moored at the mouth of the Thames; then, as now, one of the busiest waterways in the world. The first lightship was a suitably converted Dutch galliot.

1740

Press-gangs had conscripted sailors for various

A *A diving suit designed by John Lethbridge in 1715. He claimed to have used it successfully several times. It was made of wood, and strengthened inside and out with iron hoops. It had holes for the diver's arms, and a window through which he could see.*

B *The Battle of Vigo Bay, by Anna Beek. Reproduced by courtesy of the Scheepvaartsmuseum, Amsterdam.*

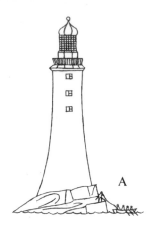

A

B

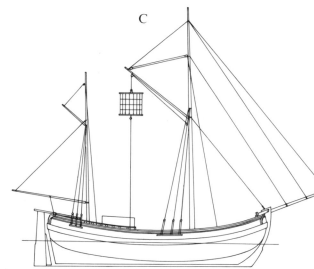

C

D

navies ever since Norman times. England needed a constant supply of men for the rapidly expanding Royal Navy. Until 1740, any male, whether an Englishman or a foreigner, serving aboard any British ship, could be impressed into the Navy. There was no appeal against the action of the press-gangs, many of which had 'recruiters' in various places. Eventually, the system became such a scandal that an attempt was made to bring some sort of order into it. The law stated that only British subjects between the ages of eighteen and fifty-five would in future be liable to be taken by the press-gangs.

Unhappily, the new law of 1740 was not rigidly observed. Indeed, one of the reasons for the outbreak of the Anglo-American War of 1812 was the insistence of press-gangs in taking American citizens off ships and forcing them to serve in English naval vessels. Finally, press-gangs were abolished in 1815, part of the tidying-up process after the end of the Napoleonic Wars.

1740
Captain George Anson's voyage round the world begins. Anson, a man of the sea since his boyhood days, was put in charge of a squadron of five men-of-war and three auxiliaries, with a total complement of 1,400 men. Although the voyage, which lasted three years and nine months, was a success, yet Anson returned with but one ship, the CENTURION.

1756-63
The Seven Years' War saw the nadir of French colonial ambitions of the eighteenth century. Many of her Indian possessions were lost to the British, as was French Canada. Britain, again, was able to call upon overwhelming sea-power. In one famous episode, however, she was very much the loser. This was in 1757, when Admiral Byng, failing to raise the French blockade of Minorca, then in British hands, fell back in order to defend Gibraltar. The great British public was so incensed at this affront to its national pride, that, persuaded by popular

E

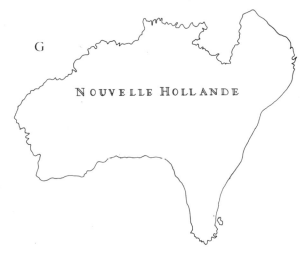

F

G

NOUVELLE HOLLANDE

that he put his telescope to his blind eye and disobeyed Admiral Parker's signal to withdraw.

1759
The new Eddystone Lighthouse off Plymouth, in south-west England, introduces a design in lighthouses that is copied to this day.

1760
Lloyd's of London is founded. It is still in business to this day. Lloyd's classification of ships has been accepted as authentic evidence of a vessel's merit for some 200 years. Its 'Lutine Bell' is sounded when any ship is overdue or lost at sea.

1768-79
Captain James Cook (1728-79) sails on his first voyage to the Pacific in 1768 in the ENDEAVOUR, with a crew of eighty men and three scientists. The object of the voyage was to proceed to Tahiti in order to observe the transit of Venus. During this voyage, Cook sailed round, and mapped, New Zealand. In 1770, he landed at Botany Bay, New South Wales, and found a country far less inhospitable than earlier explorers had described from their visits to the more northerly parts of Australia.

In 1772, Cook left on a second voyage of exploration. The purpose of this trip was to discover the legendary continent populated by millions of people. Two ships, the RESOLUTION and the ADVENTURE, made the voyage. It was during this voyage, in 1773, that he approached within 1,300 miles (2,092 km) of the South Pole, the nearest that any man had ever got to that geographical feature.

Cook's third Pacific voyage was made in the DISCOVERY and the RESOLUTION. His main purpose was to try to find a navigable passage between the Pacific and the Atlantic by way of the northern shores of Canada. In this, Cook was unsuccessful, but he was successful during this voyage in defeating the ravages of scurvy. He did this by issuing fresh fruit—especially limes—to his crews. Ever since, English sailors in those waters, and nowadays, any Englishman in the eyes of an Australian, has been referred to as a 'Limey'.

This voyage was the last that Cook ever made. On February 14, 1779, he was killed by natives on the beach at Hawaii. The voyage itself was continued, the remainder of the expedition finally reaching England on October 4, 1780.

DECEMBER 16, 1773
During late November and early December of 1773, three English ships, the DARTMOUTH, the ELEANOR, and the BEAVER, had arrived at Boston. They tied up at Griffins Wharf, unloaded their general cargo, and awaited the Tea Tax clearance certificate. A mass meeting of citizens had earlier, and on several occasions, demonstrated against the imposition of this

clamour, the Government recalled Admiral Byng, tried him for treason at one of the most blatantly political of courts-martial, and shot him at Portsmouth, for no other reason than 'Pour encourager les autres'.

Horatio Nelson was born during the Seven Years' War, on September 29, 1758, at Burnham Thorpe in the county of Norfolk, England. He joined the Royal Navy when he was only twelve years old, was commissioned lieutenant at the age of nineteen, and was captain of the BADGER when he was only twenty.

It was as commander of the AGAMEMNON that he lost his right eye during the capture of Corsica. In the attempt to take Santa Cruz de Tenerife, he was shot in the right elbow. This arm was amputated by the light of a ship's lantern. At the Battle of the Nile (Aboukir Bay) he received the wound in his forehead that resulted in the scar that he wore like a badge. It was during the Battle of Copenhagen, when the fleet was under heavy fire, particular tax; therefore, a group of young men dressed themselves up as Mohawk Indians and raided the three vessels. The cargo of tea was dumped into the harbour.

The Boston Tea Party attracted retaliation from the English Government, which attempted unsuccessfully to close the port. Now, a long, slow fuse was lit that led to the American War of Independence and to the creation of an autonomous United States of America.

1774

A Spanish explorer, Juan Perez, visits Vancouver Island, but does not land on the mainland of Canada. A year later, another Spaniard, Manuel de Ayala, entered San Francisco Bay in his ship, the SAN CARLOS. As far as is known, this was the first time that an agent of a western power had explored this territory since the time of Drake. The sound had, in fact, been noticed by José de Ortega in 1769, but he had not stopped to explore it. Indeed, the western powers were not very interested at that time in this remote part of America. Consequently, the Mexicans, who approached it from the overland route, were able to rule it from 1822 until 1844 without too much trouble.

Even then, it was not a growth area. The only boat services were operated by Englishmen. John Reed held the franchise in 1826, and William Richardson from 1841. No major expansion took place until the time that San Francisco and Oakland were connected by the steam ferry-boat KANGAROO in 1851.

SEPTEMBER 7, 1776

For the first time, a nation resorts to submarine warfare. The country is the fledgling United States of America, fighting its war for independence against Britain. The inventor of the first operational submarine is David Bushnell, and the operator is Sergeant Ezra Lee who, in the primitive hand-propelled craft, tries to screw a mine into the hull of the British man-of-war EAGLE, lying in New York harbour. The attempt fails as the hull's copper sheathing is too thick.

NOVEMBER 16, 1776

The United States ship ANDREW DORIA visits the Dutch West Indies port of Fort Orange. The Dutch accord the vessel a welcoming salute of guns, the first time such a courtesy had been extended to an American ship flying the new national ensign.

LATE 18TH CENTURY

England finds herself at war with America, France, and Holland. An American, John Paul Jones, did what was thought to be impossible: he crossed the Atlantic, and twice attacked England. Alnmouth in Northumberland was bombarded in 1778, and the following year Jones fought a naval battle off Flamborough Head. His ship was sunk, but he was saved. Jones was, in fact, a corsair who often operated with a small French squadron.

1784

Whaling is established in Nova Scotia. Governor Parr induces twenty families to leave Massachusetts and to settle at Halifax. A new settlement is built, which is named Dartmouth after the town the new settlers had recently left. A sum of £1,541 was granted to the settlers so that they might build their houses, and also a shipyard. Within a year, a fleet of three brigantines and one schooner formed the basis of the new industry.

MAY 1787-JANUARY 18, 1788

The British Government was not slow to appreciate the possibilities inherent in the discovery of Botany Bay by Captain Cook. Transportation had long been a punishment imposed under the British penal code. Cook's reports convinced the Government that Australia was the place to send convicts, now that the Americas were no longer available to receive them. In May, 1787, therefore, Captain Arthur Phillip, in command of a convoy of eleven ships, leaves England. With him go eight hundred convicts who have been sentenced to transportation. They take farm animals and seeds, in order to commence prison farms.

Australia soon came under the aegis of the British Crown, and those first convicts arrived in Australia on January 18, 1788. Between then and 1841, more than 80,000 convicts were sent from England to Australia. Many took their discharge in the new country and remained as honest settlers. It was not until 1793 that free settlers were allowed to go to Australia.

1787

Mutiny at sea, fortunately, is a rare occurrence. The absolute power of the captain, coupled with the traditional penalty of death by hanging at the yard-arm, usually acted as a sharp deterrent to would-be mutineers, and most port authorities gave mutineers short shrift. But there have been mutinies at sea, of individuals, of individual crews, of entire fleets. Let the story of the BOUNTY serve as the classic account of all mutinies.

Captain Bligh was neither fool nor coward. It is conveniently forgotten that it was Lieutenant William Bligh who was at Captain Cook's side when the latter was murdered on that Hawaiian beach. It was Bligh who counter-attacked, who stood over his captain's mutilated body, breathing defiance, until his men could rescue the body and place it in the ship's boat. Only then would Bligh leave that beach.

This, then, was the man, now Captain Bligh, who sailed the BOUNTY out of Spithead and set course for the long haul to Tahiti. His mission was to take on a cargo of bread-fruit plants and transport them to the West Indies, where it was hoped a bread-fruit industry could be established. Bligh had been chosen by the Admiralty because of his previous experience in Pacific waters. He took along a botanist to look after the bread-fruit plants.

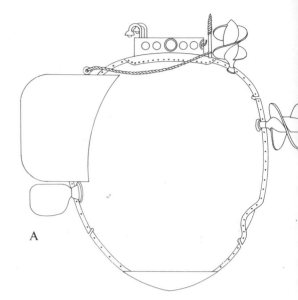

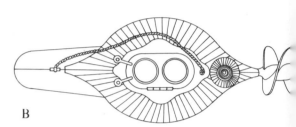

TURTLE, 1776
This submarine was designed by David Bushnell, Saybrook, Connecticut, for use during the American War of Independence. Also known as the 'Maine Torpedo', the TURTLE *was built of oak coated with tar. Water was flooded in to provide submerging ballast, and pumped out when the vessel was to surface. The air supply lasted only about thirty minutes. Underwater, the vessel was driven by a hand-cranked propeller.*
A *Side view.*
B *Plan view.*
C *Section showing interior.*
1 *Rudder*
2 *Propeller*
3 *Pump for evacuating water ballast*
4 *Glass window*
5 *Drilling screw*

Bligh was a Cornishman, one of three Blighs who saw service with the Royal Navy. Indeed, at a time when navy captains were renowned for their strictness—they had to be, for most of them commanded unwilling crews of pressed men—Bligh was no more strict than other captains. Richard Bligh was court-martialled for losing his ship to the French. He was acquitted, but a black mark was always placed against his name. John Bligh was thrown overboard from the LATONA by mutineers in 1797. These episodes, and others in which Richard and John Bligh were involved, have, by mythologization, been tagged on to Captain William Bligh.

In modern parlance, Captain Bligh 'went by the book'. He never accepted a plea of extenuating circumstances. He was strict, and he was a perfectionist. These are the worst 'charges' that can be levelled against him. His perfectionism comes through to modern times; for the charts that he drew of Hawaii are accurate to this day.

'Bread-fruit' Bligh, as he was known for a while, duly arrived in the Pacific. Unhappily, in April, 1789, when the ship had reached Tofoa Island, near the Friendly Islands, elements of the crew under Fletcher Christian mutinied. Bligh and some loyal members of his crew were set adrift in a small boat. He was virtually in the middle of the vast Pacific, thousands of miles from any main port—and all he had were his wits and the 16-foot (4.9 m) ship's boat.

Undaunted, Bligh applied his knowledge of the Pacific winds to such effect that he was able to bring that frail craft safely to Timor in the Dutch East Indies, a distance of 3,600 miles by sea. From Timor, he took a ship for London, arriving there in 1790. He reported the incident to the Admiralty, who immediately fitted out the PANDORA and despatched her to round up the mutineers and bring them back to London. Those mutineers who had established themselves on Tahiti—several with native wives

—were duly brought back to London, where they stood trial at a court-martial presided over by Admiral Lord Hood. Three of them were executed; the remainder were freed.

Some of the original mutineers had, however, left Tahiti and settled on Pitcairn Island. Their descendants live there to this day.

The Lords of the Admiralty reposed such faith in Captain Bligh that they commissioned him to return to the Pacific, where he completed his original task. He returned to England, and was paid off at Woolwich. The 'Kentish Messenger' of that time carried an article about him which stated:

The high estimation in which Captain Bligh was deservedly held by the whole crew was conspicuous to all present. He was cheered on quitting the ship and at the dock gates the men drew up and repeated their parting acclamation.

Bligh attained the rank of Admiral, but he swallowed the anchor and was appointed Governor of New South Wales. His ingrained

The feverish activity during the heat of battle on the deck of an eighteenth-century man-of-war is reconstructed here. Shot has carried away parts of the shrouds on the lower rigging. Two of the sails have fallen on the deck and are being gathered up hastily by the crew so that the decks are left clear for the gunners.

The cannon on the left has been loaded and run out. It is now being trained with the aid of a handspike, and it will then be elevated so that the shot will have the correct trajectory. The captain of gunnery is cocking the lock, and he will then step back far enough to avoid the recoil, and pull the trigger line.

On the right, an officer is directing the running out of a cannon. A cannon is run out by hauling on the side-tackle, which is also used when training the gun to the right or left. The hand-spike is also used to raise the breech during elevation. When the correct elevation is reached, a wooden wedge known as the 'coin' is pushed under the breech.

sense of discipline never deserted him. This was unfortunate, for a new philosophy had permeated the armed forces. Bligh was deposed by the Army, and placed under house arrest for two years. He was then replaced, but those responsible for deposing him were not proceeded against. Bligh returned to London, and died in bed of cancer in 1817, still faintly puzzled why the nickname of 'Bounty Bastard' had already been tagged on to him.

1789

The lifeboat is invented. A vessel was aground at the mouth of the River Tyne in northern England. It was dismasted and sorely stricken by the storm; yet it was only 300 yards (274 m) from the hundreds of sightseers who thronged the shore. Nothing could be done to save the crew, which died in front of the very eyes of the onlookers. As a result of this catastrophe, a prize was offered for the design of a Life Saving Boat. That of Henry Greathead was declared the winner and his lifeboat, the ORIGINAL, remained in service for forty years. Today, nearly thirty countries operate their own lifeboat institutions.

1791

Commander George Vancouver surveys the north-west coast of North America. He re-establishes British rule at Nootka Sound, Vancouver Island.

1792

The French Republic is proclaimed. M. Monge, the first Republican Minister of the Navy, has at his disposition 86 ships of the line, 76 frigates, and over a hundred sloops and smaller vessels.

1797

The English fleet mutinies at the Nore, which is near Chatham, in Kent. Ships are taken over by 'elected delegates', and a threat is made to hand over the ships to the French.

The mutiny was supposedly caused through grievances over bad food, insufficient pay, and tyrannical officers. However, the main cause seems to have been the spread of disaffection among the seamen by French agents sent over by the Revolutionary Movement, and by suborned English sailors. The ringleader of the mutiny, Richard Parker, was court-martialled and hanged.

1792-1815

The Napoleonic Wars are more readily identified in the public mind as land wars, with Napoleon performing prodigious feats with the Grand Army. He did; but his ultimate dream, that of being master of the world, was shattered because of England's sea-power. Had he won the Battle of the Nile (Aboukir Bay), then the way would have been open for him to have marched on to the Near East and India. But he lost that battle, as he lost most of the major

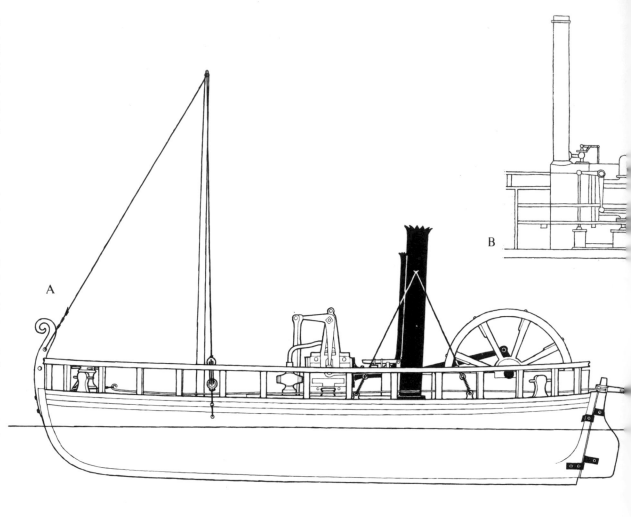

sea-battles that were fought during his meteoric career.

FEBRUARY 14, 1797

Admiral Sir John Jervis had for some time been blockading Cadiz. He received intelligence that the Spanish fleet, commanded by Don José de Cordova, had left Carthagena. Jervis, supported by fifteen ships of the line, four frigates, a twenty-gun corvette, an eighteen-gun brig, and a ten-gun cutter, set off to intercept the enemy. Soon after dawn, the Spanish fleet of forty ships, twenty-five of them being ships of the line, was sighted. The Spaniards had over 2,000 guns, which was well in excess of the 1,414 pieces that Jervis could command. The Spanish SANTISSIMA TRINIDAD of 130 guns—some records state 136—was the largest ship in the world at that time.

The battle lasted until five in the afternoon, and left Jervis the victor. A notable contribution to the success was made by Commodore Nelson in the CAPTAIN. Nelson captured two ships, the SAN NICHOLAS, 80 guns, and the SAN JOSEF, 120 guns. A delighted British Parliament elevated Jervis to the peerage, and awarded Nelson the Order of the Bath.

1798

Napoleon's fleet, en route to Egypt, stages a divertissement and captures Malta. Rather foolishly, the religious treasures of the devout islanders are seized. The Maltese immediately staged a rebellion—a classic example of David against Goliath. Nelson detailed some of his ships to blockade the French garrison. This they did for two years, until the French surrendered.

AUGUST 1, 1798

The Battle of the Nile takes place. It is often referred to as the Battle of Aboukir Bay, because it was in this inlet of the Mediterranean that Napoleon's fleet was anchored. The combined British fleet, the first ever 'modern' fleet to sail through the Straits of Messina, numbered fourteen sail, all but one of them of seventy-four guns. The total complement was 6,988 men.

The French fleet was under the command of Admiral Brueys and Rear-Admiral Villeneuve. It consisted of eighteen vessels, which in total slightly out-gunned Nelson's fleet. It had a large superiority in manpower, for there were 10,110 men at Brueys's disposal.

The upshot of the battle was that Nelson

triumphed. Perhaps the most outstanding feat in a memorable engagement was the sinking of L'ORIENT. This was Admiral Brueys's own flagship, with Casa Bianca as captain. It was a night engagement, and when the flagship exploded, the effect was spectacular. She went down firing to the last.

1800
Matthew Flinders circumnavigates Australia. He is thought to be the first man to have achieved this feat.

1800
The last decade of the eighteenth century witnessed a staggering increase in England's shipping power, with a similar increase in her trade figures. It had taken ninety years, from 1700 to 1790, for the number of registered ships in the country to increase from 3,281 to 16,079. Yet, in the last decade, the figure rose to 20,983 registered vessels in the kingdom.

APRIL 2, 1801
The Battle of Copenhagen takes place. Theoretically, Denmark was not yet at war with Britain, but it had long been held that she looked with favour upon France. It was little wonder, then, that she was a signatory to the pact known as 'The Armed Neutrality of the Northern States'. Effectively, this meant that Russia, Sweden, and Denmark could engage in acts of war against Britain without the formality of declaring war.

The British Government despatched a force of fifty-four sail under Admiral Parker to find out exactly what was happening in Copenhagen. The force was composed of eighteen ships of the line, four frigates, and various gun-brigs, bomb and fire-ships. Because of the treacherous currents, not all those ships could be deployed to take part in the battle.

The battle was a furious one. It has been estimated that something like two thousand cannon of every calibre were committed in a very small area, and that they were fired continuously for three hours. It was during this carnage that Parker, who was in the rear, sent his pre-arranged message, number thirty-nine, which was the code signal for Nelson to break off the engagement. It was then that Nelson turned his blind eye to the signal, of which he had been advised by his signal-lieutenant, issued his famous aside, and gave instructions for his own signal for closer battle to be kept flying.

1802
The first steam-boat is launched. There had been a little flirting with steam engines before, but it was not until the first Lord Dundas asked William Symington (1763-1831) to install a steam engine in a hull that the matter came to be taken seriously.

Symington had built a number of single-cylinder steam engines, so he was not without experience or skill. Lord Dundas explained that he needed a new steam paddle-ship that could be used as a tug on the Forth and Clyde Canal. A firm order was given towards the end of 1801. By 1802, the ship was ready for trials. Lord Dundas named the vessel CHARLOTTE DUNDAS, in honour of his daughter. In foul weather in mid-March, the CHARLOTTE DUNDAS made the 19½-mile (31.4 km) journey to Port Dundas, Glasgow, in 6 hours—an average speed of 3½ miles (5.6 km) an hour. A group of top-hatted, frock-coated gentlemen joined Lord Dundas and his party on the open deck of the steam paddle-tug. Everybody was impressed by the performance of the CHARLOTTE DUNDAS, despite the blustering gale that she had to cope with. Her pay-load was two barges, each of 72 tons burthen.

Despite the impressiveness of the trials, the CHARLOTTE DUNDAS did not earn her keep; for the swell caused by the passage damaged the banks of the canal. She was, therefore, tied up at Bramford Drawbridge in Lock 16, where she lay for many years.

JULY 22, 1805
Fifteen ships under the British Vice-Admiral Calder engage twenty Franco-Spanish ships under Admiral Villeneuve off Cape Finisterre. The battle is fought in misty conditions, and is inconclusive. Calder is deemed to have failed, and is relieved.

OCTOBER 21, 1805
The last large-scale fleet action under sail, the Battle of Trafalgar, takes place. Admiral Nelson had been appointed to command the British fleet, which was to seek out and destroy the Franco-Spanish fleet, known to be refitting at Cadiz.

The British fleet consisted of thirty-three sail. The VICTORY led the van, the ROYAL SOVEREIGN the rear. Collingwood was the British Vice-Admiral. First there was some sparring before the actual battle took place. On October 19, the MARS, which formed the line of communication with the in-shore scouting frigates, signalled that the combined French and Spanish fleet, under the command of Villeneuve, Don Ignatius Maria d'Alava, and Don Federico Gravina respectively, had left harbour. By a strange coincidence, the enemy fleet also numbered thirty-three sail; but the British fleet had been depleted to twenty-eight by the dispatch of five ships under Rear-Admiral Louis to Gibraltar for additional supplies.

At daybreak on October 20, the two opposing fleets make visual contact. Nelson notes that his opponents are some four leagues to leeward, and standing to the south. Throughout the day, Nelson sails slowly away from the coastline. His strategy is to draw the fleet just far enough out to make a hurried retreat impossible.

At 11.45, with the wind westering, the breeze light, and a long, rolling swell upon the water, the first shots are fired by the SANTA ANA

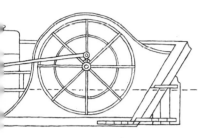

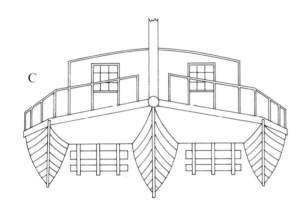

A CHARLOTTE DUNDAS, *1801.*

B *Symington's direct-drive engine which was used to drive the* CHARLOTTE DUNDAS's *paddle-wheel, which was housed in a covered stern recess.*

C *In 1787, Patrick Miller of Dalswinton in Scotland was experimenting with steam-driven boats. We show a transverse section of one of the boats he had built. It had two paddle-wheels and three hulls.*

(112 guns) at the ROYAL SOVEREIGN. Each ship engages its opposite number down the line. The VICTORY fires across the stern of the BUCENTAURE, which has Admiral Villeneuve aboard. The French vessel is disabled. The VICTORY is almost grappled by the REDOUTABLE, from one of whose fighting tops a sniper sends a bullet into Nelson, smashing his spine.

Nelson's complete strategy becomes apparent. The enemy fleet is divided into three segments, and the British are sailing through the segments in order to prevent the Franco-Spanish fleet from returning to Cadiz. Perhaps even more important, some elements of the enemy fleet are so far ahead of the battle zone that it is more than two hours before they can turn and engage the British fleet, which for a time enjoyed numerical superiority. Soon, there was little doubt as to the outcome of the action. Villeneuve was a captive, his fleet scattered. Thirteen of the enemy ships were in the hands of British prize-crews. Seventeen more Franco-Spanish vessels were dismasted.

The casualties were disproportionate. The Franco-Spanish fleet lost over 3,000 men. The British lost 454, with an additional 1,141 wounded. The BELLE ISLE—British, despite her name—was the only seriously damaged ship of that fleet: dismasted. Even the subsequent storm which lashed the area as though trying to cleanse the water of its blood-bath was kind to the British fleet which escaped unscathed, although the Franco-Spanish had three surviving vessels wrecked.

1807

Four years after the successful launching of the CHARLOTTE DUNDAS, an American engineer, Robert Fulton, turned his hand to building a steamboat. He had seen the trials of the CHARLOTTE DUNDAS, and was also worried about the escalating costs of building sailing vessels. He soon found a sponsor, Chancellor R. Livingstone, and arrangements were made for Fulton to occupy part of the shipyard of Charles Brown on the River Hudson, close by New York. The work proceeded briskly, and in 1807 the steamboat, named the CLERMONT, underwent her trials on the Hudson. She averaged five miles (8 km) an hour. Fulton decided that he would get better performance from the steamboat by raising her paddles still further out of the water. This modification was carried out, and the CLERMONT, appropriately, left New York for Clermont some 110 miles (177 km) away. Clermont was reached in twenty-four hours, the first ever lengthy trip made by a steam paddle-boat. After a short delay, she set out for the state capital, Albany, a further 40 miles (64 km) distant. Albany was reached in another eight hours. One unapprised eye-witness, on seeing the chugging, belching steamboat, ran screaming home and reported, 'I've just seen the Devil on his way to Albany in a sawmill!'

A better fate awaited the CLERMONT than had

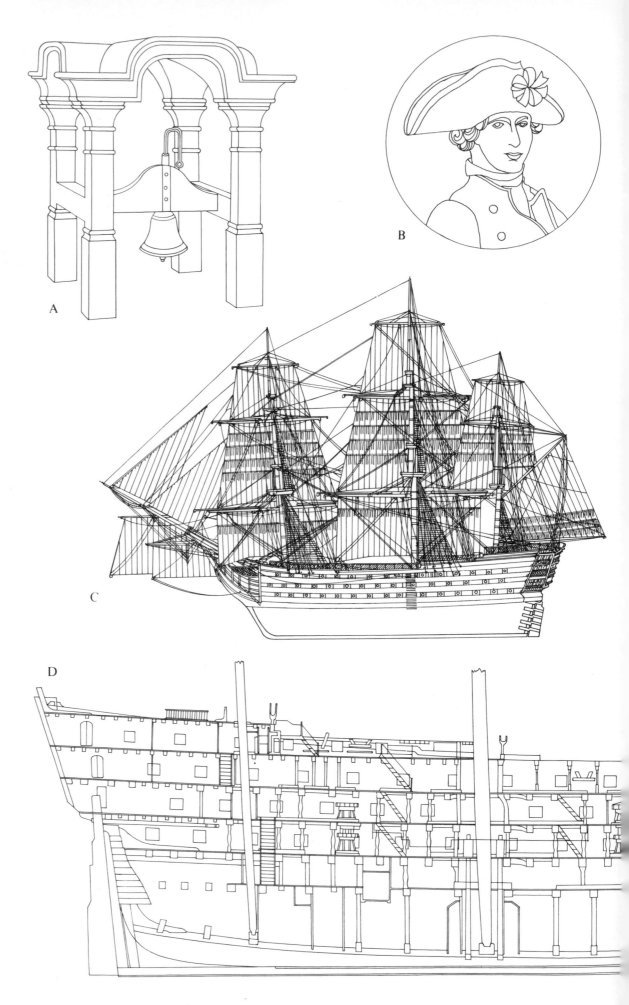

A

B

C

D

VICTORY

This was Nelson's flagship during the Battle of Trafalgar, 1805, and it was on the VICTORY *that he died from his wound. She was a first-rate ship of the line with three gun-decks and 102 guns. Her crew totalled 850 men. Launched in 1765, she took part in numerous engagements, and is one of the few preserved wooden warships in Great Britain, where she lies at Portsmouth.*

A *Ship's bell.*
B *Horatio, Lord Nelson (1758-1805).*
C *Side elevation.*
D *Longitudinal section.*
E *Midship section showing gun-decks.*
F *Stern.*

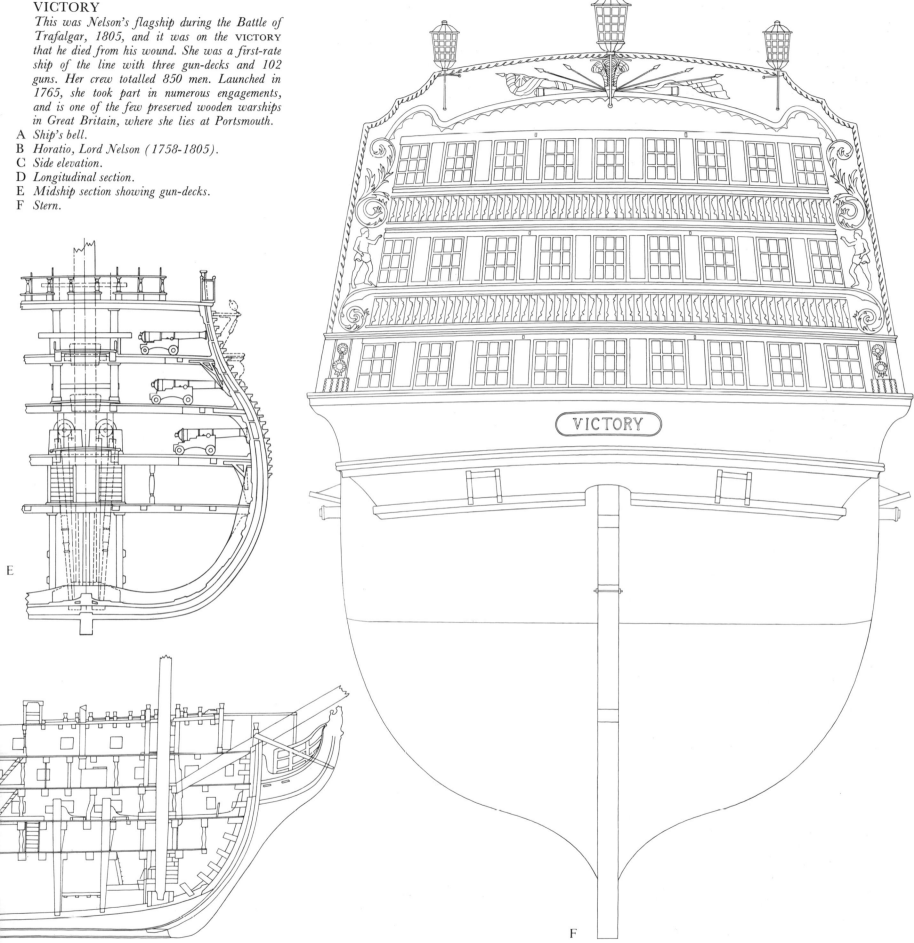

befallen the CHARLOTTE DUNDAS. The hull of the American ship was rebuilt and enlarged, after which she saw many years of extremely useful commercial service on the Hudson River, under the name of NORTH RIVER. Steam had come to stay.

1807

Despite the fact that Denmark had declared the slave trade illegal in 1802 and that various countries followed this example, yet slavery itself was not banned until 1862. This meant that shippers could still carry on with the carrying of slaves, although each trip was becoming more and more hazardous. Indeed, in 1807 the American Government classified slave trading as piracy, and maintained navy patrols, as did Britain and other maritime nations, in order to discourage shippers from trading in this aspect of human misery. In 1860, Captain Gordon of the American ship ERIE, who attempted to smuggle 820 slaves into America, was the last master to be tried, convicted, and hanged for engaging in this trade. Nevertheless, there were always those who defied the law and the risk, for it was a lucrative trade. In 1807, for example, no less than 202 ships unloaded a total of 39,000 slaves in America. The total shipped must have

been considerably more than this, for the 'wastage' on voyages was appreciable. This was a smallish number compared with the 60,000 slaves who were transported to Brazil in 1822, the year she separated from Portugal.

1812

A new dimension was brought to shipping when a steamboat reversed for the first time. The manoeuvre came about accidentally. The COMET was the pride of John Wood's shipyard at Port Glasgow, where she had been built in 1812 for Henry Bell. She was the first ever British passenger steamboat. Originally, she had two pairs of paddles, but after one pair had been trimmed from her, she performed slightly better—although the COMET would never have obtained full marks for performance, for she was under-powered. Frequently, she ran out of steam, and when the pressure dropped, the passengers had to assist in turning the fly-wheel which kept the paddles turning.

One day, the COMET ran aground. Now, in common with early steamers, the COMET had no reversing gear. She had to be poled off when she ran aground. The captain instructed the young engine-room apprentice to turn the paddles by hand. The apprentice, however, merely turned the paddles until the cylinder

B

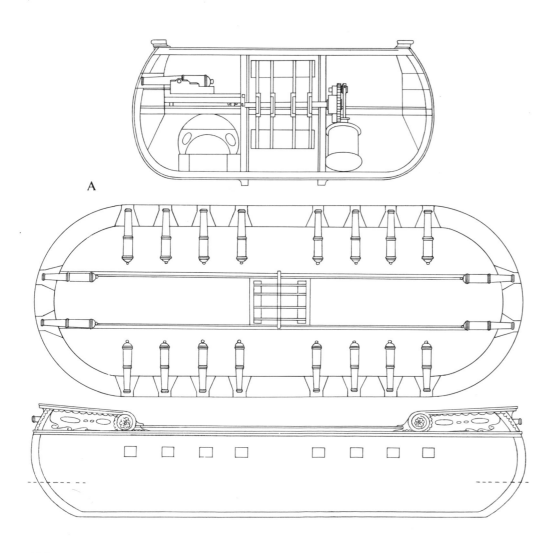

A

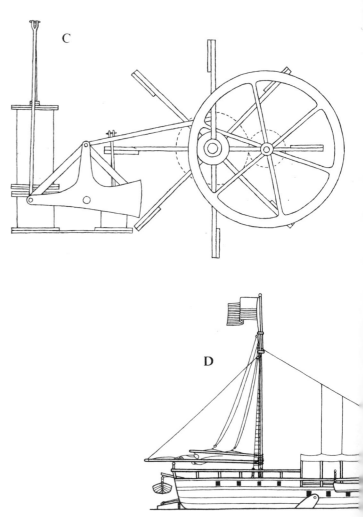

C

D

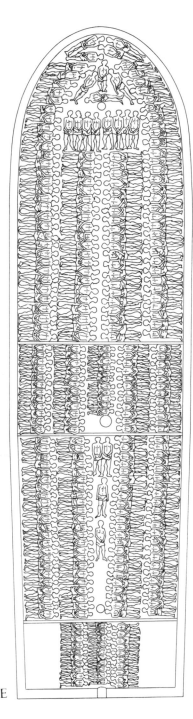

A *The American warship* DEMOLOGOS, *designed by Robert Fulton in 1812 and completed in 1815, was the first steam-driven warship in the world.*

B *The American frigate* ESSEX, *which dismasted the* ALERT *in 1812, was later the first American warship in the Pacific.*

C *The geared steam engine of the* CLERMONT, *1807.*

D *The* CLERMONT, *or* NORTH RIVER, *1807-08.*

E *The plan of a slave ship, showing how the slaves were packed under the deck.*

E

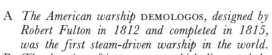

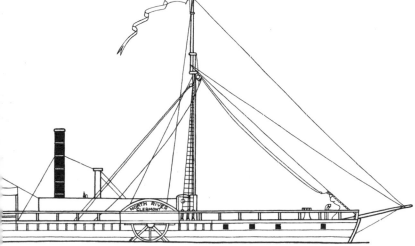

was at 'top dead centre'. Then he opened the steam valve and heaved the top paddle-blade towards himself. There was a violent cough; then, in a flurry of foam, the COMET reversed off the sandbank!

The youngster later confessed that he had performed this manoeuvre on several occasions, but had kept his mouth shut because he had feared the wrath of the captain, had he been discovered performing an unauthorized manoeuvre.

1812

Robert Fulton designs the DEMOLOGOS, the first armoured steam warship. It was a single paddle-wheel steamer, designed for the protection of New York harbour. The single paddle-wheel was placed in the centre of the hull, where it would be less vulnerable if the vessel was attacked.

JUNE 18, 1812-DECEMBER 24, 1814

Because of the slowness of communications, a totally unnecessary war breaks out between America and Britain. Neither side made any gains, but some very famous frigate actions took place. To the surprise of most Englishmen, the Americans more often than not came out on top. This put the Admiralty on its mettle, and several American ships were captured. It was during this war that the Americans introduced the forerunner of the Q-ships of the First World War. The frigate ESSEX pretended to be a merchantman, came up on the British ALERT on August 3, 1812, revealed her true colours, and dismasted the ALERT with a single broadside.

1813

Canada introduces its first steam passenger ferry, for service on the St. Lawrence River. This was the SWIFTSURE, a vessel some 140 foot (42.7 m) long.

1814

Steam comes to the River Thames when Archibald MacLachlan and William Denny build, at Dumbarton, the 63-foot (19.2 m) MAJORY. The MAJORY—sometimes the name of the vessel is spelt 'MARGERY'—was immediately acquired for the London-to-Margate ferry service. Without delay, she sailed by way of the Forth and Clyde Canal down the east coast of England, and so to the mouth of the Thames.

Off the Nore, a squadron of the British fleet was anchored. As the MAJORY thrashed into view, belching thick, black smoke, there was a flurry of signal flags. Sailors ran to action stations on the warships. The challenge streamed out: 'What ship?' Back came the reply: 'MAJORY from Scotland for London.'

This reply did not satisfy the Royal Navy. 'What sort of a ship?' was signalled. 'A steamer,' came the reply. The Royal Navy was singularly obtuse. 'Do not understand,' came from the interrogator. 'Repeat signal.'

So the little comedy was played out. The

identification of MAJORY was finally accepted, and she continued on her way to London. When she set out on her initial voyage to Gravesend, hundreds of sightseers turned out to watch her go—but only seven adventurous souls paid to make the voyage. Fortunately, after a few safe and speedy trips, people flocked to make the journey, and she was booked to capacity for the rest of the time that she was on that run. However, in the spring of 1816, she was sold to Andriel Pajol et Cie. of Paris, and she left on March 17 for the French capital. She was renamed the ELISE by her new owners, and was put into service on the River Seine. That trip from London to Paris made her the first steamer to make the crossing of the English Channel. The journey took an uncomfortable seventeen hours, for there was a stiff southerly gale blowing at the time.

Pietro Andriel, her French captain and part-owner, left Paris in the following year and settled in Naples, where he established his own shipping company of P. Andriel et Cie. It was this company that operated the first paddle-steamer in Mediterranean waters in 1818.

1816
Britain, which had pioneered the steamboat, begins to export ship-engines.

JULY, 1816
The first Swedish steamer, the STOCKHOLMS-HÄXAN—'The Witch of Stockholm'—runs her trials on Lake Mälar. Her 4-h.p. engine could propel her at a speed of 4 knots.

SEPTEMBER, 1816
The PRINZESSIN CHARLOTTE VON PREUSSEN is launched for service on the River Elbe. Her engines were British made.

1817
Early in this year, a committee of the British House of Commons sits to consider the means of preventing the 'mischief' arising from explosions on board steamships. As a result of the recommendations of this committee, all steamers had to be registered, and the boilers of passenger steamers had to be inspected regularly. Boilers had to be able to withstand three times the normal working pressure, have two safety-valves, and be made from wrought-iron or copper.

1818
The 88-ton ROB ROY becomes the first steamer on the Glasgow-Belfast ferry service.

1818
Ferdinando IV, King of the Two Sicilies, was an engineer at heart. He loved the smell of engines, and was passionately fond of anything mechanical. He gave Pietro Andriel the Royal concession to operate a steamer service from Naples to Marseilles, calling at Civitavecchia,

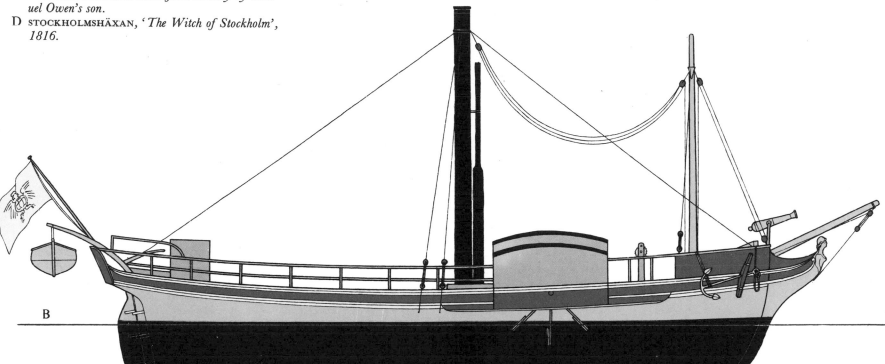

B

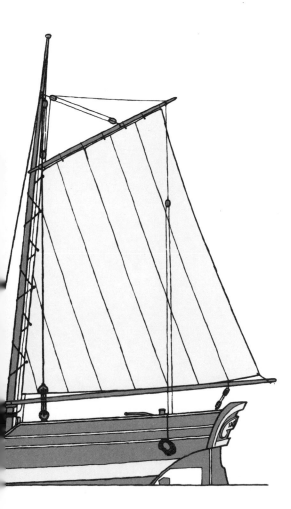

Livorno (Leghorn), and Genoa. The concession was to last for fifteen years.

Andriel tackled the project with characteristic zest. By September 27, 1818, the steamer FERDINANDO I, which had been built at the Naples yard of Stanislas Filosa, was ready to be launched, only a few days ahead of a northern concessionnaire, who had tried to inaugurate the Trieste-to-Venice run before the Naples-to-Marseilles service was ready. The CAROLINA, which steamed out of Trieste in early October, was thus the second Mediterranean steamer.

Some record books suggest that the small steam vessel ERIDANO should have the honour of heading the Italian steamboat story, for she was to be seen chugging slowly up and down the River Po long before either the FERDINANDO I or the CAROLINA was in service.

The 115-ton FERDINANDO I was 128 foot (39 m) long and 19 foot 8 inches (6 m) wide. Her hull was made of wood, and her 50-h.p. engine—of English construction—produced a speed of 6 knots. She could accommodate fifty passengers in the forward public saloon, whilst sixteen more could be accommodated in private cabins at the stern of the ship. Understandably, the chief engineer was an Englishman, although her captain was the twenty-four-year-old Guiseppi Libetta, the scion of a local patrician family. When he brought her safely into Genoa harbour, the

whole town turned out to give him a civic welcome. It had taken him a full month to make the trip from Naples to Genoa, but that did not dampen the enthusiasm of the Genoese. Libetta finally reached Marseilles on November 4, 1818, thus becoming the first steamer captain ever to put into that ancient port.

The FERDINANDO I had a very short life. A new, Clyde-built steamer replaced her in 1820.

1819
It is discovered that all samples of sea water from all parts of the world, except for river estuaries and ice-fed seas such as the Baltic, contain the same dissolved salts in the same proportions.

1819
The TALBOT is built for the Holyhead-Dublin daylight route. This was the first steamer to be provided with two engines, one for each paddle. She was able to turn in her own length.

1819
There was, as might be expected, keen competition to build the first steamer to cross the Atlantic. There are, of course, various definitions of 'steamer'. If one accepts a certain definition, then the honour of being the first steamer to make this crossing must be awarded to the SAVANNAH.

115

She was laid down in 1818 at the yard of Francis Pickett in New York, and was designed as a wooden sailing-ship for service on the New York-Le Havre route. When she was almost complete, it was decided to equip her with a small 90-i.h.p. single-cylinder steam engine. This was duly built at the Speedwell Iron Works, New Jersey.

The auxiliary steam engine—for that was what it was—powered collapsible ten-bladed paddle-wheels, which, when not in use, were folded upwards like a fan, and hinged inboard so that they could be stowed on deck. Splashing from the paddles was reduced as much as possible by the rigging of a canvas cover over iron frames that 'umbrella'd' the paddle-wheels.

The whole arrangement was in the nature of an experiment, rather than a serious form of propulsion. The basic idea, indeed, was to enable the SAVANNAH to steam on when the winds off the coasts of subtropical Georgia becalmed all other vessels.

SAVANNAH was put up for sale, and her American owners decided that Europe provided the best potential market. On May 24, 1819, therefore, she left the port of Savannah, in Georgia, and set sail for Liverpool. She was in ballast and without passengers. She duly arrived in the Mersey on June 20, after a voyage lasting 27 days and 15 hours. Her steam engine had been used for a total of 3 days and 8 hours only during the voyage, chiefly whilst leaving Savannah, and whilst arriving at Liverpool. Technically, therefore, the SAVANNAH is the first vessel with some form of steam propulsion to cross the Atlantic.

Two anecdotes are worthy of recall. The SAVANNAH was using steam to make for Kinsale in Ireland, where she planned to refuel. As she passed Cape Clear at the extreme south of Ireland, the coastguard spotted her. He reported to the Flag Admiral, Cork, that he had sighted a vessel on fire. The gallant admiral ordered a naval vessel to the rescue. To the astonishment of the officer in charge of the fast naval cutter, he was unable to catch up with the 'burning' vessel until she anchored in Kinsale harbour.

Some days later, she steamed into Liverpool Bay flying a very large 'Stars and Stripes'. At the Liverpool Bar, the officer on duty on the guardship addressed his opposite number through the loud-hailer.

'Why,' demanded the English officer, 'are you flying that pennant, Sir?'

'Because my country allows me to,' came the reply.

'My commander thinks it is done to insult him.'

'It is done as a courtesy, Sir. This is an American vessel.'

So, to the astonishment of the gathering port workers, the SAVANNAH, a steam vessel that had come all the way from America, berthed majestically alongside.

1820
Edward Bransfield, in the whaler WILLIAMS, becomes the first man to see the Antarctic mainland.

1821
The RISING STAR becomes the first steamer to plough its way through Pacific waters. She left Gravesend, England, on October 22, 1821, and sailed from port to port down the Atlantic coasts of Europe and South America, round the Cape Horn, and up to Valparaiso, a distance of more than 12,000 miles (19,300 km) from her port of departure. The voyage took six months, and detailed records were kept of the epic-making trip.

1821
The ROB ROY is taken off the Glasgow-Belfast service and transferred to the Dover-Calais route. She is the first steamer to operate a regular, scheduled cross-Channel service. The French were so impressed by her performance that they bought her to carry mails to England. She was re-named HENRI QUATRE.

1822
Lloyd's of London records the first steamer in its Register Book. This is the JAMES WATT, owned by the General Steam Navigation Co., a company which operated until quite recently.

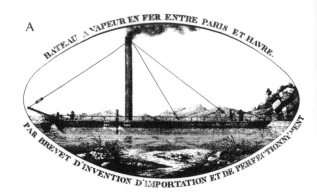

A AARON MANBY, *1822*.
B JAMES WATT, *1822*.

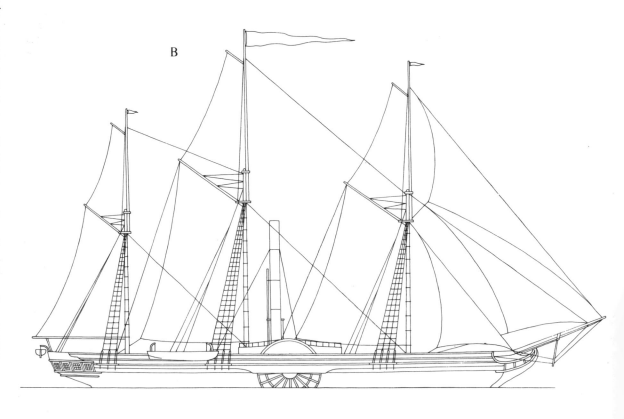

Steamer entries were sparse. By 1830, the number recorded had reached eighty-one. All these early entries refer to steamers that were built for use in estuarine or river waters, or for short cross-Channel voyages.

The main reason for the short range of the early steamers was the problems posed by fuel. In those times, coal consumption was 9 pounds (4.1 kg) per horsepower, for each engine hour. The twin 50-h.p. engines installed in the JAMES WATT required 5 tons of coal just to cross the Irish Sea at a steady 10 knots—and she was only 146 foot (44.5 m) long.

1822

The first all-iron hull is laid down at the Horseley Iron Works, at Tipton in Staffordshire, England. Here, the AARON MANBY was built as a promotional exercise to show the advantages of iron over wood as a shipbuilding material. She was built for Aaron Manby, the foremost iron-founder in France, who was also the main figure behind the Seine passenger services. In fact, he already had some experimental iron hulls in his fleet.

One of the reasons why iron was not widely used before this time was the popular preconception that iron sank, and that it would be courting the wrath of the Almighty to prove otherwise. Nevertheless, as early as 1787, an Englishman, John Wilkinson, had commenced to build iron barges at Willey in Shropshire. They were designed for river use, were 70 foot (21.3 m) long, and with a cargo capacity of 32 tons—twice as much as that carried by the usual 3-foot (0.9 m) draught barge. Accuracy demands the explanation that the Wilkinson barges were not all-iron vessels. The stem and stern-posts, together with the heel, were of wood. Iron ribs that were bolted to the heel were covered with five-sixteenth-inch (8 mm) wrought-iron plates.

When the AARON MANBY was completed, she was dismantled and taken overland to the Surrey docks in Rotherhithe, London. There she was re-assembled for her journey to Paris, and thus became the first iron-hulled paddle-steamer to make the Channel crossing. She gave admirable service on the Seine, and was not taken out of commission until 1855.

Iron-hulled ships had an inestimable advantage over wooden hulls in tropical river services: they could not be attacked by the water-beetle, the insect that ravaged wooden hulls on tropical fresh-water routes. Thus, in 1829, MacGregor Laird had the iron steamer ALBURKAK providing a service on the River Niger. India had iron-bottomed ships by 1832, when four passenger steamers, the LORD WILLIAM BENTINCK, the THAMES, the MEGNA, and the JUMNA, steamed up and down the Ganges.

1823

Holland's first steamship owner, the Nederlandsche Stoomboot Maatschappij, brings the NEDERLANDER into service.

1825

The Mediterranean Steam Navigation Co. becomes one of the first steamship companies in the Mediterranean. Services were between Marseilles and Genoa, Leghorn, Civitavecchia, Naples, Messina, and Malta. Five steamships were built for this company's initial services: the CAPRI and the VESUVIO were the first, quickly followed by the MONGIBELLO, the ERCALANO, and the MARIA CHRISTINA.

1825

Competition and rivalry inevitably followed hard in the wake of these early steam successes. Publicists were not backwards in extolling the advantages of steam as against sail. Punctuality, reliability, speed, and safety were the keynotes of an extensive propaganda campaign to get the steamship really launched on a world-wide scale. Governments and rulers joined the fray by offering handsome rewards, either monetary or by way of contracts, to companies willing to provide an efficient steamer service. The example of the Rajah of Oude in India is typical of this governmental involvement in the fledgling steamer industry.

A consortium of Indian businessmen, headed by the Rajah of Oude himself, offered a prize of 80,000 rupees to the owners of the first steamer to reach Calcutta from a European port in less than seventy days. Two voyages had to be undertaken. The prize would be paid when the steamship docked at Calcutta on the successful conclusion of the second voyage.

Apart from the direct monetary reward, there were further inducements in the shape of profitable cargoes that could be carried by the steamships both on the outward and the homeward voyage.

A group of London businessmen accepted the challenge. For the sum of £43,000, the group bought the ENTERPRISE, then being built in the Deptford yard of Gordon and Co. The ENTERPRISE, which was insured at Lloyd's as an A1 vessel, eventually left Falmouth on August 16, 1825. She was under the command of Lieutenant Johnson, and, in addition to her cargo, she also carried seventeen passengers.

The journey from Falmouth to Calcutta by way of Cape Town took 113 days, 64 of which were spent under steam. As the ENTERPRISE had not complied with the time clause, the prize was not awarded. However, the Rajah magnanimously donated half that amount, 40,000 rupees, to the owners who, although suitably grateful, decided not to continue with the competition. Instead, they sold the ENTERPRISE to the Government of Bengal for £40,000. So the London group, with half the prize money, the passenger fares and cargo charges, and the money from the sale of the ship, at least broke even.

But the ENTERPRISE does not disappear into obscurity. Fifteen years later, in 1840, the first mail steamer fusses into the port of Alexandria. The India mail is handed over for transport to the port of Suez, there to be transhipped by steamer to Bombay. And it was the ENTERPRISE that was waiting at Suez to take the mail on to Bombay.

1825

George Thompson heads a group of Aberdeen merchants who purchase three brigs: the AMITY, the MANSFIELD, and the SIR WILLIAM WALLACE. These ships form the Aberdeen Line, and the company remains in business until 1931.

1826

The KARTERIA becomes the first steamship to be involved in a naval engagement. She was the pride of the Greek revolutionaries, who mounted deck cannon on her and wrought havoc among the Turkish sailing-sloops, six of which were sunk.

OCTOBER 1826

The first steamship in the Netherlands Navy, the CURAÇAO, is acquired from the American and Colonial Steam Navigation Co. of London. Before 1830, she had made three voyages across the Atlantic to South America carrying passengers, mail, and valuable cargo. The first began on April 26, 1827, when she left Hellevoetsluis, near Rotterdam, bound for Paramaribo, Surinam. The voyage took twenty-eight days, during which she used steam power for eleven days.

OCTOBER 20, 1827

The Battle of Navarino Harbour takes place. It is the last combined fleet action to be fought under sail. Negotiations in connection with the Treaty of London were still in progress when a joint naval squadron of British, French, and Russian ships encountered a fleet of about a hundred Turkish and Egyptian vessels. A shot from a Turkish ship killed Lieutenant Fitzroy, who was in command of a boat from the British DARTMOUTH. A general engagement followed, and the battle raged until the following morning, when it was discovered that only one Turkish frigate and fifteen smaller vessels had escaped the fury of the onslaught. Allied losses amounted to 177 killed and 490 wounded. Turkish and Egyptian casualties included over 5,000 killed.

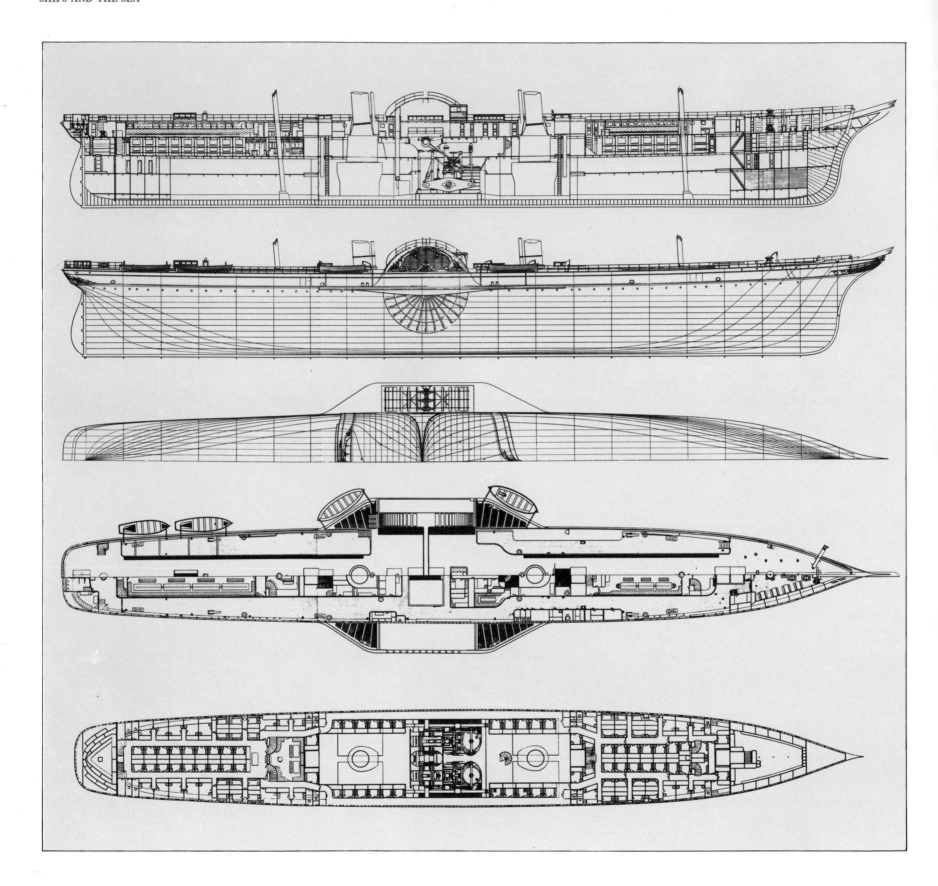

Lines and sections of a British and North America Royal Mail Iron Steamship reproduced from The Modern System of Naval Architecture *by John Scott Russell, London 1865. Russell was the man who built the* GREAT EASTERN, *although he lost his shipyard as a result of it.*

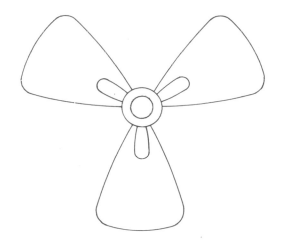

chapter 5

The end of the 1830s is a watershed in the story of the sea and of shipping. Apart from the unexplored Polar regions—and these, of course, were known about—there was little scope for pioneering voyages. Steam, too, had come to stay; and after the initial experiments with engines, the development of steam propulsion settles down to a long period of steady, rather than spectacular, improvement.

The world of shipping, too, had reached the conclusion that sail was the more economical way of carrying cargoes, but that steamships held the promise of regular sailings, and, above all, regular arrivals. This prospect, viewed against the background of expanding world trade and improving communications, held an immense attraction for the intending sea passenger.

This stance, of course, was slightly at odds with one of the original reasons for experimenting with steam propulsion: that of trying to get cost-effectiveness at a cheaper ratio than was possible with sail. However, the public demand for steamships was there, and it had to be met. As a corollary of this decision, the low-powered earlier types of steam engine would have to give way to new, tried, and tested versions which might hold out some hope of economic advantage over their predecessors.

The problems that beset the shipowner—and designer—were manifold. Coal consumption was still far too high. Boilers needed to be regularly de-salted. The steamships themselves were so small that a profitable pay-load was out of the question except on any but the shortest voyages. Above all, bunkering en route was an extremely expensive business. All these drawbacks had to be changed if the steamship was to become a truly viable method of transport rather than merely a prestigious form.

Samuel Hall's surface condenser, which he perfected in 1834, solved the problem of the boiler. The side-lever engine, with the possibility of its being built to much more powerful specifications, gave the necessary thrust. The only ingredient missing for overnight success was money—and that was to be supplied by the granting of annual subsidies in Great Britain for the carrying of the Royal Mail. Subsidies were also part of the fiscal policy of many countries where the new industry of building steamships had become established. Therefore, by 1840, the way was open for the organization of a world-wide network of steamer routes.

The choice of two forms of steam propulsion was available. There was the pioneering steam paddle-wheel method. There was also the somewhat younger screw-propulsion method. By 1845 H.M.S. RATTLER, not a very happy choice of name for a ship, had convincingly demonstrated the superiority of screw propulsion. Thereafter, paddle propulsion declined.

The death of the paddle-steamer would have come about much more quickly than, in fact, happened. The reason for this was that many Post Offices insisted upon their mail being carried at sea in ships built with a wooden hull and propelled by paddle-wheels. However, metal hulls and screw propulsion eventually led to the disappearance of this archaic rule.

By the middle of the nineteenth century, many of the shipping companies which are household names today had commenced business. Some of these companies specialized in operating steamships that were built for the carrying of mail and passengers only, as against general-purpose ships that carried both cargo and passengers.

Yet it must not be thought that sail had been completely eclipsed by this flurry of building steamships. The population explosion was just about to take off at this time. Emigration from a Europe bursting at its seams to the empty continents beyond the seas, together with a complementary impetus to world trade, meant that the demand for seagoing capacity was so great that for several decades the sailing-ship prospered and multiplied alongside its cousin, the steamship.

After 1880, the decline in sail tonnage accelerated. Strangely, the largest sailing-ship ever built was not launched until well into the twentieth century. This was the famous FRANCE.

In order to enter into any sort of competition with steamships, sailing-ships had to become both faster and bigger. The solution was the clipper ships—designed to 'clip' days off the time taken for voyages by earlier sailing-ships. In 1855, the world's largest ship was still a sailing-ship, the WHITE STAR, although the ARABIA of the Cunard Company was longer overall.

It was in 1855 that an engineer, John Elder, brought the compound engine to the marine world. In a compound engine, steam is fed into a small, high-pressure cylinder, and is then re-used in a larger, low-pressure cylinder, thereby doubling the efficient use of the steam. John Elder intended the compound engine to be used on what he called the 'Coalless Routes', mainly those to South America.

The idea was a good one, but it did not find favour with marine engineers. In 1866, Alfred Holt installed compound engines in his Blue Funnel Far East steamers, the AGAMEMNON, ACHILLES, and AJAX. It was another five years before the compound engine came to the Atlantic. This time it was the National Line which installed such an engine in its HOLLAND. With this breakthrough on the world's busiest shipping routes, the fashion of re-engining gathered momentum.

The famous GREAT EASTERN is a classic anachronism of the middle years of this phase of the story of the sea. It is true that, in concept, and in size, she was a good fifty years ahead of her time. Yet her double propulsion was both unique and anachronistic. In crude commercial terms, she was far too big to handle. There was hardly a dock, quay, or dredged anchorage in the world that could accommodate her bulk.

Whilst resources were being diverted to such prestigious exercises as the building of the GREAT EASTERN, still more resources were being used in building many fine ships which incorporated the maximum potential that an improving technology could offer a voracious shipbuilding industry. After 1860, the emphasis was always on building bigger, better, and faster ships—often with a mail contract as the tempting bait.

It was in 1869 that, amidst scenes of great splendour, the Suez Canal was opened. This short-cut to the East made the sailing-ship voyage via the Cape not only unattractive to shippers, but also uneconomic to owners. The accelerating decline in sail dates from the very day that the Suez Canal was opened to traffic. Within a decade, steam tonnage had overhauled that of sail, which never recovered its first place.

The last thirty years of the nineteenth century were ones of unmatched progress in the world of shipping. Ships were now lit by electricity. Extra passenger decks amidships were incorporated into liners, giving additional suites, single cabins, dining saloons, and ornate lounges. The concept of the floating luxury liner-cum-hotel was emerging. Sails and yards disappeared from the masts, which for years bore an almost naked look. Bilge keels gave extra seaway stability. New designs with straight stems and more funnels gave the ships a new profile.

Twin screws arrived. Three-cylinder engines with triple expansion of the steam were followed by those with quadruple expansion. Refrigeration allowed frozen meat and fruit to be transported. And always, ships were designed for higher speeds.

Warships kept pace with the general improvement of ships as development raced towards the twentieth century. Indeed, it is arguable that each main step forward came from the experience of war. For example, the Crimean War demonstrated the effectiveness of steam and the efficiency of armour plating. Again, the American Civil War rehearsed the idea of commerce raiders. This war also saw the introduction of the mine; and the fight between the MONITOR and the MERRIMACK foreshadowed the sea battles of the end of the century and the beginning of the next.

The navies of the world were shedding sail by the 1870s, and were producing a new breed of battleship. The British DEVASTATION, which lacked the masts, yards, and sails of the past, epitomized this new breed of battleship.

Whitehead's torpedo not only sank ships; it sank the arguments of those who still hankered for wooden hulls. It was the most potent weapon yet invented, and in its turn it was responsible for the torpedo-boat, the torpedo-boat destroyer, for secondary armament on capital ships, and, ultimately, for the submarine.

By the last decade of the nineteenth century, then, the navies of the world had re-styled their images, their silhouettes, and their strategies. They now stood ready to test their weaponry in the only suitable testing-grounds—the cockpit of war. The arms race had started. The urge for supremacy had overtaken events. The First World War was a brief fourteen years away.

But even the dying years of the century saw the introduction of improvements and inventions at sea. In 1894, for instance, the TURBINIA dashed through the Spithead Naval Review at a spanking 34.5 knots. She was the first turbine-driven ship and, demonstrably, the fastest vessel afloat. But—and here is the classic example of war accoutrements presaging peaceful equipment—it was not until 1900 that the first commercial turbine entered into service.

In June, 1897, Dr. Rudolf Diesel brought a new concept to engines when he unveiled his diesel engine to the world. Shipping, this time, lagged behind commercial acceptance; for it was not until 1912 that the first diesel motor vessel slipped out to sea.

Finally, on the very threshold of the twentieth century, in 1899, Guglielmo Marconi boarded the American ship ST. PAUL, en route for Europe. Whilst on board, he assembled a little gadget, a gadget with which he soon established direct and remote contact with the Needles Lighthouse off the Isle of Wight. His invention, the wireless, gave a new dimension to the world, and especially to the world of shipping.

This, then, is the next phase of our story; the phase during which steam propulsion comes to maturity, with, paradoxically, the apotheosis of sail, as seen in the lines of that classic type, the clipper. It is the phase that sees the transformation of the warship from the muzzle-loader sailing-ship to the turret-gunned, steel-hulled battle fleets of the leading maritime powers. It is a phase that begins with a handful of pioneering steamship owners trading mainly within European waters, but which ends with world-wide trade routes thronged with efficient ships flying the ensigns of more than a hundred different nations. It is, above all, the phase which marks the maturity of the propeller-driven ship; for the twentieth century sees nothing radically new in the steamship until the advent of the atomic-powered ships of recent years.

That is the outstanding achievement of the men and women responsible for this phase of our story, that they did with steam in less than a hundred years what it had taken their ancestors nearly five thousand years to do with sail.

EARLY STEAMBOATS

PRINZESSIN CHARLOTTE VON PREUSSEN

This was the first steamboat to be built in Prussia (1816). She had twin wooden hulls with one paddle-wheel working between them. PRINZESSIN CHARLOTTE VON PREUSSEN *was built by John Rubie at Pichelsdorf near Spandau. A Boulton & Watt one-cylinder side-lever engine powered her. A large steering wheel, visible on the aft deck, controlled her three rudders.*

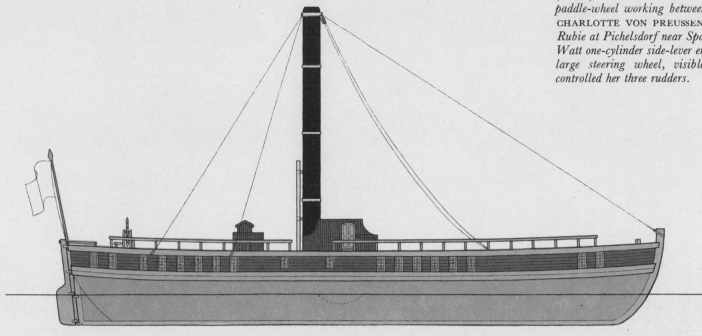

CALEDONIA

Built on the Clyde in Scotland in 1815, the CALEDONIA *saw service on the Thames before crossing the North Sea to Rotterdam in 1817, from where she went to Coblenz. She was the first steamboat on the Rhine. In 1818, she was sold to Steen Andersen Bille and operated on the Copenhagen-Kiel route, thus becoming the first steam-propelled vessel in Denmark.*

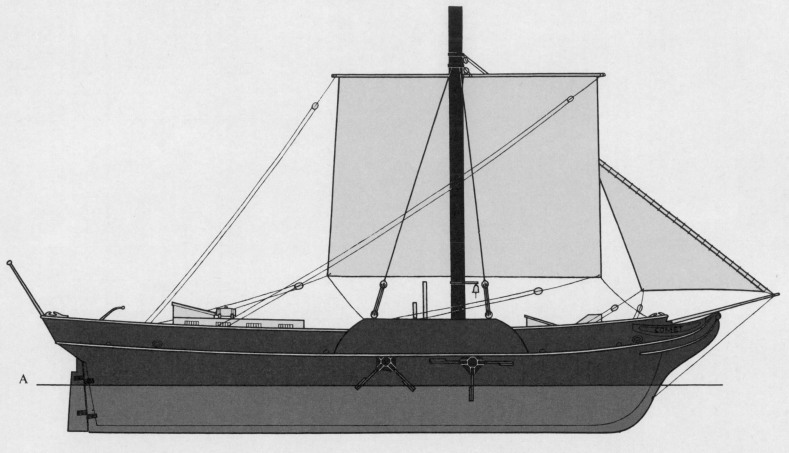

COMET

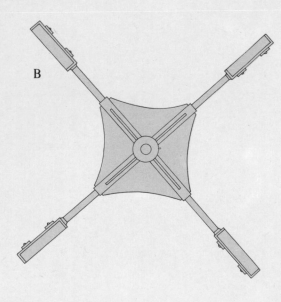

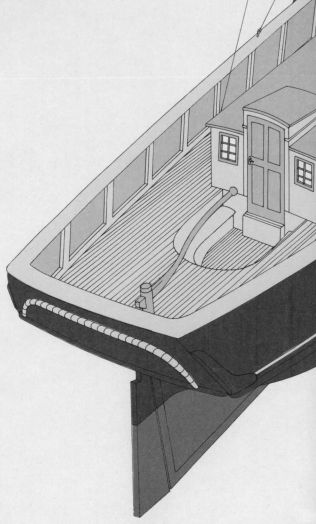

The first steamer to operate commercially in Europe, the COMET was built in 1812 to the order of Henry Bell. He was the proprietor of the Helensburgh Baths on the Clyde in Scotland, and he wanted to use the COMET to convey guests to his hotel from Glasgow. After consulting Robert Fulton, the American engineer responsible for the CLERMONT, Bell had the COMET built at the shipyard of Messrs John Wood & Co. at Port Glasgow.

Henry Bell considered the COMET more as an exercise in public relations than as a viable alternative to the usual sailing packets, but the little steamer created such an interest in steam navigation that, by 1815, ten steamboats were operating on the Clyde.

The COMET was launched in July, 1812. Accomodation for passengers consisted of a second-class saloon forward, in which the passengers could only sit, there was so little headroom. In the first-class saloon aft, there was standing headroom.

A low-pressure horizontal boiler, mounted in brickwork and fired externally, was placed on the starboard side of the boat, and it supplied steam to the engine on the port side. John Robertson, of Glasgow, supplied the vertical single-cylinder engine, which had a nominal horse power of four. The single funnel also functioned as a mast.

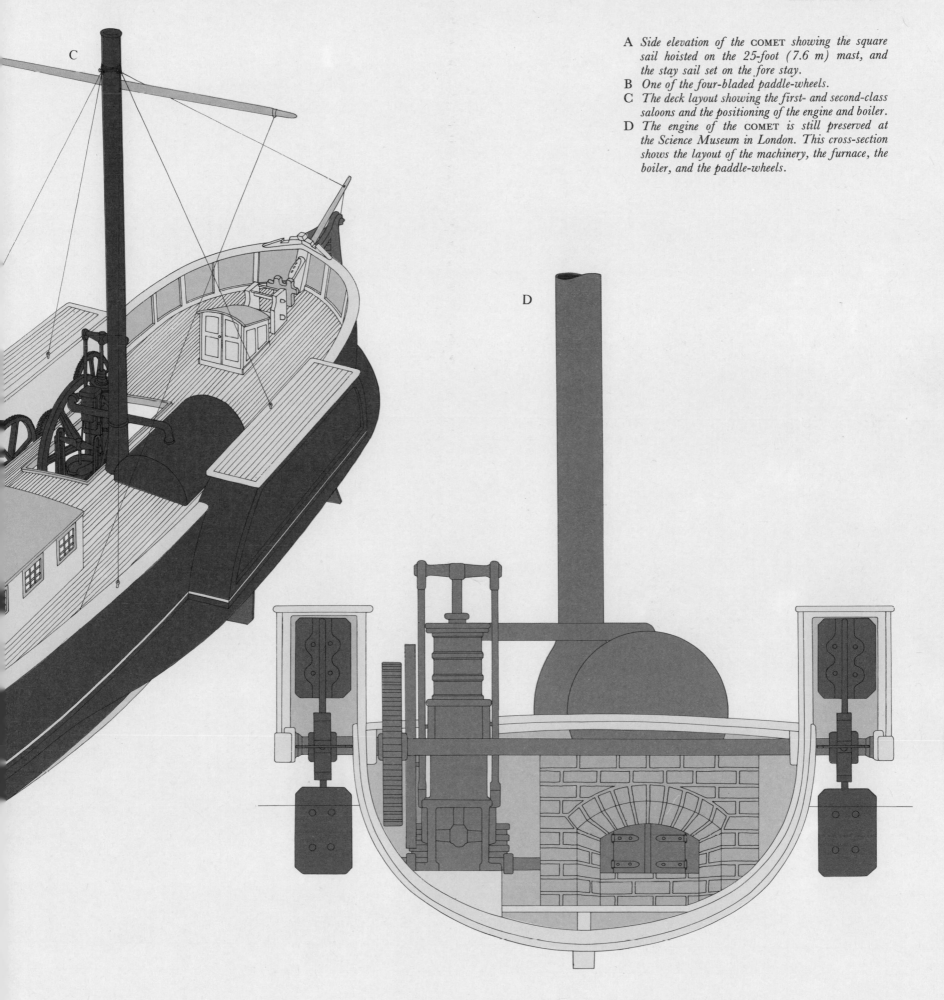

A *Side elevation of the* COMET *showing the square sail hoisted on the 25-foot (7.6 m) mast, and the stay sail set on the fore stay.*

B *One of the four-bladed paddle-wheels.*

C *The deck layout showing the first- and second-class saloons and the positioning of the engine and boiler.*

D *The engine of the* COMET *is still preserved at the Science Museum in London. This cross-section shows the layout of the machinery, the furnace, the boiler, and the paddle-wheels.*

NEDERLANDER

This, the first steamboat of the Nederlandsche Stoomboot Maatschappij, was built in 1823 at the Hoogendijk yard at Capelle aan de Ijssel. The engine was imported from Henry Maudslay in England. In regular service, she connected with the coaches from Brussels to Antwerp and from Rotterdam to the Hague.

FERDINANDO I

This was the first steamboat to operate in the Mediterranean (1818). She was built at the Stanislas Filosa shipyard near Forte Vigliena and fitted with two side-lever vertical cylinder engines, probably imported. Her accommodation consisted of sixteen private cabins aft and a public saloon forward.

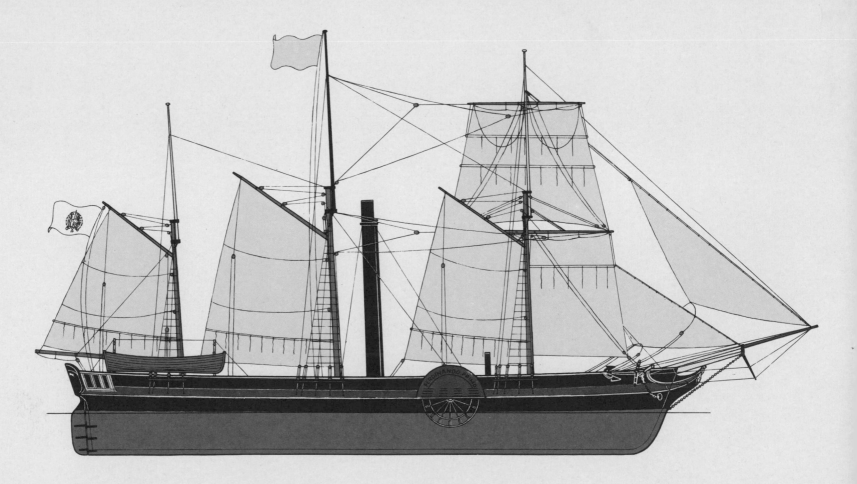

A *Return flue boiler, c. 1850.*
B *Side lever engine, c. 1840.*
C *Inverted vertical reciprocating compound engine, c. 1870.*
D *Samuel Hall's surface condenser, 1834.*
E *Oscillating engine, c. 1840.*

F *Detail of oscillating engine showing section of the cylinder.*
G *The river boat* NATCHEZ, *1869, which took part in the famous race on the Mississippi against the* ROBERT E. LEE, *1870.*

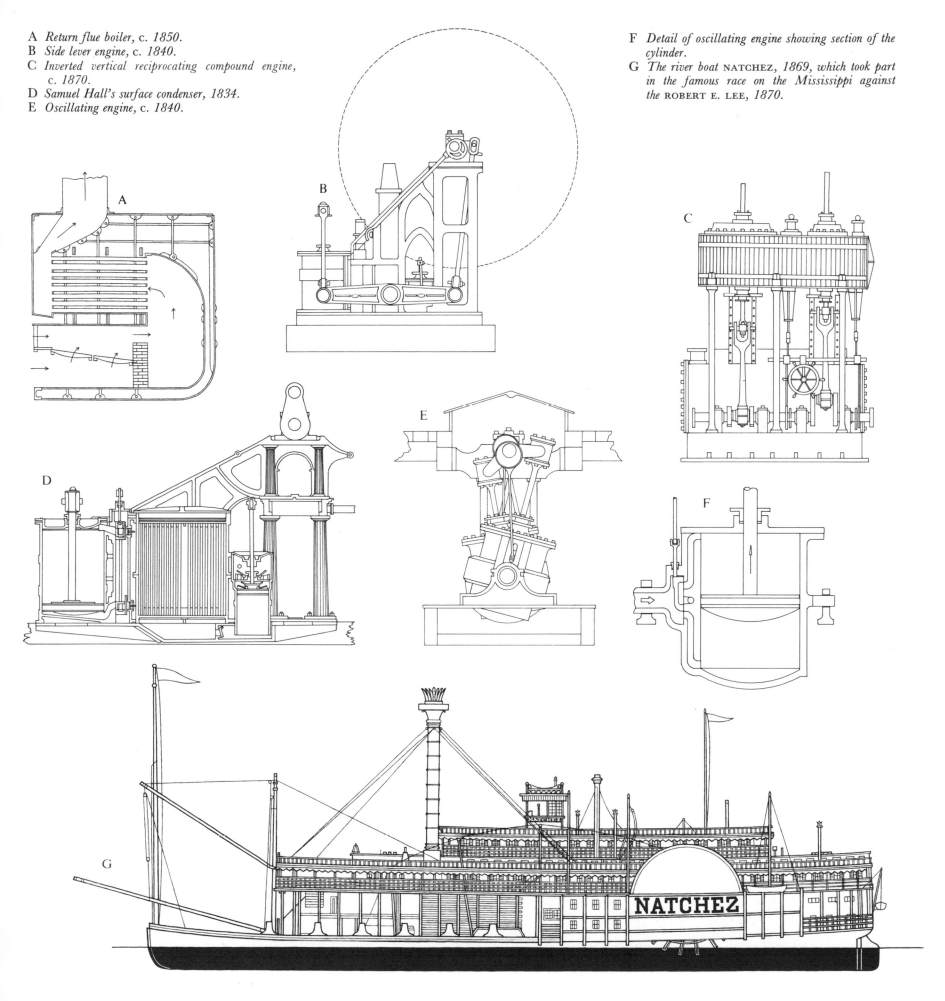

1830

The SPHINX, of 777 tons, is the first paddle corvette to see service. She was built for the French Navy, but the authorities there, and elsewhere, did not take too kindly to this type of ship.

Naval opinion held that the vulnerability of paddles, the wasted space for fuel, and the low speed occasioned by the weight of the engine, made steam propulsion unsuitable. The SPHINX was present at the Siege of Algiers when the last lair of the Barbary pirates was destroyed. However, despite her contribution, naval opinion was confirmed in its dislike of this type of vessel.

1833

As far back as 1805, Francis Tudor of Boston had shipped 130 tons of local lake ice to Martinique. He soon built up a thriving trade to the West Indies in this commodity. By 1833, his ships were venturing much farther afield. In that year, 180 tons of ice were shipped aboard the TUSCANY to Calcutta. One hundred tons arrived in perfect condition.

The trade proved very lucrative. Soon, the Norwegians joined in. They sold their lake ice mainly to fishermen, and very soon British trawling smacks were freezing their catches with Norwegian ice. As a result, the British ships were able to fish much farther from their usual haunts.

The Norwegians built runways, and ran the blocks of ice from the lakes down the mountainsides to the loading berths. As soon as the waiting ships were fully loaded, the runways were diverted into heavy wooden warehouses, in which the ice could be efficiently stored for several months.

Ice-ships — nicknamed 'freezers' - carried their cargoes packed in sawdust. The fumes given off by the wet saw-dust were inflammable, and ice-ships caught fire easily. Lloyd's classified them as a bad fire risk.

From the beginning of the twentieth century, this trade was threatened by the manufacture of artificial ice, which, however, was costly to produce. Demand, too, varied enormously, according to the season. The First World War interrupted the ice trade, and it never revived.

1833

The ANN MCKIM is launched. She is the first vessel known to have been built in the clipper ship style. She was built by Kennart & Williamson of Fells Point, Baltimore, for Isaac McKim.

1834

The boilers of early steamers used sea-water. Although the steam that was produced in these boilers was uncontaminated, yet the residue of the process was pure caked salt. This meant that every four days, the boiler fires had to be drawn, and the inside of the boilers had to be de-scaled.

Samuel Hall's solution to the problem was

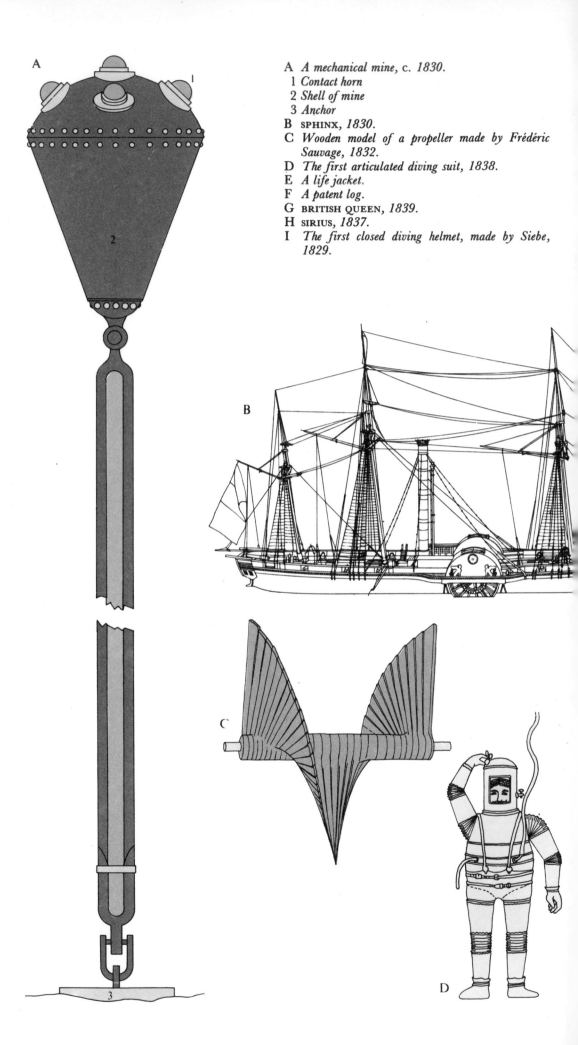

A *A mechanical mine, c. 1830.*
1 *Contact horn*
2 *Shell of mine*
3 *Anchor*
B SPHINX, *1830.*
C *Wooden model of a propeller made by Frédéric Sauvage, 1832.*
D *The first articulated diving suit, 1838.*
E *A life jacket.*
F *A patent log.*
G BRITISH QUEEN, *1839.*
H SIRIUS, *1837.*
I *The first closed diving helmet, made by Siebe, 1829.*

E

F

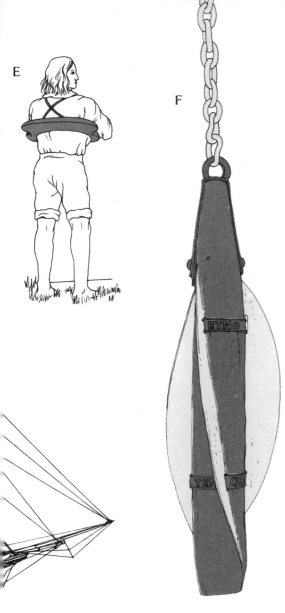

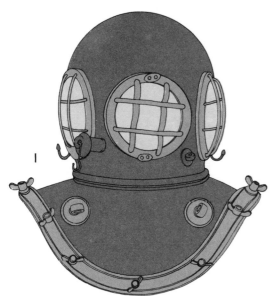

I

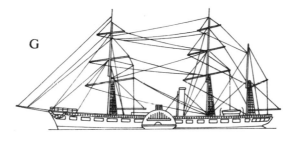

G

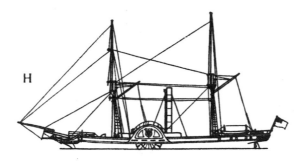

H

the surface condenser. This used fresh water in a closed circuit to produce steam. The used steam was then re-condensed back to produce fresh water.

Hall's invention was used to the greatest advantage by the three great transatlantic rivals, the BRITISH QUEEN, the SIRIUS, and the GREAT WESTERN. The use of the Hall condenser enabled ten days to be lopped off the crossing. The one disadvantage was that an additional load of fresh water had to be carried by ships using this type of condenser—a relatively small price when set against the many advantages.

JULY 2, 1835

The French Government starts a state-owned steamer service between Marseilles and the major ports of Asia Minor. The first steamers on this service are the EUROTAS, LEONIDAS, LYCURGUE, MENTOR, SCAMANDRE, and TANCREDE. The company later developed into the famous shipping company Messageries Maritimes, which still exists, and which has grown into one of France's two greatest shipping companies.

1836

The Dramatic Line, a shipping company owned by Mr. E. K. Collins of New York, inaugurates a regular passenger service between New York and Liverpool in his specially designed sailing-packets. The time for the eastbound passage varied between eighteen and twenty-one days. The westbound passage was something over thirty days. These voyage times were the target which the supporters of steam set out to better.

1836

The BEAVER is the first steamer on the West Coast of America. She is used to survey thoroughly the American coastline from San Francisco to Alaska. Built on the Thames to

the order of the Hudson Bay Co., the BEAVER steamed from London to Vancouver by way of Cape Horn. Although basically a survey ship, she carried four brass cannon for her protection. She remained in service until 1880, when she suffered shipwreck off Vancouver.

It was not until the Californian gold-rush of 1849 that regular steamer services began in this part of the world.

1836

In shipping circles, gossip and informed newspaper comment are on the subject of crossing the Atlantic using only steam as the method of propulsion. Generally, opinions are sceptical. A Dr. Lardner gave an interesting lecture in Liverpool in December, 1836. What he said reflects current thinking on the problem: 'As to the project of crossing the Atlantic entirely by steam—it is chimerical. They might as well talk about making a voyage from New York or Liverpool to the moon.'

THE GREAT TRANSATLANTIC RACE OCTOBER 1836

The British and American Steam Navigation Co. is incorporated with a capital of £500,000, following the publication on June I, 1835, by Dr. Junius Smith of a prospectus for a steamship line from London to New York. The new company places an order with Curling and Young of London for a 2,000-ton wooden paddler.

1837

The new ship is laid down as the ROYAL VICTORIA. Upon the accession of Queen Victoria, the ship is renamed BRITISH QUEEN. Misfortune strikes when Claude Girwood and Co., builders of the engine, go bankrupt, thus occasioning at least a year's delay in the completion of the vessel.

1837

Meanwhile, the Great Western Steamship Co. is also building a steamer for the North Atlantic route. Their splendid challenger, the GREAT WESTERN, is expected to be ready in the spring of 1838. Her designer is the great Isambard Kingdom Brunel, who is later to design the GREAT EASTERN. The directors of the British and American Steam Navigation Co. hear of this, and are determined to find a ship to take their sailings until the BRITISH QUEEN is ready. It so happens that three of the directors are connected with the St. George Steam Packet Co., which operates a service between London and Cork, and this company happens to have a new 703-ton steamer, the SIRIUS. She is chartered to make two voyages.

MARCH 28, 1838

The SIRIUS leaves from London, making for Cork, where she will pick up more passengers, the London mail, and coal supplies.

APRIL 4, 1838

The SIRIUS leaves Cork harbour at noon, under the command of Lieutenant Roberts, with 40 passengers, 20 tons of water, and 450 tons of coal. There was no room for cargo. As it was, she was dangerously low in the water, with her paddle axles just above the surface.

APRIL 8, 1838

The GREAT WESTERN leaves Bristol with only seven passengers on board, bound for New York. She is the first steamer specifically designed for the purpose to cross the Atlantic.

APRIL 23, 1838

After a stormy, difficult, and, some say, nearly mutinous voyage, the SIRIUS reaches New York, 18½ days out from Cork. She had beaten her rival by the astonishingly short margin of four hours, for no sooner had she berthed at Battery Place than the cry went up that another steamer was pounding up the Verrazzano Narrows. It was the GREAT WESTERN, 15 days and 5 hours out of Bristol. If it was any consolation to the owners, builders, and crew, she had completed the voyage in over three days less than the SIRIUS.

JULY 5, 1838

The SIRIUS was an Irish Sea cross-channel ship. Her owners' fiercest competitors were the City of Dublin Steam Packet Co., and the directors of that company wanted to match their rivals. Therefore, they transferred their steamship, the ROYAL WILLIAM, to the Atlantic route, and she left on her first voyage on July 5, 1838.

The ROYAL WILLIAM was the first vessel to be designed with her hull divided into five watertight compartments. A contemporary description gives an interesting account of the rigours attending the loading of these early steamers. Despite the fact that she carried no cargo, and only thirty-two out of a maximum of eighty passengers, 'coal filled her bunkers, her holds, and even her well deck, so that her paddles were buried six feet. Her sponsons were submerged, and it was possible by the act of leaning over the bulwarks to wash one's hands in the water that surged the vessel's sides.'

OCTOBER 20, 1838

The City of Dublin Steam Packet Co., well satisfied with the performance of the ROYAL WILLIAM, founds the Transatlantic Steam Ship Co. On the same day, the newly-built LIVERPOOL, which had been bought from Sir John Tobin, leaves Liverpool for New York on the company's inaugural voyage. The ROYAL WILLIAM, her hour of glory passed, is returned to the Irish Sea service. The LIVERPOOL is the first steamer to have two funnels—large, black, shiny ones. Furthermore, she had hot and cold water in the bath-rooms. For all that, her first seven voyages were unprofitable, and she was laid up until sold to the P. & O. Line, which renamed her the GREAT LIVERPOOL, so as not

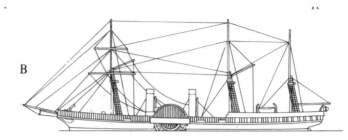

A ROYAL WILLIAM, *1837*.
B GREAT LIVERPOOL, *1837*.
C *Stern view of the* ROBERT F. STOCKTON, *1838, showing the original arrangement of two propellers abaft the rudder. After trials, this was changed to a single propeller positioned in the accepted manner.*
D GREAT WESTERN, *1837*.

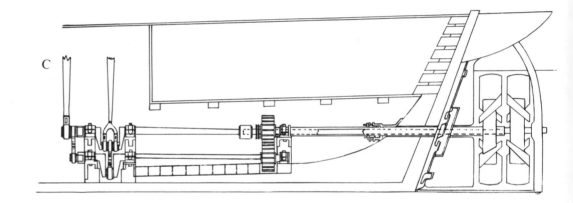

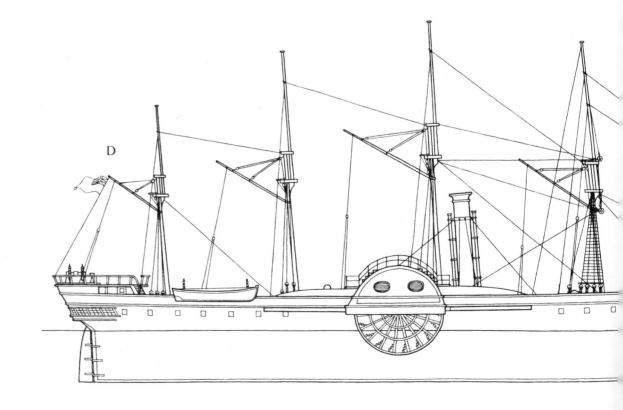

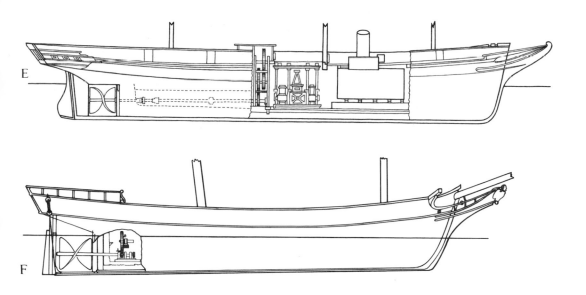

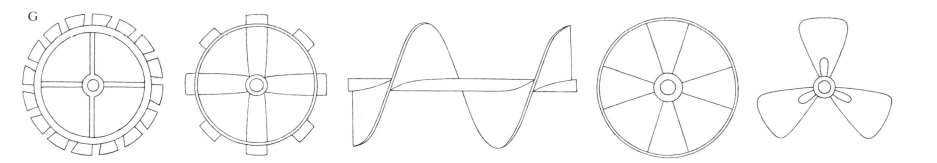

E CIVETTA, *built in 1829 at Trieste by Joseph Ressel and Ottavio Fontana. As early as 1812, Ressel, an Austrian, had sketched an Archimedean screw which had two blades of half a turn each.*

F *Francis Pettit Smith's patent propeller was used to drive the* ARCHIMEDES, *which was built in 1838 by Henry Wimhurst. The original propeller had one complete turn and was 7 foot (2.1 m) in diameter. Finally, after trials, the propeller fitted had two blades with a diameter of $5\frac{3}{4}$ foot (1.75 m).*

G *Five stages in the early development of the propeller. Reading from the left, they are dated 1785, 1800, 1812, 1840, and 1860, respectively.*

to confuse her with the LIVERPOOL already in her service. That LIVERPOOL was immediately nicknamed the 'LITTLE LIVERPOOL'.

SCREW PROPULSION

The story of the propeller is the story of neglect and missed opportunities. Almost a hundred years earlier, a mathematician, Daniel Bernoulli, had proposed the screw as a method of propulsion for ships. This was in 1752, but it was not until 1794 that a Mr. William Lyttleton took out a patent for the screw drive. Six years later, in 1800, a certain Mr. Shorter, staking his claim to immortality, had his sailing barque DONCASTER moved at a speed of $1\frac{1}{2}$ miles (2.4 km) an hour by means of a propeller that was driven by eight men running round a capstan!

In 1802, the first propeller-driven craft took to the water. Colonel John Stevens fitted his 18-foot (5.5 m) rowing-boat with a single windmill-bladed propeller. He plied the River Hudson with this vessel until 1806.

Colonel Stevens soon discovered that a right-hand rotating screw deflects the vessel gradually to the left. The opposite was also true. He cured this fault by mounting twin counter-rotating screws driven off the one cylinder. However, his invention provoked little interest. It was not until 1838 that the ROBERT F. STOCKTON and the ARCHIMEDES adopted his revolutionary idea. Yet, by 1845, the supremacy of the propeller over the paddle had been established. The pity is that, had engineering technology been able to transfer what was workable in an 18-foot (5.5 m) 'model' to the size of ships that were then coming from the shipbuilding yards, the life of the paddle-steamer would have been even shorter than it actually was.

Despite the tardiness in developing a specific technology that could translate Colonel Stevens's invention into a major shipbuilding adjunct, there was, nevertheless, a steady stream of marine engineers who worked at the idea of a propeller. One of the first of these was an Austrian, Joseph Ressel, who experimented with the helical Archimedean screw fitted to a river vessel that sailed the Danube

WHALING

Illustrated is an American whaler from the middle of the nineteenth century, together with a selection of American and English whaling gear, used for hunting spermaceti whales. The whaleboats are hoisted under fixed oak davits, ready to be lowered as soon as the lookout at the main top-gallant mast head has sighted a whale. On the deck, the blubber tryworks are in use, so the lower sails are furled.

The whaling gear illustrated includes harpoons, lances, blubber knives, and prickers, drawn after the illustrations of Captain Scammon and William Scoresby Jr.

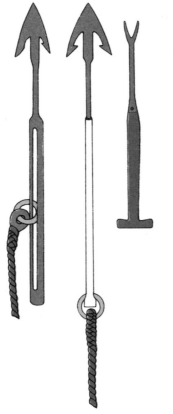

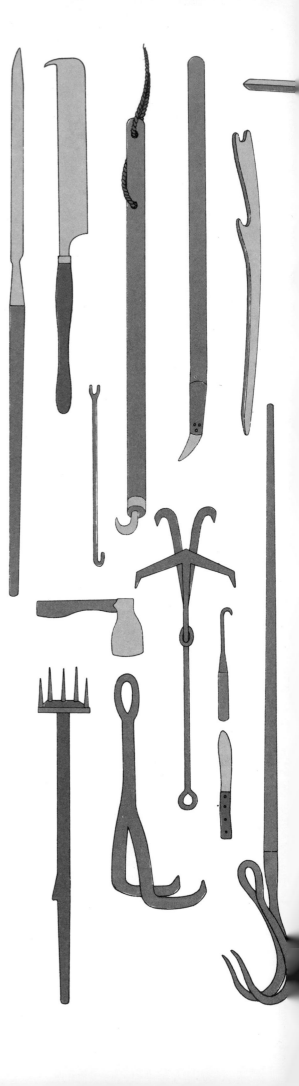

in 1812. Another attempt was made in Europe in 1829 to use a ship with screw propulsion on the Venice-Trieste service. The authorities banned this ship, because it was alleged that the boiler was faulty.

The first major breakthrough for this method of propulsion came in 1836. An Englishman, Francis Pettit Smith, experimented on the Paddington Canal in London with his six-ton steam launch FRANCIS SMITH. She was a successful craft, although small. In the same year, a Swedish engineer, John Ericsson, who was resident in England, built the highly successful FRANCIS B. OGDEN that was screw-propelled. The ship was named for the then U.S. consul in Liverpool.

Then, in 1838, Lieutenant Robert F. Stockton privately orders a small 63-foot (19.2 m) iron-hulled Ericsson screw-steamer from the shipbuilding firm of Lairds at Birkenhead. Not unexpectedly, he named the ship the ROBERT F. STOCKTON, and in the spring of the following year, she crossed the Atlantic under sail. After a series of trials, some of which were

rather tricky, the position of the screw and rudder were interchanged to the present-day style of having the rudder abaft the propeller. This made all the difference to her performance. She was renamed the NEW JERSEY, and for several years after the change in 1840 she saw excellent service in American waters, the first ever commercial screw-driven vessel on that side of the Atlantic.

The patents held by Francis Pettit Smith were taken over by the Ship Propeller Co. in 1838. The company built the ARCHIMEDES at the yard of Henry Wimhurst at Blackwell, in the East End of London. Her screw was set into the deadwood of the hull's keel, and she reached a speed of nine knots. In 1840, the ARCHIMEDES made a demonstration voyage around the ports of Britain. As a direct result of her call at Bristol, the GREAT BRITAIN, which was built in 1843, was fitted with screw propulsion. Thereafter, it was just a question of time before the screw ousted the paddle as the main method of propulsion for steam-ships.

(33.2 m) long and 28 foot (8.5 m) wide, was by then so rotten that she had to be broken up on the spot. Her cargo of whale oil, so laboriously acquired, came home to St. John's in the SIGNET.

Whaling ships, which were nicknamed 'spouters', never enlisted seamen—only whalemen and greenhorns. The reason was that a whaling voyage was so long and so boring that a trained seaman could jump ship at any port-of-call and be certain of getting another, and more congenial, berth. Shore leave from whalers was granted only on remote Pacific atolls, from which there could be no escape. Whalers avoided as far as possible any commercial port. The entire crew had shares, called 'lays', in the venture of a whaler, and these lays were calculated on the net profit of a voyage. Whaling captains traded with their own crews in such things as clothing, tobacco, and other comforts. Unfortunately, whalemen often bought recklessly so that they had little or nothing to come in cash at the end of a voyage that might have lasted for three or more years.

Whales, too, were not plentiful. The record catch on a nineteen-month voyage was only thirty-four whales. Some ships took three or four years to record such a catch. The size of a whale was measured in barrels. A large whale was a sixty-barrel whale. In those days, a barrel was worth £100.

The record day's catch was that of the MARGARET RAIT out of St. John's. She took three sixty-barrel whales on the same day, proceeded to London in order to sell her full cargo, and received £18,600 for it—and that was more than the entire cost of the ship!

Although 'spouters' were generally ill-kept, poorly rigged, and usually appeared neglected, yet accidents on them and to them were comparatively rare. Complete losses or disappearances at sea were almost unknown; but they seldom arrived at their home port with the same crew with which they had left.

Canadian whalers were given to seek the company of British whalers, no matter how distant the other vessel might be. The reason was not one of kinship. There was a far more prosaic reason than that. British whalers had to carry a doctor aboard. Canadian and American whalers had no such luxury.

WHALERS AND WHALING
1820-50

The Cunard family of Halifax, Nova Scotia, was one of the families interested in the whaling industry, which was established in that province in 1784, when Governor Parr welcomed the twenty emigrant families from Massachusetts. It was these two places, the one in Canada, the other in America, that were to become the centres of the world's whaling industry. Incidentally, the Cunard family was to give the sea one of its most illustrious sons, Samuel Cunard, the founder of the Cunard Shipping Co. More, one of the most famous whalers, the SAMUEL CUNARD, sailed out of Halifax in 1837 to continue the Cunard family's involvement in the whaling industry.

The heyday of the sail whaler was short-lived. By 1850, the industry began to dwindle because of the very long duration of the whaling voyages, and the reluctance of sailors to be so long from their homes, and also because of the boom in world-wide general trading, which made it easier to earn a living by transporting cargoes rather than by chasing whales.

The voyages of exploration of medieval sailors were often long. One recalls, for instance, the three years and more that Magellan was away from his home port on a single voyage of discovery. But such voyages could be capped by the voyages of whalers. Perhaps the longest whaling voyage was that of the PACIFIC, which left St. John's, Newfoundland, in April, 1841. Four years and nine months later, in January, 1846, she limped into Valparaiso—all 347 tons of her. Her once sturdy framework, 109 foot

One problem remained that might have jeopardized the take-over by the propeller. In the early days of screw propulsion, there was no metal bearing that could stand up to the wear caused by the rotating, thrusting screw. In 1840, fortunately, a Mr. Penn discovered that the extremely hard wood, *Lignum vitae,* would, when lubricated with water, remain as hard as metal and would not show any appreciable signs of wear. The impending reversion to the paddle, therefore, was avoided.

SAFETY ON BOARD
1817-39

Over the centuries, very little had been done by the British Government to make statutory safety measures for ships at sea. Then, in 1817, the British Parliament drew up some rules and regulations for the construction and testing of boilers. A parliamentary report, dated 1836-37, called for the registration of all steamers. To the astonishment of the commissioners who drew up the report it was discovered that, on the River Mersey, only thirty-nine ships out of a total of seventy-six that were inspected had been registered. Two Liverpool owners alone had more

GREAT BRITAIN, 1843.
A *Side elevation.*
B *The six-bladed propeller which was used during the trials. Later, a four-bladed propeller was substituted.*
C *The midship section, showing the positioning of the engines.*

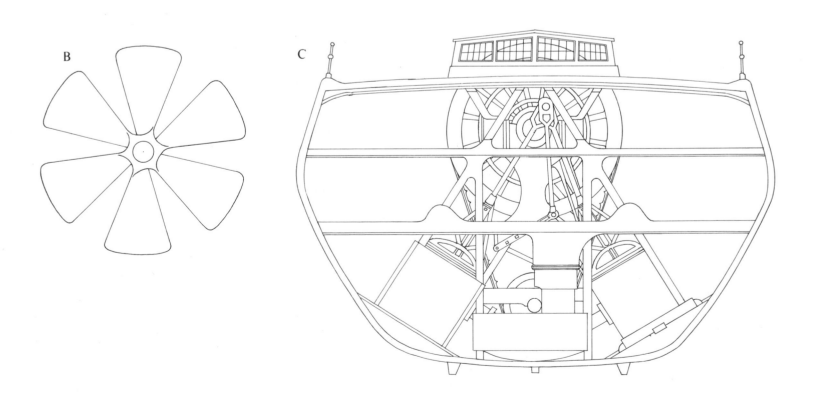

vessels than the total number that were registered there.

The story was the same throughout the country. The River Thames had a tally of sixteen unregistered ships, the River Humber twenty-six; and there were literally hundreds of others scattered on the rivers and in the ports of the country. Significantly, ninety-five per cent of Liverpool shipping was in Irish ownership.

An urgent instruction went out to all port agents throughout the British Isles to make a physical count of the steamers under their nominal control. The tally came to 766, of which 484 were river and estuarine vessels, including numerous tugs, whilst 282 were large coasters and seagoing vessels. Yet a bare nine years before this count, Lloyd's Register, then a fairly definitive document, had contained the names of only 81 steamers.

The first regulations demanding the carrying of lifeboats, in addition to a ship's normal cutter and gig, stem from the adoption of the Commission's report. For, as the 'London Gazette' cogently put it, 'Floating wreckage will no longer suffice for the saving of lives.'

In order to comply with the new regulations, a number of companies experimented with lifeboats that were carried upside down on the paddle-boxes. Other companies employed designers to plan lifeboats to be the top of the paddle-box itself. Thus, it is often possible to date old illustrated prints by the lifeboat.

A further close look at safety regulations was made after the experiment embodied in the design of the COLUMBUS. This 330-ton paddle-steamer was planned for the North Atlantic route. However, she never undertook such a voyage.

The COLUMBUS attracted great interest when she made her trial voyage from Liverpool to London. Steam was generated in her by an entirely revolutionary manner. A jet of water was injected onto a pan of mercury that was heated to a temperature of 350°C. Instant steam was thus produced. The remainder of the engine was of conventional design.

During her trials, the COLUMBUS reached 8¼ knots. Her fuel consumption of only three tons a day represented a saving of fifty per cent. Unfortunately, before the COLUMBUS could go into service, there was a serious engine-room explosion. This led to the banning of the 'quicksilver' type of boiler, and the idea was never taken up again. The year following the explosion, in 1839, the British Parliament appointed another Commission charged with the duty of producing a report and to draw up a more 'modern' Code of Safety.

MAIL BOATS
1837-39
The North Atlantic was not the only ocean attracting the attention of pioneering steamship owners. The difficulty, however, of looking to the other oceans of the world was that over great distances the early steamships could not carry a profitable pay-load. Too much space was needed for the coal that had to be carried to fuel the boilers. Bunkering en route was a very costly business.

Nevertheless, the importance of developing and encouraging regular, punctual, and profitable steam services was not lost on the governments of Europe and of the Americas.

There was one area of activity in which governments could help. This was mail delivery. Hitherto, sailing-packets had been extensively used, but were unreliable. The post was growing enormously, and its prompt delivery became a matter of sheer commercial need.

The British Government began asking for tenders to carry its mail from steamship owners as early as 1837, three years before the introduction of the Penny Post.

Up to this time, postal charges had been paid for by the addressee. Sir Rowland Hill's Bill changed this system. In future, the sender would buy a stamp, affix it to the envelope, and the Post Office would then deliver it to the addressee.

The idea received world-wide acclaim. Soon, other countries adopted the system. It became one of the most significant social indicators in history. In Great Britain, for example, 73 million letters were posted in 1840. By 1870, the number of pieces had risen to 630 million.

From the revenue collected by the Government from the Post Office, substantial payments could be made for carrying the overseas mail by steamer.

The first contract made for the carrying of mail by steamer was between the British Government and the Peninsular and Oriental Steam Navigation Co.—the famous P. & O. The contract was dated August 22, 1837, and was for the carrying of mail to Spain and Portugal. In September, 1837, the company advertised its first sailings in the London papers.

Two years later, the Royal Mail Steam Packet Co., also of London, was founded for the purpose of carrying mail to the West Indies, the Caribbean area, and to the west coast of South America. Anticipating a heavy need, the company placed one of the largest shipping orders of all time. Fourteen transatlantic steamers were contracted for. In 1841, the CLYDE was completed and became the first of the new company's fleet. The CLYDE carried the prefix R.M.S., thus indicating that she was a Royal Mail Steamer. This prefix became identified with most ships carrying the Royal Mail.

Other contracts were awarded. In 1839, for example, Samuel Cunard gained the contract for the North Atlantic services to Canada and to New York, with feeder services to Boston and Quebec. His company was originally named 'The British and North American Royal Mail Steam Packet Co.' This long name was quickly changed by those who had to use it to the 'Cunard Line', although the company itself did not officially recognize, and use, the shorter name until 1878. The first steamer on this particular run was the BRITANNIA.

In October, 1839, the Postmaster General of the United States of America invited tenders for a series of mail services from New York to Liverpool, Bristol, Southampton, Antwerp, Bremen, and Hamburg, with feeder services to Le Havre, Brest, and Lisbon. Few serious tenders were submitted to accommodate this mammoth order. The lowest tender that was submitted was that of a Mr. Edward Mills, who came from New York, and who wished to operate a service between that city and Le Havre. Mr. Mills offered to perform a specific service for a tender fee of $1,300,000 annually. The Postmaster General accepted the tender on behalf of the U.S. Government. In 1846, Mr. Mills founded the Ocean Steam Navigation Co. to carry the mail. Its first steamer was the WASHINGTON, which was closely followed by a sister ship, the HERMANN.

France was the third country to offer mail contracts. The firm of Heroult et de Handel established the first French transatlantic service, also in 1839, with the UNION. Thereafter, it was just a question of time before other governments were seeking tenders from steamship owners and managers for the conveyance of their overseas mail.

1840
Captain James Clark Ross, an Englishman, takes an expedition to the Antarctic in ships that have been especially strengthened to withstand the pressure of the ice. He maps the coast of Victoria Land, named in honour of the young British Queen, but does not effect a landing.

1845
Despite the performance of screw-ships since the launching of the ARCHIMEDES, despite the rapid spread of screw propulsion, the world of shipping was still arguing as to which was the better method of propulsion; the paddle or the screw. The argument of the pro-paddlers could be summed up as follows: How could the puny, rotating screw be better than the power of the two revolving paddles, with blades 10 foot (3 m) across and 3 foot (0.9 m) deep, biting into the water?

The only way to settle the argument once and for all was by a practical demonstration. The British Admiralty, therefore, had two sister ships built, the one paddle-driven, the other screw-propelled. The sister ships were, indeed, twin sisters, of equal size, equal tonnage, and equal engine horsepower.

On a calm, windless April day, the two ships were tethered stern to stern by stout cables. The word was given. RATTLER, the screw-driven ship, took up the strain. ALECTO, the paddle-driven steamer, started her engines. A pre-determined and monitored time-scale had been worked out. The two captains increased

the revolutions of their engines until both were flat out. Slowly, RATTLER inched forward, towing the threshing ALECTO. Within ten minutes, the discomfited ALECTO, despite the protest of her engine, was being pulled stern first by the RATTLER at a steady 2.8 knots.

The result was conclusive; yet, the Lords of the Admiralty were slow to throw the paddle overboard completely. Admiralty mail contracts still contained two anachronistic clauses. One called for ships with wooden hulls, and the other called for paddle propulsion. But for these demands, screw propulsion would have made even quicker inroads into sail and paddle. Such companies as Cunard had to build two types of vessels to stay in business; screw-driven ships for the mounting passenger traffic, and wooden-hulled mail ships in order to abide by the terms of the Admiralty mail contracts.

JULY 26, 1845

The GREAT BRITAIN, the first screw-driven Atlantic liner, leaves Liverpool bound for New York.

Isambard Brunel, the builder of the GREAT WESTERN, started work on her in 1843. She was to be a massive, screw-driven ship, the second and final ship of the Great Western Shipping Co. to be designed by Brunel. She was so large that the name originally chosen for her was MAMMOTH. Brunel liked this kind of name for his ships, thinking, quite rightly, that they gave a better impression of size and majesty than did the names that were ultimately chosen for his vessels. The third ship he built, the GREAT EASTERN, was to have been given the name of LEVIATHAN. However, neither the Prince Consort nor Queen Victoria liked the name MAMMOTH, and as the Prince Consort named her on July 19, 1843, the alternative of GREAT BRITAIN was used.

No slipway was large enough to accommodate the mammoth vessel. Therefore, she was built in a dry dock at Bristol by the Railway Co. with construction under the supervision of William Patterson. Unhappily, the draught of the vessel had been miscalculated. To the consternation of all those present at the ceremony, it was discovered that the ship could not be floated over the sill of the dry dock. It took a full year to make the alterations necessary to

free her from her dry-dock 'prison', and a further year to fit her out for service.

The GREAT BRITAIN was designed by Brunel in 1838, the year in which the GREAT WESTERN made her belated maiden voyage to New York. Therefore, seven years had passed since the inception of the GREAT BRITAIN until that July day when she left on her maiden voyage, also to New York. She had been designed to accommodate 360 passengers, but only 60 took passage in her. The crossing was slow: 14 days and 21 hours. But, slow as she was, the GREAT BRITAIN was the pioneer of all screw-driven liner services.

She fell on evil days. For years, she lay a rusting hulk in the Falkland Islands. Eventually, she was salved in April, 1970, and made her forty-eighth and final voyage home to Bristol. There she is to remain, restored to her former glory, a floating museum to Brunel's genius.

SAIL AND COTTON

Despite the monster steamers that were coming from the shipyards, in some areas the sailing-ship was more than holding its own. The cotton industry is a typical example of

A *The Siamese engine of the* RATTLER.
B *The famous tug-of-war between the* RATTLER *and the* ALECTO, *in which the* RATTLER *demonstrated the superiority of the propeller over the paddle-wheel.*

B

under sail, both her funnel and propeller were retracted. She was the first ship-of-the-line steamer.

1847

Frederick William III, King of Prussia, calls the first meeting of the National Assembly of the Germanic Federation, an organization that was formed in 1815 from the leading Germanic states of that time. Germany had no corporate existence until after the Franco-Prussian war, but the North German Federation formed a naval unit when Denmark attempted to annexe the two border provinces of Schleswig and Holstein. The unit was formed by the purchase of two Cunarders, the BRITANNIA and the ARCADIA. These ships were each armed with nine 68-pounder guns, and were re-named the BARBAROSSA and the ERZHERZOG JOHANN respectively. The Federation's first armoured steam frigates were commissioned in 1867. These were the KRONPRINZ and the FREDRICH CARL. The rivalry for sea power that commenced a hundred years and more ago has lasted down to modern times.

1847-48

These years are marked by an intensifying of the rivalry that had already arisen among the maritime powers of the world. Great Britain was the undoubted leader in the shipping stakes. America felt this keenly, particularly in respect of the Atlantic where, between 1838 and 1847, every regular liner flew the British flag.

It is true that the excellence of the American transatlantic sailing-packets retarded American steamer development. Yet prestige, and presumably national honour, rested with steam.

1847-48

Another fillip is given to sail as an indirect result of the terrible Irish potato famine of 1847-48. The failure of the staple crop in Ireland over such a long period led to the emigration of hundreds of thousands of the Irish to Canada and the United States. Most of them sailed in emigrant sailing-ships. Conditions aboard ship were overcrowded and unhygienic. The dreaded disease, 'Ship Fever'—a generic term for dysentery, typhoid, and cholera—killed many hopeful emigrants. Indeed, it is estimated that 25,000 Irish died on their way across the Atlantic to Canada, and a similar number died on the way to the United States. Records show that 10,000 Irish emigrants are buried on Grosse Island, the quarantine station for Quebec, and that another 6,000 are buried at Montreal.

JANUARY 1847

The directors of the Red Cross Line, which specialized in sailing-packets, wished to operate steam vessels from the United States to Europe. They are forced to charter a British vessel, the SARAH SANDS, a propeller steamer. She

this reliance upon sail. Mobile and Savannah developed into the two foremost American cotton ports. Sail contributed handsomely to their prosperity.

The cotton crop was pressed into 500-pound (227 kg) bales, which were strapped on the outside, but which were left open at both ends. It was in this form that the cotton was delivered to the sailing-ships. In order to stow the cargo, a process known as 'screwing' was employed. This involved the operating of a Jack Screw by a team of four. The object of the screwing was to squeeze the bales so tightly that three could be stowed where there was nominal space for two only. One end of the Jack Screw was placed against the ship's beam, and the other against the line of bales that had already been placed in the hold. The team of four then turned the Jack Screw until they were able to insert another bale in the line. This process was continued until it was impossible to insert another bale. Brawny men were needed in the teams, for the work was tough and heavy. The teams even dossed down at night on top of the cargo they were stowing. Screwers were paid by results only. Their enthusiasm to get

yet another bale into a line has been known to lift a deck off its stanchions.

The screwers, who were mainly loggers from the far north, came to the southern ports only at cotton time. They were a very rough crowd indeed. In fact, the local police paid no attention to a body that might be found in the harbour—unless it was the body of a local resident, when the police would open a murder investigation.

1845

The explorer John Franklin heads an expedition to try to discover the North West Passage. His two ships, the EREBUS and the TERROR, incorporated the latest equipment that the explorers could need. The expedition was never seen again.

1846

A 60-gunner, the AJAX, is commissioned by the British Admiralty. She was screw-driven by a Maudslay, Sons and Field 4-cylinder engine of 450 horsepower, that gave her a top speed of 9 knots. Basically, the AJAX was merely a sail-assisted man-of-war, her engine being used mainly for manoeuvring. When the vessel was commences the first of her ten chartered voyages in January, 1847.

JUNE 2, 1847
The WASHINGTON becomes the first American steamship to cross the Atlantic. Owned by the Ocean Steam Navigation Co. of New York, she sails from New York, thus inaugurating the U.S. Mail contract between New York, Southampton, and Bremen.

APRIL 1848
The Black Ball Line, fierce competitors of the Red Cross Line, are so anxious to compete on the Atlantic run with them that they buy the UNITED STATES, which was already committed to the New York-New Orleans route. She commences her career as an Atlantic steamer on the New York-Liverpool service.

1849-51
Another mass movement of hopefuls hastens the introduction of steam to the Pacific coast of America. This mass movement is the Californian Gold Rush of 1849-51.

The initial services on the west coast ferried prospectors from the Isthmus of Panama to San Francisco. The ferries consisted mainly of old vessels, nearly all of them sailing-craft. The Gold Run ships earned a very unsavoury reputation indeed. In 1850, the COLUMBIA was built in New York. She was a paddle steamer —what the Americans called a 'side wheeler'— and she was the first such craft designed and built for the San Francisco run. She operated between San Francisco and Portland, Oregon, for her owners, the firm of Holland Aspinwall which, in the fulness of time, became the Pacific Mail Steamship Co.

1849
Halfway through the nineteenth century, steam was gathering momentum on the seas of the world largely because trade itself was increasing enormously. One of the contributory factors was the decision of the British Government to repeal its Navigation Acts. This was done in 1849. Thus, ships flying a foreign flag could carry cargoes to British ports with impunity.

THE CLIPPER ERA
Despite the increase in the number and percentage of steamers, sail still had another twenty years of growth ahead. That period of growth was to encompass numbers, speed, and size. Indeed, the zenith of sail as regards speed was the clipper, the ship par excellence of the middle of the nineteenth century.

Sail and steam played a sparkling duet in the area of design. Undoubtedly, for a long time, sheer grace remained with sail. This was notable in the lines of the hull. Roughly speaking, speed increased under the same square frontage of sail as the lines of the hull changed at the bows from a blunt 'U' shape to a fine 'V' shape. The so-called 'hollow

water-line' technique produced actual inward curves from the cutwater to the fullest width of beam.

Another development was the composite sailing-ship. In this type of ship, the frames of the hull were made of iron, which bore a cover of wooden planking. Below the water-line, the wood was sheathed in copper or yellow metal. This was a protection against the ravages of the teredo bore-worm.

These two major developments in sail combined to produce the light-hulled, sleek clipper ships, which raced like yachts across the oceans, outdoing each other in making record voyages, 'clipping' days off previous best timings.

The earliest description of American-built clippers depict them as being the sharpest ships afloat. This turn of phrase referred to the shape of the forward parts of the hull.

Even before the clipper ships reached their peak of performance, there was at least one sailing-ship that had carved out a little niche in history. This was the Canadian vessel MARCO POLO. She started her life under a cloud, for on her launching in 1851 she ran across the river and heeled right over, throwing a young boy clean into the water. She had been built at St. John's for James and Thomas Smith, but at the end of her maiden voyage, which was on May 31, 1851, she was sold to James Baines for his Black Ball Line of Liverpool.

Baines placed her on the Melbourne run, and she managed a seventy-six-day passage. From then on, the MARCO POLO was his favourite ship. She remained on the Australian run for

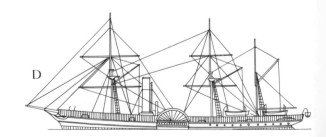

A MARCO POLO, *built in 1851, was labelled the 'fastest ship in the world' in 1852.*

B WASHINGTON, *1847.*

C SARAH SANDS, *1847.*

D UNITED STATES, *1848.*

E *This is a midship section of a composite ship, a wooden vessel with iron frames, from the latter half of the nineteenth century.*

E

fifteen years, before ending her days rather more humbly in the guano trade, sailing out of Huanillos in Chile, where she once waited fifteen months for a full cargo. In 1883, her thirty-fourth season, the MARCO POLO had to be grounded off Cavendish, Prince Edward Island, in order to save the cargo. The crew reported that she was so rotten that the pumps could not hold the rush of water through the leaky timbers.

For most of the time when the MARCO POLO was on the Australian run, her captain was the renowned 'Bully' Forbes. He was a man, so it was alleged, who could not be bested; but he was once—by a fish. It so happened that on one particular voyage, the MARCO POLO was being shadowed by a 16-foot (4.9 m) shark. An irate Forbes ordered that the fish be caught, and winched aboard. This was accordingly done. The moment the monster was on deck, it thrashed around madly. To the consternation of the crew, who were powerless to do anything, the shark smashed the skylight over Forbes's day cabin, and disappeared, hook, line, and sinker. There, it just flashed past the captain, who had never had such a fright in his life, and then proceeded to break everything in the cabin. History does not tell if Forbes enjoyed shark-fin soup!

1850

The French Government decides to introduce steam propulsion into her ships of the line. The NAPOLEON was, therefore, laid down to the design of Stanislas Dupuy de Lôme, an eminent French naval architect. She ranked as a second-rate ship of the line, a 92-gunner, with a top speed of 13.8 knots. She was of 5,057 tons burthen, her overall length was 235 foot (71.2 m), and her engines developed 900 horse-power. These statistics show that she was the leading warship of the time.

The building of the NAPOLEON piqued the British into retaliation. Their reply, in 1852, was to build the far larger AGAMEMNON.

1852

MacGregor Laird founds the African Steam Co.—the Elder Dempster Line of today.

Laird had long associations with Africa. In July, 1832, accompanied by the explorer Richard Lander, he had left for the River Niger in order to open up its hinterland to trade with the African Commercial Co. The venture was well provided for, for the company put two small river paddle-steamers and a 200-ton brig at Laird's disposal. Unfortunately, sickness led to the early death of Lander. This incident, coupled with poor trading results, made the company give up the attempt to open up the Niger territory.

Laird returned to Liverpool in 1834, became a partner in the consortium that bought the SIRIUS, and immersed himself in shipping. Ten years later, in 1844, he founded the shipyard of Laird Bros. and Co. Ltd., which achieved

EMIGRATION TO THE NEW WORLD

The mass emigration from almost all the European countries, which began about 1840, brought millions of people to America, where land and opportunity awaited the poor, the landless, and the adventurous. A big increase in population during the peaceful years after the Napoleonic Wars, insufficient harvests, natural disasters such as the Irish potato blight, and the lure of the gold finds in California, all combined to make the New World a very desirable alternative to the home countries.

For the millions of peasants who emigrated, the sea journey was an appalling experience, marked by bad food, illness, sea-sickness, and the fear of storms. For many, the worst problem was, however, getting to the port. One Swedish family, for instance, walked from the middle of Sweden to the western port of Gothenburg, took a ship from there to London, and then walked from London to Liverpool, where they embarked for America.

NINETEENTH-CENTURY SHIP DECORATION

The origins of the ship's figurehead go back to the very beginning of the history of ships. The Nubian Desert carving of a ship with a horned figurehead on pages 12-13 is about seven thousand years old. It was probably meant to frighten away evil spirits. Later on, ship decoration was used as a means of identification, to frighten enemies, and to display the skill, pride, or prestige of the owner.

A *Figurehead from the* VANADIS, c. *1860.*
B *Name board of the* ALBION, *1800s.*
C *Figurehead of the* AJAX, *1807.*
D *Unidentified figurehead, c. 1850.*
E *Unidentified wood carving, c. 1850.*
F *Unidentified wood carving, c. 1820.*
G *Figurehead of the* HORATIO, *1807.*
H *Unidentified wood carving, c. 1800.*

C

H

world-wide fame under the name of Cammell Laird.

In 1852, Laird was awarded the contract for a monthly service to West Africa. Amongst the partners in this new venture were Alexander Elder and John Dempster. Their names are perpetuated in the present-day Elder Dempster Line.

MAY 1852

Gibbs Bright and Co. had operated sailing-ships on the Australia service since 1830. In 1852, however, they buy Brunel's GREAT BRITAIN for £18,000. She was modified according to the requirements of the new owners, and received four masts and twin funnels placed abreast. By this time, the Australian Gold Rush was at its height. The new GREAT BRITAIN immediately went into service, and on her first voyage as a four-master carried 636 passengers on an 83-day 'dash' to Sydney.

JANUARY 3, 1852

The wooden mail ship AMAZON, belonging to the Royal Mail Line, catches fire 110 miles (208 km) west of the Scillies, whilst on her maiden voyage. Thirty-seven of the 161 passengers, together with 68 members of the crew, lost their lives in the ensuing holocaust.

As a direct consequence of the loss of the AMAZON, future mail ships had to be built with iron hulls and be driven by screw propulsion. In fact, during this same year, the Cunard Line introduces screw propulsion on its Liverpool-New York sailings. The first ship so equipped was the ANDES. Ironically, she was not permitted to carry the mail.

1853

One of the most ambitious but least successful services was that inaugurated in 1853 by the New York and Australian Navigation Co. The name gives a clue to the proposed itinerary, which was New York to Liverpool, Liverpool to Cape Town, and then Cape Town to Sydney. The GOLDEN AGE was the ship selected to pioneer the route. Unhappily, the response was so poor that the company stopped the service after the one run. The GOLDEN AGE was then switched to the Pacific run, for which she had been intended originally.

1853

The Cunard Co. builds its last wooden paddler, the ARABIA, which is laid down only because the British Post Office still persists in requiring wooden hulls in those ships awarded a mail contract.

1853

Ships are remembered usually because there is something different or spectacular about them. Few have been given the accolade of fame for being ordinary. If such an award were made, then the MILES BARTON would undoubtedly qualify for it. She was a 963-tonner

belonging to the Golden Line, operated by Mr. Beazley. Even the company name is lost in oblivion, whilst its contemporaries, the Cunard Line, Elder Dempster, General Steam, and so on, continue to make a little bit of history.

The MILES BARTON was on the Liverpool-to-Melbourne run. Her first three voyages were completed in 74, 76, and 79 days respectively. These times were a matter of only a few days outside the record-breaking times of the fastest sailing-ships, and well inside the slowest times of the steamers. The MILES BARTON continued to give years of exemplary, reliable service. Perhaps these are the attributes that make the true story of the sea and of ships, rather than the spectacular events of the better-known ships.

JULY, 1853

The American commodore, Matthew Perry, steams into Sagami Bay and forces Japan to open her ports to world trade.

1854

The BRANDON is launched, the first ship to be installed with diametrically opposed high and low-pressure cylinders. Jubilantly, the owners reported on her economic operating costs. Other companies, however, were slow to convert to the new compound engine.

The compound principle for steam engines had been patented by Charles Randolph and John Elder in 1853. The principle was easy. By using both high and low-pressure cylinders, steam could be utilized twice. The obvious effect was to cut coal consumption by half. This would mean that a ship using the new type of engine could have a far better pay-load than ships using the conventional method. With growing cynicism and disbelief, the inventors saw their brain-child ignored for an appreciable time. Eventually, the principle was adopted by marine engineers and ship designers.

1854

One splendid achievement of this year is the record-making run of the LIGHTNING, one of the new breed of sailing-ships. She clipped the Sydney-to-London trip to sixty-four days.

MARCH 1854

Despite the improving safety precautions imposed upon ship designers by governments and by companies, 1854 proves to be a year of disaster. The first major catastrophe is the loss of the CITY OF GLASGOW in March. The ship left Liverpool with a total complement of passengers and crew numbering 480. She was never heard of or seen again. It must be assumed that she struck an iceberg some days out from New York, her port of destination, and sank without trace.

JULY 17, 1854

The second loss this year involves the FRANKLIN,

A *A capstan from a sailing ship*, c. *1850.*
B AGAMEMNON, *1852.*
C GOLDEN AGE, *1852.*
D ANDES, *1852.*
E ARABIA, *1852.*
F NAPOLEON, *1850.*

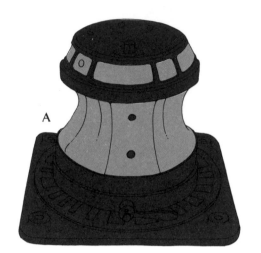

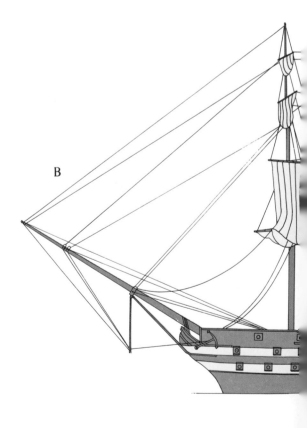

belonging to the New York and Havre Steam Navigation Co. She struck off Long Island, New York, and broke up. Fortunately, there was no loss of life.

SEPTEMBER 9, 1854

The Inman Line, which had lost the CITY OF GLASGOW earlier in the year, suffers another shattering blow when their CITY OF PHILADELPHIA is wrecked off Cape Race. This fine ship had commenced her maiden voyage only ten days before. Again, happily, there was no loss of life resulting from this accident.

SEPTEMBER 27, 1854

The fourth shipping tragedy of the year involves the ARCTIC, a vessel belonging to the Collins Line, which collides with the French ship VESTA. Within four hours, the ARCTIC sank. Three hundred and twenty-two passengers and crew died as a result of this terrible accident. Among those drowned were the wife, son, and daughter of Mr. Collins, the dynamic proprietor of the Dramatic Line and the New York and Liverpool United States Mail Steamship Co.

1854-56

The Crimean War takes place. Although a land war, it had a profound influence on the future of naval vessels. By its end, governments and naval architects were convinced that future sea warfare would be conducted by fully powered vessels. Again, the Crimean War demonstrated the need to protect naval vessels with armour plating. Napoleon III of France ordered the construction of three floating howitzer batteries: the TONNANTE, the LAVE, and the DEVASTATION. All of them were protected with several layers of armour plating, to a total depth of 8 inches (203.4 mm). On October 14, 1854, they shelled a Russian fort and demolished the gun emplacements. Although all three of the floating howitzers received direct hits from the cannon of the defending Russians, they were virtually undamaged.

The war broke out in March, 1854. Great Britain, Piedmont—a kingdom of Italy—and France, all of whom were allies of Turkey, declared war on Russia, which had encroached upon Turkish territory. Vice-Admiral Dundas, a British flag officer, was in charge of a military landing that commenced on September 14, 1854, at Sebastopol, situated on the Crimean peninsula, which juts out into the Black Sea. This was the first large-scale movement of troops since the advent of steam.

Most of the early passenger steamships were contracted to the Government for mail transport. A clause in the agreements stipulated that the ships could be used for trooping purposes. Therefore, many of these ships were immediately chartered, but the HIMALAYA was purchased for £130,000. In all, twelve P. & O. ships went into service as troop-carriers, and transported a total of 62,000 soldiers and 15,000 horses.

Because of this re-deployment of its vessels, the P. & O. had to cancel its services to Australia. Similarly, Cunard had to suspend its North Atlantic sailings when most of its vessels were taken into government service as troopships. Additionally, the Cunarder ANDES was chartered at a fee of £505 a month to serve as a hospital ship between the Crimea and Scutari, where Florence Nightingale had established her hospital.

Other companies that contributed vessels to the authorities were the Inman Line, the Allan Line, Bibby Brothers, the Union Steam Collier Co.—the forerunner of the famous Union Castle Line of present times—and the Royal Mail Line. The French Government used some of the ships of Messageries Maritimes, as well as chartering a certain amount of foreign tonnage.

One of the greatest losses of naval vessels in modern times occurred towards the end of the Crimean War. It was an act of maritime suicide. On September 10, 1855, the Russians abandoned Sebastopol and destroyed their entire fleet of 117 warships. Among the vessels lost were five 120-gunners, eight 84-gunners, one 80-gunner, and four 60-gun frigates.

The keel of this colossal ship was laid down on May 1, 1854 at the yard of Messrs. John Scott Russell & Co. on the Isle of Dogs on the River Thames in London. Her designer was the famous engineer, Isambard Kingdom Brunel.

The launching was due to take place on November 3, 1857, but it was not successful, and the great ship remained there for more than a year until she finally floated. She had been christened LEVIATHAN, but was finally registered GREAT EASTERN.

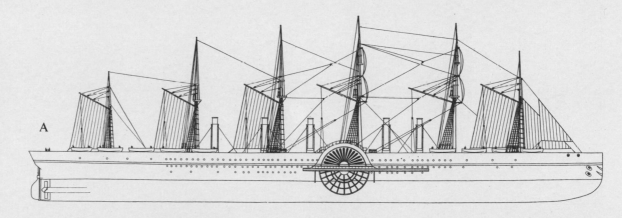

GREAT EASTERN

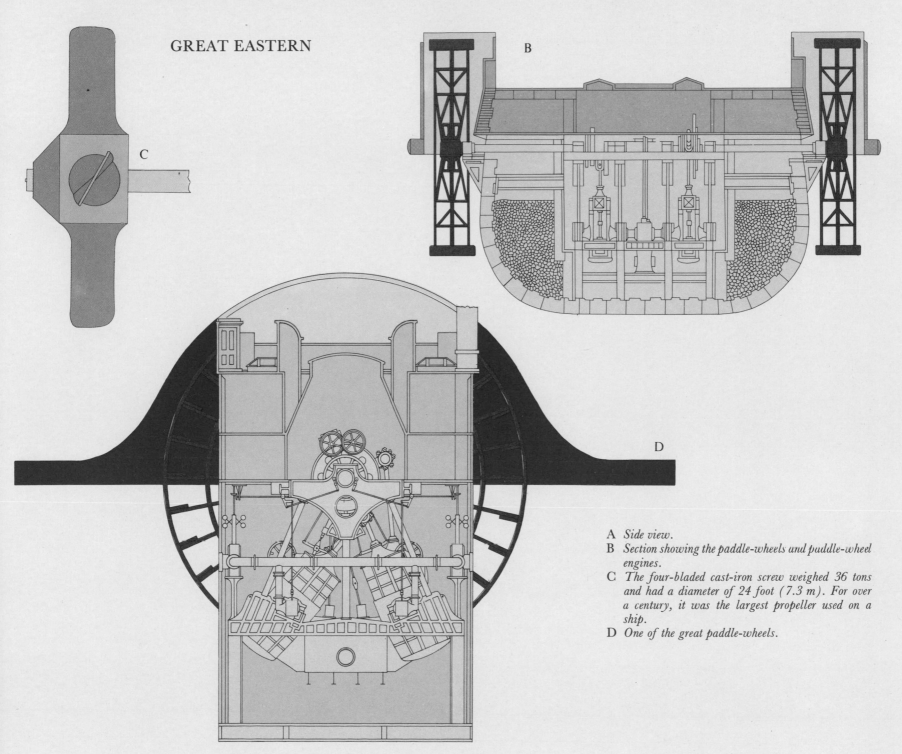

A Side view.
B Section showing the paddle-wheels and paddle-wheel engines.
C The four-bladed cast-iron screw weighed 36 tons and had a diameter of 24 foot (7.3 m). For over a century, it was the largest propeller used on a ship.
D One of the great paddle-wheels.

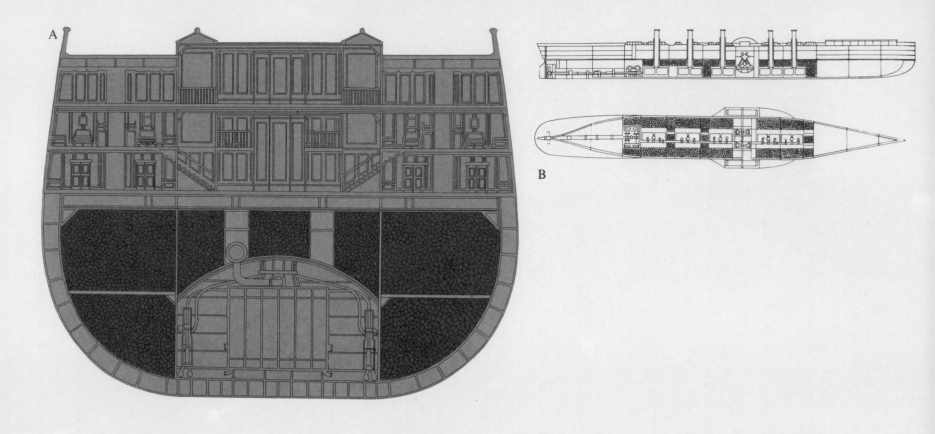

A *Transverse section.*

B *The* GREAT EASTERN *was first intended to carry large cargoes to Ceylon, from where smaller steamers would distribute these to ports in India and Australia. Her coal bunkers were built to hold 12,000 tons of coal for the journey, and were situated above and around the ship's ten boilers. Some experts consider that the ship might have* been an economic success if she had been used as originally intended.

C *The paddle engine room was located between the second and third boiler rooms. The four oscillating cylinders weighed 38 tons each, inclusive of piston and piston-rod. They were built by Scott Russell.*

D *The pompously decorated deck compass.*

E *The longitudinal section shows the complicated* layout of the engine rooms and gives an idea of the huge size of the ship compared to the human figures visible.

The ten rectangular, double-ended, tubular boilers were situated two at the base of each of the five chimneys. The 150-foot (45.7 m) long screw-shaft was driven by steam from the six boilers between the screw engine and the paddle

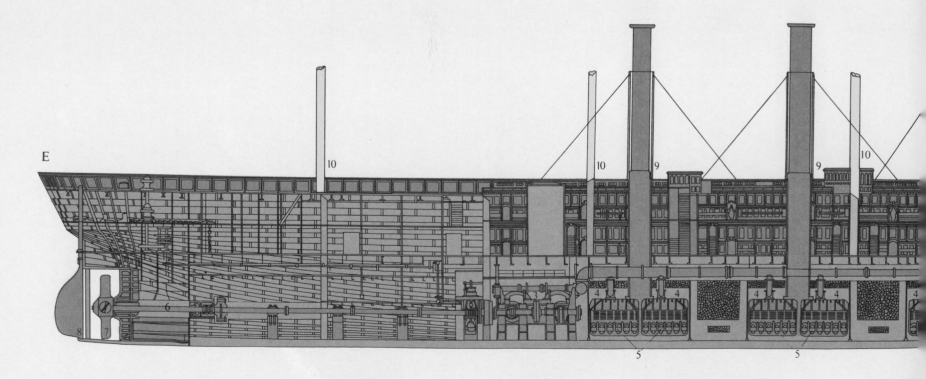

C

D

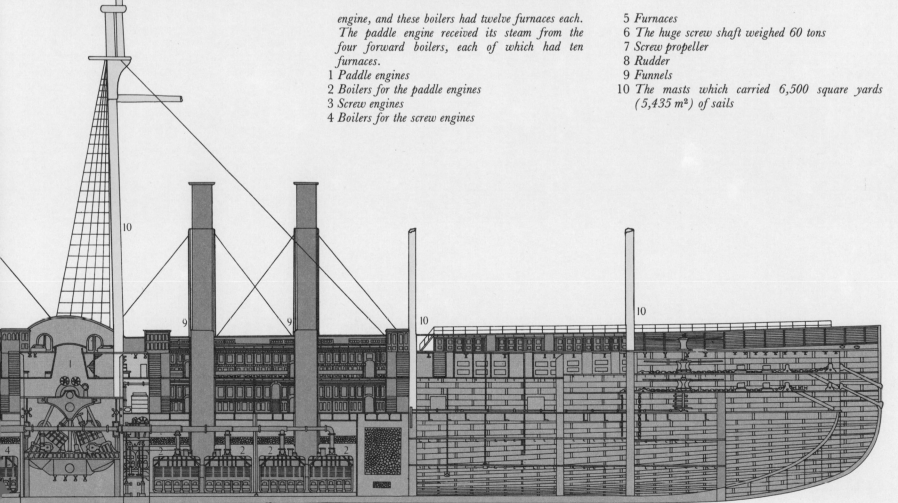

engine, and these boilers had twelve furnaces each. The paddle engine received its steam from the four forward boilers, each of which had ten furnaces.

1 Paddle engines
2 Boilers for the paddle engines
3 Screw engines
4 Boilers for the screw engines
5 Furnaces
6 The huge screw shaft weighed 60 tons
7 Screw propeller
8 Rudder
9 Funnels
10 The masts which carried 6,500 square yards (5,435 m²) of sails

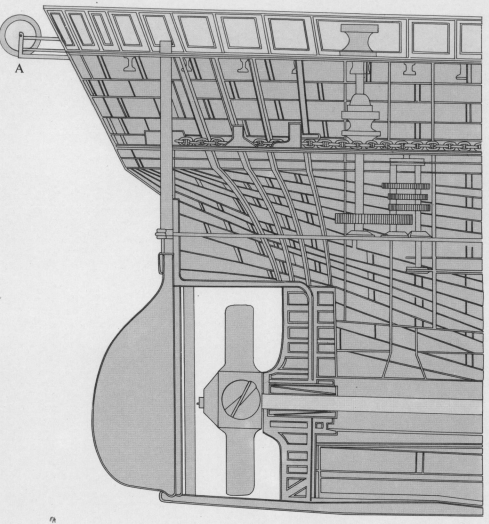

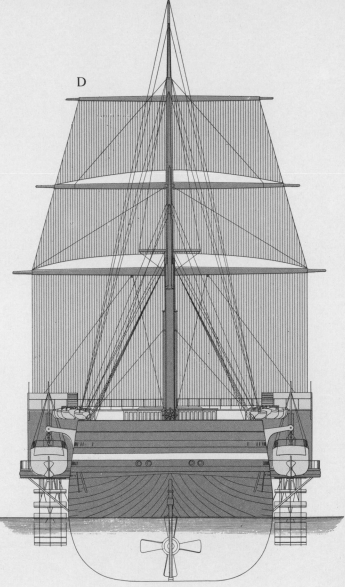

Between 1865 and 1874, the GREAT EASTERN was employed to lay cable lines across the Atlantic and between Bombay in India and Suez in Egypt.

A The pulley through which the telegraph cable was paid out.

B A contemporary print of the great ship laying the transatlantic cable.

C The anchor chain.

D Stern view of the ship showing the spread of her sails and the fine lines of the hull.

E The designer of the GREAT EASTERN was Isambard Kingdom Brunel (1806-59), known popularly as 'The Little Giant'. He was one of the most famous engineers of his era. He died when his colossal brainchild was making her maiden voyage.

A ERICSSON, *1853.*
B FRANKLIN, *1850.*
C HUDSON, *1858.*
D NORTH STAR, *1851.*

A
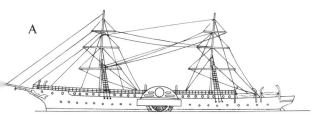

B
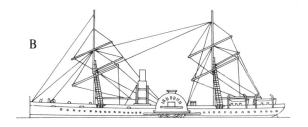

C
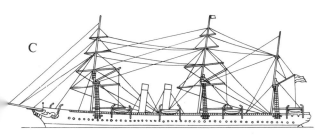

D
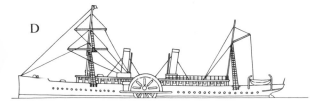

1855

The ERICSSON goes into service for her owner, John B. Kitching. Technically the most advanced ship of her time, she was initially a failure. She was the first ever four-funnelled ship, although the funnels were little more than two pairs of stove-pipes. Each of her 32-foot (9.8 m) diameter paddles was driven by two enormous cylinders, 137 inches (3.5 m) and 168 inches (4.3 m) in diameter respectively. However, her engines, which were of the caloric type and which depended on heated, compressed air, were not considered suitable. She also had the misfortune to sink in shallow water. When she was rehabilitated, the opportunity was taken of replacing her caloric engines with the normal steam engines. Eventually, the ERICSSON was chartered by the Collins Line when their PACIFIC disappeared in 1856.

1855

The Vanderbilt Line commences operations in the North Atlantic.

Commodore Vanderbilt's first steamer was the NORTH STAR, which was commissioned in 1853, and in which he and his family cruised to Europe. Her sister ship was the ARIEL, and in 1855, the Commodore put the two steamers on the North Atlantic run. He was taking a calculated commercial risk, for at that time the Vanderbilts did not have a mail contract. They were awarded a limited one in 1857. This called for thirteen round voyages between New York and Bremen during the ensuing year. The subsidy, however, was fixed at the face value of the mail only.

At the same time that Congress was fixing the rate of subsidy for the Vanderbilt contract, it also cut by half a million dollars a year the subsidy that had been paid to the Collins Line. That move precipitated the end of that famous shipping line. Further retrenchments were imposed. The Ocean Steam Navigation Co. refused to match the ridiculously low tender of the Vanderbilt Line, and they, too, went out of business. This left the Atlantic services to the Vanderbilt interests, but the mail freight proved to be significantly less than had been hoped for. The Vanderbilt vessels were taken over in 1861 by the Federal Government for service in the Civil War. This ended the Vanderbilt involvement in the Atlantic services.

1856

The PERSIA is built for the Cunard Line. She is the first Cunarder to be built with an iron hull.

1856

The Cie. France-Américaine is founded in order to operate services to North and South America. The company bought eight screw-steamers from among the ships that were sold after the end of the Crimean War. The BARCELONE, ALMA, LYONNAIS, and VIGO worked the service to New York. The CADIX, FRANÇOIS ARAGO, JACQUART, and FRANC-COMTOIS worked the Rio de Janeiro and Havana runs.

Once again, experience proved that there was little or no French demand for these routes. The LYONNAIS was run down on November 21, 1856, and 120 people were killed. This gave the company the opportunity to suspend the services. All the ships were sold and reverted to traders.

1856

Germany begins to operate a service in the North Atlantic. H.A.P.A.G.—the Hamburg America Line—had actually been formed in 1847, but it did not begin to operate steamers until 1856, when the BORUSSIA and the HAMMONIA entered service on the Hamburg-New York route. These two vessels were followed by the SAXONIA and the AUSTRIA, which, before entering the H.A.P.A.G. service in 1858, were chartered in 1857 for the carriage of troops to India, where they served during the Indian Mutiny.

1856

Randolph and Elder make one more attempt to popularize their compound engine. They build two ships, the INCA and the VALPARAISO, to the order of the Pacific Steam Navigation Co. These vessels are all equipped with compound engines.

1856

During this year, the Hamburg Brasilienische Co. open an unsuccessful service to various Brazilian ports. When the venture collapsed, the two vessels which had operated the service, both of them sister ships of the BORUSSIA, were sold to H.A.P.A.G. The PETROPOLIS was renamed the BAVARIA by her new owners. The other ship, the TEUTONIA, became H.A.P.A.G.'s reserve steamer.

SEPTEMBER 1857

William Mackinnon obtains the mail contract between Calcutta and Rangoon, and founds the Calcutta and Burmah Steam Navigation Co., which immediately buys three steamers: the CAPE OF GOOD HOPE, the CALCUTTA, and the BALTIC. The company rapidly expanded. Soon, it was operating services to Madras, Ceylon, Bombay, Karachi, and Penang. In 1862, the British India Steam Navigation Co. Ltd. was founded with a capital of £400,000. William Mackinnon's original firm of Mackinnon Mackenzie and Co. was appointed managing agents of B.I. Again, the rate of expansion was enormous. When the NOWSHERA was launched in 1883, she was the hundredth ship to join the B. I. fleet.

NOVEMBER 23, 1857

The last—and largest—wooden-hulled vessel specifically designed for the Atlantic run goes into service; the ADRIATIC of the Collins Line.

A WARRIOR, *the first iron-hulled armoured warship, 1860.*

B *Midship section of the* WARRIOR, *showing the horizontal trunk engines and two of the smooth bore muzzle-loaders originally used.*

C GLOIRE, *the first 'ironclad', 1859.*

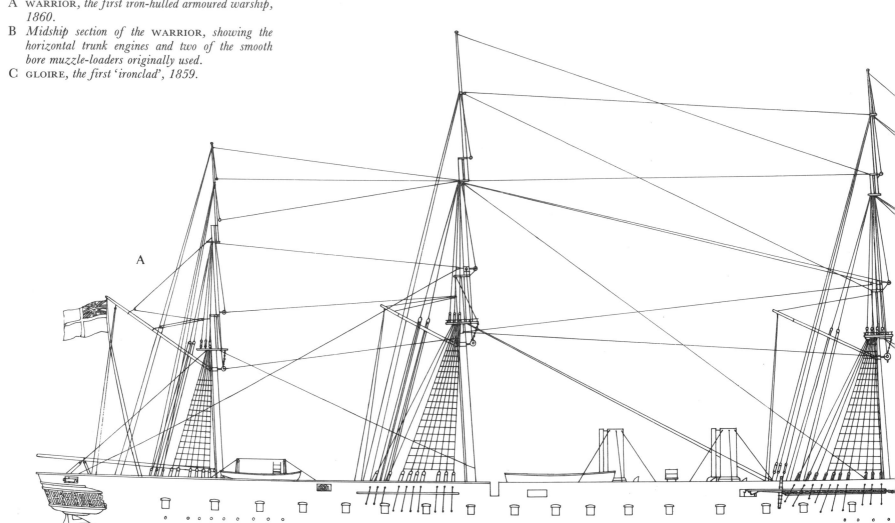

She managed only one voyage before the service was ended in February, 1858. This resulted in the ship being laid up for two years.

The reason for the abandonment of the service was the loss of half a million dollars in revenue when the American Congress slashed the company's subsidy from $858,000 to $385,000. The ADRIATIC had cost the company $250,000. It was a combination of these two factors that caused the Collins Line to go out of business.

JUNE 19, 1858
The BREMEN leaves Bremen for New York. She carries 115 passengers, the first of a steady stream that Norddeutscher Lloyd were to ferry across the Atlantic.

Norddeutscher Lloyd was founded because of the success of the Hamburg America Line (H.A.P.A.G.), which had stirred the ambitions of other German ports, notably Bremen. So

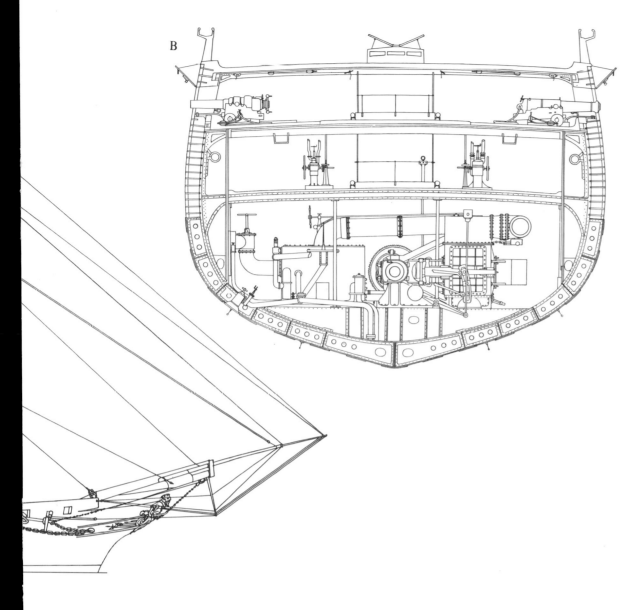

B

was 5,675 tons, her length was 235 foot (71.6 m), and she could reach a maximum speed of 12 knots.

1860

The WARRIOR, the first British ironclad, is commissioned for the Royal Navy as a direct reaction to the building of the GLORIE by the French. Her hull was constructed of iron that was further reinforced by armour plating along a 200-foot (61 m) section amidships. The WARRIOR mounted twenty-eight 7-inch (177.8 mm) muzzle-loading guns. Her displacement was 9,210 tons, and her length 380 foot (115.8 m).

1860

At this time, the U.S.A. could boast the largest merchant navy fleet in the world. Her ocean-going tonnage was less than half that of Great Britain, but America's lake and coastal shipping was enormous. The U.S.A.'s total tonnage was 2,500,000; Britain's was 2,000,000. No other nation topped the million mark. Understandably, America lost this supremacy from 1861 onwards. Four years of the Civil War were followed by the gathering momentum of expansion westwards across the open plains, and this at a time when America had little or no capital for spending on world sea trade.

JUNE 17, 1860

The maiden voyage of the GREAT EASTERN commences from Southampton.

Brunel had contracted to build for the Eastern Steam Co. a ship 'no less than five times as large as any ship previously built'. He wanted to call his new ship the LEVIATHAN, but when the MAMMOTH was renamed GREAT WESTERN, he agreed upon GREAT EASTERN.

The idea was that the ship should be large enough to carry sufficient coal to steam from England to Ceylon without having to bunker en route. At the time when the GREAT EASTERN was planned, the HIMALAYA, a P. & O. ship, was the largest vessel afloat. She was 340 foot (103.6 m) long, and 3,500 gross tonnage. Brunel's new ship was to be a staggering 680 foot (207.3 m) in length, and 118 foot (36.0 m) wide over the paddle-boxes. Her displacement was 27,400 tons, and her gross tonnage 18,915. She was driven by both propeller and paddles, the only vessel ever to have been built with this combination of propulsion units.

Her keel was laid sideways on to the River Thames on May 1, 1854. It was not until January 31, 1858, that she became waterborne. By this time, £750,000 had been spent on her, and she was still unfinished. The Eastern Steam Ship Co. could not complete her, so she was sold for £160,000 to the Great Ship Co. for the North Atlantic service. She was finally completed in September, 1858.

The GREAT EASTERN left Southampton on her maiden voyage on June 17, 1860. The

---

the City Fathers of Bremen decided to give a charter, dated December 8, 1856, to H. H. Meier. In order to indicate to intending passengers the excellence and reliability of the ships—the BREMEN, NEW YORK, HUDSON, and WESER—H. H. Meier called his company 'Norddeutscher Lloyd'—North German Lloyd.

Later, this introduction of the name 'Lloyd' became fairly common practice. The word appears in many shipping companies' names.

SEPTEMBER 13, 1858

The H.A.P.A.G. vessel AUSTRIA is destroyed by fire at sea. The tragedy was caused during the routine fumigation of the emigrants' quarters. In those days, fumigation was carried out by dipping a red-hot chain into a bucket of tar. On this singularly unlucky, windy thirteenth, the chain was too hot. The tar ignited and spilt onto the deck. The ship was engulfed; 471 of the 538 aboard the ship perished.

1859

Oil has been known as a scientific curiosity for a very long time. Surface oil has been used even by primitive peoples for various purposes. In 1859, a Colonel Drake struck oil at Titusville in the U.S.A. There immediately began an export trade in the commodity.

1859

The first 'ironclad', the French GLOIRE, is launched. She had the conventional wooden hull, but this was covered from a point 6 foot (1.8 m) below the water-line right up to the main deck with two layers of iron plating, to a total thickness of 4½ inches (114.3 mm). Originally, the GLORIE mounted thirty 36-pound smooth-bore muzzle-loading guns. However, these were replaced with the new breech-loading type gun. She carried the at that time incredible armament of six 9.4-inch (238.8 mm), and two 6.4-inch (162.6 mm) guns. Her displacement

151

John Ericsson's MONITOR *(top right), 1862, the first ship to be equipped with a gun turret, was one of the many designs which came from the fertile imagination of the Swedish-American engineer. On this page, we illustrate an earlier Ericsson design for a monitor. This was to have been driven by hand-cranked propellers.*

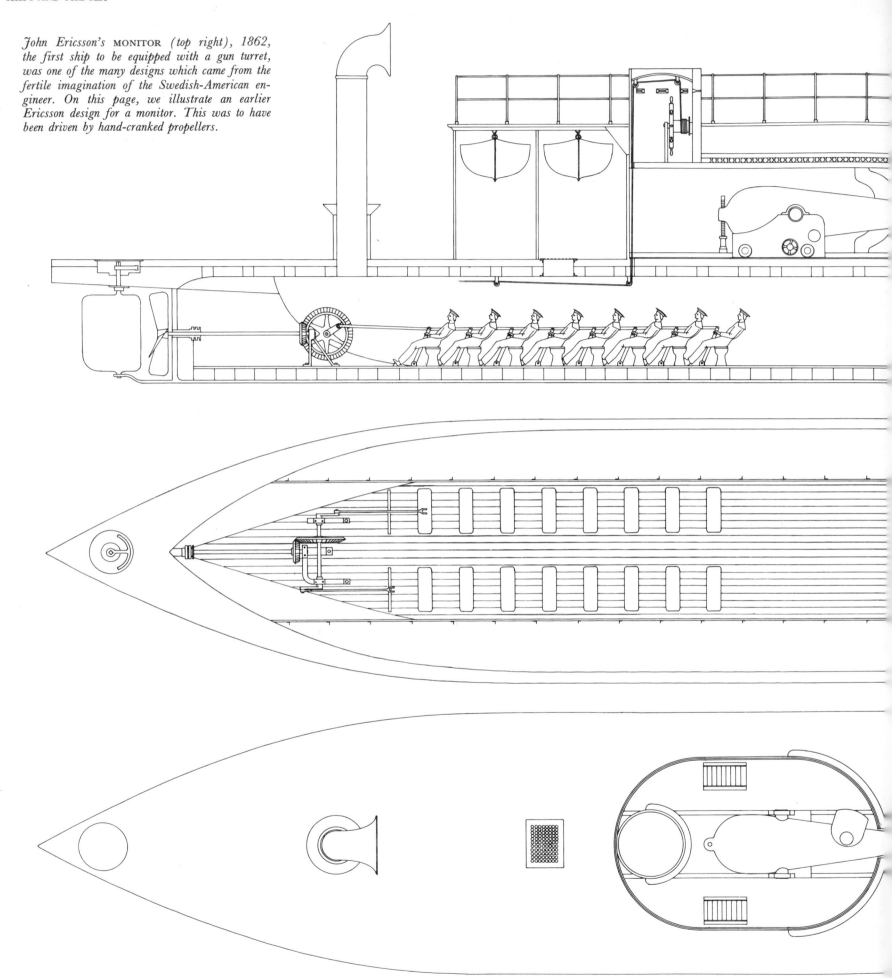

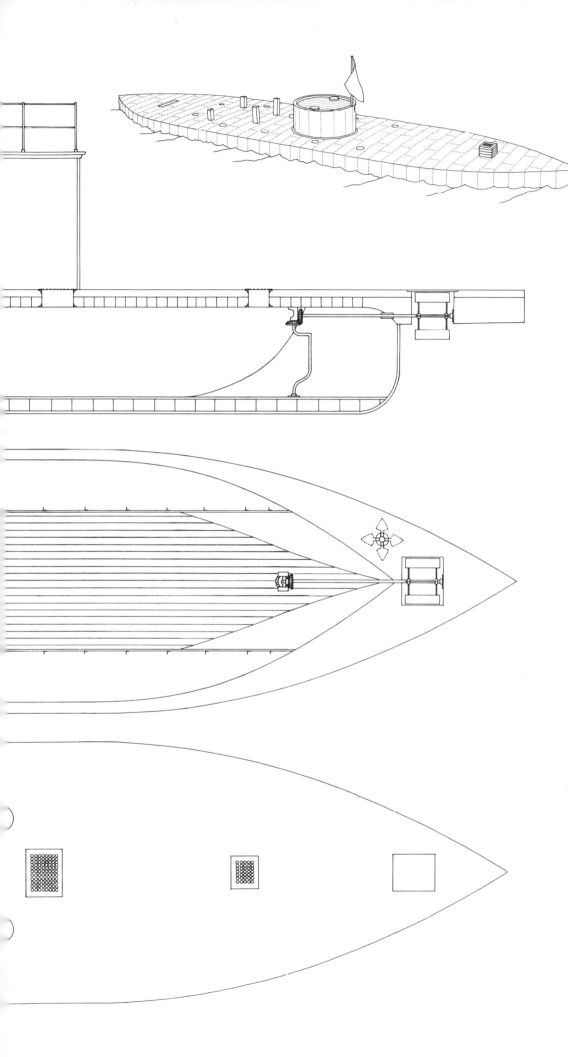

crossing took 11 days and $13\frac{1}{4}$ hours, compared to the record at that time of 9 days and 18 hours. She had a crew of 400, first-class accommodation for 800, second-class for 2,000, and third-class for 1,200. On that maiden voyage, she carried only 40 passengers, who had each paid £75 for the trip.

This, unfortunately, was to be the pattern of the economics of the GREAT EASTERN. Great as she undoubtedly was, she was a continuing loss-maker. In fact, she only made eleven transatlantic voyages. For Brunel had overlooked one fundamental point which dogged his masterpiece all her life: her enormous size. In the 1860s, the ports of the world were just not equipped to receive such a Goliath among ships. Safe anchorages were too shallow to accept her. Docks could not take her. Piers and jetties were too small. The ship also had one disturbing characteristic: she rolled considerably and alarmingly. Within five years of her completion, the mighty GREAT EASTERN had become an embarrassing white elephant.

Although taken off the Atlantic run, yet she performed many less glamorous tasks. From 1864 to 1866, she laid the transatlantic cables. Her vast holds were capable of carrying over 1,000 miles (1,600 km) of cable at a time. In 1867, she was used as a special excursion ship taking Americans to France for the Paris Exhibition. Towards the end of her comparatively long life, she, too, became an exhibition —a floating one, at Liverpool. In 1888, she was dismantled piecemeal at Birkenhead.

The GREAT EASTERN was a liability to those who owned her. She managed to survive in one capacity or another for twenty-eight years, and during all that time she was the largest ship in the world. It was not until 1899 that the White Star Co. built the OCEANIC that exceeded her in length, and then built the CELTIC in 1901—the first ship to exceed her in tonnage.

It was the late A. C. Hardy, who summed up the GREAT EASTERN when he remarked to the author: 'For forty years that darned ship ruined every record book, upset all average tables, and was the exception to every rule. Brunel had no right to play about with history like that!' But then, Brunel built three ships only, and all of them were 'Great'.

1861-65

Considerable naval activity takes place during the American Civil War. The Confederate, or Southern, States put privateers to sea. The Northern States blockade the Southern ports. In support of troop movements, numerous actions are fought between single ships from the two sides.

The most famous encounter of the Civil War is between the MERRIMACK of the Confederate States and the MONITOR of the Northern States. Their encounter on March 8, 1861, on Hampton Roads, was the world's first engagement between ironclads.

The MERRIMACK was a converted steam screw frigate with ten guns and a ram-bow. The screw-driven MONITOR had two 11-inch (279.4 mm) guns in a revolving turret, and was little more than a floating gun platform. The duel lasted for four hours without either vessel sustaining any real damage. The engagement proved the value of armoured ships.

Some Confederate privateers had astonishing records. The ALABAMA, for example, ranged the Atlantic and Indian oceans for two years. She captured thirty-eight ships before the Federal, or Northern, ship KEARSARGE finally sank her. The FLORIDA sank thirty-seven ships in just over a year.

The Confederate torpedo-sloops were small steam launches which had a mine, called a torpedo, fastened to the end of a long pole projecting over the bow. The mine detonated on impact with the side of an enemy vessel. The defence against the torpedo-sloop was a floating boom rigged 15-20 foot (4.6-6.1 m) away from the hull.

It was the Northern States that introduced the underwater mine. These early mines were connected by wires to electric plungers on shore, and were detonated at the appropriate moment.

1861

The Spanish Government awards its Central American mail contract to A. Lopez of Alicante. Spain still had direct control of several South American and Central American areas at this time. The Lopez enterprise expanded over the years. In 1881, it was reorganized to form the Compania Transatlantica, a company which is still thriving today under the name Compania Transatlantica Española.

1861

The first oil-tanker is launched. She is the sailing-ship ELIZABETH WATTS, built on the River Tyne, in England, specifically for the carriage of oil. She was fitted with eight tanks, thus giving rise to the expression 'oil-tanker'. Two of her masts were hollow so as to allow for the expansion of the oil.

JULY 1861

Two brothers, Emile and Isaac Periere, obtain the French mail contract between France and the United States, Mexico, the West Indies, and Central America. The following month, the Emperor Napoleon III gave the company which the brothers formed its present name, the Compagnie Générale Transatlantique—the C.G.T. or the French Line. It is now one of the foremost shipping companies in the whole world.

1862

A Spanish inventor, Monturiol, has the claim to be called the 'father of the modern submarine'. His vessel, EL ICTINEO, may still be seen at Cartagena in southern Spain. This

A MERRIMAC, *1855, which fought the famous duel against the* MONITOR *in the American Civil War.*
B EL ICTINEO, *the first Spanish submarine, 1862.*
C LE PLONGEUR, *the first French submarine, 1863.*
D WASHINGTON, *1864.*
E NORTHUMBERLAND, *1864.*
F *A French-designed propeller, 1860s.*
G KEARSARGE, *the Union ship which sank the Confederate* ALABAMA *in the English Channel, 1864.*

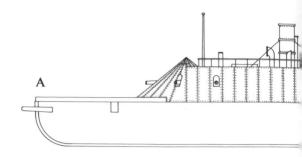

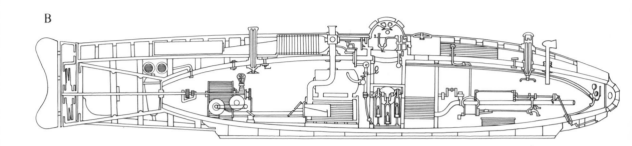

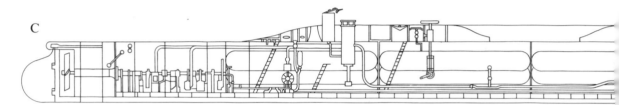

submarine has a double hull, steam propulsion, ballast tanks, and a chemical plant that produces oxygen. The EL ICTINEO was well ahead of her time.

1863

The most serious rival to EL ICTINEO, LE PLONGEUR, is built in France. The French submarine was driven by compressed air.

All early submarines had problems of stability, and they were extremely sensitive under water. The slightest inbalance in the trim would send them straight to the bottom. Later, bow hydroplane rudders were devised to prevent plunging.

1864

Money Wigram and Co. commences its regular steam services to Australia. The company had, in fact, operated a service there since 1837, using sailing-ships. Now they experimented with auxiliary-engined sailing-ships. Sail was utilized whenever possible, but in periods of calm or light breezes, the auxiliary engine was used. The NORTHUMBERLAND, which went into service in 1864, is a typical auxiliary-engined sailing-ship. This type of vessel enjoyed some success on long voyages, and some were kept in service until 1882.

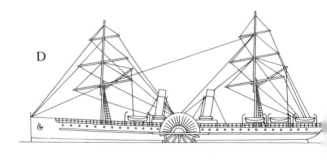

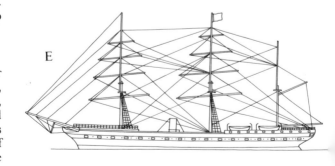

F

G

JUNE 15, 1864
The Cie. Générale Transatlantique inaugurates its transatlantic service when the WASHINGTON, a paddle-steamer, sails out from Le Havre bound for New York.

THE TEA TRADE

Tea, of course, had been well-known in Europe since soon after the middle of the seventeenth century. Samuel Pepys mentions it in his famous diary as early as 1661. It was China tea, and must have come by the overland route. It was not until 1664 that the East India Co. brought a cargo of tea by the sea route. Part of the consignment, some two pounds and two ounces (1 kg), valued at £85, was given as a gift to Charles II.

Tea found a continuing market. The East India Co., therefore, quickly built tea factories and warehouses, as did the Dutch East India Co. on the other side of the Channel. Their tea was much cheaper than that which was imported into England. A thriving tea-smuggling industry soon developed and kept the revenue men busy in the early years of the eighteenth century.

The tea trade was very profitable. Tea could be bought in China for the equivalent of five pence a pound (0.5 kg), and be sold on the

London market for sixty pence a pound. It was also, as far as England was concerned, a monopolistic business, for the East India Co. did not lose its monopoly until the passing of the Repeal Act of May 22, 1834. Three days later, the first free trade ships left China. The China tea trade had begun.

Initially, there was no urgency in bringing supplies to Europe. The 'Tea Wagons', as the cargo vessels were nicknamed, were a motley assortment of craft whose size and speed varied enormously. In 1849, as we have seen, foreign vessels were legally permitted to carry cargoes to England. In that same year, the Californian Gold Rush commenced. The two disparate events were made for each other. The New York clippers took miners and cargoes out to San Francisco. However, they could find no return cargoes for transhipment to the Atlantic seaboard ports of America. Therefore, they hurried across the Pacific, loaded up with tea, and raced back to London.

This could have been built up into a lucrative trade for the American clipper owners. The speed of their ships justified a freight price in Hong Kong of £6 per forty cubic foot (1.1 m³) of space. This compared with the £3.50 per forty cubic foot of space in the much slower Tea Wagons.

Unfortunately for the Americans, their clippers were far too numerous for everybody to share in the tea trade. They were also too big. The British clippers were somewhat smaller. At first, they suffered from various defects. They were too narrow in the beam, too fine in the hull, and were known as 'wet' ships because they took too much water aboard, which could damage the cargo. However, when these defects were rectified in later designs, the British clippers were able to dominate the profitable tea trade.

It was now the British clippers that had it all their own way, particularly when the Indian tea trade bid fair to rival the China tea trade, although Indian tea was a late arrival on the English market. Smith's City Line, which operated between Calcutta and London, very quickly established itself as the leading specialist tea carriers. But not even the English clippers could compete with the Suez Canal when it was opened in 1869. Steam, as has already been noted, was going to push sail from the oceans of the world.

THE CHINA TEA RACE
Perhaps the most famous China tea race was that between the two clippers ARIEL and TAEPING. They both left Foochow on May 30,

A *Lantern from Broström's* MATHILDA.
B MATHILDA, *bought by Broström in 1865.*

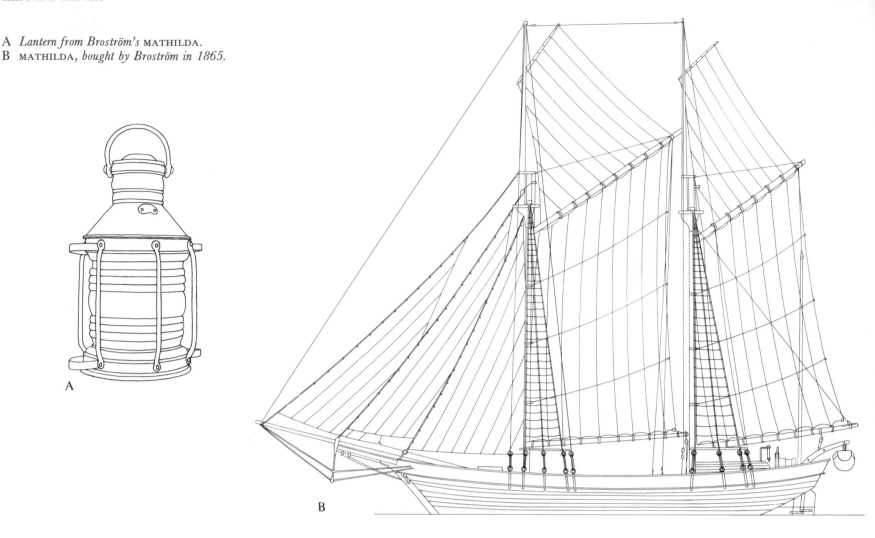

A

B

1866, loaded with tea for the London market. They set the same homeward course—and never lost sight of each other! On September 5, on the ninety-ninth day of the voyage, they both raced up the English Channel at a spanking thirteen knots. Less than an hour separated the two clippers. ARIEL reached the waiting tugs first. Forty minutes later, the TAEPING reached the same point.

This was not all. Behind these two clippers came the SERICA, with her sails visible from the deck of the TAEPING. From the SERICA could also be seen the FIERY CROSS and the TAITSING screaming along an hour or so in the rear. In fact, all five clippers docked on the same tide.

There was more than mere prestige in being the first clipper home. The first tea landed of the new crop had a scarcity value, and could command a premium on the market. In that memorable race of 1866, five clippers docking on the same day, bringing five cargoes of tea, actually had the effect of depressing the market considerably, so that the tea merchants were unable to obtain premium prices—much to their annoyance!

Yards that specialized in the building of clippers employed designers who knew to a fraction the right degree of curve to give to the lines. The Greenock yard of Robert Steele and

Son was fortunate to have one such designer. ARIEL, TAEPING, and SERICA were all 'Steele'-built clippers. Deep-sea sailors could look at a four-master, and say with accuracy not only who built her, but also who designed her. Bernard Waymouth, the designer of the THERMOPYLAE, and Hercules Linton, who designed the CUTTY SARK, the TWEED, and many other equally famous clippers, left such a distinctive imprint upon their ships that they might just as well have signed them with their own names.

THE GUANO TRADE
Not so glamorous as the tea and wool trades was the trade in guano, which aided the world's farming industry long before nitrates and other types of fertilizers were used.

For centuries, sea birds, such as the cormorant, pelican, penguin, and albatross, had reared their young on isolated islands in the Pacific. The droppings accumulated over the years, and became veritable hoards of fertilizer, in which a lucrative trade developed.

The Peruvian islands of Chincha, Ballestas, Lobos, and Guanape were the main sources of supply. The islands were all inhospitable and completely arid. Loading the precious cargo of guano could take as long as three

months. The ships engaged in the trade had to call at Callao first. There they were inspected, provisioned, and received their sailing orders. Between 1851 and 1872, ten million tons of guano were lifted from Chincha alone. Five thousand ship loads were needed to shift this mountain of droppings.

The trade was largely controlled from England. Anthony Gibbs and Co. of Liverpool had the franchise from 1856 to 1862.

1865
The twenty-seven-year-old Axel Broström, an ambitious young Swede, borrows the equivalent of £110 and buys the eighty-ton wooden ketch MATHILDA. Broström's home town was Kristinehamn on Lake Väner, from which the sea was reached by way of the Trollhätte Canal and the Göta River to Gothenburg. When he bought the MATHILDA, only four ships were registered at Kristinehamn.

When he was thirty-one, Broström bought his first steamer, a converted schooner named JOHN. Thereafter, the Broström enterprises flourished. When the centenary of the purchase of that first ketch was celebrated in 1965, the Broström fleet numbered eighty-five ships, controlled by the Tirfing Co., the Swedish American Line, the Swedish East Asiatic Co.,

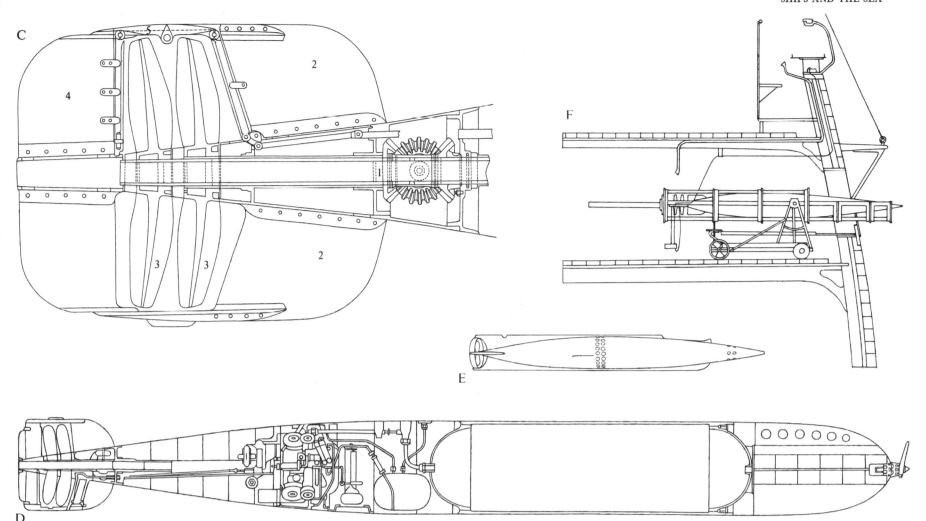

C *The tail assembly of a typical torpedo of the type developed from the Whitehead torpedo, 1866.*
1 *Propeller shafts*
2 *Fins*
3 *Contra-rotating propellers*
4 *Warhead*
5 *Horizontal rudders*
D *Longitudinal section of a torpedo.*
E *The first Whitehead torpedo, 1866.*
F *Torpedo-launching system for an early type of Whitehead torpedo.*

the Swedish Orient Line Ocean Co., the Timex Co., the Fern S.S. Co., the Motor Tank Co., the Broström Tender Service, and the Albatross Co.

1865

Alfred Holt installs compound engines in his new Far East traders, the AGAMEMNON, the AJAX, and the ACHILLES. They are twin tandem compound engines driving one screw. The vessels' average fuel consumption was twenty tons of coal a day each. They carried enough fuel to make the voyage to China and back, re-coaling only once on each leg, at Mauritius.

THE WOOL TRADE

English wool had been exported since Roman times. From 1660, manufactured woollen goods only were allowed to be exported, the exporting of wool itself being prohibited until 1825. Similarly, the importing of wool was banned. The ban on imported wool was lifted in 1828, and Spain became the first source of imported wool into England.

In 1788, sheep had been taken to Australia as food for the penal colonies. Once again, shippers were confronted with the age-old problem of having adequate outbound and poor homeward cargoes. The sheep that had been

taken to Australia were crossed with an Indian breed, and this produced prolific herds. In 1820, wool began to be shipped to England.

Freight cost 4½ pence per pound (0.5 kg), and the London selling price was 43 pence. By 1850, 130,000 bales were shipped to the value of £2,600,000. Thereafter, all companies regarded wool as the most important inbound cargo.

New Zealand received her first sheep in 1848. By 1856, the largest exporters of wool from New Zealand were a Mr. Shaw and a Mr. Savill, who founded the Shaw-Savill Line, later the Shaw, Savill and Albion Line.

The loading of wool, like cotton, was achieved by screwing. The bales of wool were first loaded, and were then forced apart so that a third bale could be introduced. By screwing, the CUTTY SARK once carried 5,010 bales of wool, which was 800 more than her official capacity.

One unhappy by-product of wool was fleas. They made life intolerable in the tropics. To avoid them, the crew often slept on deck in the centre of a wet patch.

Some fine runs were achieved by wool ships. Three of the fastest from Australia were those of the CUTTY SARK, 67 days; the PATRIARCH, 68 days; and the CRUSADER, 69 days.

CUTTY SARK
A *The albatross was the sailor's friend, the herald of fair winds and good fortune.*
B CUTTY SARK, *one of the greatest of the clipper ships, was built in 1869.*
C *How the tea chests were packed in the hold of a clipper ship.*

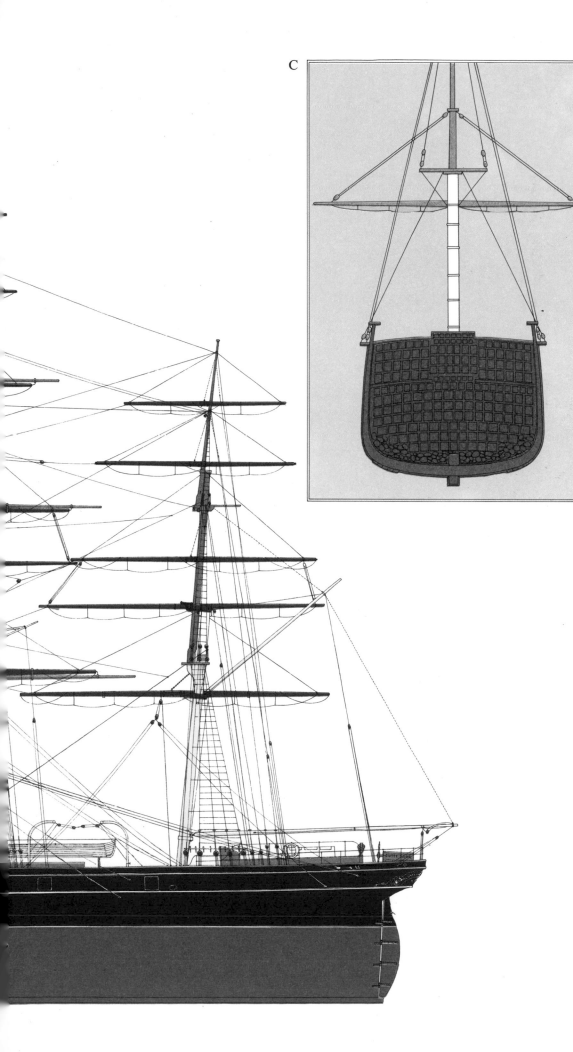

C

JULY 20, 1866

The first fleet action with ironclads takes place. The occasion was the Battle of Lissa, during the Third Italian War of Independence from Austria. A fleet of Italian warships, twenty-four strong, formed in three squadrons under the leadership of Admiral Carlo Pellion di Persano, attempted to take the island of Lissa which is off the Dalmatian coast in the Adriatic. He acted in such a dilatory manner that a smaller force of Austrian warships under the command of Admiral Wilhelm von Tegetthoff was able to take him by surprise. The ensuing battle lasted some three hours. Admiral Tegetthoff's flagship, the FERDINAND MAX, sank the Italian flagship, RE D'ITALIA. An Italian ironclad, PALESTRO, commanded by Captain Alfredo Cappellini, was also sunk, whilst the AFFONDATORE was severely damaged.

THE TORPEDO
1866

The torpedo is developed by a marine engineer, Robert Whitehead, working at Fiume for the Austrian Government, in association with a Captain Luppis. His prototype weighed 300 pounds (136.1 kg), and had a war-head filled with 18 pounds (8.2 kg) of dynamite. The torpedo was fired from a special tube, and was screw-propelled by a compressed-air engine.

In 1871, Whitehead's patent was purchased by the British Navy for £15,000. He returned to London, where he continued to work on the weapon.

Progressively, various improvements have been incorporated. For example, the hydrostatic valve gives it a depth-keeping control. In 1876, the introduction of a servo-motor counteracted the 'porpoising' effect. Still later, in 1895, the gyroscope was added to ensure a straight run. There have been other refinements added, but Whitehead's basic design has not changed fundamentally since its inception. Yet, when the weapon was first fired in anger—in 1877 by the cruiser SHAH against the Peruvian monitor HUASCAR, whose crew had mutinied—it failed. A few months later, in January, 1878, the Russian CONSTANTINE sank a Turkish patrol-boat off Batoum in the Caspian Sea.

The German rival to the torpedo was the 'Schwartzkopf', whilst those of the U.S.A. were the 'Bliss-Leavitt' and the 'Howell'.

SEPTEMBER 6, 1869

The Oceanic Steam Navigation Co. is founded by Thomas Ismay and Gustave Schwabe. It operates the famous White Star Line, whose first four ships are built by Harland & Wolff in Belfast. Schwabe's nephew was Gustav Wolff, co-founder of the shipyard. The four vessels were named OCEANIC, ATLANTIC, BALTIC, and REPUBLIC, thus starting a tradition of naming all the ships specifically built for the line with a word ending in -ic.

The White Star Line's four ships were much in advance of other ships then existing, in design as well as performance. In order to compete, other lines were forced to re-think their own designs, and to build bigger and better vessels.

NOVEMBER 17, 1869

The Suez Canal is opened by the Empress Eugènie, aboard the French royal yacht L'AIGLE, which leads a procession of sixty-nine steamships through the Canal from the Mediterranean. The previous night, the Egyptian steam frigate LATIF had grounded near Kantara. Luckily, the waterway was cleared five minutes before the procession was due.

Plans to build a canal connecting the two seas survive from 1504, but nothing was done until Napoleon Bonaparte occupied Egypt in 1798, and resuscitated the scheme. Unfortunately, the surveyor Le Père announced that the level of the Red Sea was 32 foot (9.8 m) above that of the Mediterranean, and the scheme was shelved once more.

An English expert, F. R. Chesney, disproved this eventually, but the British, who at the time occupied Egypt, were then engaged in building a railway between the two seas, and nothing was done.

In 1854, Said Pasha, the Khedive of Egypt, granted permission to the French engineer, Ferdinand de Lesseps, to go ahead with his canal scheme. It took him five years to collect the funds and the technical experts, but at last, construction work began at Port Said on April 25, 1859.

At first, the Suez Canal was little used. In 1870, only 486 steamers, with an average size of only 1,000 tons, passed through. But when Egypt nationalized the Canal in 1956, 14,600 ships, with an average tonnage of 8,000, were using the waterway each year.

1870

The Dominion Line is a name that is known all over the world, yet it is only a nickname! In 1870, the Liverpool and Mississippi S.S. Co. had a fleet of steamers trading between England and the former Confederate States, now firmly incorporated within the new United States of America. In 1872, the company's MISSISSIPPI inaugurated a new service to the Dominion of Canada. This route not only became the company's principal service; it also provided the nickname by which the company was known throughout several changes of name. In 1903, the name was changed to the White Star-Dominion Line. In 1926, the White Star Line was taken over by the Royal Mail Line, although it kept its name.

1870

The Papal Navy had been in existence for nearly a thousand years. At the Battle of Lepanto, 1571, the Papal fleet played a decisive role. In 1754, Pope Benedict XIV bought two 30-gun English frigates, and renamed them S. PIETRO and S. PAOLO respectively. There was even a Papal dockyard at Civitavecchia. Three steam

A

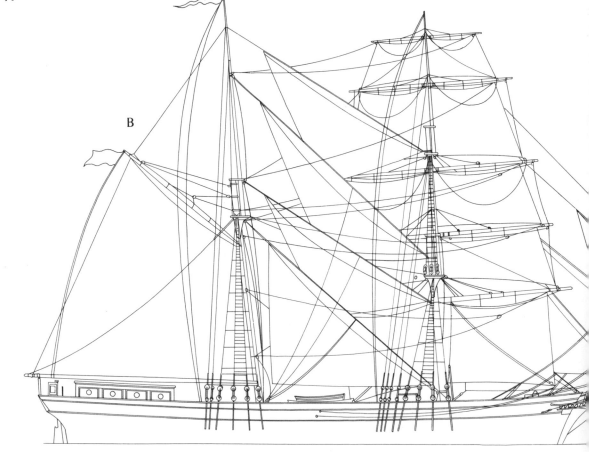

B

A *The opening of the Suez Canal, 1869.*
B *The ill-fated brigantine* MARY CELESTE, *built in 1861 as the* AMAZON.

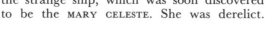

tugs, the ARCHIMEDES, the PAPIN, and the BLASES DE GARAY, operated a service on the River Tiber in 1842. In 1859, the last Papal ship was completed. She was the IMMACOLATA CONCEPZIONE, which looked like an elegant yacht, but which was designed to protect the fishing fleets.

Pope Pius IX decided that it was time to divest the Papacy of its maritime interests. In 1870, he donated the IMMACOLATA CONCEPZIONE to the French, who renamed her the LOIRE in 1883. She was finally lost in the Mediterranean in 1905.

1870

The compound engine is introduced on the Atlantic run. Norddeutscher Lloyd's HUDSON, sold after a fire to the National Line (who named her the LOUISIANA), is lengthened, fitted with compound engines, and entered on Atlantic service as the HOLLAND.

1870

The New Zealand Shipping Co. is formed with a capital of a quarter of a million pounds by a group of Christchurch businessmen, who were dissatisfied with the poor and unreliable services to and from New Zealand. The company would charter vessels, not build them, and their first chartered ship was an iron sailing-vessel, the WAITARA. All N.Z.S.Co. ships were given Maori names. In 1883, the company decided to buy their ships, and the first vessel bought was the steamship TONGARIRO.

DECEMBER 4, 1872

There have always been stories of mysteries at sea. Indeed, several of these have been recorded in this work, mysteries that often have to do with the total disappearance of vessels. However, the story of the MARY CELESTE is not that of another disappearance—on the contrary. For the MARY CELESTE did not disappear. Her crew did!

The departure of the MARY CELESTE out of her home port of New York was just another ordinary sailing. She went about her business in deep waters. Everybody connected with her knew that she had embarked on just another voyage, and that, in the fulness of time, she would return to New York and carry on with her rather humdrum task of carting cargo various distances for various shippers.

On December 4, 1872, the Nova Scotian brigantine DEI GRATIA, scudding along some 600 miles (1,110 km) off the coast of Portugal, noticed a sailing-ship nearby. The DEI GRATIA moved closer. Her crew noticed that the ship with which she was closing had her jib and fore-topsail set, but that the lower fore-topsail was hanging down. All other canvas was furled.

Repeated hailings from the DEI GRATIA failed to elicit any reply. A party was sent aboard the strange ship, which was soon discovered to be the MARY CELESTE. She was derelict.

The ship's log showed that her master, a thirty-eight-year-old competent mariner named Benjamin Briggs, had made his last entry on November 24 of that year. Everything seemed in order. Indeed, the table was set for a meal. There was preserved meat in the galley. The ship carried sufficient food to last for six months. Strangely, the ship's boat, the sextant, chronometer, and navigation books were not on board the ship.

The forecastle showed clear signs of having been hastily abandoned. But there was no apparent reason for the desertion. The vessel was in good trim and undamaged. True, the fore and lazarette hatch covers lay upside down on the deck. But her cargo of 1,700 barrels of alcohol was untouched except for one barrel which had been broached.

The story of the MARY CELESTE moves on to Gibraltar, where an exhaustive court of enquiry was held. Even the crew of the DEI GRATIA were suspect, for they could have murdered the captain, his family, and the crew of the MARY CELESTE, although why they should have done that is beyond logic. Had there been some sort of mutiny on the ship, which alone survived to bear mute testimony of such an outrage? But the stains on the deck were not blood-stains. Even Barbary pirates came under suspicion, although nobody explained what any coastal pirate was doing so far out to sea.

Deep as the court delved, the members could not find a single clue. Mystified, the court closed its hearing without coming to any sort of conclusion.

For years, people waited for some sign of the missing crew. But the silence has continued down the still reticent years.

And history is still silent about the greatest unsolved mystery of the sea. All that is positively known is that Captain Briggs and his entire crew vanished from the face of the earth leaving only one clue, a frayed and severed rope trailing alongside the ship. Volumes have been written, promoting theory after theory to explain the mystery. But the sea, like the Sphinx, is as enigmatic and inscrutable as ever.

JANUARY 19, 1873

The first service of the newly-founded Red Star Line commences when the VADERLAND leaves Antwerp for Philadelphia. Named after its house flag, the Red Star Line was owned by the Société Anonyme de Navigation Belge-Américaine, a subsidiary of the International Navigation Co.

Soon, a service to New York was started and, within five years, this had become more important than the Philadelphia service. To consolidate this position, the parent company, the International Navigation Co., purchased the American Line in 1884, and the Inman Line in 1886. By 1901, I.N.C. had grown to become the International Mercantile Marine Co., and had absorbed the White Star, Dominion, Atlantic Transport, and Leyland Lines.

A *A lighthouse lamp with four wicks which burned
paraffin oil, c. 1880.*
B *The frames and plating of a riveted steel ship, late
nineteenth century.*

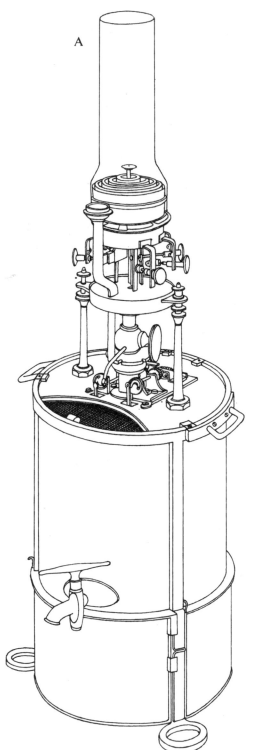

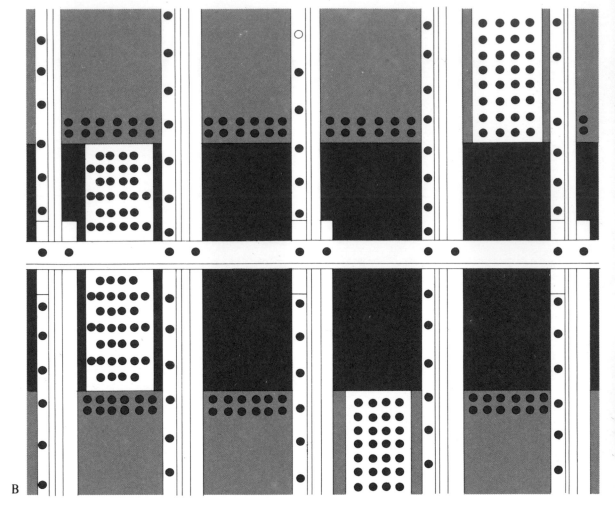

Further, it had links with H.A.P.A.G., N.D.L.,
and Holland-America.

APRIL 1, 1873
The White Star Line's ATLANTIC is wrecked off
Halifax with a loss of 585 souls. This is the
worst sea disaster up to this time.

APRIL 18, 1873
The Holland America Line—H.A.L.—is founded in Rotterdam from the Plate, Reuchlin
and Co. concern, which sells the ROTTERDAM
and the MAAS to the new line. A year later,
H.A.L. buys the W. A. SCHOLTEN and the
P. CALAND.

1874
Smoking is permitted for the first time on
Atlantic liners.

1875
James Anderson was a Scot from Petershead.
In 1828, he joined James Thompson and Co.,
and in 1869, his family took it over. In 1874,
the Pacific Steam Navigation Co. could not
keep all its steamers fully occupied, so in 1875,
Anderson, Anderson and Co., of which James

Anderson was the progenitor, offered to operate
the vessels in partnership with Frederick Green
and Co. Further, they offered to operate a
service to Australia by way of the Cape.
   The offer was accepted. In March, 1877, a
sailing schedule for the LUSITANIA, CHIMBORAZO,
and CUZCO, all belonging to the Pacific Steam
Navigation Co., was advertised under the name
of the Orient Line. A year later, the Orient
Steam Navigation Co. Ltd. was formed,
purchased the three vessels that it was already
operating under the guise of the Orient Line,
purchased a sister ship, the GARONNE, from
the Pacific Steam Navigation Co., and commenced trading in its own right.

DECEMBER 8, 1875
The TORRENS commences her maiden voyage,
the last composite, fully rigged passenger clipper
to be built in Britain, at James Laing's shipyard
in Sunderland. Her stern and keel were of
elm. She had iron frames with teak planking,
was copper fastened, and sheathed to the
water-line in yellow metal. The TORRENS was
of 1,276 tons, and she cost £27,257.

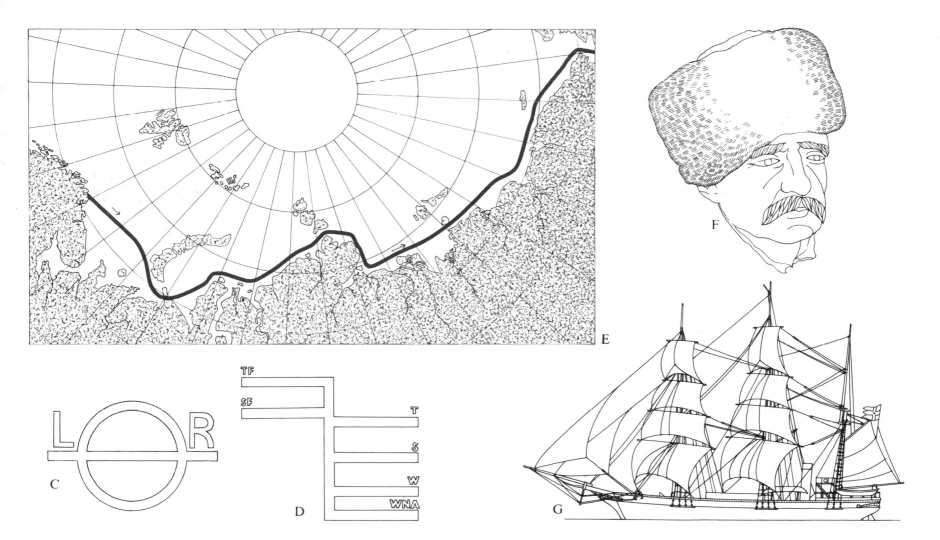

1876

One of the more unfortunate results of this upsurge in trade from 1830 onwards was that an increasing number of owners, agents, and managers tried to make a fast penny. This was often obtained by the unscrupulous and inexpert loading of ships, which resulted in an ever-increasing number of losses at sea. Old, rotten ships, called 'coffin ships', were continually and excessively overloaded, often deliberately so as to ensure their loss.

Samuel Plimsoll, a British Member of Parliament, campaigned for a law to compel owners to accept the safe load line. His campaign came to a successful conclusion in 1876, when the 'Plimsoll line' was adopted, together with other safety measures, such as the method of stowing deck cargoes.

1878

The Swedish explorer, Adolf E. Nordenskiöld, sails in the steam whaler VEGA to the east by way of the North East Passage, along the coast of northern Russia. The journey took a full year, from July, 1878, to July, 1879. The Russians call the route that he pioneered the 'Northern Sea Route'. It is used regularly between July

and October, although merchant ships have to be led by ice-breakers.

1879

Electric navigation lights had been fixed to the French Line's AMÉRIQUE in 1876. Three years later, the Inman Line's CITY OF BERLIN lit its dining saloon with electric lights.

1880

The Thingvalla Line is established in Denmark, taking its name from a steamer called the THINGVALLA, which had been built in 1874 for the Danish company, Sejl- og Dampskibsselskabet. The Thingvalla Line operated small and ageing steamers. In 1898, Det Forenede Dampskibs-Selskab of Copenhagen took over Sejl- og Dampskibsselskabet, and the New York service eventually blossomed into the Scandinavian-American Line.

1880

The BUENOS AYREAN, belonging to the Allen Line, is the first steel-hulled ship to enter Atlantic service.

By this time, steel hulls were becoming more common. The P. & O. Line found that their

C *Plimsoll mark.*
D *Ordinary loadlines. The letters indicate:*
  TF: fresh water tropical loadline
  SF: fresh water summer loadline
  T: salt water tropical loadline
  S: salt water summer loadline
  W: salt water winter loadline
  WNA: winter North Atlantic loadline
E *The route taken by Nordenskiöld on the first successful North-East Passage, 1878-79.*
F *Baron Nils Adolf Erik Nordenskiöld (1832-1901).*
G VEGA, *Nordenskiöld's ship.*

steel-built RAVENNA was much more satisfactory than both their iron-built ships, the ROHILLA and the ROSETTA, and after that all P. & O. vessels were made of steel.

1882

The Pennsylvania Railroad Co. had already backed the American Line in the Philadelphia-to-Liverpool service. Now, in conjunction with B. N. Baker, a Baltimore-to-Liverpool service was started. A new company, the Atlantic Transport Line, was formed to deal with this part of the trade.

Already, American wages and costs had shot ahead of British charges. In these circumstances, the new company's vessels flew the British flag, the 'Red Duster'.

NOVEMBER 23, 1882

The French shipping company, Messageries Maritimes, opens services to Australia, with the NATAL. The line offered sailings by way of Port Said, Mahe, Reunion, Mauritius, and Noumea to the various Australian ports. Seven vessels were built for the service.

1883

At this time, the Oceanic Steamship Co. begins to operate the steamers ALAMEDA and MARIPOSA from San Francisco to Honolulu. When Pacific Mail declined to renew its Australian mail contract in 1885, the Oceanic Steamship Co., in partnership with the Union Steamship Co. of New Zealand, took over the responsibility for carrying the mail. The ZEALANDIA was purchased from Pacific Mail, and Oceanic extended its passenger service to Australia. It is from these beginnings that the famous Matson Line originates.

1884

All the major navies of the world invest in torpedo-boats. Russia has most, a total of 115. France owns 50, but two years later orders another 34. Britain, strangely enough, has only 19.

1884

Charles Parsons invents an engine in which a jet of steam turned a multi-bladed shaft which was connected directly to the propeller. Pistons were thus dispensed with.

1885

The GLÜCKAUF, the first 'real' oil-tanker, with the characteristic profile, is built. Designed by Henry Swann and built by Armstrong Mitchell at their Newcastle shipyard in Britain for the Deutsche Amerikanische Petroleum Co., she had nine purpose-built tanks.

1887

The British Navy acquires its first submarine, the NAUTILUS, which is operated by a two-man crew. It is an experimental vessel only.

A GLÜCKAUF, *1885.*
B *Parsons's steam turbine engine, 1884.*
C TURBINIA, *1894.*

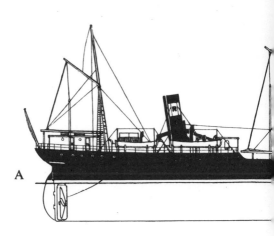

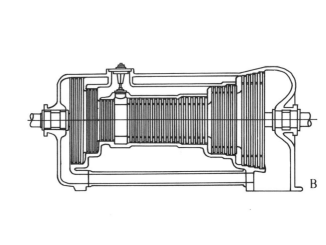

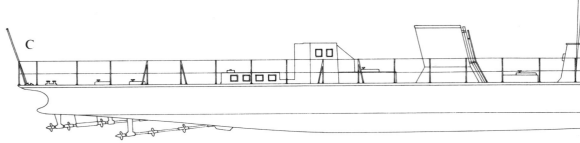

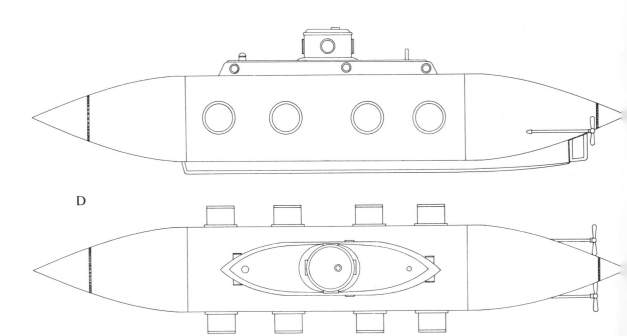

D NAUTILUS, *one of Britain's first submarines.*
E FRAM, *1893.*
F *The voyage of the* FRAM, *1893-96.*

1893
Fridtjof Nansen, the Norwegian Arctic explorer, drifts with the ice in his specially built ship FRAM from the Bering Strait to the Norwegian Sea. The voyage took three years.

1895
Stories concerning the disappearance of ships abound. Many ships which have 'disappeared' have, however, reappeared elsewhere after a lapse of time. Perhaps the HONRESFELD holds the record; she took a very long time indeed to disappear completely.

On December 20, 1892, the HONRESFELD caught fire some 100 miles (85 km) off the coast of Mexico. Her crew, unable to contain the flames, abandoned their vessel. Three years later, on December 28, 1895, the whaler ALICE KNOWLES sighted her 700 miles (1,296 km) beyond Midway Island. She was never seen again.

1896
The Italian Navy builds its first submarine, EL DELFINO, designed by Pullino.

1896
John P. Holland, the American submarine expert, builds his first experimental craft, the PLUNGER. This leads to the 'Holland Boat', the U.S. Navy's first underwater boat, 1899.

These boats were driven on the surface by a 50-h.p. petrol engine at 7 knots, and, whilst underwater, by a 50-h.p. electric motor that could run for three hours. They were armed with two internally-loaded torpedo-tubes.

1896
By the end of the century, nautical history was preoccupied with steam. But sail was still very much to the fore. Indeed, the famous Aberdeen Line was building sailing-ships right up to the end of the century. Their distinguished, green-hulled, immaculate ships had provided a connoisseur's service to Australia ever since the company's ANEMONE of 205 tons burthen first called there in 1840. In 1896, with its reputation still as high as ever, the Aberdeen Line was operating a mixed fleet that included at least five steamers, and nine sailing-ships.

AUGUST 17, 1896
Gold is found at Bonanza Creek, on the Klondyke River in the Yukon. As a result, about forty thousand people arrive in all manner of ships.

1897
At the Spithead Naval Review of 1897, the TURBINIA, a new craft named after Parsons's turbo-engine, dashed through the lines of assembled warships at 34.5 knots. Torpedo-boats that were sent to intercept her were left far behind. One very interested spectator was the German monarch, Kaiser Wilhelm.

The TURBINIA was fitted with three shafts. The engine drove the starboard shaft by way of a high-pressure turbine. The middle shaft was turned by the intermediate turbine. Lastly, the port shaft was turned by the low-pressure blades. The last element of the mechanism also incorporated a small reversing turbine.

Experiments with a model had shown that, at the high r.p.m.-speeds that were achieved, the propellers produced cavitation; that is, a hole in the water resulted. In order to get a grip of the water, three propellers were fitted to each shaft.

1898
The Cuban revolt against Spain was at its height when, in order to protect American interests on the island, the U.S. Government despatched the MAINE to Havana. Mysteriously, the MAINE blew up and sank. The Americans accused the Spanish of the deed, and, despite the fact that Spain was willing to go to arbitration, declared war. Hostilities lasted over seven months, by which time the Spanish fleets in the Philippines and in Cuba had been defeated.

THE CATTLE TRADE
It has been noted that the absence of homeward cargoes had exercised shipowners both in Europe and America during the middle years of the nineteenth century. The problem was largely resolved by bringing tea and wool to England and other European markets. The same kind of problem worried shipowners, agents, and managers from the 1880s, when the highly industrialized countries were exporting goods in ever-increasing quantities, without being able to obtain full cargoes for the inbound voyages. The bulk carriage of wheat and cattle was the answer to the shippers' problems.

Initial experiments in the carriage of live cattle were successful. At first, the cattle were carried on deck in collapsible wooden stalls. Later, the cattle were carried 'tween decks with electric light and adequate ventilation systems. In 1888, the White Star Line built the CUFIC, followed the next year by the RUNIC. These were the first two ships designed specifically for the cattle trade. Each could accommodate a thousand head of cattle. The

A *Illustrations showing the layout of the machinery of the first turbine-driven destroyer, the* VIPER, *1899.*
B CUFIC, *1888.*
C *Cattle-pens on the* CUFIC.
D *The first modern submarine, the* HOLLAND, *1897.*
E PLUNGER, *1896.*

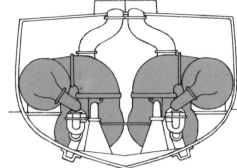

A

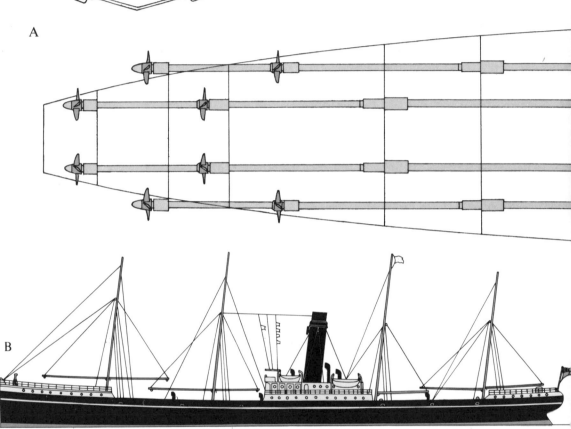

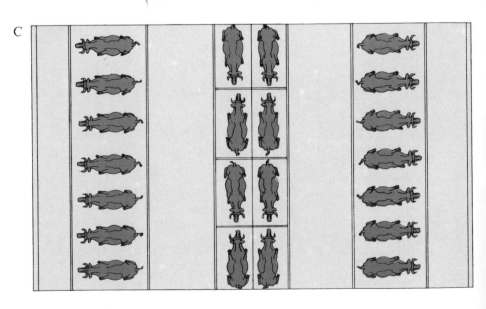

B

C

D

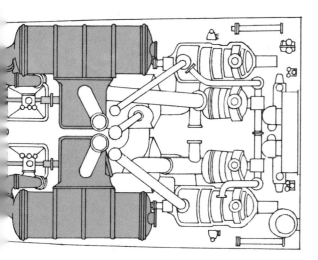

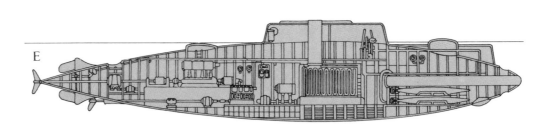

E

GEORGIC, built in 1894 for the White Star Line, was the largest ever cattle-ship.

Almost every North Atlantic operator equipped some ships with cattle stalls. The export of live cattle became a major feature of all the main ports of America and Canada. Chicago was the main centre of the cattle trade.

THE TORPEDO-BOAT

Whilst shippers were worried about cargoes, navies were worried about torpedoes. Robert Whitehead, as has been shown, made the torpedo a practical weapon for the navies of the world. There was one technical difficulty about the use of the torpedo; that of getting close enough to the enemy in order to be able to launch it with some hope of success. The solution was the torpedo-boat.

Britain was the innovator of the torpedo-boat, although other countries built them more extensively than did Britain. The prototype was the LIGHTNING, which, although she was only 84 foot (25.6 m) long, was capable of a speed of 20 knots. She was armed with two Whitehead torpedo-tubes. The LIGHTNING quickly demonstrated the devastating effect of her 'attacks'. During exercises, she 'sank' every capital ship against which she launched one of her torpedoes.

In order to offset the potential of the

torpedo-boat, the British Admiralty had built two torpedo-boat catchers, the GOSSAMER and the RATTLESNAKE. These two catchers, however, were only two knots faster than the prey they were supposed to hunt. Consequently, they failed to deter the attacks of the torpedo-boats.

Alfred Yarrow was accepted as the best builder of the fastest torpedo-boats. His firm, therefore, was given the problem of producing the deterrent to the torpedo-boat. He came up with the destroyer, and two were immediately ordered by the Admiralty. They were the HAVOCK and the HORNET. Each was capable of a speed of twenty-seven knots, and thus had the edge on the torpedo-boats. They were also armed with one 12-pounder and three 6-pounder guns, together with two beam torpedo-tubes.

The destroyers were an immediate success. Within a few years, all the major navies of the world possessed harbour and coastal defence torpedo-boats, whilst destroyers lurked in deep waters waiting to pounce on invading torpedo-boats. The race was soon initiated to possess the fastest and most seaworthy destroyers. These two criteria demanded that the destroyer must be of greater size than the original designs. Indeed, the destroyer became so much larger, so much more sophisticated, that by

1965 it had replaced the cruiser. Again, Britain led this particular armament race. The VIPER, which was built in 1899, was far in advance of any destroyer at that time. She was capable of thirty-seven knots, and was armed with the usual two torpedo-tubes. The VIPER was turbine-driven—the first destroyer to be equipped with this type of engine. However, the moving pistons and crankshafts of the reciprocating engine proved to be a serious handicap at speeds above thirty knots. Vibration and metal fatigue caused severe damage to the engines. Accidents were frequent. At thirty knots, the moving parts were only a blur of metal.

By the end of the nineteenth century, that is, just fifty years after the NAPOLEON had become the first real propeller-driven ship of the line, the navies of the world had changed out of all recognition. Armour plating, revolving turrets, speeds in excess of thirty knots, breech-loading guns, rifled barrels, torpedoes, mines—all these added to the increased efficiency of the warship. The Battle of Lissa can be seen to be a rehearsal for what was to come. However, it was not until the beginning of the twentieth century that the strategies, tactics, and equipment of modern navies could be proved in battle.

The first such proving-ground was to be the Russo-Japanese War.

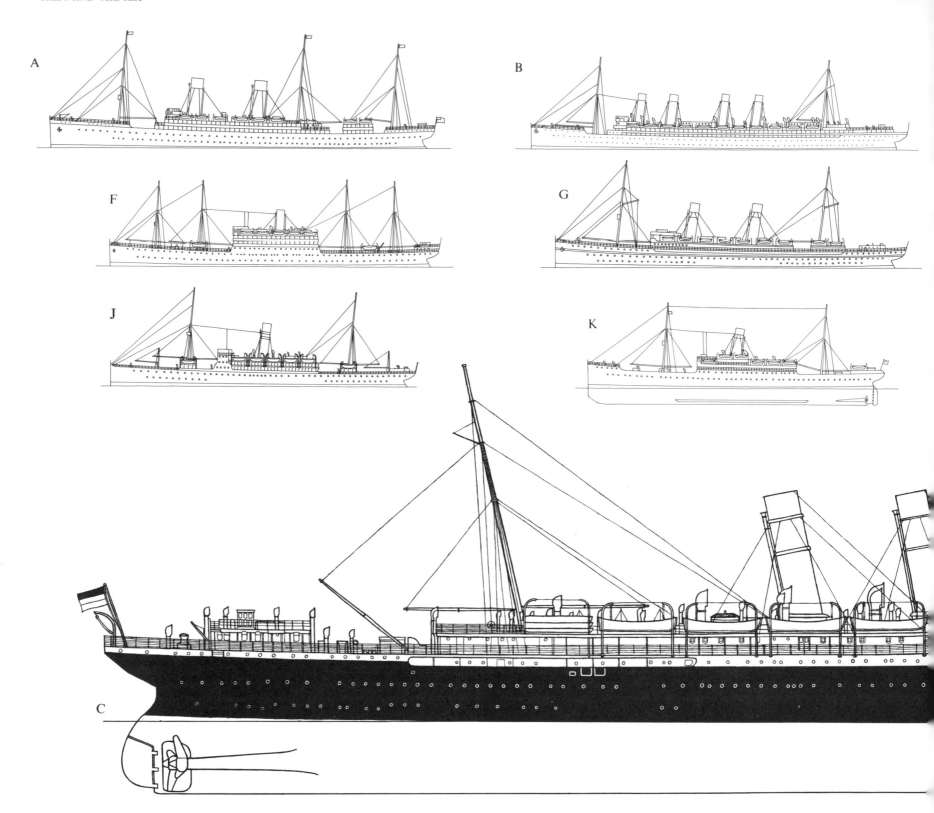

THE BIGGEST SHIPS IN THE WORLD,
1899

A OCEANIC, *1899. Owned by the White Star Line.
17,274 tons. 686×68 foot (209×20.8 m).*

B DEUTSCHLAND, *1899. Owned by the Hamburg
America Line. 16,703 tons. 663×67 foot (202.1
×20.4 m).*

C KAISER WILHELM DER GROSSE, *1897. Owned
by Norddeutscher Lloyd. 14,349 tons. 627×66
foot. (191.1×20.1 m).*

D LUCANIA, *1893. Owned by the Cunard Steamship Company. 12,950 tons. 601×65 foot (183.2
×19.8 m).*

E SAXON, *1899. Owned by the Union Line. 12,385
tons. 586×64 foot (178.6×19.5 m).*

F PENNSYLVANIA, *1893. Owned by the Hamburg
America Line. 12,261 tons. 560 × 62 foot
(170.7×18.9 m).*

G ST. PAUL, *1895. Owned by the American Line.
11,625 tons. 535×63 foot (163.1×19.2 m).*

H NEW ENGLAND, *1898. Owned by the Dominion Line. 11,394 tons. 550×59 foot (167.6×18 m).*

I LA LORRAINE, *1899. Owned by the Compagnie Générale Transatlantique. 11,146 tons. 563×60 foot (171.6×18.3 m).*

J STATENDAM, *1898. Owned by the Holland America Line. 10,491 tons. 515×60 foot (157×18.3 m).*

K BAVARIAN, *1899. Owned by the Allan Line. 10,376 tons. 501×59 foot (152.7×18 m).*

L EGYPT, *1897. Owned by the P. & O. Line. 7,912 tons. 500 × 54 foot (152.4 × 16.5 m).*

M FRIESLAND, *1899. Owned by the Red Star Line. 7,116 tons. 437×51 foot (133.2×15.6 m).*

This sectioned view of the Compagnie Générale Transatlantique's LA PROVENCE, *1906, gives an idea of what life was like aboard the great liners on the North Atlantic route at the turn of the century.*

chapter 6

The twentieth century opened auspiciously for the nautical world with three shipbuilding 'firsts' before it was five years old: the first vessel to exceed 20,000 tons gross, the White Star Line's CELTIC, built in 1901; the first commercial turbine-driven ship, the KING EDWARD, also built in 1901, and the first triple screw liner, the Allan Line's VICTORIAN, built in 1905. Another 'first' was also recorded during these years, one which was to change the face of naval warfare, and that was the first effective mass use of mines, which occurred during the Russo-Japanese War, in 1904.

The demonstration of speed by Sir Charles Parsons's TURBINIA had impressed the shipbuilders W. Denny & Brothers, of Dumbarton, Scotland, who had a reputation for building fast steamers. Unable to interest the shipping companies in the idea of turbine-driven merchant vessels, Denny and Parsons founded the Turbine Steamers Syndicate together with a Clyde shipowner, Captain Williamson. The KING EDWARD was built at Denny's yards, and launched on May 16, 1901. During trials, she averaged 20.48 knots. She was put on passenger service on the Firth of Clyde where she ran until 1951, with spells as a troopship during both World Wars.

The next commercial turbine-ship was the cross-Channel packet QUEEN which, in 1903, operated the Dover-Calais route faster and more economically than the reciprocating-engined steamers which had operated that route for many years.

The success of the steam turbine-engine was assured when the Cunard Line tried it out, in 1905, on their liner CARMANIA, and compared her performance to that of her sister ship, the CARONIA, which was fitted with quadruple expansion engines. Cunard was so satisfied with the CARMANIA's performance that, when the LUSITANIA and the MAURETANIA were ordered in 1905, the propelling machinery for these liners was to be steam turbines driving four shafts.

To many people in the nautical world, the appearance of a ship is important, and departures from traditional profiles are sometimes avoided. False funnels are often added to 'give proper balance' to the superstructure's silhouette. When the SELANDIA entered service in 1912 as the first ever ocean-going motor vessel, she was rigged as a three-masted schooner, and had no funnel. It was purposely omitted by her owners, the Danish East Asiatic Co., who were among the principal early advocates of the diesel engine. But most owners of motor

vessels preferred to keep the funnel profile and to run the exhaust from the engines up through the funnels.

The major steamship services between North America and Great Britain, France, Holland, Italy, and Germany were the only ones on which large high-speed vessels could be economically operated. Rivalry between the shipping companies on the North Atlantic routes was based on a curious mixture of economics, publicity, and the sporting instinct. The holder of the Blue Riband was indeed a proud ship. This competitiveness produced, from the beginning of the century, a stream of bigger, faster, and more luxurious liners. Norddeutscher Lloyd launched the KRONPRINTZ WILHELM in 1901, the KAISER WILHELM II in 1902, and the KRONPRINZESSIN CECILIE in 1906, each marking an increase in size and speed. Cunard answered these with the LUSITANIA and the MAURETANIA in 1907, and the latter had the unique distinction of holding the Blue Riband for twenty-two years until Norddeutscher Lloyd's BREMEN came into service in 1928.

The Hamburg America Line's policy was to avoid excessive speed, and to concentrate instead on size and comfort. In answer to Cunard's liners, they built the biggest liners in the world, the first of which was the IMPERATOR, of 51,969 tons gross, launched in 1912. Ironically, she was given to the Cunard Line after the First World War, and renamed the BERENGARIA.

Following the war, most shipping companies had to engage in shipbuilding programmes to replace their lost vessels, but there was no rush to build challengers for the Blue Riband. The tendency was, rather, to build moderate-sized vessels with good cargo capacity and comfortable passenger accommodation at reasonable rates. Some fine ships were built during the 1920s, and an innovation in ship construction methods was made by the FULLAGAR, built at Birkenhead in 1920. She was the first sizeable merchant ship to be all-welded, without any rivets in her hull.

The GRIPSHOLM, built at Newcastle in 1925 for the Swedish America Line's service between Gothenburg and New York, was the first North Atlantic liner to be propelled by diesel engines. Although not in the same class as the great liners from the point of view of size and speed, the GRIPSHOLM had a distinguished career on the North Atlantic for over thirty years. During the Second World War, she became famous as a repatriation ship.

The international economic depression of the late 1920s and the early 1930s caused a serious set-back to the shipping world, which is always the first to feel the cold winds caused by financial crises. Many ships were laid up or sold for scrap, and many lines had to close down. Work on the Cunard Line's QUEEN MARY was stopped in 1931, and not recommenced until the British Government stepped in with financial backing in 1933. The economic turmoil had scarcely died down when the clouds of war gathered again.

This part of the twentieth century produced three types of warship which came to transform war at sea. Two of these, the submarine and the aircraft carrier, were new. (Although the submarine had been invented in the previous century, it was not until the First World War that it became an effective fighting vessel.) The third was the transformed battleship, which for a brief forty years became the major capital ship of the world's navies.

The Russo-Japanese War of 1904-05 saw the first mass torpedo-boat action, the first effective mass use of mines, and the establishment of the superiority of the turret-mounted big gun in naval battle. The various actions between the opposing squadrons of armoured warships demonstrated to the naval strategists that long-range gunfire with big guns was more effective than the indiscriminate use of mixed calibres at short range. Also, the efficacy of the smaller guns on the armour of the warships was minimal, all the damage being caused by the 12-inch (304.8 mm) shells. This soon led to the development of the all-big-gun battleship, the first of which was the British DREADNOUGHT, launched in 1906, whose design and perform-

ance outstripped that of every other battleship afloat.

Mines had been used before the Russo-Japanese War, but with no casualties. The Russian battleship PETROPAVLOSK, returning from a sortie against the blockading Japanese, struck a mine and sank, with 600 casualties, including the Russian Admiral Makaroff, commander of the fleet. Later, the Japanese lost two battleships to Russian mines. The efficiency of the mine was beyond doubt.

During the First World War, over a quarter of a million mines were laid by both belligerent and neutral countries. This time-consuming procedure was done by ships. Minelaying became much more efficient during the Second World War, when aircraft, as well as ships, were used to do the job. It is estimated that the Allies laid about 600,000 mines, while the Axis Powers laid over 300,000. Almost 2,500 merchant and naval vessels were lost by mines during the Second World War. Even today, mines from both World Wars are being drawn up by the fishing nets of both deep-sea and inshore trawlers.

In the opening phase of the First World War, the pre-Dreadnoughts were demonstrated to be no match for the Dreadnought type warships, which, on their part, soon found their supremacy threatened by the submarine. The battle for the sovereignty of the seas became one of surface ships against underwater vessels. Merchant shipping, carrying vital supplies, took a tremendous pounding from the U-boats, and it was not until the convoy system was re-introduced that the U-boat threat was beaten.

In 1917, a new dimension in naval warfare was created with the introduction of the aircraft carrier. Carrier-borne aircraft developed their potential so well that they contributed decisively to the outcome of many of the sea-battles of the Second World War, especially in the Pacific arena. Again, submarines very nearly strangled the transportation of vital supplies to Britain and Russia, but the convoy system proved a match for the U-boat once more.

Following the First World War, several conferences were held in an effort to slow down the re-armament race, but these had a diminishing effect on the size and number of the warships built. In 1935, an agreement was signed in London, whereby Germany was permitted to rebuild her navy. Japan had already accelerated the building of her navy; the stage was set for another war, even more terrible than that of 1914-18.

The Second World War followed a similar pattern to the First, with German submarine power playing a decisive role in the early years, and with America joining the Allies at a later stage. The course of this war has been dealt with in many thousands of books. It is sufficient for our history to say that the end of the war saw the merchant and naval fleets of

the world in a sorry state. The process of rebuilding had to begin again. At the same time, however, this gave the shipping lines the opportunity to concentrate on the building of specialist ships for the transport of crude oil and other bulk commodities. This specialist type of ship was to increase in importance in the following decades.

NORMANDIE

A *The pride of the Compagnie Générale Transatlantique when she was launched in 1932, the
quadruple-screw* NORMANDIE *offered the ultimate
in service to its 1,975 passengers.*
B *A contemporary poster advertising the ship.*
C *The exhaust system was built around the first
class dining room (1), cabins (2), and the main
lounge (3).*

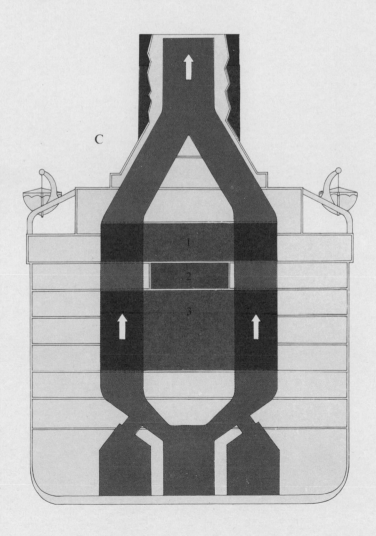

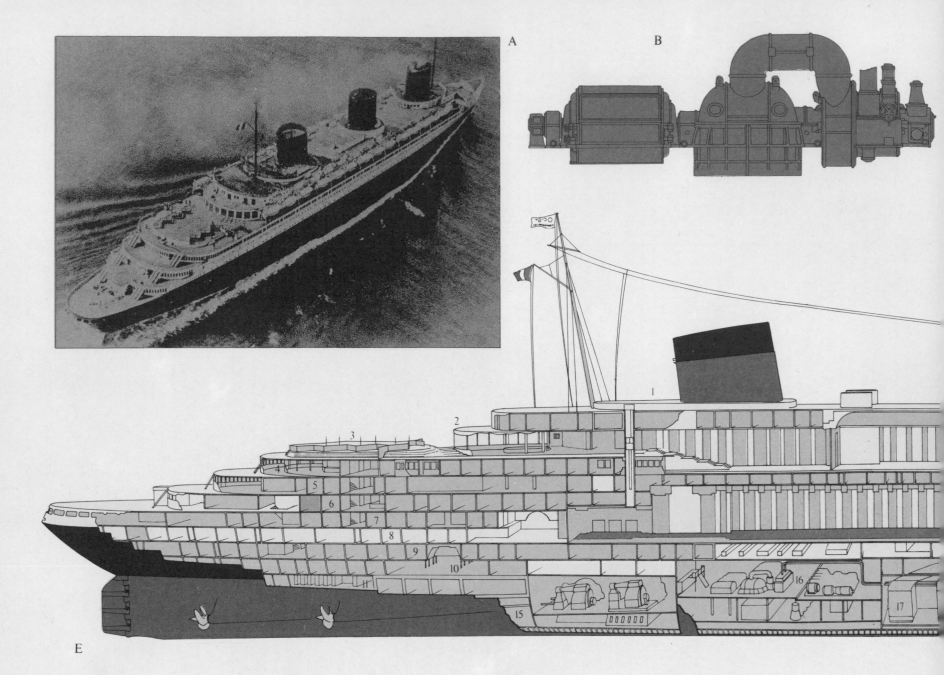

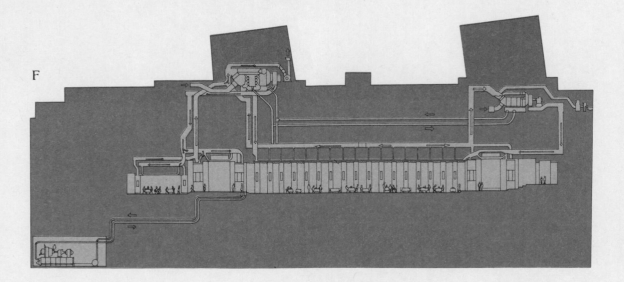

A NORMANDIE *under way.*

B *Elevation of one of the two-casing main turbo-alternators.*

C *The house flag of the Compagnie Générale Trans-atlantique, the French Line.*

D *One of the main water-tube boilers of the ship. They were equipped with superheaters.*

E *Longitudinal section.*

  1 *Upper sundeck*

  2 *Sundeck*

  3 *Lifeboat deck*

  4 *Promenade deck*

  5 *Main deck*

6-13 *The A to H decks*

14 *Bottom of ship*

15 *Propeller shafts and chairs*

16 *Turbo-alternators compartment*

17 *Boilers*

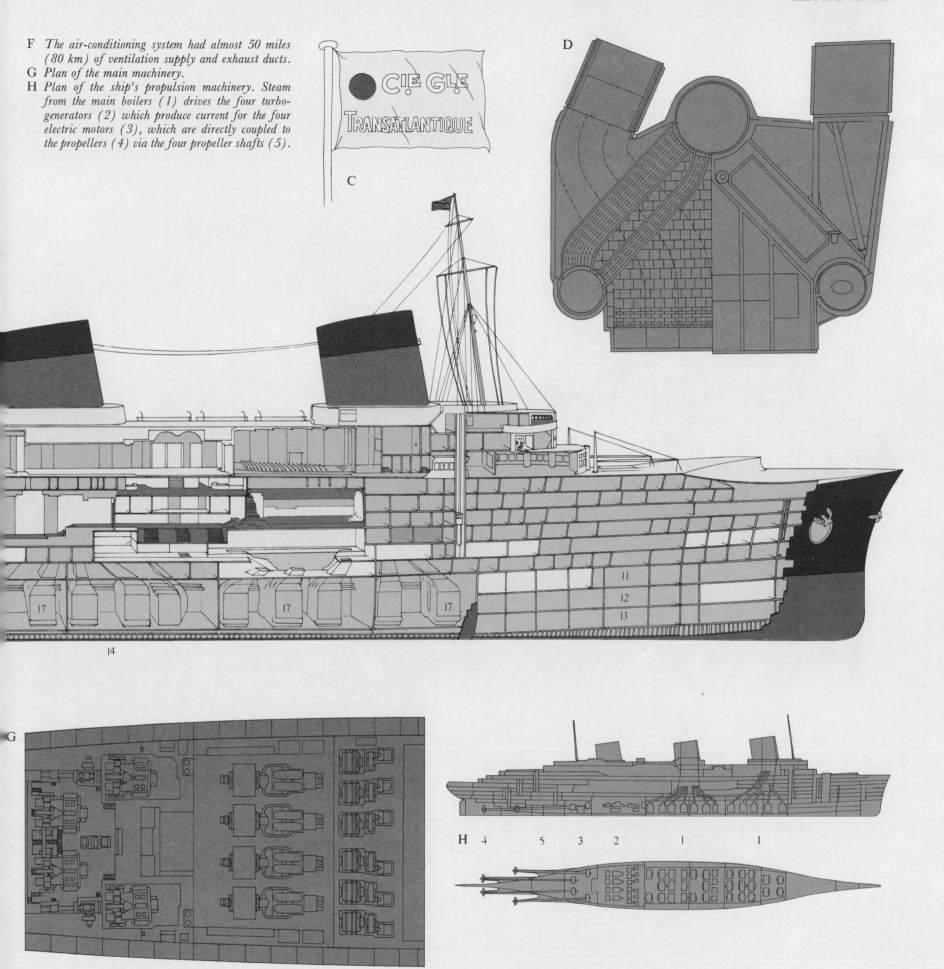

F The air-conditioning system had almost 50 miles (80 km) of ventilation supply and exhaust ducts.
G Plan of the main machinery.
H Plan of the ship's propulsion machinery. Steam from the main boilers (1) drives the four turbo-generators (2) which produce current for the four electric motors (3), which are directly coupled to the propellers (4) via the four propeller shafts (5).

A *Cross-section of one of the transformers.*
B *The V-shaped structure forward was a break-water.*

A

B

NORMANDIE

A *The famous Pelorus Jack, who was protected by New Zealand law, was a Risso's dolphin.*
B KING EDWARD, *1901.*
C NARRAGANSETT, *1903.*

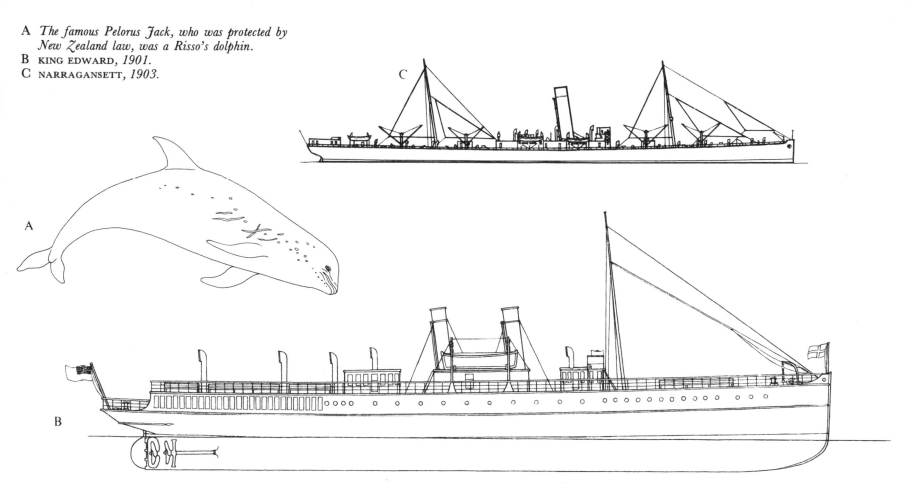

JULY 1900

The DEUTSCHLAND, belonging to the Hamburg America Line, takes the Blue Riband on an eastbound crossing of the Atlantic. This is the second time that a German ship has won this speed record, the KAISER WILHELM DER GROSSE having won it in 1897. Just to show that it was no fluke, between 1900 and 1901 the DEUTSCHLAND breaks the record no less than seven times.

1901

The KING EDWARD becomes the first commercial turbine ship. She is used for coastal duties on the River Clyde and its estuary.

1901

The White Star Line builds the CELTIC, which is the first vessel to exceed 20,000 tons gross. With her sister ship, the CEDRIC, she is the largest ship afloat. True, the OCEANIC, which was built in 1899, was 5 foot (1.5 m) longer, but she was much narrower. Neither of the sister ships was built for breaking speed records. Indeed, company policy was to build comfortable ships in the intermediate speed range, and this made the White Star Line one of the most popular shipping lines in the North Atlantic.

1902

The International Navigation Co., to give the American Line its full title, is re-organized under the name of The International Mercantile Marine Co.—the I.M.M., for short. Pierpont Morgan, the American banker, increases the capital of the new company from £3,000,000 to £24,000,000. The I.M.M. then acquires the shares of the White Star Line, the Dominion Line, the Atlantic Transport Line, and the Leyland Line. In addition, it takes substantial shareholdings in several other shipping companies, including fifty-one per cent of the Holland America Line.

In return for the co-operation of the Hamburg America Line and Norddeutscher Lloyd, I.M.M. guarantees a dividend of six per cent on their capital, provided I.M.M. receives fifty per cent of any sum paid in excess of six per cent. The deal is favourable to Norddeutscher Lloyd, whose dividends averaged four per cent from 1902 to 1911; but H.A.P.A.G., whose dividends are declared at over seven per cent, must forfeit substantial sums to the American banker.

1903

The NARRAGANSETT, belonging to the Anglo-

American Oil Co., is launched, thus becoming the largest oil-tanker in the world. Her engines are amidships, not aft as had been the custom since the introduction of real, purpose-built tankers. However, the engines of subsequent oil-tankers were all placed aft.

1903

The Cunard Line is appointed the official agent for Austro-Hungarian emigration to the United States. Services are opened from Trieste, Fiume, and Venice to New York. The AURANIA inaugurated this service.

1903

The GJÖA, carrying the famous Norwegian explorer, Roald Amundsen, sets off to sail through the North West Passage. Amundsen knew that he would be able to sail only during the short summer months, and that he would be ice-bound for the greater part of the year. It took him three years to complete the voyage.

1904

One of the happiest of all marine laws is passed by the New Zealand Government. This law makes it a crime for anybody to interfere with the friendly dolphin Pelorus Jack, who met all incoming vessels making Wellington harbour. Pelorus Jack was a well-known character, who for years gambolled about the liners which travelled half-way round the world to fetch up in the Antipodes.

Wellington was just about as far as ships could steam from the Old World. For example, the distances from New Zealand to London by way of the Cape, Suez, and Panama were 13,200 miles (24,450 km), 12,450 miles (23,055 km), and 11,309 miles (20,945 km) respectively.

1904

Charles Roux is appointed president of the French Line, the Cie. Générale Transatlantique. Between 1905 and 1911, he added seventeen new ships to the French Line. The largest liner in the fleet was LA PROVENCE, of 13,750 tons gross, which was built in 1906.

THE RUSSO-JAPANESE WAR
1904-05

By the terms of the Treaty of Shimonoseki, 1895, Japan occupied Port Arthur, together with the Liao-Tung peninsula, and received treaty rights in Manchuria. Two years later, the Russians, who had been forced to cede these territories, regained them with the help of Germany and France. Port Arthur was critical to the Russian economy, for it was the most northerly of the ice-free ports. A deaf ear was turned to the protests of Japan. Indeed, Admiral Alexieff, the Russian Viceroy in the Far East, indulged in a calculated policy of provocation.

Tension between the two countries mounted. On February 5, 1904, with tension at breaking point, Admiral Heihachiro Togo, the Commander-in-Chief of the Imperial Japanese Navy, called a conference aboard his flagship, the MIKASA. His unsheathed Samurai sword on the table proclaimed war to all who saw it. Admiral Togo's strategy was to be the same as that at Pearl Harbour some forty years later: an undeclared, pre-emptive strike against the enemy. There would also be the first ever mass attack by torpedoes.

FEBRUARY 8-9, 1904

Five Japanese destroyers enter the harbour of Port Arthur. Russian recognition signals are given, so they steam forward unmolested. A swarm of nine torpedoes hit the Russian battleships TSESAREVITCH and RETVIZAN, and the cruiser PALLADA. Completely undamaged, the Japanese destroyers withdraw.

The following day, sixteen Japanese warships, led by the MIKASA, return. They bombard the port installations and nine major Russian ships from a distance of 8,000 yards (7,300 m). This time, the Russians return fire, and five ships on each side are damaged, but casualties are light.

A cat-and-mouse naval war now developed. Although the Russian fleet outnumbered the Japanese, yet the Russians decided to hole-up

A VICTORIAN, *1904.*

B KNIAZ SOUVAROFF, *1903, was Admiral Rozhestvensky's flagship at the Battle of Tsu-shima, 1905.*

C *The Japanese flagship at Tsu-shima was the* MIKASA, *1899.*

D *During the Russo-Japanese War, the Russian mines were activated by the Herz horn, invented by the German, Herz, in 1868.*

1 *Horn cover*
2 *Lead horn*
3 *Electrolyte container*
4 *Electrodes*

E *The Japanese mines were exploded by a more modern device known as a pendant connector. When the mine was struck by a ship, the spring weight in the middle (1), was forced against the rim, thus completing the circuit to the charge.*

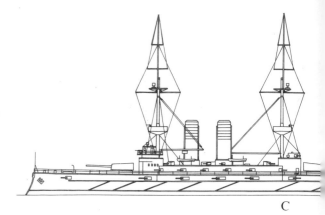

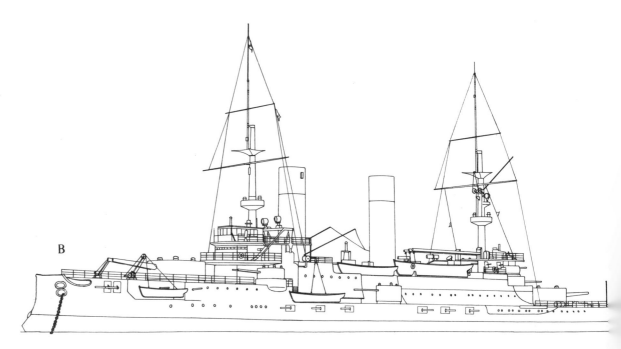

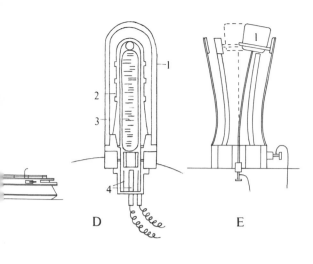

D   E

for long periods, interspersing these periods of inactivity with quick hits against the Japanese. For their part, the Japanese seemed content to rely upon a policy of blockading the enemy.

FEBRUARY 25, 1904
Five Russian warships venture out of Port Arthur. They are confronted by a patrol of seven Japanese warships, which drive the Russians back into the safety of the port.

MARCH 11, 1904
Destroyers from the two belligerents skirmish in similar fashion off Lao-Ti-Shan.

MAY 1904
The blockading Japanese battleships, HATSUSE and YASHIMA, sink after entering a defending Russian mine-field. This, the first effective mass use of the mine, reduces the number of Japan's capital ships by a third.

AUGUST 10-11, 1904
The Battle of Round Island takes place. Fifteen Japanese warships engage ten Russian warships. The first round of the battle is in-

decisive. Indeed, the most severely damaged ship is Admiral Togo's own flagship, the MIKASA.

The next day, the two sides clash in the straits that separate the islands of Tsu-shima, which are midway between Japan and the Korean mainland. The Russian fleet is badly mauled, losing by scuttling the RURIK, which had been damaged beyond repair.

Russia, smarting under these reverses, decided to re-think her naval strategy. She had more than a hundred naval vessels in European waters. In the shipyards, four large, modern battleships were being built. Plans to send sizeable elements of the European fleets were put in hand. By the beginning of October, 1904, forty-two warships were ready to leave European waters.

OCTOBER 16, 1904
Reinforcements for the Russian Far East fleet leave the Baltic for Port Arthur. The brand-new battleship KNIAZ SOUVAROFF is the flagship, with Admiral Rozhestvensky in overall command. The BORODINO, ORYOL, and ALEXANDER III, all sister ships of the KNIAZ SOUVAROFF, formed the Second Pacific Squadron. In addition, there were numerous cruisers and torpedo-boats.

Russia had no overseas bases, and the neutral countries were disinclined to coal such a large fleet. Therefore, the Russians ordered half a million tons of coal to be ferried to the fleet in sixty-two colliers belonging to the Hamburg America Line. The arrangement was that bunkering should take place either at sea or at neutral roadsteads, whichever was the more convenient. In addition, this formidable Russian fleet was accompanied by its own hospital and repair ships.

OCTOBER 21, 1904
The passage of the Second and Third Squadrons through the North Sea caused an international incident that almost precipitated war between England and Russia. The Gamecock Fishing Fleet out of Hull was trawling in an area that turned out to be right across the path of the Russian warships. The trawlers sent up two green identification flares. The Russians mistook the flares for Japanese signals. A furious shooting-match ensued. Russian warship even fired at Russian warship. Unhappily, the trawler fleet was caught in the cross-fire. The little CRANE was sunk, and two of her crew were killed. Several other trawlers were hit—as were some of the Russian battleships.

Britain retaliated by mobilizing twenty-eight battleships and by putting Gibraltar on a war footing. Tempers were running high when the Russian fleet put into Vigo. The worried Spanish authorities gave the Russians twenty-four hours only to quit the port. When the Russians left Vigo, the British fleet was waiting in open waters, with searchlights playing on the Russian armada.

Peace trembled on the brink. Fortunately,

wiser counsels prevailed. Explanations and apologies took the heat out of the situation. War was narrowly averted over the Dogger Bank incident. The Russians continued on their way.

THE BATTLE OF TSU-SHIMA
MAY 27-28, 1905
The Russian reinforcements reached a point off the island of Tsu-shima, still two days' sailing from the intended destination, Vladivostok. But the way was barred by Admiral Togo's waiting fleet.

Action stations sounded. Battle ensigns flapped from Russian masts, for the sea was rough, the weather bleak. Indeed, the scouting Japanese torpedo-boats were ordered back to port. The remaining formations of the two opposing fleets confronted each other.

Admiral Togo had deployed twenty capital ships and seventy torpedo craft. Admiral Rozhestvensky commanded thirty fighting ships, the remainder of his fleet being of the auxiliary category. More, the Russian fleet had been at sea some seven months. All of the ships needed some sort of dockyard attention.

Admiral Rozhestvensky, on the KNIAZ SOUVAROFF, placed the four newest and most formidable ships to starboard in order to bear the brunt of the Japanese attack, whilst Admiral Togo took his fleet directly across the bows of the advancing Russians, turning the whole line through 180° so as to sail parallel with the enemy on the weaker side.

All the day, at a range of 9,000 yards (8,200 m), the bombardment continued. That night, as the waters became calmer, the seventy Japanese torpedo-boats mounted repeated attacks on the Russians, sinking several of their ships.

The battle continued throughout the next day. The Russian fleet was annihilated. No Japanese ships were lost, although most sustained damage of one sort or another. The casualty list of Admiral Rozhestvensky makes tragic reading. Eleven ships were sunk, four were captured, one was wrecked, and three were interned in Manila.

MAY 29, 1905
With all Russia awaiting the news, one lone cruiser, the ALMAZ, limps into Vladivostok. The destroyers BRAVI and GROZNYI slowly follow. The ALMAZ had escaped only because she had been detailed to escort the transport ships.

Against all odds, Japan defeated Russia. No world power had thought this possible. America acted as mediator to procure peace.

1905
The Allan Line's VICTORIAN becomes the first turbine liner on the North Atlantic routes. She is also the first triple screw liner.

JULY 1905
The crew of the Russian battleship POTEMKIN

mutiny at the Black Sea base of Odessa, murdering their officers and hoisting the Red Flag.

AUGUST 1905

The UNTERSEEBOOT NO. I, the first German U-boat, is launched. Designed by a French-born Spanish citizen named d'Equevilley, it weighed 235 tons, and employed a petrol engine for surface propulsion and battery charging.

AUGUST 1, 1906

The Russian America Line commences North Atlantic sailings from Libau to New York. The first voyage is made by the KOREA.

OCTOBER 1906

Britain launches the DREADNOUGHT. Her performance and design are so successful that all other battleships afloat are made obsolete.

1907

The Cunard Line's LUSITANIA takes to the water, a double 'first': the first liner to exceed thirty thousand tons gross, and the first ship to be equipped with quadruple screws. On November 16, 1907, her sister-ship, the MAURETANIA, sets off on her maiden voyage. This she accomplishes at a record speed of 23.69 knots, thus capturing the Atlantic record. For more than a year, she and the LUSITANIA vie with each other to improve the time for the Atlantic crossing. Regularly, they break each others' records. Eventually, the MAURETANIA emerges as the clear-cut winner, holding the record no less than nine times in her career. She proved herself to be the fastest flier of her generation.

JUNE 13, 1908

The Holland America Line enter their ROTTERDAM, a then giant of 24,170 tons gross, on the North Atlantic service. She did yeoman service until she was laid up in 1915 for the remaining years of the First World War. The ROTTERDAM came back into service after that war, and ended an honourable career in 1940, at the beginning of yet another war.

APRIL 1909

The White Star Line's LAURENTIC introduces a new form of propulsion to shipping. Her triple screws are driven by a combination of quadruple expansion and a low-pressure turbine on the centre shaft.

APRIL 1909

The Red Star Line inaugurates another service between Antwerp and New York with the LAPLAND, of 17,540 tons gross.

JUNE 12, 1909

Norddeutscher Lloyd puts the GEORGE WASHINGTON into service. She was for a long time Germany's largest vessel, and was third only to the MAURETANIA and the LUSITANIA in the world ratings. However, her maximum

A DREADNOUGHT, *1906.*
B UNTERSEEBOOT NO. *1, the first German U-boat, 1905.*
C SELANDIA, *1912.*
D *The* SELANDIA's *diesel engine.*
E *An early Marconi telegraph.*

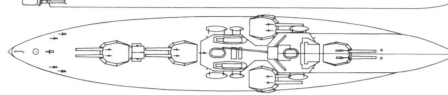

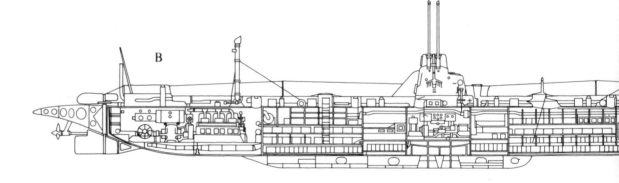

speed was only nineteen knots, so she was not exactly a threat to those ocean greyhounds. Norddeutscher Lloyd, however, set comfort before speed. The GEORGE WASHINGTON became an American troopship in 1917, and was not broken up until 1951.

JULY 26, 1909

The WARATAH, the largest ship of William Lund's Blue Anchor Line, leaves Durban for London on the inward leg of her Australian maiden voyage, with 92 passengers and a crew of 119. Early on July 30, she is sighted by Clan Line's CLAN MACINTYRE, and is then never seen again. No trace of her, not even floating wreckage, has ever been found, despite strenuous efforts to find her. Only the sea knows the enigma of the WARATAH.

SEPTEMBER 1909

The MAURETANIA breaks the existing record by crossing the Atlantic in 4 days, 10 hours, and 51 minutes, at an average speed of 26.06 knots. It was a record that was to stand supreme for another twenty years, until the BREMEN clocked a faster time in July, 1929.

JANUARY 23, 1909

The White Star Line's REPUBLIC collides with the FLORIDA, belonging to the Lloyd Italiano Line. Fortunately, wireless had just been installed, and a radio message summoned help. Another White Star liner, the BALTIC, picked up the message and rescued all the passengers and crew of the REPUBLIC, which, unhappily, sank. This is the first instance of wireless being used at sea to summon aid.

JUNE 14, 1911

The White Star Line's OLYMPIC becomes the largest ship afloat, at 45,324 tons gross, when she leaves Southampton on her maiden voyage. She reaches New York 5 days and 16 hours later.

1912

Cunard acquires the shares of the Anchor Line. This makes Cunard one of the shipping giants.

FEBRUARY 22, 1912

The SELANDIA, the world's first ever ocean-going

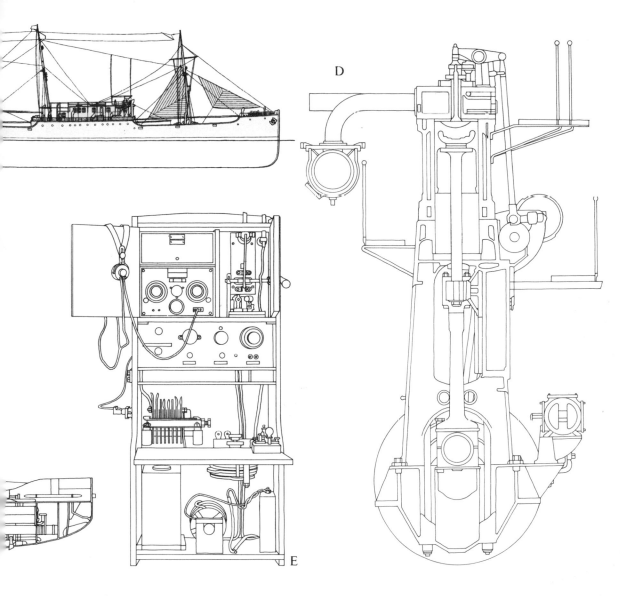

has been designed to keep afloat with five of the watertight compartments flooded. Despite riding calmly on that glass-like water, one compartment too many has been damaged. She is doomed.

At 00.05, the orders are given for the lifeboats to be uncovered and for the passengers to be mustered. Minutes later, the wireless operator, Phillips, is told to send the official 'C.Q.D.'— Come Quick, Danger. This is followed by 'MGY'—the TITANIC's call sign. A new alarm call, 'S.O.S.', has recently been recommended by the marine authorities. Phillips sends this as well, the first time that the call has been used in earnest.

Only 10 miles (18.5 km) away, the 6,000-ton Leyland liner, CALIFORNIAN, has seen and identified the TITANIC. Captain Stanley Lord, master of the CALIFORNIAN, has already stopped his ship, for he knows that the way ahead on his trip from London to Boston is blocked by ice. He intended to send the TITANIC the Morse ice-warning signal, when the liner appeared to change course to port. Tragically, TITANIC's C.Q.D. goes out at 00.10. Closing-down time for the CALIFORNIAN is 23.30.

The lifeboats on the TITANIC are being prepared. There are sixteen wooden lifeboats, eight on each side. In addition, there are four 'Englehardts'—collapsible canvas boats. The total capacity of these twenty boats is 1,178 persons. And there are 2,207 people aboard.

Inevitably, the bridge order from Captain Smith is, 'Women and children first.' The chairman of the White Star Line himself, J. Bruce Ismay, is aboard, and, knowing the discrepancy in the accommodation of the lifeboats, he moves about the ship urging the passengers to get away. Uncomprehending, many of the passengers refuse to obey the order. Half-empty lifeboats pull away.

On deck, the ship's orchestra is playing.

At a quarter to one, the TITANIC starts sending up distress rockets to attract the attention of the CALIFORNIAN, clearly distinguishable on the horizon. Even now, there is no real panic. For the response to the C.Q.D. call is encouraging. Four vessels have already acknowledged it: N.D.L.'s FRANKFURT, which is only 150 miles (277 km) away; a Russian ship, the BURMA; the Allan Line's VIRGINIAN; and the Canadian Pacific's MOUNT TEMPLE. Even better, the Cunarder CARPATHIA is only 58 miles (106 km) distant, no more than four hours' steaming from the TITANIC; and the world is beginning to know what has happened, for Cape Race has picked up the signal, and so has New York, although the port of destination hears it only as a whisper.

The race to rescue the people aboard the TITANIC begins at almost the same time that Captain Smith is telling his officers that Mr. Andrews, the managing director of Harland & Wolff, the builders of the vessel, who is making the voyage in his expert capacity, is of the opinion that the ship will sink in about an hour's

motor vessel, makes her maiden voyage. She was ordered by the East Asiatic Co., a Danish shipping line. On her first call to London, Winston Churchill, then First Lord of the Admiralty, inspected her. The SELANDIA notched up fifty-five round voyages, totalling a stupendous 1,200,000 nautical miles for her owners. She was sold in 1935, and saw service until she was wrecked on January 26, 1942, off the coast of Japan. She still had her original machinery installed.

The SELANDIA had two sister ships, the JUTLANDIA and the FIONIA. When the FIONIA visited Kiel in Germany, on July 12, 1912, Albert Ballin, the head of the Hamburg America Line, paid a very high price for her. Soon afterwards, Kaiser Wilhelm came aboard. He renamed the ship CHRISTIAN X.

APRIL 15, 1912

The TITANIC was a companion vessel to—almost the sister of—the OLYMPIC, the largest liner in the world. When she left on her maiden voyage on April 10, 1912, the tag 'unsinkable' had already been placed on her.

With 1,310 passengers and 897 crew, she left Southampton for New York, via Cherbourg and Queenstown. A priceless, bejewelled copy of the 'Rubaiyat of Omar Khayyám' had been safely locked in her strong-room.

Four days out from Southampton, Lookout Frederick Fleet, high in the crow's nest on the foremast, saw ice in the distance. Immediately, he clanged the crow's nest bell and reported to the bridge, 'Ice ahead'.

First Officer William Murdoch immediately orders, 'Hard a-starboard', and rings down, 'Full speed astern', to the engine-room.

The bows begin to turn, but the iceberg, a hundred foot (30.5 m) tall, nudges gently along the hull of the TITANIC. Survivors later describe that 'gentle nudge' as being reminiscent of a ship coming along the quay-side.

First Officer Murdoch issues a third order: 'Close all watertight compartments.' He feels the judder of ice upon steel, as do so many of the passengers. It is a slight contact, so slight that some of the passengers do not even feel it, but the iceberg has torn a gash 300 foot (91.4 m) long in the first six watertight compartments on the starboard side. The 'unsinkable' TITANIC

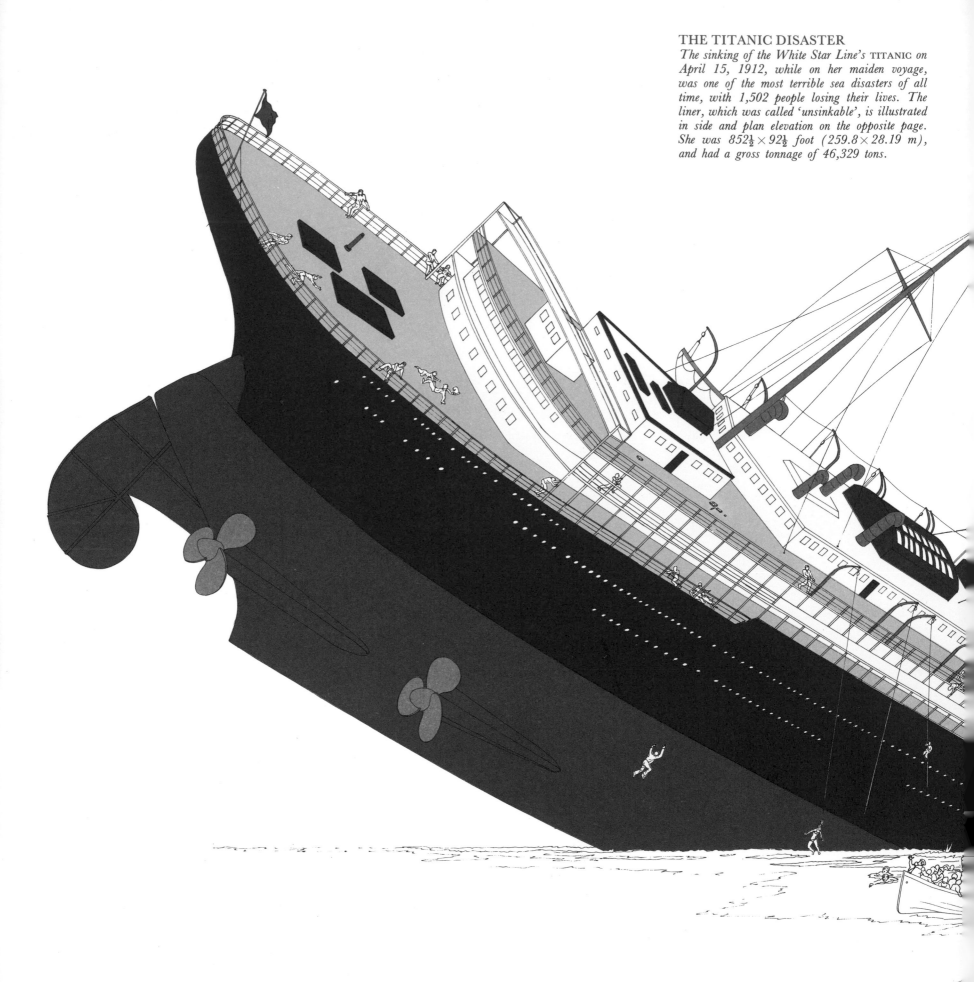

THE TITANIC DISASTER
The sinking of the White Star Line's TITANIC *on April 15, 1912, while on her maiden voyage, was one of the most terrible sea disasters of all time, with 1,502 people losing their lives. The liner, which was called 'unsinkable', is illustrated in side and plan elevation on the opposite page. She was $852\frac{1}{2} \times 92\frac{1}{2}$ foot (259.8 × 28.19 m), and had a gross tonnage of 46,329 tons.*

time—at the most, an hour and a half. Down in the engine room, Chief Engineer Bell keeps steam up. The generators are still running smoothly, giving normal light. This is what puzzles the people watching aboard the CALIFORNIAN; for they can see the distant TITANIC, on an even keel, lights ablaze, apparently hove-to; just as they are. Even as the watchers puzzle over the night-piercing rockets, they do not appreciate that the unsinkable TITANIC has already entered her death throes and that the end is near.

By 01.45 on the Monday morning of April 15, 1912, even the most sceptical aboard the TITANIC knows what is happening. Water flushes over the bow. There is a distinct list to port. Chief Officer Wilde gives the command for everybody to move to starboard. At the same time, Second Officer Lightoller, responsible for the loading and despatching of the lifeboats, stands by number four. It is the last boat left aboard. It has places for forty-seven people. Sixteen hundred are still on the TITANIC.

When the last boat has left the TITANIC, Captain Smith instructs the wireless officers to close down and abandon ship. One seaman who should have gone with one of the boats is found on deck. 'What are you doing here?' he is asked. 'Plenty of time to get away, Sir,' is the reply.

At 02.15, the sea is washing over the bridge. The crow's nest on the foremast is at sea level. The TITANIC is again listing to port.

The remaining passengers move towards the rising stern. To some, this move is merely prolonging the agony. A growing torrent of people starts jumping into the icy waters.

There is a forward movement of the ship, for all the world as though she is getting under way. But it is an illusion. The movement is downward. The descent of the TITANIC to her Atlantic grave has begun.

Three minutes later, at 02.18, all the lights go out—except for one solitary oil lamp on the mainmast. Seconds later, the forward funnel collapses in a shower of angry sparks.

Death comes at 02.20. The TITANIC stands perpendicular, her stern probing the night sky, her fourth funnel above water. A thunderous noise rends the air. Her twenty-nine boilers have fallen from their beds. The TITANIC quickens her downward movement. She disappears, leaving an agonizing silence, pierced only by the cries of those struggling in the water.

Too late, the rescue ships start to come to the scene of the disaster. By 08.30, Captain Rostron on the CARPATHIA has picked up 705 survivors. He holds a brief service for the 1,502 people who have gone down with the ship, and then alters course from his original destination of Trieste, and makes for New York. He arrives there two days later.

The shipping world, the entire world, was stunned by the tragedy to the TITANIC. Funds were set up to help the survivors. More im-

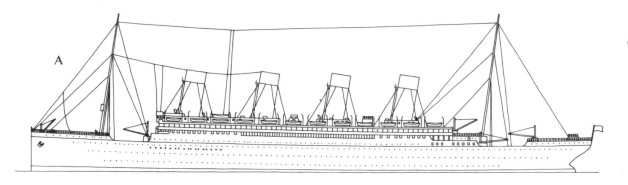

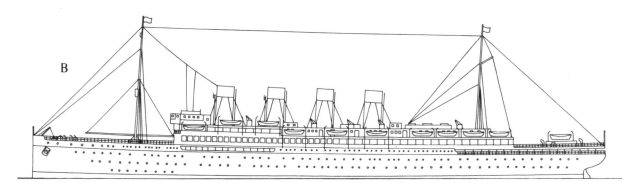

PACIFIC OCEAN

portant, Boards of Inquiry were held, both in America and in Great Britain.

There are so many imponderables in the tragedy of the TITANIC. Why did not Captain Smith heed the six ice warnings that he received on April 14, 1912? That which emanated from the MESABA at 21.30, a little more than two hours before the tragedy, was explicit in the extreme.

Why was speed not reduced when the ice warnings had been given? This would have been prudent seamanship. Yet speed was maintained throughout the critical hours of potential danger.

The progressive drop in the temperature of the water had been recorded during the Sunday evening. Why did no one realize the importance that should have been attached to this information?

Why, above all, did the people aboard the CALIFORNIAN not believe the evidence of their own eyes? Why did they rely on the publicity material that the TITANIC was unsinkable?

The 'if's' are just as imponderable as the 'why's'. If only the designer of the TITANIC had taken those watertight bulkheads beyond F deck, then even the flooding of the six compartments would not have doomed the vessel.

If only there had been a bright moon shining, or choppy water; then that would have revealed the outline of the iceberg earlier.

If only First Officer Murdoch had slammed into that iceberg instead of ordering hard a-starboard; then the TITANIC would have telescoped her bows but remained afloat.

Various recommendations were made by the Courts of Inquiry. Several of these recommendations were adopted and implemented. Soon, an international ice patrol had been inaugurated. It was made mandatory for ships to reduce their speed, once ice had been reported. The wireless watch on all passenger ships was extended to cover the full twenty-four hours of the day, not selected times. It was made compulsory for all passenger ships to carry enough lifeboats to accommodate all the passengers aboard.

The unhappy truth of the matter is that, although the TITANIC was technically the most advanced ship of her time, yet the rules and regulations under which she was operated were archaic. Indeed, they had been little changed since the introduction of the first 'giant' liners, many decades before the TITANIC had been built. The main safety requirement under the old regulations was that British ships over ten

ATLANTIC OCEAN

thousand tons were obliged to carry sixteen lifeboats, with an additional number of rafts for carrying up to seventy-five per cent of the lifeboat capacity. Thus, legally, when the TITANIC set out on her disastrous maiden voyage, she needed only to carry lifeboats to accommodate 962 persons. Actually, she had capacity for 1,178 persons. This, whilst well over the legal minimum, was still only sufficient for thirty per cent of her total capacity of 2,584 passengers and 900 crew.

The implementation of the recommendations of the Boards of Inquiry meant that there was greater safety at sea in the future. It was a lesson that had been learnt the hard way. The loss of the TITANIC, and those 1,502 souls, was a high price to pay for the inescapable conclusion that administrative advances did not match the technological advances that were being made. It is debatable if the full lesson will ever be learnt; for in other places, other times, oil is the classic example where technology has moved beyond the parameters in which it could operate without harm to others.

APRIL 20, 1912

The largest French liner afloat, the Cie. Générale Transatlantique's FRANCE commences her maiden voyage. She is twice as large as any other C.G.T. vessel, and the third fastest ship in the world after the MAURETANIA and the LUSITANIA.

1913

The Hamburg South America Line puts into service the CAP TRAFALGAR. At 18,710 tons gross, she is the largest vessel yet built for the South American run.

JUNE 18, 1913

The monster IMPERATOR goes into service for the Hamburg America Line. At 51,969 tons, she is the first vessel to top the 50,000 tons gross mark. Like other giant 'firsts' before her, she had her teething troubles. She was scheduled to leave on her maiden voyage on May 24, but she ran aground in the River Elbe, and the voyage had to be postponed. Further delay occurred as the result of an explosion in her boiler room. The outbreak of the First World War halted her North Atlantic career. After the war, she crossed the North Sea and joined the Cunard fleet, being renamed the BERENGARIA.

THE FIRST WORLD WAR
JULY 28, 1914-NOVEMBER 11, 1918

When war broke out, the German Navy had three groups overseas. The largest group was the East Asiatic Squadron, under the command of Vice-Admiral Maximilian, Graf von Spee. The squadron comprised the SCHARNHORST, GNEISENAU, EMDEN, LEIPZIG, and the NÜRNBERG. The small Caribbean Squadron comprised the DRESDEN and the KARLSRUHE. The third unit was the KÖNIGSBERG, which was based at Dar-es-Salaam, in German East Africa.

None of these ships ever came back to Germany. The story of the EMDEN is, perhaps, the most embarrassing to the Allies.

On August 13, von Spee held a conference attended by his captains at Pagan, in the Marianas. As the result of various decisions arrived at, the EMDEN was detached from the squadron and despatched to the Indian Ocean. She was attended by her collier, the MARKO-MANNIA, a H.A.P.A.G. vessel. During the month of September, the raider destroyed twenty-three British steamers, and bombarded the oil depot at Madras. She then doubled back, and sank the Russian cruiser JEMTCHUG in Penang Roads on October 28. The pursuing French destroyer, MOUSQUET, was also sent to the bottom.

SEPTEMBER 14, 1914

The German vessel CAP TRAFALGAR, under the command of Commodore Wirth, had been fitted out as an armed merchant cruiser with guns taken from an obsolete gunboat, the EBER. The CARMANIA, a British armed merchant cruiser recruited from the Cunard Line, came upon the CAP TRAFALGAR, coaling from colliers off Trinidad. In the ensuing battle, the CARMANIA fired 417 rounds. The CAP TRAFALGAR was sunk, but not before she had registered 79 hits on the CARMANIA.

SEPTEMBER 22, 1914

U-9, commanded by Lieutenant-Commander Weddigen, sinks the three cruisers ABOUKIR, CRESSY, and HOGUE, within one hour.

The potential of the submarine had been underestimated until this. At the outbreak of war, Britain had eighty submarines, while Germany had only thirty-five, with another seventy being planned or built. Under international law, the sinking of merchant ships without warning was forbidden. Indeed, a crew had to be given time to abandon ship before it was torpedoed. However, merchant ships were quickly armed, and on February 15, 1915, the seas around Britain were declared by the Germans to be a War Zone. This gave the U-boats the right to attack neutral shipping there. Unrestricted sea warfare ensued.

NOVEMBER 1, 1914

The first fleet action of the war is fought. The forces were small ones, and Germany won the day. After sending the EMDEN on her raiding mission, von Spee had taken the remainder of

A *The German super-dreadnought* BAYERN, *1915.*

B *The Davis torpedo, developed for the U.S. Navy, 1912.*

C *The British* INVINCIBLE, *1907, which played a successful part in the Battle of the Falkland Islands, 1914.*

D *The German battle-cruiser* HINDENBURG, *1915, which joined the High Sea Fleet in 1917.*

E *Motor torpedo boat of the British Navy, 1915-18.*

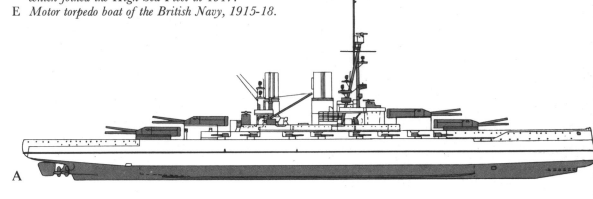

A

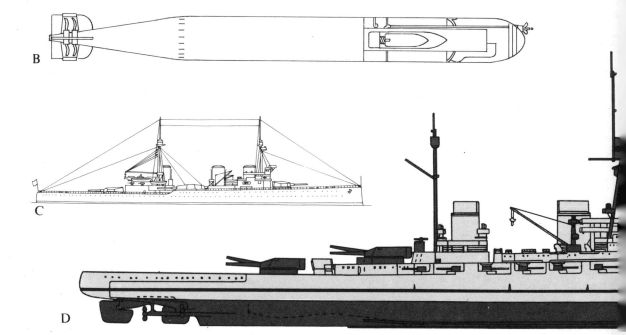

C

D

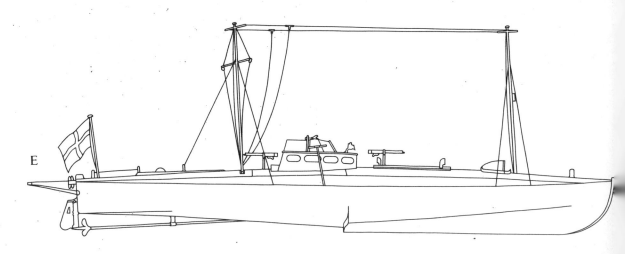

E

THE FIRST WORLD WAR
1 *The Battle of the Falkland Islands, off the south-west coast of South America*
2 *The sinking of the* ABOUKIR, *the* HOGUE, *and the* CRESSY
3 *The Battle of the Dogger Bank*
4 *The Battle of Jutland*
5 *Scapa Flow*

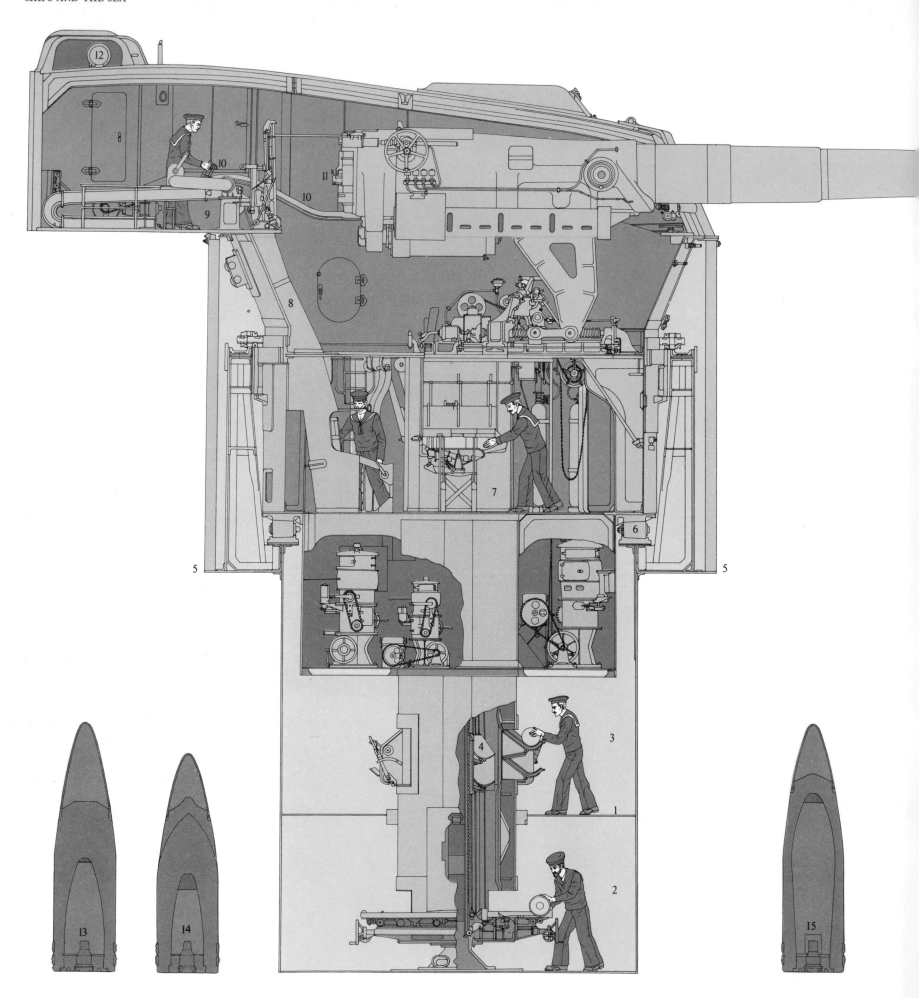

BOFORS TWIN TURRET GUN, 1912.
28 cm (11 inches)
1 *Loading was carried out on the lower deck*
2 *Shell magazine*
3 *Powder magazine*
4 *Ammunition hoist to 'tween-deck*
5 *Rotating turret*
6 *The turret rotated on these roller bearings*
7 *'Tween-deck*
8 *Ammunition hoist to loading bridge*
9 *Loading bridge*
10 *Loading rack*
11 *Breech*
12 *Range finder*
13 *Armour piercing shell*
14 *Semi-armour piercing shell*
15 *High explosive shell*

his fleet south towards Chile, where the DRESDEN joined them. The nearest Allied force was that under Rear-Admiral Sir Christopher Cradock, whose flagship was the cruiser GOOD HOPE. In addition, Cradock could dispose of the cruisers MONMOUTH and GLASGOW, and the armed merchant cruiser OTRANTO. The force was outnumbered and outgunned by the fleet under the command of von Spee.

The two fleets made contact at sunset off Coronel, in Arauco Bay, Chile. The result was a foregone conclusion. The GOOD HOPE and the MONMOUTH were sunk with all hands. The GLASGOW and the OTRANTO managed to make good their escape. They were joined by the pre-Dreadnought battleship CANOPUS, which had been hurrying to assist Cradock.

There was consternation back in London when the outcome of the Battle of Coronel was known. The Dreadnoughts INVINCIBLE and INFLEXIBLE, under Vice-Admiral Sir Doveton Sturdee, were ordered to the Falkland Islands, with instructions to sink von Spee's fleet.

NOVEMBER 9, 1914
The EMDEN destroys the telegraph station on Cocos Islands. However, the telegraphists there managed to send a message, which was picked up by the SYDNEY, an Australian cruiser, which was in the vicinity. Within three hours, the SYDNEY arrived on the scene. Her 6-inch (152.4 mm) guns outmanned the raider's 4.1-inch (104.0 mm) guns. The EMDEN was forced inshore. Soon, she was on fire, and half-sunk. She had already lost seven of her officers and 104 men. Faced with total destruction, she struck her colours and ran ashore as a wreck.

DECEMBER 8, 1914
Meanwhile, von Spee had been ordered back to Berlin. En route, he decided to destroy the Port Stanley wireless station on the Falklands. By a strange chance, Sturdee and von Spee arrived within twenty-four hours of each other. Sturdee was coaling his fleet when the SCHARN-HORST was sighted. All von Spee had to do was attack, but shells from the CANOPUS and the exit of the KENT from the harbour made him pull off southwards. When von Spee was told that tripod masts of the Dreadnoughts had been seen, he refused to believe it. But when the British fleet had finished coaling and put out to sea, von Spee realized that the odds were against him. Nevertheless, he decided to engage the enemy.

In the ensuing battle, the INVINCIBLE sank the SCHARNHORST, and the INFLEXIBLE dispatched the GNEISENAU, while the armed P. & O. merchantman MACEDONIA and the BRISTOL accounted for the supply ships BADEN and SANTA ISABEL. The CORNWALL sank the LEIPZIG, and the KENT finished off the NÜRNBERG.

Of the warships, only the DRESDEN managed to escape from the battle; but three months later, on March 14, 1915, she was cornered at the Juan Fernandez Islands by the KENT, the GLASGOW, and the ORAMA. Her commander, Captain Ludecke, was forced to surrender. As soon as his crew was ashore, he blew the ship up.

JANUARY 23, 1915
The Battle of the Dogger Bank takes place. A German task force had left the Jade, intent on destroying the minesweeping and trawler fleets in the Dogger Bank area of the North Sea. It consisted of the battle-cruisers SEYDLITZ, MOLTKE, DERFFLINGER, and BLÜCHER, with supporting cruisers and destroyers.

The British battle-cruisers LION, TIGER, PRIN-CESS ROYAL, NEW ZEALAND, and INDOMITABLE challenged the German fleet and, at a range of 25,000 yards (22,860 m) the battle commenced. The opposing flagships, SEYDLITZ and LION, both suffered direct hits. The BLÜCHER was also damaged, and had her speed reduced by five knots. The German fleet tried to form a defensive circle, but the SEYDLITZ had to retire, and the BLÜCHER was left to her fate. After another seventy direct shell hits and seven torpedoes, she capsized with a heavy loss of life.

MAY 7, 1915
The Cunard liner LUSITANIA is sunk by U-20, commanded by Lieutenant-Commander Schweiger, with a loss of 1,198 lives, many of them American. Neutral public opinion is enraged.

JULY 1915
In December, 1914, the German KÖNIGSBERG put to sea from her base, Dar-es-Salaam, making for the Gulf of Aden. While she was away, the ASTREA arrived off Dar-es-Salaam, and shelled the wireless station. The Germans scuttled the graving dock across the mouth of the harbour as a protective barrier. This left the KÖNIGSBERG without a communications base and, also, without a harbour. Instead, she was forced to use the nearby Rufigi delta. From there, she attacked Zanzibar, and sank the cruiser PEGASUS, whereupon she was bottled up in the Rufigi.

Soon afterwards, the two shallow-draught monitors SEVERN and MERSEY arrived in tow from England, manoeuvred within range of the KÖNIGSBERG, and destroyed her.

AUGUST 1915
U-24 sinks the White Star liner ARABIC, again

A *The British light cruiser* GALATEA, *1914.*
B *The Italian super-dreadnought* CAIO DUILIO, *1913, survived the First World War, was modernised, and served in the Second World War.*

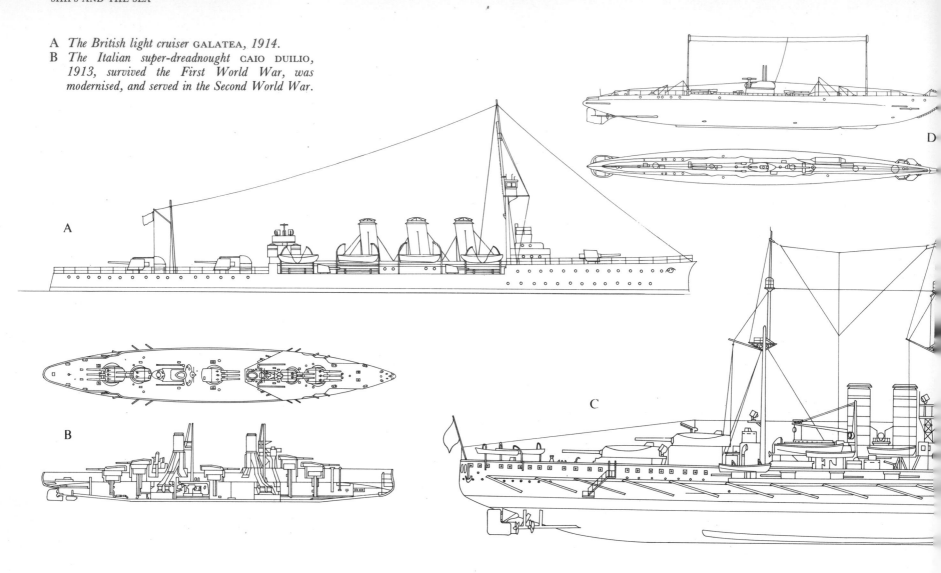

with heavy loss of life. This time, the Germans see themselves forced to bow to public opinion and call off U-boat attacks on passenger ships; but they continue building submarines.

DECEMBER 1915

One of the famous German merchant raiders, the MÖWE, leaves Hamburg to make two cruises during which she sinks or captures thirty-four British merchant ships, and lays the mines that are later to sink the KING EDWARD.

One of her prizes is the YARROWDALE, which the Germans disguise and rename the LEOPARD. Her disguise was not pierced until March, 1917, when she tried to break through the British blockade and was sunk by the cruiser ACHILLES.

JANUARY 1916

President Wilson requests Britain to stop arming her merchant vessels, since this is the excuse for Germany's U-boat attacks. Britain refuses, and Germany re-opens her unrestricted submarine campaign. Some weeks later, the SUSSEX is torpedoed, and many Americans lose their lives.

Britain mines the Straits of Dover, so that the U-boats are forced to go around the north of Scotland to get into the Atlantic.

FEBRUARY 1916

The German raider GREIF on her first sortie, two days out of port, meets with the COMUS and two former Royal Mail ships, the armed merchant cruisers ANDES and ALCANTARA. Both the GREIF and the ALCANTARA are lost in the engagement that follows.

MAY 31, 1916

The Battle of Jutland takes place. Two German fleets under Admirals von Hipper and von Scheer had set out from Wilhelmshaven northwards towards Norway. The British fleet under Admirals Jellicoe and Beatty had left its British bases for a sweep of the North Sea. In the vicinity of the north end of Jutland, ships from the advance squadrons sighted each other when they went to inspect the same neutral Danish ship.

Von Hipper turned round from north to south, to rejoin his main fleet. Beatty followed in pursuit. The Germans harassed their pursuers

with destroyer action, and the QUEEN MARY and the INDEFATIGABLE were both sunk by single salvoes. On seeing the destruction of the second ship, Beatty made his now famous comment: 'There seems to be something wrong with our bloody ships today'.

At this point, the main German fleet was seen to the south, and Beatty swung north to lure it into the path of the greatly superior British Grand Fleet. When Jellicoe's fleet arrived, a furious general engagement took place. Hipper's flagship LÜTZOW was put out of action; the British INVINCIBLE, DEFENSE, and WARRIOR were lost. When dark came, the engagement was broken off, with the Germans moving southwards towards home. Skirmishing during the night caused the sinking of the British BLACK PRINCE, while the Germans lost the FRAUENLOB, the POMMERN, and the ELBING. By daybreak, the German fleet was close to its home base, and Jellicoe, fearing minefields and the possibility of submarine attacks, broke off the engagement and, at 11.00, sailed for home. A summary of the battle is given above in table form.

Thus, the statistic evidence shows that the

C *The Austrian dreadnought* VIRIBUS UNITIS, *1911.*
D *U-boat type 46, First World War.*
E *The British battleship* HOOD, *laid down during the First World War, was not completed until 1920.*

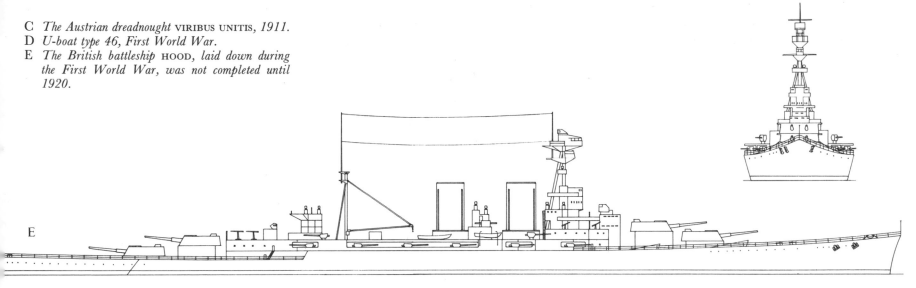

E

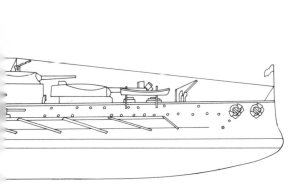

THE BATTLE OF JUTLAND

	German	British
Battleships	22	28
Battle-cruisers	5	8
Cruisers	11	34
Torpedo-boats	61	77
Seaplane carriers	0	1
Minelayers	0	1
	Total: 99	**Total: 150**
Reported losses:		
Ships	11	14
Men	2,551	6,097
Other statistics:		
Big guns used	200	264
Torpedo-tubes fired	475	457

German fleet bested a larger and more heavily armed adversary. But, as the *New York Times* put it: 'The prisoner attacked his jailer, but is still in jail.' Britain's mastery of the seas was not challenged again on a large scale during the remainder of the war.

JUNE 5, 1916
U-75 lays mines which sink the HAMPSHIRE, with Field Marshal Lord Kitchener, the British Commander-in-Chief, on board. Kitchener is drowned.

OCTOBER 4, 1916
The ex-Cunarder FRANCONIA is torpedoed near Malta, while serving as a troopship. All but twelve on board are saved.

FEBRUARY 1, 1917
Germany resumes her total blockade of Britain. By April, Britain had lost one and a half million tons of shipping. By August, the total had reached three million tons.

APRIL 6, 1917
America enters the war on Britain's side. All

interned German ships are seized. Among the largest passenger liners are: N.D.L.'s KRON-PRINZESSIN CECILIE, GEORGE WASHINGTON, KAISER WILHELM II, GROSSER KURFURST, BARBAROSSA, PRINZESS IRENE, PRINZ EITEL FRIEDRICH, NECKAR, and RHEIN; and H.A.P.A.G.'s VATERLAND, PRESIDENT GRANT, PRESIDENT LINCOLN, AMERIKA, CINCINNATI, HAMBURG, and PENNSYLVANIA.

DECEMBER 1917
The British fleet is augmented by the U.S. 6th Battle Squadron, comprising the nine battleships NEW YORK, TEXAS, UTAH, NEVADA, ARIZONA, ARKANSAS, WYOMING, FLORIDA, and OKLAHOMA.

APRIL 22, 1918
The ports of Zeebrügge and Ostend are attacked with the object of sinking block ships in the harbour entrances. The attack on Ostend failed, but at Zeebrügge the mole was breached by the VINDICTIVE, and three old cruisers, the THETIS, the INTREPID, and the IPHIGENIA, were sunk at the entrance to the Bruges Canal. Within a week or so, however, the Germans could use the harbour again, but the raid was

valuable for the consternation it caused along this strongly held German coastal line.

NOVEMBER 11, 1918
The Armistice is declared, and the First World War comes to an end. The German fleet is interned at Scapa Flow in the Orkneys. It consists of ten battleships, six battle-cruisers, eight light cruisers, and fifty destroyers.

JUNE 21, 1919
This was the date assigned for the signing of the Treaty of Versailles, although it was not, in fact, signed until June 23. At 10.00, Admiral von Reuter ordered the scuttling of the entire German fleet. Of the major ships, only the BADEN, the FRANKFURT, the NÜRNBERG, and the new EMDEN were saved. The EMDEN was ceded to France, the FRANKFURT to the United States, and the other two to the British.

1920
The bulk of Germany's merchant navy is sold in order to satisfy, in part, the reparation demands that are made upon her under the terms of the Treaty of Versailles.

In 1916, Germany possessed more than four million tons of merchant shipping. Only a small amount of this total was lost as the result of war action. By the end of 1920, the German merchant navy grossed no more than half a million tons, the average size of a vessel being 600 tons. All the rest, representing some 434 merchant ships, were sold to various new owners. For example, forty passenger ships were sold to Great Britain. These included the BISMARCK and the IMPERATOR. The United States retained all the vessels she had seized when she entered the war in April, 1917.

1921

Some pre-war ships can still be used in the post-war era, although not necessarily for the same owners as originally. The Hamburg America Line is a sufferer in this respect. In 1921, for example, the IMPERATOR, 52,226 tons gross, enters Cunard's service as the BEREN-GARIA. The BISMARCK, 56,621 tons gross, which never even flew the H.A.P.A.G. flag, was operated by the White Star Line under her new name, the MAJESTIC; whilst the VATERLAND, 54,282 tons gross, joined the United States Line as its flagship, the LEVIATHAN.

Holland also benefited from this handing over of German ships as part of the reparations programme. Two H.A.P.A.G. ships were completed in 1921 for the Holland Lloyd Line. The original JOHANN HEINRICH BURCHARD, 19,582 tons gross, became the LIMBURGIA; the WILLIAM O'SWALD became the BRABANTIA, of 19,653 tons gross. Indeed, the Hamburg America Line was so depleted of her shipping stock through war losses and reparations that for a time she was reduced to operating one ship only, the ageing HANSA, 16,703 tons gross.

1924

Gustaf Erikson, a shipowner of Mariehamn in Finland, swimming against the rip-tide, is the sole person left operating a fleet of commercial sailing-ships.

1925

The first major passenger motor-ship is built. She is the Swedish America Line's GRIPSHOLM, 17,993 tons.

1926

The last trading sailing-ship, the PADUA, is built for the German company Laeisz, which put her into service on the Chile run. Her cargo outwards was coal and coke, whilst she brought nitrates to Germany on the homeward run. She always went by way of the Horn.

1926

In England, the directors of the Royal Mail Line purchase the shares of the White Star Line, thus emphasizing the move towards huge conglomerates in the shipping world, a phenomenon that was also noticeable in other aspects of the commercial world.

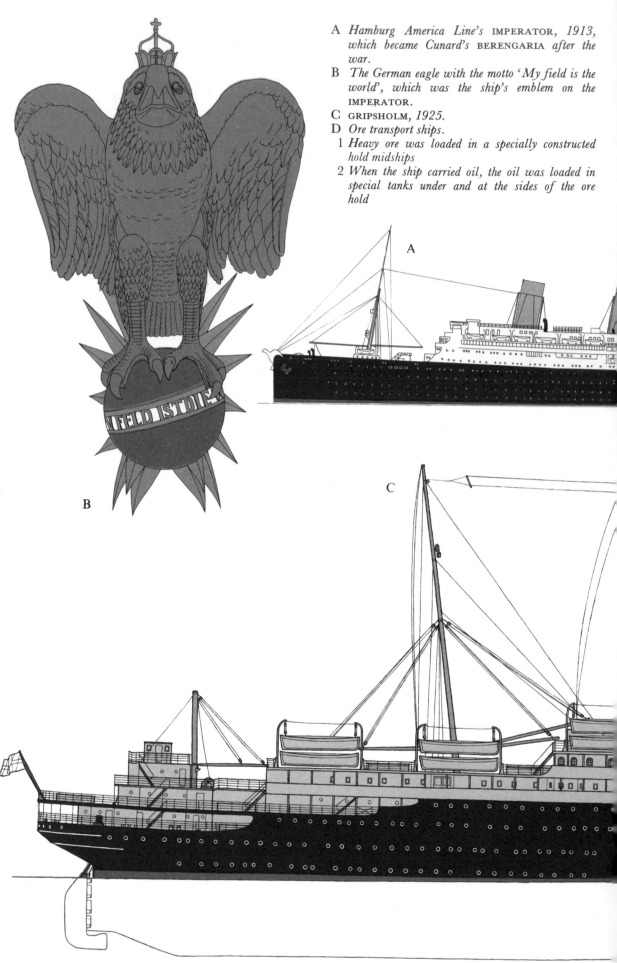

A *Hamburg America Line's* IMPERATOR, *1913, which became Cunard's* BERENGARIA *after the war.*

B *The German eagle with the motto 'My field is the world', which was the ship's emblem on the* IMPERATOR.

C GRIPSHOLM, *1925.*

D *Ore transport ships.*

1 *Heavy ore was loaded in a specially constructed hold midships*

2 *When the ship carried oil, the oil was loaded in special tanks under and at the sides of the ore hold*

E *This bulk carrier of the 1920s was constructed to carry both heavy ore, which only filled part of the hold, and lighter loads such as grain or phosphates, which filled the hold completely.*

F STRÅSSA, *1921, built for ore transport in Arctic waters.*

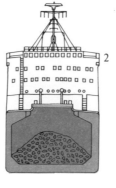

D

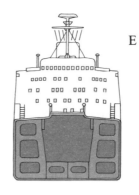

E

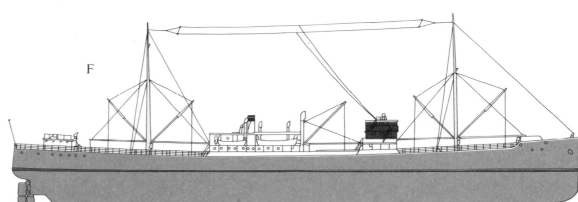

F

A *In 1924, Gustaf Erikson added the* ARCHIBALD RUSSELL, *1905, to his fleet of sailing-ships.*
B KØBENHAVN, *1921, which vanished with all hands in 1928.*
C BREMEN, *1928, which won the Blue Riband from the* MAURETANIA *in 1929.*

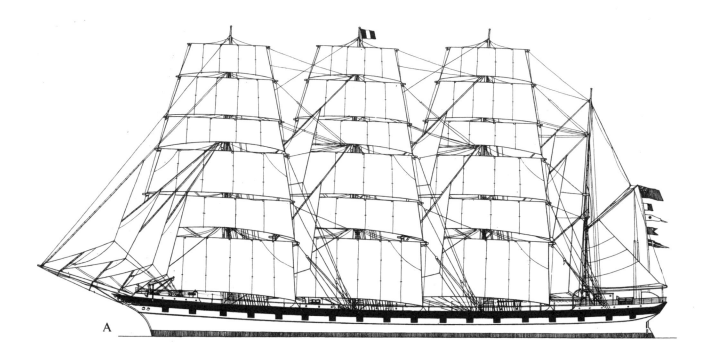

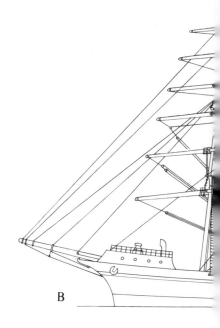

OCTOBER 1927

The PRINCIPESSA MAFALDA, belonging to the Navigazione Generale Italiana of Italy, was steaming off the coast of Brazil when her propeller-shaft snapped. Normally, such an accident would be an inconvenience rather than a major tragedy. On this occasion, however, the rotating screw pulled the shaft clear of its housing. At once, before even the alarm could be raised, water rushed into the vessel. In a very short time, she filled and went to the bottom.

1928

The Panama Pacific Line builds the PENNSYLVANIA, the VIRGINIA, and the CALIFORNIA, the first turbo-electric-driven liners.

NOVEMBER 1928

Seatrain Lines, owned by the Overseas Steamship Co. of Montreal, inaugurates a new transport service between New Orleans and Havana. This service involves one great innovation: the shipper placed sealed containers onto railway flats, and these were not unloaded until they reached their destination. Seatrain was the ancestor of the modern container ship.

Of course, railway wagons had been carried aboard ships in Europe since 1849, when the Edinburgh, Perth and Dundee Railway Co. inaugurated such a service with the LEVIATHAN, and in Canada, on the Great Lakes, since 1858 when the International Buffalo and Lake Huron Railway operated a similar service on the INTERNATIONAL.

DECEMBER 14, 1928

The five-masted barque KJØBENHAVN, 1,921 tons gross, the sail training ship of the Danish East Asiatic Co., leaves Buenos Aires bound for Melbourne. She is never seen again. She disappeared without word or trace, to join that ever-increasing roll-call of vanished ships.

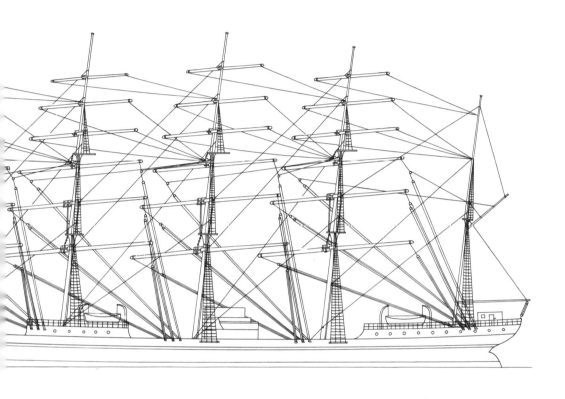

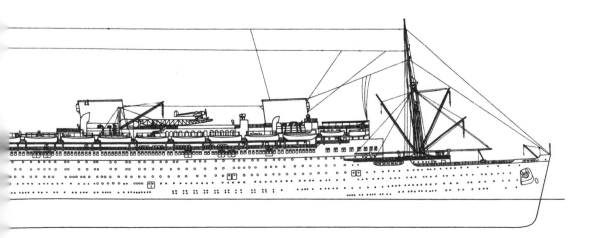

1929
The MAURETANIA, which had held the speed record for so many years, has to yield pride of place to the BREMEN, which breaks the record both to and from America with the speeds of 27.83 and 27.92 knots respectively.

1931
Spain becomes a republic. Cia. Transatlantica reflects this change by renaming two of her distinguished ships. The ALFONSO XIII, 10,551 tons, becomes the HABANA; the REINA VICTORIA EUGENIA, 10,137 tons, is changed to the ARGENTINA.

JUNE 1931-NOVEMBER 26, 1932
Perhaps the most unlucky ship of modern times is the BERMUDA, built in 1927, and belonging to Furness Withy of Great Britain. Until June, 1931, there was no sign of a jinx upon her. Unhappily, she then caught fire whilst in port at Hamilton, in Bermuda, and was ninety per cent destroyed. She was taken in tow and delivered to the repair yards of Harland & Wolff in Belfast. A fine rehabilitation job had almost been completed when, on November 26, 1932, she caught fire once again. This time it was decided that the damage was beyond repair, and she was sold for scrap. The United Towing Co. was given the contract to tow the hulk to the scrap-yard. A storm broke out while the tug SEAMAN had her in tow, and she was wrecked off the coast of Scotland.

JANUARY 2, 1932
The depression of the late 1920s and early 1930s causes the formation of the Italia Line by the amalgamation of the Cosulich Line, the Sabaudo Line, and the Navigazione Generale Italiana. The new company owned twenty-two vessels.

MAY 16, 1932
The GEORGES PHILIPPAR of Messageries Maritimes of France catches fire off Cape Gardafui, on the inbound leg of her maiden voyage. Forty-four lives are lost. Fortunately, the Russian tanker SOVETSKAYA NEFT is near at hand, and takes 400 survivors aboard. These are later transferred to the Greek ship ATHOS II, and landed at Djibouti.

JANUARY 4, 1933
L'ATLANTIQUE, belonging to the Cie. Sud-Atlantique, catches fire at half past three in the morning at a point 22 miles (40.7 km) west of Guernsey. At eight o'clock, her captain gave the order to abandon ship, satisfied that she was doomed. Unfortunately—for the company—the ship was salvaged. Disputes immediately arose over the hulk, and, after a protracted law-suit, she was broken up at Port Glasgow, over two years after she had been abandoned.

A QUEEN MARY, *1934, won the Blue Riband in 1936 and again in 1938. During the Second World War, she was used as a troopship, and she was capable of carrying 15,000 troops at a time. After travelling over 500,000 miles (926,600 km) in war service, she was recommissioned on the North Atlantic run in 1947. She is now anchored at Long Beach, California, where she is used as a maritime museum.*

B *One of the* QUEEN MARY's *stabilizers.*

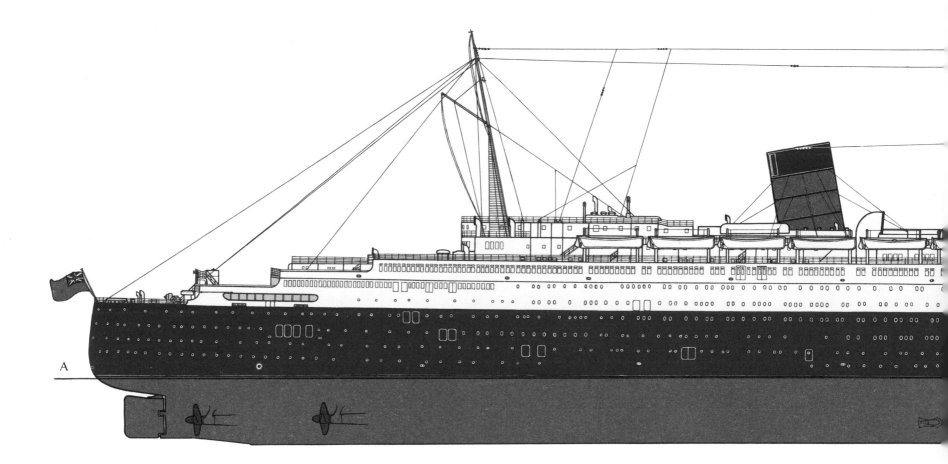

AUGUST 1933

Italia Line's REX takes the Atlantic Blue Riband. She steamed from Gibraltar to New York in 4 days, 13 hours, and 58 minutes, at an average speed of 28.92 knots. The REX thus became the first Italian vessel ever to achieve this honour.

1934

One effect of the depression in world trade was that many vessels were broken up whilst they still had many years of useful life before them. The Atlantic Transport Line's MINNEWASKA and MINNETONKA, both of 22,000 tons gross, were broken up in 1934. Neither was more than ten years old. Their owners

also became a casualty of the depression, and went out of business in 1936.

In England, the White Star Line felt the cold wind of depression. She disposed of four of her ships, a small number when set alongside the twenty medium-sized Italian ships that were laid up. Laying-up was the fate of scores of useful ships in most of the major maritime countries.

APRIL 1934

One small pointer to the coming dissipation of the dark clouds of economic gloom is the decision that was made to re-start work on the giant Cunarder QUEEN MARY. Government

aid, however, had to be given before work recommenced.

The QUEEN MARY had actually been laid down in the Clyde-bank shipyard of John Brown in May, 1930. A year later, this prestigious project became a victim of the depression. In December, 1933, the Government agreed to advance the company the sum of £3,000,000 in order that the ship should be completed, on the understanding that a further £5,000,000 would be made available should her proposed sister ship also be built. Additionally, in order to effect economies of scale, the Cunard Line and the White Star Line were forced to amalgamate.

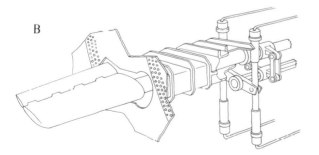

B

SEPTEMBER 26, 1934
The QUEEN MARY is launched by Queen Mary of England.

1935
The London Naval Agreement is signed. This permits Germany to rebuild her navy. The German Government concentrated its resources on Plan Z, which called for the building of six 45,000-ton battleships. In 1939, Plan Z was abandoned in favour of U-boat construction. German strategists later claim that this delay in the starting of U-boat building cost them the war. Another hundred U-boats would have won the war for Germany.

MAY 27, 1936
The maiden voyage of the QUEEN MARY breaks no records but, in August, she establishes new records in both directions. She crosses from Bishop's Rock to Ambrose Light, 2,907 nautical miles, in 4 days and 27 minutes, at an average speed of 30.14 knots.

JULY 17, 1937
The maiden voyage of the DELIUS, belonging to Lamport and Holt, takes place. She is the first vessel to have her bridge, wireless cabin, and wireless operations room actually built into the funnel.

1938

The Greek Line is founded. This small shipping line purchased the TUSCANIA from the Anchor Line, renamed her the NEA HELLAS, and early in 1939 put her on the Piraeus-New York service. This was one of the last peaceful shipping acts before all shipping throughout the world had to face the hazards of war as well as the perils of the seas.

MARCH 6, 1938

The most severe naval loss of the Spanish Civil War (1936-39) is the sinking of the 10,670-ton BALEARES by torpedoing.

THE SECOND WORLD WAR
SEPTEMBER 3, 1939-AUGUST 14, 1945
The Second World War breaks out. The first naval casualty is the German destroyer LEBERECHT MAASS, sunk by Polish guns at Hel, within hours of the declaration of war.

SEPTEMBER 3, 1939

At 21.00 U-30, commanded by Lieutenant-Commander Lemp, torpedoes the Donaldson liner ATHENIA, off Ireland. One hundred and twelve lives are lost, twenty-eight of them American. Public opinion in the United States is outraged against this repetition of history.

Admiral Dönitz, Commander-in-Chief of the German submarine forces, had fifty-seven U-boats under his command at the outbreak of hostilities, twenty-six ocean-going and the rest coastal. A submarine fleet can, however, only be one-third operational. For each operational craft, there is one on passage and one at base re-arming.

SEPTEMBER 5, 1939

The U.S. Government passes the Neutrality Act. Under the terms of this statute, all passenger sailings to Great Britain, France, and Germany were suspended. Sailings to Italy were excluded from the ban, and this loop-hole allowed American shipping lines to continue some sort of service to Europe, using Genoa as the port of disembarkation. Also, in an attempt to circumvent the provisions of the Neutrality Act, the board of the United States Line transferred eight of their ships to the Société Maritime Anversoise, in order that they might be operated under the Belgian flag—a stratagem that was perfectly legal.

SEPTEMBER 14, 1939

U-39 tries to torpedo the British aircraft carrier ARK ROYAL, but is herself sunk.

SEPTEMBER 17, 1939

U-29, commanded by Lieutenant-Commander Schuhardt, torpedoes the aircraft carrier COURAGEOUS off north-west Ireland. Captain Makeig-Jones and 518 of her crew are lost, and 682 are rescued by the VEENDAM of the Holland America Line.

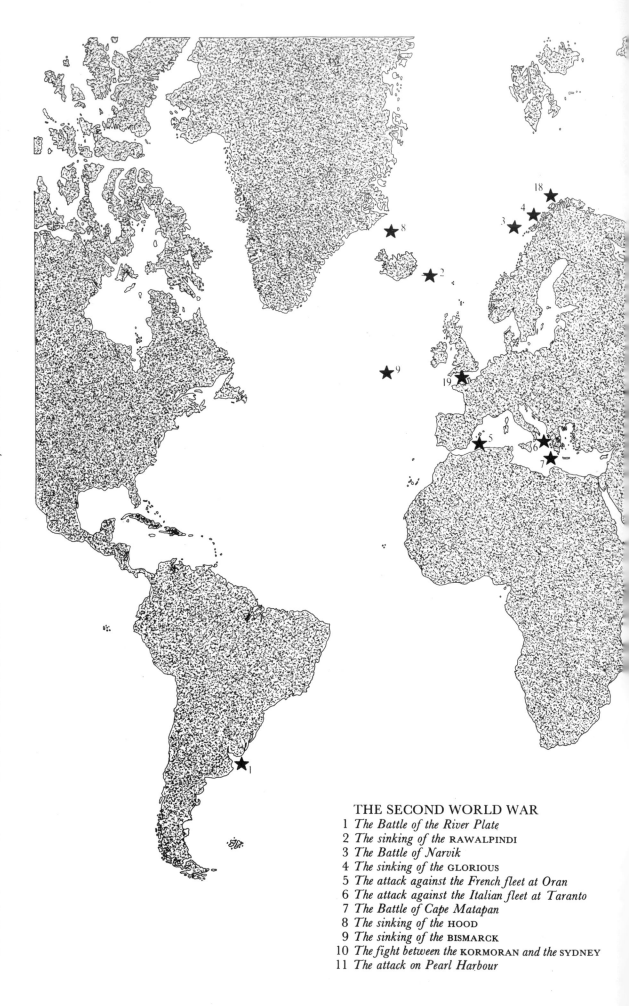

THE SECOND WORLD WAR
1 *The Battle of the River Plate*
2 *The sinking of the* RAWALPINDI
3 *The Battle of Narvik*
4 *The sinking of the* GLORIOUS
5 *The attack against the French fleet at Oran*
6 *The attack against the Italian fleet at Taranto*
7 *The Battle of Cape Matapan*
8 *The sinking of the* HOOD
9 *The sinking of the* BISMARCK
10 *The fight between the* KORMORAN *and the* SYDNEY
11 *The attack on Pearl Harbour*

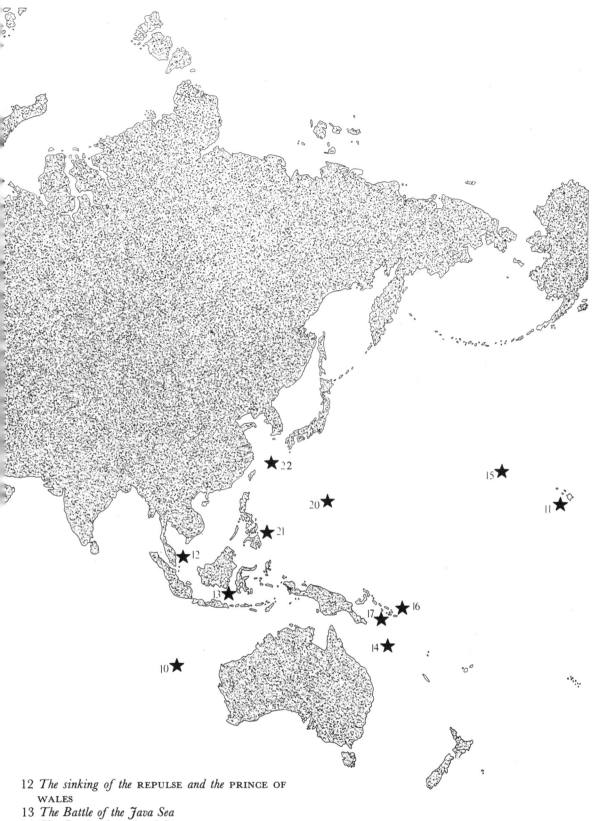

SEPTEMBER 26, 1939

The 'sinking' of the ARK ROYAL. Lieutenant Adolf Francke of the Luftwaffe, in a Heinkel, bombs the ARK ROYAL. An incredibly near miss deluges the ship, and Francke sees her disappear in a fountain of water. He reports that he 'believes' he has hit the ARK ROYAL. A German reconnaissance plane locates three British warships, but no aircraft carrier. Germany therefore claims that the ARK ROYAL has been sunk. What the plane, in fact, saw was a different group of warships.

OCTOBER 14, 1939

U-47, commanded by Lieutenant-Commander Günther Prien, creeps through the boom into Scapa Flow and torpedoes the ROYAL OAK, which capsizes, leaving 833 dead.

NOVEMBER 1939

A new German weapon, the magnetic mine, sinks twenty-seven merchant ships and the destroyer BLANCHE, while the cruiser BELFAST is badly damaged. Fortunately, one of the mines is captured, and the new weapon is countered by de-gaussing wires around the hull of each ship. These wires neutralize the hull's magnetic field.

NOVEMBER 1939

The German ship DEUTSCHLAND is renamed LÜTZOW to prevent the Allies making capital out of a possible sinking of a ship with such a name.

NOVEMBER 1939

The ADMIRAL GRAF SPEE sinks nine British merchant ships. Under the command of Captain Hans Langsdorff, she had left Wilhelmshaven for the South Atlantic eleven days before the outbreak of war.

In Britain, Force G is instructed by the Admiralty to hunt down the GRAF SPEE. Force G consists of the cruisers AJAX, EXETER, and ACHILLES, under the overall command of Commodore Henry Harwood.

NOVEMBER 23, 1939

The armed merchant cruiser RAWALPINDI, commanded by Captain E. C. Kennedy, is sunk by the SCHARNHORST and the GNEISENAU. Thirty-eight survivors are picked up.

Fifty-six British ships, mainly liners, were used as armed merchant cruisers in 1939 and 1940.

DECEMBER 13, 1939

The Battle of the River Plate takes place. The three British cruisers encounter the GRAF SPEE near the River Plate. The EXETER is badly damaged, but her torpedoes force the GRAF SPEE to turn and to make smoke, in case the others also fire torpedoes. The EXETER follows her, and all three ships attack. After one and a half hours, the GRAF SPEE has received twenty direct hits, and the last turret of the EXETER is silenced.

Unable to fight through to home, the GRAF SPEE makes for Montevideo, trailed by the ACHILLES and the AJAX. The EXETER, with fifty-three dead, limps off to the Falkland Islands. At Montevideo, the GRAF SPEE is given three days for repairs and then must leave. Captain Langsdorff decides on a dash to Buenos Aires, but a British merchant ship quickly leaves the harbour, and this means that, by international law, the GRAF SPEE may not now sail for twenty-four hours.

DECEMBER 17, 1939
At 18.15, the GRAF SPEE, her battle ensigns flying, sails out from Montevideo accompanied by the TACOMA, a H.A.P.A.G. merchantman. At the three-mile (5.6 km) limit, she stops and scuttles herself. The crew transfers to the TACOMA, which sails for Buenos Aires.

FEBRUARY 16, 1940
GRAF SPEE's oil-tanker supply ship ALTMARK reaches Norwegian waters with 299 British prisoners aboard. The British destroyer COSSACK follows, and boards her in the neutral fjord. All the prisoners are rescued. The machine-guns on the ALTMARK disprove her 'unarmed' claim and prevent a diplomatic incident with Norway.

FEBRUARY 27, 1940
The largest liner ever built, the QUEEN ELIZA- BETH, is completed at John Brown's Clyde-side yard. To safeguard her against bombing, she is sent secretly to New York. En route, she passed a battleship which flashed the one word 'SNAP!' to her. It was her namesake, the battleship QUEEN ELIZABETH!

The liner was converted to a troopship, capable of carrying 15,000 troops, and served as such until the end of February, 1946.

APRIL 6, 1940
The German invasion of Norway starts, fore-stalling the Allies, who are planning a similar step only days later. The battleships SCHARN- HORST and GNEISENAU go north, and the ADMIR- AL HIPPER and fourteen destroyers head for Trondheim. The battleship LÜTZOW, the heavy cruiser BLÜCHER, and a screen of light cruisers head for Oslo.

APRIL 8, 1940
The day before the landing, the HIPPER meets the British destroyer GLOWWORM and sinks her, but not before she has been rammed by the GLOWWORM and received a 120-foot (36.6 m) gash in the bow.

On the same day, the British mine Norwegian waters across the path of the Germans, and the Polish submarine ORZEL sinks the German troopship RIO DE JANEIRO.

APRIL 9, 1940
In violent seas off Narvik, the SCHARNHORST

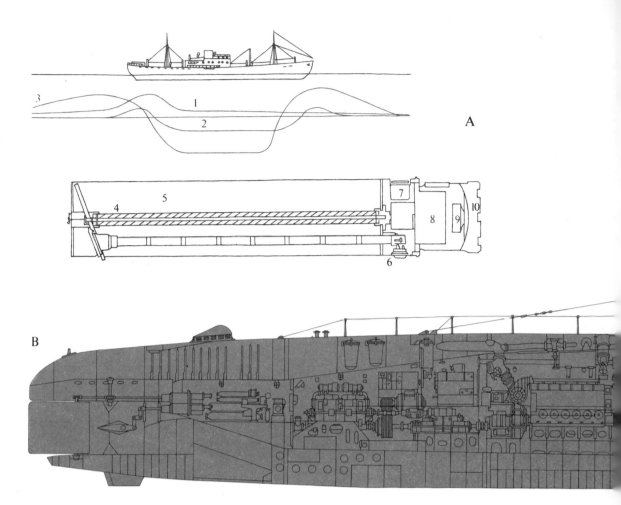

A

B

and the GNEISENAU meet the RENOWN, ex-change fire, and then race off in the storm. Meanwhile, Trondheim capitulates to the HIPPER, and Bergen is taken by the cruiser KÖNIGSBERG. At Oslo, the BLÜCHER is sunk by torpedoes from the forts. Near Kristiansand, the British submarine TRUANT torpedoes the cruiser KARLSRUHE.

By nightfall, Norway has been occupied. Denmark suffers the same fate on the same day.

APRIL 10, 1940
Skua aircraft from the ARK ROYAL destroy the KÖNIGSBERG at Bergen in a dive-bombing attack. This is the first major warship to be lost in this manner. The significance of this is missed by the British, but marked well by the Germans and the Japanese.

The First Battle of Narvik takes place on the same day, when five British destroyers, the HARDY, the HUNTER, the HAVOCK, the HOTSPUR, and the HOSTILE, steam right into Narvik Bay and engage a superior force of German de-stroyers. The ANTON SCHMITT is sunk, and the DIETER VON ROEDER, the GEORG THIELE, the BERND VON ARNIM, and the HANS LÜDEMANN are all damaged. The HERMANN KÜNNE has

her engines put out of action. The German commodore, Friedrich Bonte, is killed aboard the WILHELM HEIDKAMP, which is sunk.

British losses are heavy. The HARDY and the HUNTER go down, and Captain Warburton-Lee, commander of the ships, is killed.

APRIL 13, 1940
The Second Battle of Narvik follows three days later. The battleship WARSPITE with her seven destroyers sinks eight German destroyers, in-cluding all the survivors named above from the First Battle. The U-64 is caught on the surface by aircraft, and sunk. The British COSSACK is beached but, eventually, she is towed to safety.

MAY 26-JUNE 2, 1940
Following the German break-out across France, 338,000 Allied forces are evacuated from Dun-kirk. Every ship of less than 1,000 tons, from Weymouth in the south-west to Harwich in the south-east, is used, including scores of private river launches. Only 2,000 troops are lost in the crossing.

JUNE 8, 1940
The British and French forces finish evacuating Norway on June 7. On her way home, the

A *The magnetic (magnetic-acoustic) mine, Second World War.*
1 *Variation of earth's magnetic field under a ship*
& *with permanent magnetism (1), and under a*
2 *degaussed ship (2).*
3 *Variation of sound pressure*
4 *Induction coil*
5 *Charge*
6 *Primer with detonator*
7 *Safety device*
8 *Instrument box (with relay, ship counter, etc.)*
9 *Acoustic device*
10 *Parachute container*
B *U-boat type* XXI, *Second World War.*

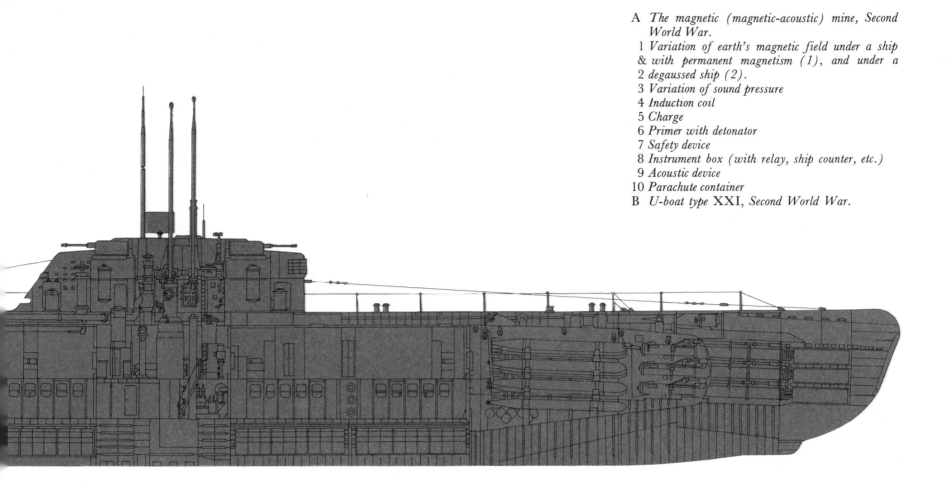

aircraft carrier GLORIOUS is caught by the SCHARNHORST and the GNEISENAU and sunk, together with her destroyers, the ARDENT and the ACASTA.

JULY 3, 1940
The British Navy attacks the French fleet under Admiral Gensoul at Oran, North Africa, in order to prevent the Germans from taking over the French ships. If the French fleet had defected to Britain, then Vichy France would face the consequential wrath of the Germans.

The British fleet demands that the French ships be neutralized. Admiral Gensoul signals his ships, 'Get under way ready for action.' At 18.00, the British attack. Sixteen minutes later, it is over. The battleship STRASBOURG, the only one to escape, flees towards Toulon. The BRETAGNE has been blown up, the DUNKERQUE is beached in paralyzed condition, and the PROVENCE, afire, has gone aground. The destroyer MOGADOR receives a direct hit, and her stern blows off when her mines explode. One thousand three hundred Frenchmen are dead.

JULY 19, 1940
The Australian cruiser SYDNEY disables the Italian cruiser BARTOLOMEO COLLEONI north-west of Crete. Torpedoes from the destroyers ILEX and HYPERION finish her off.

SEPTEMBER 13, 1940
Ninety British children, being evacuated to Canada, are on board the Ellerman liner CITY OF BENARES when she is torpedoed and sunk. Only thirteen children survive.

NOVEMBER 5, 1940
Convoy HX 84, in mid-Atlantic, is sighted by the German pocket battleship ADMIRAL SCHEER. To allow the convoy to scatter, its escort, the armed merchant cruiser JERVIS BAY, makes a smoke screen and steams to meet the battleship. The JERVIS BAY is sunk, but only five ships in the convoy are caught by the ADMIRAL SCHEER.

NOVEMBER 11, 1940
The Italian fleet in Taranto, at the 'toe' of Italy, is attacked by twenty-one Swordfish aircraft from the aircraft carriers ILLUSTRIOUS and EAGLE. The battleship CONTE DI CAVOUR is sunk, and two others put out of commission.

MARCH 8, 1941
U-47, commanded by one of Germany's greatest

submarine commanders, Günther Prien, is sunk by the destroyer WOLVERINE when she attacks convoy OB 293.

MARCH 17, 1941
U-99 and U-100, commanded by two other ace commanders, Otto Kreschmer and Joachim Schepke respectively, are sunk by the destroyers VANOC and WALKER.

MARCH 28-29, 1941
The Battle of Matapan is fought by night. The Italian fleet, under Admiral Angelo Iachino in the battleship VITTORIO VENETO, clashes with the British Mediterranean Fleet led by the battleships BARHAM, VALIANT, and WARSPITE. For once, the Luftwaffe air cover is poor, and aircraft from the carrier FORMIDABLE score hits on the VITTORIO VENETO and on the cruiser POLA, which is forced to stop.

The Italian fleet breaks off and races for port, leaving the cruisers ZARA and FIUME to protect the stricken POLA. All three cruisers are sunk, as well as the destroyers GIOSUE CARDUCCI and VITTORIO ALFIERI.

MAY 22, 1941
A British Fleet Air Arm reconnaissance crew

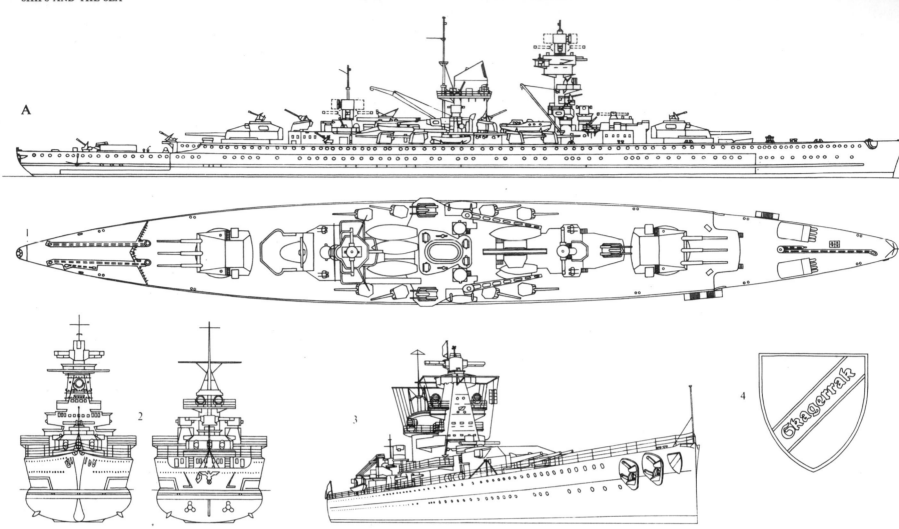

reports that the BISMARCK, the biggest and one of the most powerful battleships afloat, and the heavy cruiser PRINZ EUGEN are no longer at their berths in Bergen, Norway. The British Admiralty alerts all ships.

MAY 23, 1941
The patrolling cruisers SUFFOLK and NORFOLK sight the BISMARCK and the PRINZ EUGEN on the Denmark Strait, off Greenland. The BISMARCK fires at the NORFOLK without hitting her.

MAY 24, 1941
The battleship PRINCE OF WALES arrives with the Royal Navy's largest cruiser, the HOOD. At twelve miles (22.2 km) range, the HOOD opens fire on the PRINZ EUGEN, the leading German ship, but the PRINCE OF WALES concentrates on the BISMARCK. A direct hit from the PRINZ EUGEN starts a fire on the HOOD. The BISMARCK, firing salvoes every twenty-two seconds, concentrates on the HOOD, which, rent by a huge explosion, disappears in a cloud of smoke and flame. Only three survive from a crew of 1,419. But the BISMARCK has been damaged by direct hits and, with her speed reduced, is leaking oil. Admiral Lütjens directs her course southwards towards St. Nazaire,

the only port with a large enough dry dock for her. PRINZ EUGEN slips away on her own.

MAY 25, 1941
The BISMARCK finds herself alone. She can still detect enemy radar, but makes a fatal mistake when, unaware that the return radar echo is not bouncing back as far as her searchers, she sends a radio signal, thus giving away her position. The Royal Navy had, in fact, lost the BISMARCK six hours earlier, and were searching for her frantically.

MAY 26, 1941
The sea is still empty, but the trap is closing. Swordfish planes from the aircraft carrier ARK ROYAL are launched and, racing out of the mist, attack. Eleven magnetic torpedoes are released before the pilots realize that their victim is the SHEFFIELD. Miraculously, five torpedoes detonate prematurely, and the rest miss.

The aircraft return to the ARK ROYAL, re-arm with contact torpedoes, and attack, this time, the right ship. The fourteenth torpedo hits the BISMARCK amidships, doing no damage. The fifteenth and last strikes her aft in the steering compartment, jamming the tiller hard a-starboard. She is crippled, and can only

steam in a circle. In the vicinity, U-556 is powerless to help as she is without torpedoes.

MAY 27, 1941
Firing begins at 08.47. The battleships RODNEY and KING GEORGE V attack, with support from the battle-cruiser REPULSE and the cruisers NORFOLK and DEVONSHIRE.

At 10.40, it is over. The BISMARCK, her flag still flying, turns slowly over and sinks.

SEPTEMBER 27, 1941
The first 'Liberty' ship, the PATRICK HENRY, is launched. The 'Liberty' ship was the equivalent of the First World War's 'standard' ship, and was occasioned by the same reason—appalling losses of merchant shipping from the onslaught of the U-boat. In late 1940, the British Merchant Shipping Commission had visited the United States and ordered eighty-six ships. Initial plans were for fifty ships a year. The Canadian Government contracted for 450 ships and, ultimately, a total of 2,710 Liberty ships were built.

NOVEMBER 12, 1941
The British aircraft carriers ARK ROYAL and ARGUS strengthen Malta's air defence by trans-

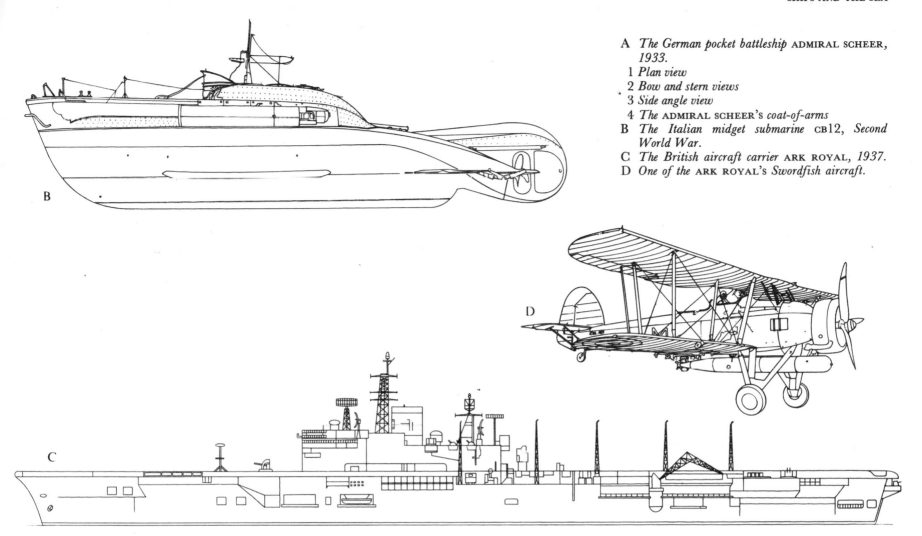

A *The German pocket battleship* ADMIRAL SCHEER, *1933.*
  1 *Plan view*
  2 *Bow and stern views*
  3 *Side angle view*
  4 *The* ADMIRAL SCHEER'S *coat-of-arms*
B *The Italian midget submarine* CB12, *Second World War.*
C *The British aircraft carrier* ARK ROYAL, *1937.*
D *One of the* ARK ROYAL'S *Swordfish aircraft.*

porting aircraft to within flying distance. Seven Blenheim bombers and thirty-seven Hurricanes arrive safely in Malta.

NOVEMBER 13-14, 1941
At 15.40, the ARK ROYAL is torpedoed by U-81, commanded by Lieutenant-Commander Guggenberger. Listing heavily, she is taken in tow by the tugs THAMES and ST. DAY at 02.00. But she continues to heel over and, at 06.13, she sinks.

NOVEMBER 19, 1941
The German raider KORMORAN, 150 miles (241.4 km) off west Australia, meets the Australian cruiser SYDNEY. To avoid battle, KORMORAN pretends to be the Dutch STRAAT MALAKKA. Steaming cautiously closer to the bristling raider, SYDNEY signals, 'Show your secret sign.' The KORMORAN opens fire. The cruiser is too close for effective fire, and is disabled by a torpedo. Down at the bows, the SYDNEY tries to ram the KORMORAN, which is ablaze in the engine-room. The raider dodges, and they draw apart. By now, the KORMORAN's engines are on fire, and useless. Her crew abandons ship. Some hours later, the stricken SYDNEY has gone too.

NOVEMBER 25, 1941
U-331 hits the BARHAM amidships with three torpedoes from such close range that the submarine is blown to the surface. The BARHAM explodes with a loss of 862 lives.

THE ATTACK ON PEARL HARBOUR
DECEMBER 7, 1941
The Japanese attack Pearl Harbour, thus bringing the full power of the United States into the war.

Commanded by Admiral Chuichi Nagamo, six aircraft carriers, AKAGI, KAGA, SORYU, HIRYU, SHOKAKU, and ZUIKAKU, the battleships HIEI and KIRISHIMA, three cruisers, three submarines, destroyers, and oil-tankers, sailed from Etorofu on November 26. Admiral Yamamoto, using the signal 'Climb Mount Niitaka', ratifies the war strike on December 1.

At a distance of 275 miles (509.3 km) off Hawaii, the 183 strike aircraft take off. It is Sunday, and, even when the planes are seen on radar, the sleeping U.S. Pacific Fleet is not alerted. At 07.55, the first attack begins. At 08.10, the ARIZONA explodes, killing 1,100 men, including Fleet Admiral Kidd.

The second strike, with 170 re-armed aircraft, follows at 09.15, and lasts forty minutes. By 10.00, Pearl Harbour is a pillar of smoke. Of the eight battleships in port, the ARIZONA, the OKLAHOMA, and the CALIFORNIA lie wrecked at their berths. The WEST VIRGINIA is ablaze and sinking. The NEVADA is aground. The MARYLAND is a shambles forward. Both the TENNESSEE and the PENNSYLVANIA have been hit. The target ship UTAH and the destroyers CASSIN and DOWNES sink within a short while. The cruisers HELENA, HONOLULU, and RALEIGH are severely damaged. Other ships suffer damage to a varying degree.

At the airfields, 188 aircraft are destroyed, and 159 damaged.

The Americans lost 2,403 killed, and a further 1,178 were injured. The Japanese losses were trivial: twenty-nine aircraft, one large submarine, five of the advance force of midget submarines, and 125 men.

In just two hours, the Japanese had won for themselves the balance of naval power in the Far East. On the very day that Pearl Harbour was struck, the Japanese, under Admiral Goto, occupied Guam.

DECEMBER 10, 1941
The British Force Z is destroyed in the South China Sea. The previous day, the battleship

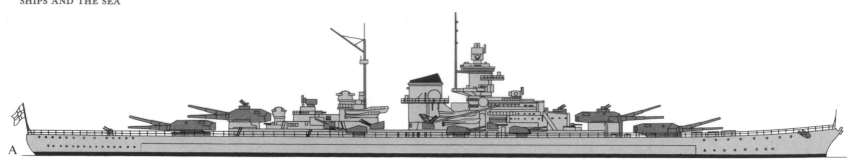

A

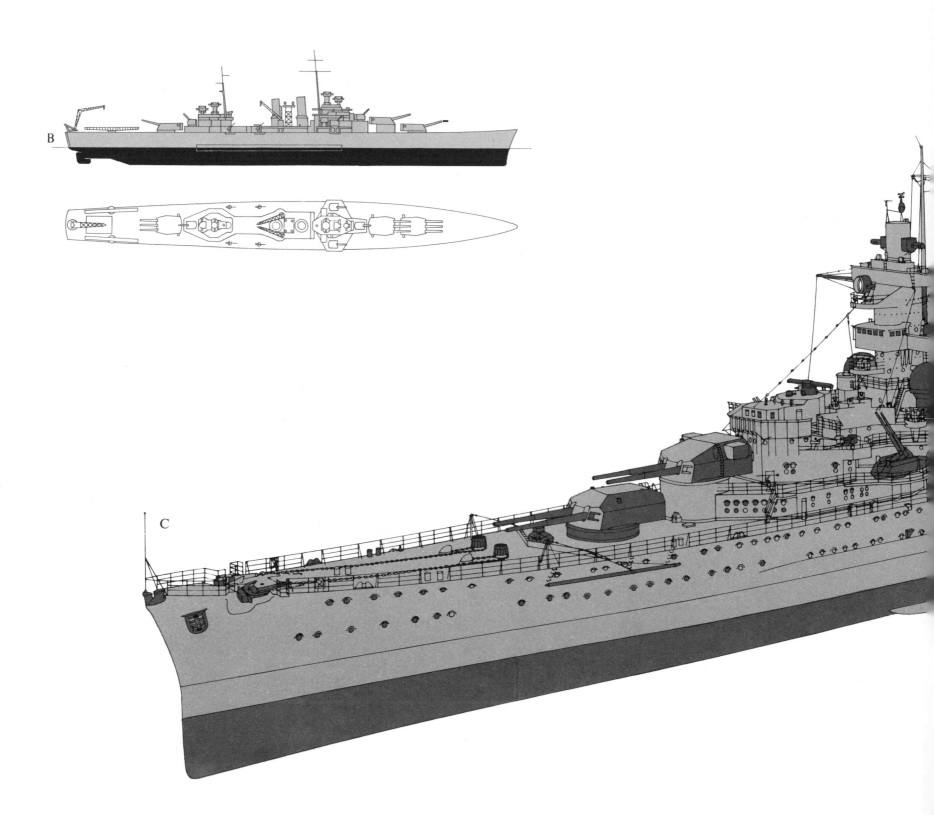

B

C

A *The German battleship* BISMARCK, *1939.*
B *The American heavy cruiser* WICHITA, *1937.*
C *The German heavy cruiser* ADMIRAL HIPPER, *1937.*

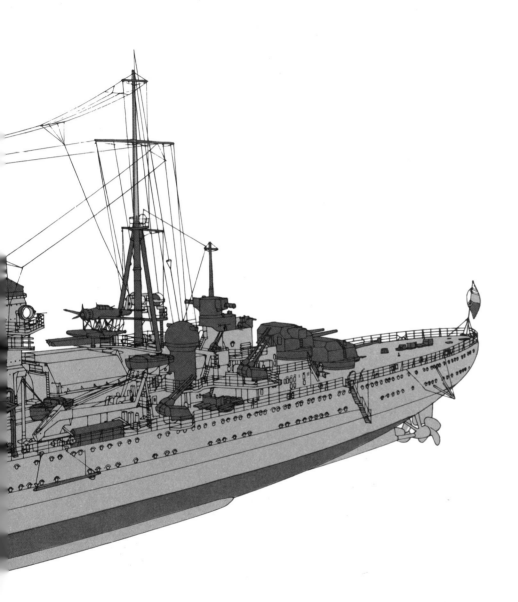

PRINCE OF WALES and the battle-cruiser REPULSE, escorted by the destroyers EXPRESS, ELECTRA, and VAMPIRE, were spotted by the Japanese submarine I-65 while racing to meet the Japanese invasion fleet at Kuantan. Aircraft scouts from the cruisers KINU and KUMANO report that the fleet has no air cover.

Ninety-five aircraft from the Japanese 22nd Air Flotilla take off from Saigon. They find first the destroyer TENEDOS, but she escapes their bombs and proceeds.

In the main attack on Force Z, two aerial torpedoes cripple the screws and rudder of the PRINCE OF WALES; the REPULSE, although damaged, manages to avoid seventeen torpedoes before being struck by eight more. Direct hits with three torpedoes and nine bombs are made on the PRINCE OF WALES.

Both ships are doomed. The destroyers rescue 1,924 men, and bring them to Singapore.

The end of Force Z marks the end of the era of the battleship. No new battleships have since been ordered by any navy.

DECEMBER 19, 1941
As if to underline the vulnerability of the battleship, two Italian 'human torpedoes' breach the harbour defences at Alexandria and badly damage the British battleships QUEEN ELIZABETH and VALIANT with limpet mines.

FEBRUARY 9, 1942
The 83,000-ton United States Line's liner LAFAYETTE, the ex-NORMANDIE, is burnt out at her berth on the Hudson River, and is eventually scrapped.

FEBRUARY 12, 1942
The German ships SCHARNHORST, GNEISENAU, and PRINZ EUGEN, under Vice-Admiral Otto Ciliax, were at Brest, within reach of British aircraft and French sabotage. Increasing numbers of Allied convoys were getting through to Murmansk. The ships are ordered to sail through to Germany.

On the night of February 11, they set off at high speed along the English Channel. Next day, they are favoured by the expected low cloud and mist. Massive German air cover is afforded them.

The ships are not spotted until they reach the Straits of Dover, 350 miles (648.2 km) from Brest. The escorting small craft lay down smoke-screens, radar jamming is effective, and the few British attacks are pitifully small and unco-ordinated.

Two and a half hours after passing Dover, the SCHARNHORST hits a mine and is stopped for half an hour, without being attacked. As night falls, GNEISENAU strikes a mine, and the SCHARNHORST hits her second mine. Nevertheless, by dawn on February 13, all are safely in Germany. However, the next bombing raid puts the GNEISENAU out of action, and she is finally sunk as a block-ship at Gdynia, Poland, in 1945.

FEBRUARY 27, 1942

The Battle of the Java Sea takes place as the Japanese continue to sweep through the Dutch East Indies. An ABDA fleet had been assembled to protect Java, the next Japanese objective. 'ABDA' took its name from the assortment of American, British, Dutch, and Australian cruisers and destroyers which made up the fleet.

It is appreciated that all these ships can do is buy time. They manage to clear the area, but several are lost. The remaining ships are commanded by Admiral Karel Doorman in the Dutch cruiser DE RUYTER. His strike force leaves Surabaya, and hastens towards the reported position of the Japanese invasion fleets.

At dawn, Admiral Doorman has not made contact but, by 09.30, Japanese aircraft bomb the fleet. No damage is done. Admiral Nishimura, in the cruiser NAKA, leads six destroyers and the heavy cruisers NACHI and HAGURO, and Admiral Tanaka, in the cruiser JINTSU, leads eight destroyers comprising the 2nd and 4th Destroyer Flotillas, against the ABDA fleet.

Away to the east, the old U.S. aircraft carrier LANGLEY dashes towards Java with thirty-two P.40 fighter bombers ready to fly, and a further twenty-seven crated in the accompanying freighter SEAWITCH. But the LANGLEY is spotted and bombed out of action. The SEAWITCH escapes, but lands her P.40s at Tjilatjap too late to assist Admiral Doorman.

The ABDA fleet consists of the cruisers DE RUYTER and JAVA (Dutch), the EXETER (British), the HOUSTON (American), and the PERTH (Australian).

Ahead are the British destroyers ELECTRA, ENCOUNTER, and JUPITER. To the rear are the American destroyers JOHN D. EDWARDS, PAUL JONES, JOHN D. FORD, and ALDEN. On the port beam steam the Dutch destroyers EVERTSEN, WITTE DE WITH, and KORTENAER.

Visual contact is made at 16.12. Four minutes later, a general engagement ensues, with the Japanese having numerical and fire power advantage. The NAKA and her destroyers execute a parallel torpedo attack, but all forty-three torpedoes launched miss, or explode prematurely. There are smoke-screens everywhere, and the spouts of water are coloured with different dyes to help spot the fall of shot.

The Japanese close the distance, and fire sixty-four torpedoes. At this moment, a shell disables the EXETER's engine-room, and she drops out of the line. At 17.15, a torpedo strikes the KORTENAER, and she blows up. The EXETER is ordered to Surabaya, accompanied by the damaged WITTE DE WITH. Meanwhile, the ELECTRA is sunk.

The fleet has now lost four ships, and ammunition is running low. The Japanese pull away to protect their troop convoy, but return after nightfall. The fleets meet again in bright moonlight.

Twelve torpedoes are fired at the DE RUYTER,

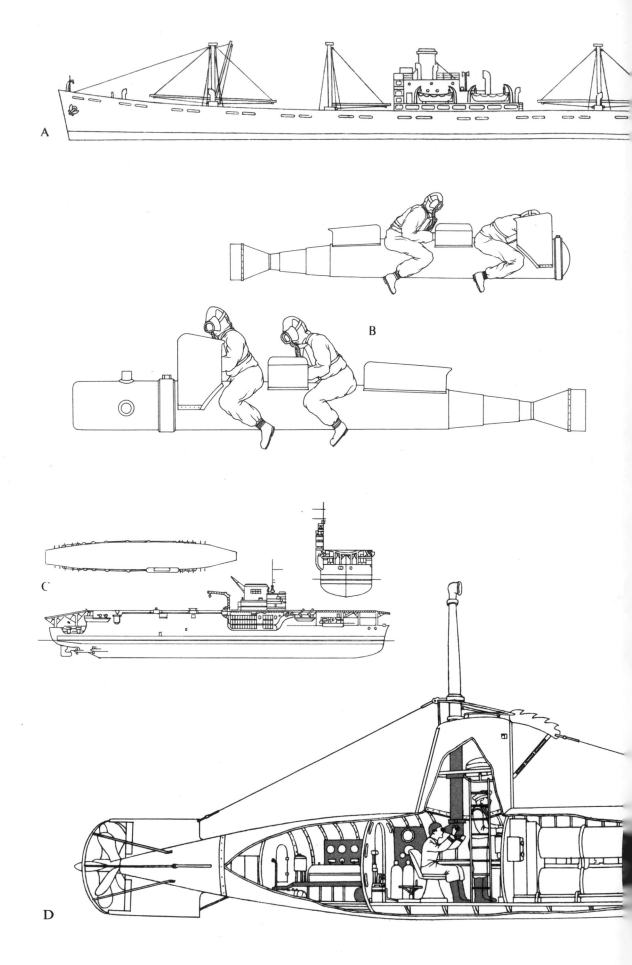

A *A 'Liberty' ship, Second World War.*
B *An Italian 'human torpedo', Second World War.*
C *The French aircraft carrier* BÉARN, *1927.*
D *A Japanese midget submarine, Second World War.*

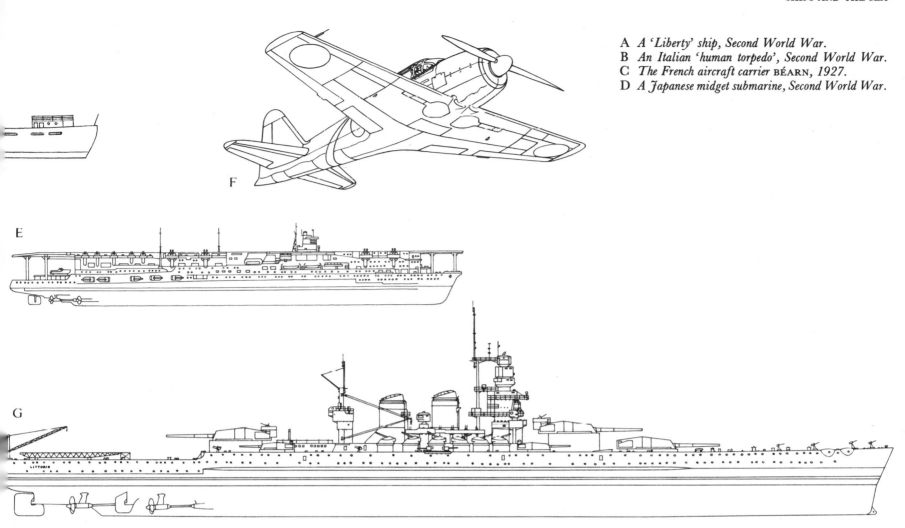

E *The Japanese aircraft carrier* KAGA, *1925.*
F *A Japanese Mitsubishi Zero naval fighter, 1942.*
G *The Italian battleship* LITTORIO, *1937.*

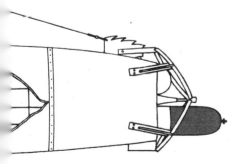

and she bursts into flames. The JAVA is also hit and, catching fire, explodes. The defiant survivors, struggling in the water, call for three cheers for their Queen, Wilhelmina of the Netherlands. Doorman orders the PERTH and the HOUSTON to escape. DE RUYTER sinks, taking with her Doorman and 344 crew.

Java is now open to the Japanese invasion fleets, which land almost unopposed.

FEBRUARY 28-MARCH 1, 1942
The PERTH and the HOUSTON, en route to Australia, are sunk by Japanese cruisers.

MARCH 1, 1942
The EXETER, and the destroyers POPE and ENCOUNTER, are attacked and sunk.

MARCH 27-28, 1942
The raid on St. Nazaire in France takes place. The aim of the raid is to prevent the TIRPITZ, the BISMARCK's sister, from using the Normandie Graving Dock at St. Nazaire, the only dry dock capable of accommodating her.

The former U.S. destroyer CAMPBELTOWN has twenty-four time-fused depth charges concreted into her bows and, escorted by the destroyers ATHERSTONE and TYNEDALE, the motor gun-boat MGB 314, the motor torpedo-boat MTB 74, and sixteen motor launches, she sails into St. Nazaire. There, under intense fire, the lock gates are rammed and the CAMPBELTOWN is sunk in position. Next day at noon, the ship explodes. Operation Chariot has succeeded.

APRIL 5, 1942
Carrier-based Japanese aircraft sink the two British cruisers DORSETSHIRE and CORNWALL in the Indian Ocean. Four days later, the aircraft carrier HERMES is sunk.

APRIL 18, 1942
Aircraft from the U.S. carriers HORNET and ENTERPRISE bomb Tokyo. This is the first time the Japanese capital has been attacked. The immediate Japanese reaction is to recall the Indian Ocean Fleet, to postpone the invasion of Australia, and to start plans to invade Midway and Hawaii in order to protect Japan from aerial attack. These changes in strategy will eventually lose them the war.

MAY 7-8, 1942
Early in May, the plans to invade Australia are taken up again, and the island of Tulagi is invaded. Port Moresby, in New Guinea, is

the main objective. Unknown to the Japanese, the Americans have broken their code, and plan their counter-move. Admiral Nimitz is concentrating on the defence of Port Moresby, and he has the aircraft carriers YORKTOWN and LEXINGTON, supported by the cruisers CHICAGO, HOBART, and AUSTRALIA, with destroyers.

First contact is made when a Japanese reconnaissance aircraft spots the destroyer SIMS and an oil-tanker, but does not find the main force. The SIMS is sunk by a force of seventy-eight planes. The tanker escapes. However, the YORKTOWN's aircraft find the aircraft carrier SHOHO, and sink her.

The next day, May 8, the Japanese fleet attacks. The YORKTOWN is severely damaged. The LEXINGTON is set on fire, and is eventually sunk by her own forces. No Japanese carrier is sunk, but the carrier SHOKAKU is hit by three bombs, and withdraws with the rest of the invasion fleet. The Battle of the Coral Sea, as it came to be called, halted the Japanese southward advance.

JUNE 1942
U-boats sink 627,000 tons of shipping during this month, two-thirds of it off the east coast of the United States.

In the Mediterranean, it is becoming increasingly difficult to get supplies to Malta. The convoy 'Harpoon' with six ships, heavily escorted, falls prey to the Italian cruisers EUGENIO DI SAVOIA and RAIMONDO MONTE-CUCCOLI. The eleven-ship convoy 'Vigorous' is attacked by the battleships VITTORIO VENETO and LITTORIO. Of these two convoys, only two ships reach Malta. Escort losses include the cruiser HERMIONE, the destroyers BEDOUIN, HASTY, AIREDALE, the Australian NESTOR, and the Polish KUJAWIAK, and two mine-sweepers.

JUNE 4-6, 1942
The Battle of Midway Island finally destroys the myth of Japanese invincibility. At this time, Japan still had twice as many aircraft carriers as the United States. The fleet consisted of over two hundred ships, of which eleven were carriers, eleven battleships, twenty-two cruisers, sixty-five destroyers, and twenty-one submarines. Not all of these were engaged at Midway.

Two unsuccessful strikes are first made by American aircraft based on Midway. These are followed by an attack from carrier-based aircraft. This, too, achieves nothing. At this point, the Japanese modify their plans, and their returning aircraft are re-armed with torpedoes instead of bombs. With their decks crowded with re-arming aircraft, the Japanese are attacked again.

The three carriers KAGA, AKAGI, and SORYU, are repeatedly hit. Bombs explode everywhere, aircraft fuel blazes across the decks, and the three are reduced to a shambles, sinking within twenty-four hours.

A third American carrier strike proves un-

successful, but the fourth leaves the HIRYU in a sinking condition. The battle ends in an American victory.

JUNE 27-JULY 9, 1942
The P.Q. 17 convoy leaves Reykjavik for Murmansk. It consists of thirty-six ships, escorted by six destroyers which are led by the KEPPEL, four corvettes, three mine-sweepers, four anti-submarine trawlers, two submarines, the Hurricane-fighter-equipped Catapult Cam ship EMPIRE TIDE, and two anti-aircraft ships.

To the south, the British cruisers LONDON and NORFOLK are on patrol with the American cruisers TUSCALOOSA and WICHITA. Heavy cover is given by the battleships DUKE OF YORK and WASHINGTON, and the aircraft carrier VICTORIOUS is in the area with accompanying cruisers and destroyers. Furthermore, a dummy convoy sails as if for Norway.

The German Admiralty mounts operation *Rösselsprung* (Knight's Move). The battleships TIRPITZ, HIPPER, and SCHEER, with twelve destroyers, move to intercept and destroy the convoy, after the U-boats have scattered it.

As the German fleet prepares, the British Admiralty orders the 'big ships' to make for Norway. U-boats get in among the convoy, which scatters over thousands of square miles of ocean. The German support fleet returns to port after only twelve hours, for it is not needed. Two of the convoy return to Reykjavik, ten are sunk by U-boats, aircraft sink another thirteen, and only eleven make it to Murmansk.

AUGUST 10-14, 1942
The fourteen-ship convoy 'Pedestal' is escorted by a full battle fleet from Gibraltar to Malta. Five out of the fourteen come through, including the deeply-laden oil-tanker OHIO. The voyage was a running battle all the way. The aircraft carrier EAGLE, the cruisers CAIRO and MANCHESTER, and the destroyer FORESIGHT are all sunk.

AUGUST 24, 1942
At the Battle of the Eastern Solomon Islands, the Japanese aircraft carrier RYUJO is sunk off Malaita Island by bombing attacks from the U.S. carrier SARATOGA.

SEPTEMBER, 1942
The Liberty ship JOSEPH N. TEAL is built in ten days at the Oregon Shipbuilding Corporation, Portland, U.S.A. This is the all-time record for ship construction.

SEPTEMBER 12, 1942
The LACONIA incident takes place. U-156, commanded by Lieutenant-Commander Hartenstein, torpedoed the LACONIA and surfaced to capture an officer. To Hartenstein's horror, he discovered that, out of the 4,000 people aboard the LACONIA, 1,800 were his Italian allies, prisoners of war. Soon U-156 had 193 Italians

The aircraft carrier proved its worth during the Second World War, especially in the Pacific arena.

aboard, so that diving was impossible. Hundreds more were in the water, and several lifeboats were taken in tow.

Frantic signals were sent to Germany and Dakar, and, finally, Hartenstein sent an open call in English to all allied ships, asking for assistance in picking up survivors. He undertook not to attack, provided his U-boat was not molested. Several ships answered, but before they could reach the scene, an American Liberator appeared and attacked the U-boat, despite the string of lifeboats it had in tow and the Red Cross flag draped over the U-boat's deck. In order to dive, the U-boat crew had to throw the rescued overboard. Only 1,091 persons were eventually rescued.

After the incident, Admiral Dönitz issued the 'Laconia Order', forbidding the rescue of survivors. He was tried at the Nuremberg War Trials for this and other things, but was acquitted.

OCTOBER 11, 1942
In the Battle of Cape Esperance, American cruisers and destroyers sink the Japanese cruiser FURUTAKA and one destroyer, while they sink their own destroyer DUNCAN by cross-fire.

OCTOBER 25, 1942
The American aircraft carrier HORNET is irreparably damaged in the Battle of Santa Cruz Island. She has to be sunk by gunfire. Her sister carrier ENTERPRISE is severely damaged.

NOVEMBER 8, 1942
During the Allied landing at Casablanca in French North Africa, the French battleship JEAN BART opens fire on the American battleship MASSACHUSETTS, and her supporting cruisers and destroyers. During this exchange, the French cruiser PRIMAUGUET, with seven destroyers and eight submarines, tries to prevent the American sailors from bringing the troopships in. In the general engagement that follows, all but four submarines are lost, the JEAN BART is silenced, and the destroyers FOUGUEUX, MILAN, BOULONNAIS, FRONDEUR, and ALBATROS are sunk.

NOVEMBER 14, 1942
The Battle of Guadalcanal, in which the Japanese Admiral Kondo tries to retrieve the Guadalcanal situation, takes place. Far from righting things, the Japanese suffer a severe defeat. Kondo's flagship, the battleship KIRISHIMA, has to be destroyed after damage received from the American battleships SOUTH DAKOTA and WASHINGTON. The Japanese also lose the cruiser KINUGASA, and the destroyers AYANAMI and YUDACHI. The American cruiser ATLANTA and three destroyers are lost.

NOVEMBER 30, 1942
The Battle of Tassafaronga, near Savo Island, is a hit-and-run night attack by eight Japanese destroyers, which seek out four American cruisers and hit them in a lightning torpedo attack. All four cruisers are damaged, but only the NORTHAMPTON sinks. The Japanese lose one destroyer, the TAKANAMI.

APRIL-AUGUST 1943
One critical factor in the turning of the tide for the Allied cause is the victory that the Allied Forces achieve in the Battle of the Atlantic—in other words, the virtual end of the U-boat menace.

The calendar of U-boat losses in the North Atlantic reads as follows: fifteen U-boats sunk in April, forty-one in May, seventeen in June, thirty-seven in July, and twenty-five in August.

Thus, in the five months of the campaign, no less than 135 U-boats were lost. Equally important to the Axis war effort: most of the crews were also lost. Experienced submariners were, perhaps, more difficult to replace than the submarines in which they fought.

Many Allied ships were lost despite these successes, but the losses dropped sharply. When air cover reinforced the efforts of the fleets, then losses plummeted dramatically. The experiences of Convoy ONS 5, one of the last convoys to lose a fair proportion of merchant vessels—thirteen in all— may be cited to show that attacking convoys was now a dangerous occupation for U-boat commanders. The chronicle of U-boat losses during the voyage of Convoy ONS 5 is: U-710, destroyed on April 24, U-630 on May 4, U-192 and U-638 on May 5, and U-125, U-531, and U-438 on May 6.

Seven U-boats were lost for the thirteen merchantmen that were sunk—an impossible ratio of losses for the Germans to sustain.

JULY 9, 1943
The Allied invasion of Sicily takes place. The landings were a triumph for detailed planning. A vast armada of 580 warships and about 2,600 landing craft, with a host of gliders and parachutists, land 66,000 American and 115,000 British troops along eighty miles (128.7 km) of the Sicilian coast during a period of twenty-four hours.

SEPTEMBER 22, 1943
Six British midget submarines, x5, x6, x7, x8, x9, and x10, set out to attack the German battleships TIRPITZ, LÜTZOW, and SCHARNHORST, which are sheltering in the almost inaccessible Altenfjord in north Norway. En route, x9 is lost, and x8 has to be scuttled because of defects. In the vicinity of the TIRPITZ, x5 is lost. (Her wreckage was located in July, 1974.) x10 finds the SCHARNHORST gone. Meanwhile, the crews of x6 and x7 drop their charges beneath the TIRPITZ, but are trapped and captured. Severe damage is caused to the engines.

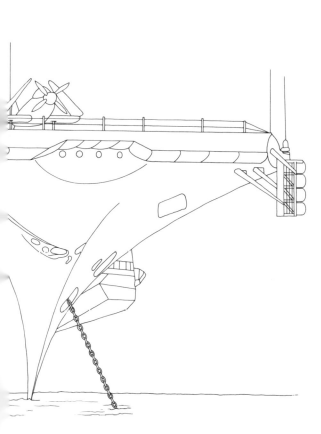

OCTOBER 22, 1943

Another attack on the TIRPITZ shatters her hull. It is about a year before temporary repairs enable her to move to Tromsø, where, in November 1944, she is destroyed by R.A.F. bombers.

DECEMBER 26, 1943

The SCHARNHORST is sunk while trying to get through to attack the Arctic convoy JW 55B, which is guarded by the command destroyer ONSLOW and thirteen others. Three cruisers, the BELFAST, the SHEFFIELD, and the NORFOLK, patrol the sea near Norway. Remote cover is given by the battleship DUKE OF YORK, her screen of four destroyers, and the cruiser JAMAICA.

It is pitch dark and blowing a gale when the BELFAST picks up the SCHARNHORST on her radar. The first the German battleship knows about it is when a star shell bursts above her and a shell from the NORFOLK hits her. When the SCHARNHORST tries to go north around the cruisers to get at the convoy, she is again blocked by the cruisers. This time, the NORFOLK is hit.

Meanwhile, the DUKE OF YORK has been called to the scene. Another star shell illuminates the SCHARNHORST, and she receives direct hits from the DUKE OF YORK and the JAMAICA. She begins to flood but speeds away, trying for the safety of the darkness. Suddenly, a destroyer gets home a torpedo, and the SCHARNHORST turns across the path of the other destroyers, who hit her with three torpedoes. The DUKE OF YORK now fires accurately from close range. The SCHARNHORST rolls over, and sinks.

APRIL 14, 1944

The FORT SIKINE, carrying a cargo of 1,400 tons of explosives and 124 bars of gold, catches fire at Bombay. Despite Herculean efforts to control the fire, the flames reach the explosives stacked in the forward holds and they blow up, devastating a vast area.

The Scindia Line's JALAPADMA was lifted clean out of the water. She finished draped across Shed No. 2, with just her bows touching the water. Where No. 1 Berth had been, there was now nothing but a vast crater.

The fire still raged on the FORT SIKINE. At last, the after holds were breached, and the 780 tons of explosive stored there went up in another cataclysmic shock. Fire engulfed the docks to a radius of a mile (1.6 km). Buildings guttered like huge torches or fell asunder. Eleven other ships were lost. The FORT CREVIER, a sister ship to the FORT SIKINE, simply disappeared from the adjacent berth. Casualties ran into thousands. The exact total was never known.

JUNE 6, 1944

D-day. The invasion of Normandy takes place. A vast armada of troop landing craft is escorted from the south of England to Normandy by heavy naval forces. At Arromanches, a 'Mulberry' harbour is erected for the landing of vehicles and supplies. A breakwater of blockships to protect the harbour is made from the target battleship CENTURION, the cruiser DURBAN, and the Dutch cruiser SUMATRA. No Allied vessel larger than a destroyer is lost.

JUNE 19-20, 1944

The Battle of the Philippine Sea takes place between a Japanese force consisting of five battleships, nine aircraft carriers, cruisers, and destroyers, and the American fleet comprising fifteen carriers with 956 aircraft, supporting cruisers and destroyers, and a submarine screen. Two of the submarines penetrate the Japanese destroyer screen. The ALBACORE torpedoes and sinks the aircraft carrier TAIHO, while the CAVALLA puts three torpedoes into the SHOKAKU. The Japanese force withdraws eastwards.

The next day, planes from the U.S. 58th Task Force search for and, almost at the end of their bombing range, find the Japanese fleet. The aircraft carrier HITAKA is sunk, and the carrier CHIYODA is set on fire.

The American planes, almost out of fuel, have to land on their carriers in the pitch dark. Fifty-nine aircrew out of 209 are lost.

OCTOBER 20, 1944

United States forces invade the Philippines.

OCTOBER 23-28, 1944

The Battle of Leyte Gulf takes place. The Japanese commit their South Pacific Fleet against the massive U.S. 3rd and 7th Fleets, and lose their battleships FUSO, MUSHASHI, and YAMASHIRO; the four aircraft carriers CHITOSE, CHIYODA, ZUIHO, and ZUIKAKU; and ten cruisers and light destroyers. American casualties are the destroyer HOEL and three small aircraft carriers, one of whom, the ST. LO, is the first ship to be sunk by a Kamikaze suicide attack.

This was the largest naval battle of all time, with 282 ships and several hundred aircraft taking part.

FEBRUARY 19, 1945

American Marines land on Iwo Jima after the heaviest and most prolonged bombardment and aerial attack of the Pacific war.

APRIL 1, 1945

The Americans land on Okinawa, only 350 miles (648.2 km) from the Japanese mainland. The Battle of Okinawa sees the peak of the Kamikaze attacks. Ten destroyers are lost to these suicide planes.

In addition, the following carriers are damaged, although not sunk, by Kamikaze attacks: FORMIDABLE (British), FRANKLIN (American), WASP (American), YORKTOWN (American). Altogether, 34 naval craft were sunk and 368 damaged during the Kamikaze attacks in the Pacific zone.

APRIL 6, 1945

The giant battleship YAMATO leaves Japan. She has only fuel enough for the one-way journey to Okinawa, and no air cover. Everybody aboard her knew that she was going on a suicide voyage.

APRIL 7, 1945

A little after midday, she is picked up by aircraft from Admiral Mitscher's carrier force. A swarm of 380 aircraft swoop into the attack. There is no real defence against the blanket bombing of the planes. The YAMATO is hit repeatedly, and goes to the bottom.

MAY 8, 1945

The Second World War ends in Europe.

MAY 14, 1945

All the U-boats that had not been accounted for in battle surrender at Londonderry, Northern Ireland.

MAY 15-16, 1945

The Japanese cruiser HAGURO, victor of the Java Sea battles, is intercepted by the British 26th Destroyer Squadron, led by the SAUMERAZ, and is sunk by three torpedoes. The SAUMERAZ scores three hits. The VERULAM, the VENUS, and the VIGILANT score two each before the ship sinks. This is the British Navy's last major surface action of the Second World War.

JULY 29, 1945

The American cruiser INDIANAPOLIS is torpedoed by the Japanese submarine I-58 north-east of Leyte. She is the last American ship sunk in the war.

AUGUST 15, 1945

The war with Japan ends. On the very same day, the following message is sent from the Commander-in-Chief, U.S. 5th Fleet, to his colleague of the 5th Fleet Pacific:

The war with Japan will end at 12.00 on 15th Aug. It is likely that Kamikazes will attack the fleet after this time as a final fling. Any ex-enemy aircraft attacking the fleet is to be shot down in a friendly manner.

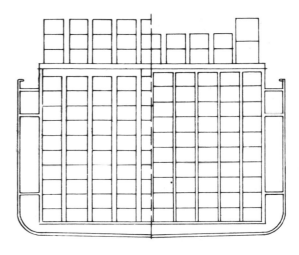

chapter 7

In the long history of ships and the sea, there has always been some degree of specialization. This usually took the form of minor modifications to the standard shipping designs of the age. However, the commencement of real specialization in ships came when general cargo ships were rivalled by the building of ships for the transport of one specific commodity.

The sail whaler appears to be the first type of seagoing cargo carrier which was designed from the very beginning for a continuous, separate, and different form of commercial life. In modern terms, however, the oil carrier saw the commencement of the age of specialization. 'Modern', nevertheless, is only a relative term; for the ELIZABETH WATTS, which was built in 1865, can claim to be the forerunner of all specialized ships. Even this claim would be disputed by the champions of the LEVIATHAN, a 167-foot (50.9 m) paddle train ferry that was built for the Edinburgh, Perth, and Dundee Railway Co. as far back as 1850.

Generally, then, specialization began in the 1860s when ordinary cargo vessels were adapted for a particular cargo. Often, the adaptation was made for the homeward leg of a journey only. This was logical, for the outward journey from Europe invariably offered facilities both for passengers and for general freight. It was the inbound voyage that was uneconomic. Ingenuity had to be exercised in order to find suitable pay-loads for the homeward run. Spices, tea, wool, rice—these came from the Far East and from Australasia. From North America came wood and then live cattle, which were carried in purpose-built stalls on the decks of ships.

The CUFIC was the first specifically designed cattle-boat. She was commissioned in 1888 by the White Star Line. New Zealand, Australia, and South America were too remote for the carriage of live cattle. This problem was solved by the introduction of refrigerated ships, which carried the frozen carcasses of cattle and sheep. The ELDERSLIE of 2,761 tons gross, built for Turnbull Martin in 1884, was the first ship specifically constructed for the carriage of frozen meat, although the German Sloman Line had partially adapted one of its steamers, the SORRENTO, in 1880 for this trade.

The process of specialization was slow. It is not until 1920, well after the end of the First World War, that there is any significant departure from the principle of carrying general cargo. It was then that a number of prominent companies had their fleets rebuilt with ships that conformed to the needs of specific requirements and trades. It is at this time that the oil-tanker settled down to its familiar silhouette of engines aft-bridge amidships, whereas before they had been built with the conventional outline of having the funnel amidships. Refrigerated ships looked somewhat box-like, with a profusion of deck houses and light-weight derricks. Fruit carriers, nick-named 'Banana Boats', were smaller and faster vessels than the two previous types of carrier. They were painted white, and often had lines more like a yacht than a cargo carrier. They contrasted vividly with colliers, which had large hatches, uncluttered decks, and few aids for unloading.

Whale factory ships appeared in the 1920s. Although at first they were adapted from liners, yet they were unrecognizable as such in their new guise. Another innovation, the heavy-lift ship, was introduced in 1924 by the Norwegian company Christen Smith. This was the BELDIS, which was provided with one 40-ton, and one 100-ton derrick. On her maiden voyage, she carried seventeen railway locomotives to Buenos Aires.

But the real age of the specialist ship did not come until the Second World War had ended. More specifically, it was the nationalization by President Nasser of the Suez Canal in 1956 that triggered off the transformation. European governments as well as shipping fraternities everywhere realized what would be the consequences of political control, of increased transit charges, of the ever-present threat of unilateral closure for other than commercial reasons.

Nowadays, scarcely any general-purpose ships are built. Each new vessel is constructed for a specific role. This constraint often makes such design demands that the resultant vessel scarcely resembles any ship that was once known and recognized as a ship. The size, engines, power, speed, and carrying capacity of the modern specialist ships make them economically sound, but all too frequently aesthetically offensive.

The first sign that a new age of shipping had arrived came with a rush of large tankers owned by such entrepreneurs as the Greek tycoons Aristotle Onassis and Stavros Niarchos. These ships, which were some 30,000 tons gross and more than 750 foot (228.6 m) long, looked big. Contrasted with the giants of today, they were puny vessels.

The ever-enlarging oil-tanker was followed by a breed of merchant ships that were designed for speeds in excess of twenty knots, and that were capable of carrying specialist cargoes. The hulls of these ships lost their ‘bluff appearance and adopted a clipper-like sleekness. Bulbous bows appeared. Heavy-lift gear proliferated. The superstructure was moved either right aft or two thirds of the way back. These ships became box-like and slab-sided. Their funnels were modernized into conical pepper-pots.

Many of the immediate post-Second World War ships that were replaced by this new breed of merchantmen were, of course, scarcely a decade old, and had plenty of life left in them. For the most part, they were sold to create the new fleets of the ‘emerging nations’.

Between 1955 and 1965, the profiles of the new ships became bizarre in the extreme. Change is now so fast that new types of ships emerge before the idiosyncrasies of their immediate predecessors can be absorbed.

But the sea-change has scarcely started. The Six Day War between Egypt and Israel closed the Suez Canal completely. Overnight, the Middle East oil-fields were another 6,000 miles (11,112 km) distant. The route to the Far East by way of Cape Town, thought to be an historical anachronism, was once more a stark reality. Tankers were the first ships to have changes imposed upon them by this political upheaval. Their size, speed, and cargo capacity burgeoned to such an extent that the ‘giants’ of ten years ago are the ‘pigmies’ of today. Cargo ships followed the example set by the tankers. Then came the container ships with their pre-boxed cargoes. Some containers remained on the lorries, and this development gave rise to the roll-on roll-off ship.

One post-war development that did not have much success was the atomic-powered commercial vessel. The SAVANNAH was the prototype of this type of ship, but it did not gain general acceptance. Of course, atomic-powered warships are now becoming commonplace, and the atomic submarine with its Polaris, or similar, missile, is claimed to be the ultimate in deterrents.

Estuarine work is now frequently handled by ‘LASH’ ships. These vessels obtain their name from the initials of the ‘Lighter Aboard SHip’ scheme, in which lighters are loaded intact upon a ship, which delivers them by hoisting them back into the water at the destination. A complementary smaller version called ‘Bacat’—Barge aboard Catamaran—has also been developed.

There is also a sudden profusion of new, short sea-routes, with mini-liners providing the service. Finally, a totally new breed of ship has appeared on the modern scene: the service vessel that supplies the forest of rigs that are being set up to exploit the oil to be found beneath the bed of shallow coastal waters.

The passenger liner is not quite obsolete, despite the truncating of transatlantic, and similar, services. Cruising is becoming increasingly popular, and those ships which can deal with this type of passenger traffic have been given a new lease of life.

In the winter of 1973-74, the oil-producing nations doubled, then quadrupled, the price of oil. Again, the world has had to suffer an enforced pattern of economic change. What the long-term effects of this change will be on the shipping industry is difficult to assess. Time alone will tell. Presumably, the ‘economy’ type engine will appear, and speed will no longer be the main criterion for cargo carrying.

One further point worthy of mention is that the size of house fleets is reduced. Where a shipping company might once have operated a fleet of fifty ships, its complement in 1975 is more likely to be ten. However, the cubic cargo capacity of those ten ships is likely to be superior to the cubic capacity of the earlier fifty ships.

Throughout the history of shipping, the ancillary matter in connection with the business of carrying passengers and cargoes has also developed. Several of the customs that emerged during the long story of ships have already been explained.

The carrying of goods by sea is almost as old as the story of man himself. Curiously, the rules and conditions that have emerged to cover the practice of cargo carrying have changed little with the passage of time. By definition, cargo is the name given to the goods to be transported. Freight is the price paid for the facility.

The contract entered into for the carrying of goods is called the Bill of Lading. When it has been signed, the shipowner assumes re-

sponsibility for the care of the goods, and for their transport to the agreed destination.

Two types of charter exist: ‘Bare boat’, and ‘Normal’. Bare boat, or charter by demise, means the hiring of the ship as she is, and where she is, with the charterer finding the crew, fuel, stores, and everything else he needs for his venture. The charterer pays a flat rate per day, month, or even year. The charterer under this arrangement treats the ship as if he owned it.

In the case of the normal charter, the owner finds the officers and crew. In this type of contract, the charterer hires only the cargo space or the passenger accommodation. The shipowner operates the ship.

The word ‘charter’ comes from the Latin expression ‘carta partida’, and when both parties have signed a charter, the following responsibilities obtain:

The shipowner warrants that the vessel is tight, staunch, and strong. The carrying capacity—the deadweight—is accurately stated, and the insurance rating of the vessel, e.g. 100 A1 at Lloyd’s, is declared. The statement is made explicit that the ship is ready to sail at a convenient speed to the loading port. There, the ship will load, the usual wording to this effect being that the vessel is ‘always afloat, the full cargo of legal merchandise, not exceeding that which she is permitted to carry in excess of her tackle, apparel, provisions, and furnishings’. When she is loaded, the ship will proceed, as ordered in signed Bills of Lading, to the port indicated, or as near to it as she may safely get, and upon being paid the agreed freight will deliver the cargo.

These stated responsibilities form the basis of the charter, but other clauses are laid down. These may be summarized as follows:

(a) How the freight is to be paid.

(b) What advances the master shall receive at the port of loading.

(c) The rights of the charterer’s agents at the port.

(d) Details of the holds and of the stowage facilities.

(e) The availability of space for deck cargo, on the understanding that accepting deck cargo is always at the shipper’s risk and with the assent of the master of the ship.

(f) The number of days allowed for discharging the cargo before penalties for delay—demurrage—are incurred.

The next series of clauses deals with the essentially maritime aspects of the charter. These include such things as:

(a) Acts of God.

(b) Perils of the sea.

(c) Fire on board.

(d) Barratry, that is, fraud by the ship’s master or crew without the consent of the owner.

(e) Acts occurring from enemy causation, from piracy, or by restraint by princes or rulers.

(f) Acts caused by collisions, accidents of navigation, and similar events.

The shipowner also makes specific disclaimers, divesting himself of liability for damage or loss arising from explosion, burst boilers, defects in the machinery, or loss of the propeller, providing that these do not occur 'from want of due diligence by the owners, ship's husband, or manager'.

The shipowner also specifically claims the right for the ship to call en route at any port or ports that the master of the vessel deems necessary in order to obtain fuel or supplies, or for the purpose of landing the sick. The right is also reserved for the master to tow or to assist any vessel in distress, and for him to deviate from the agreed route in order to save life or property.

When the vessel is loaded, the master signs the Bill of Lading only when he has the mate's receipts for the cargo. When this has been done, the shipowner has a lien on the cargo for freight, until such time as the unloading has been completed, and payment has been made.

The charterer is protected in many ways. For example, the Bill of Lading sets out the 'Lay Days', that is, the time during which the ship must be ready to load or to discharge her cargo. If the ship is not ready at the end of the Lay Days, then the contract may be cancelled. This right is of considerable importance where seasonal cargoes are involved.

The intention of these clauses is simple; the variations are limitless. Differing cargoes, different port conditions, varying types of ship, local customs and legal codes—all these can produce an infinite range of possibilities and problems. Yet even with this complexity of possibilities and problems, the basic law is simple. It may be expressed in this way: the owner of a passenger ship is a floating inn-keeper; the cargo ship is a floating warehouse or cold storage depot; the same laws apply on land as on sea.

Two examples will suffice to illustrate this basic principle of law. For centuries, it was held that a shipowner could be liable only up to the value of his ship. Yet, logically, a sunken ship could have no value. Therefore, insurance against such a contingency became acceptable practice. Further, the insurer could—and does—seek redress for negligence as a contributory factor to loss.

Again, let it be assumed that two ships collide and the blame for the collision is equally shared. Further, let it be assumed that the damage suffered by one cargo is in excess of the damage suffered by the other. In law, the damage to the cargoes of both is aggregated, and that quantified sum is divided equally to arrive at the damage suffered by each.

A ship, in common with other property, can have a lien—a first charge—placed upon it for materials, labour costs, or for debts due. A ship can be arrested in any port, and be held until the debts are paid. If the debts are not met, then the ship may be sold and the proceeds used to meet the debts. By common consent, the crew have first call on the sums realized for any monies due to them.

In the last two hundred years, the 'Common Carriage' shipowner has emerged. This is the owner who accepts job lots of cargo at tariff rates from anyone for carriage to any of the ports advertised.

Since the end of the Second World War, a complete change in cargo carrying techniques has come about. The first change was the use of 'parcels' of cargo, in which everything that went aboard was put into packages. Then pallets were introduced, whereby the cargo was pre-loaded onto flat racks, and the racks themselves were then loaded. Finally, the container arrived—the technique whereby the cargo is loaded at the factory or warehouse, and arrives at the ship ready for embarkation. One interesting change in the law also evolved. Hitherto, deck cargo was always carried at the shipper's risk. Of course, there was a corresponding reduction in the freight. Today, however, when containers are designated as deck cargo, the liability for the safe delivery of the containers is thrust upon the shipowner.

The latest advances in shipbuilding technology have produced this automatic stabilizer system, which can reduce a 30 degree roll to only 8 degrees. The U-shaped tank visible in the illustrations is filled with what is called 'counter-weight water'. When the vessel reaches its maximum roll (far left), the counter-weight water rushes to the lower half of the tank. As the ship rights itself, the water is locked in its last position by an automatic compressed air system, thus stopping the roll to the other side. The arrows at the top of the ship show the direction of the roll, those at the bottom show the direction of the counter-weight's thrust.

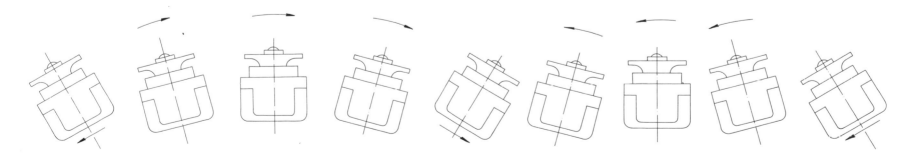

A

B

B

A MGB 2009, *the first ship powered by gas turbine, 1948.*
B *The installation of the Metropolitan Vickers Gatric gas turbine.*

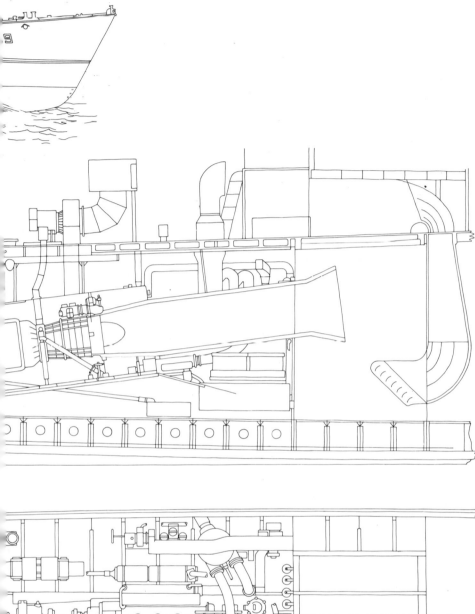

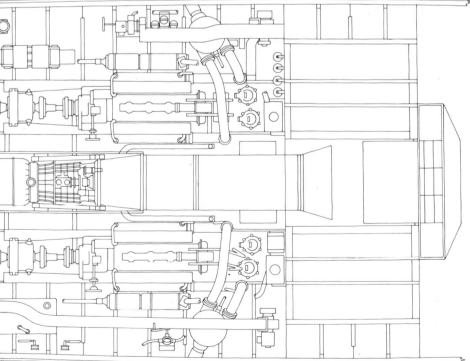

1947
The replacement of passenger ships lost during the war begins in earnest this year with the building of Cunard's MEDIA and PARTHIA, and Swedish America Line's STOCKHOLM.

1947
The American President Line convert two P2 hulls into the PRESIDENT CLEVELAND and the PRESIDENT WILSON.

AUGUST 19, 1947
The Union Castle Line's PRETORIA CASTLE is launched in England by the wife of General Smuts, using radio telephone from Pretoria, South Africa.

1948
Cunard's CARONIA is launched. She is known as the 'Green Goddess', and is built for summer service on the North Atlantic and winter 'round the world' cruising. The ratio of one crew member per passenger makes her expensive to operate.

1948
The Orient Line's ORCADES introduces the so-called 'vertical' look in shipping.

1948
The South American Saint Line builds the ST. ESSYLT and ST. THOMAS for cargo traffic. They introduce a new outline at sea.

1948
The Silver Line builds the SILVERBRIAR and the SILVERPLANE, which are the forerunners of the streamlined cargo vessels of the 1960s and 1970s. Both have two large, squat funnels, of which the fore funnel makes up most of the bridge.

MAY 28, 1948
The ex-British VENERABLE becomes Holland's first aircraft carrier. She is named the KAREL DOORMAN after the Dutch Admiral who led the ABDA fleet in the Battle of the Java Sea, and who died when the DE RUYTER was sunk.

1949
Tragedy befalls the Royal Mail Line's MAGDALENA, on her maiden voyage between Rio de Janeiro and London, when she is lost whilst navigating the Cagarras reefs.

1949
The British frigate AMETHYST, supported by the cruiser LONDON, is trapped by the Chinese up the Yangtse River. She races through a hail of gunfire to rejoin her fleet.

1950
The Korean War breaks out. The United States re-activates many naval ships from its 'moth-balled' fleets. In particular, there is demand for transports.

A

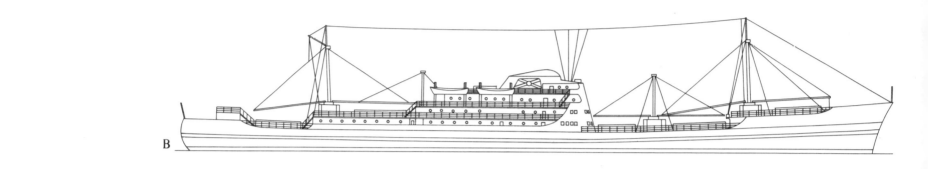

B

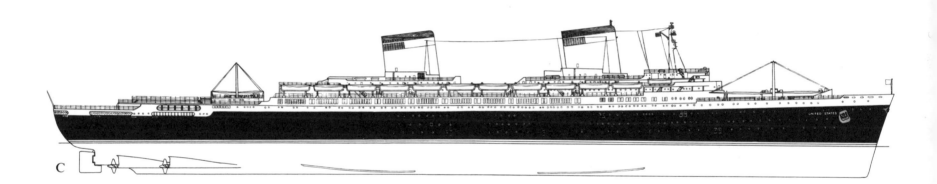

C

AUGUST 25, 1950
The American hospital ship BENEVOLENCE sinks off San Francisco after a collision.

1951
Among the ships built this year are the seven which the Lloyd Triestino Line needed for its East African and Australian services. Two very similar classes were built, the AUSTRALIA, NEPTUNIA, and OCEANIA forming one, and the AFRICA, ASIA, EUROPA, and VICTORIA forming the other.

1952
American interests order thirty-five vessels of the highly successful standard C4-S-Ia type. Originally, all the ships were given names ending in MARINER. Deliveries began to various American shipping companies in 1952, and the

ships were then renamed according to house policy.

JULY 1952
The liner UNITED STATES becomes the fastest North Atlantic liner ever when she crosses to Europe at an incredible 35.59 knots average and returns at an equally impressive 34.51 knots average. She thus clips ten hours off each normal voyage time. These speeds are a full 4 knots faster than the QUEEN MARY's best. The UNITED STATES was built for speedy conversion to a troopship and was completely fireproofed.

1953
A number of wartime escort aircraft carriers are re-converted back to passenger liners. Two such vessels are the COVADONGA and the GUADALUPE, both of which go into service with the Spanish Compania Transatlantica.

A SILVERBRIAR, *1948*.
B ST. ESSYLT, *1948*.
C UNITED STATES, *1952*.

OIL DRILLING AT SEA

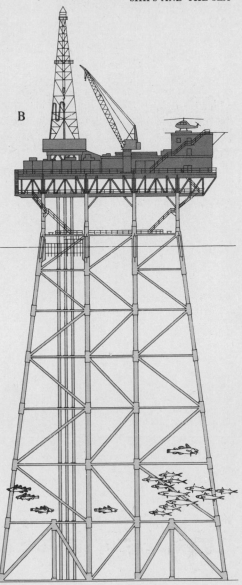

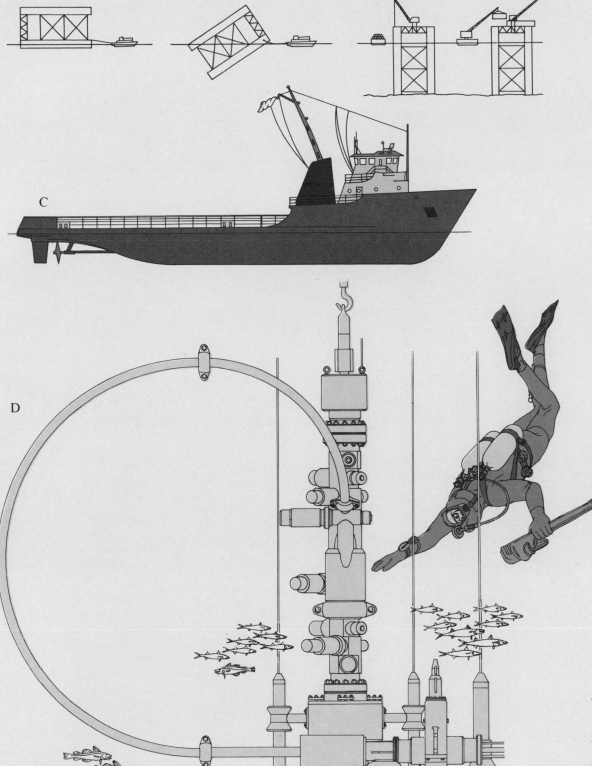

In recent years, the search for oil has moved out to sea. It is believed that most of the earth's remaining oil and gas lies under the ocean bed. This has meant the development of a whole new range of technologically ingenious machinery to bring the oil up from underneath the sea.

A Drilling and production platforms are built ashore, towed into position over the drilling site, and then flooded with water.

B One of these drilling and production platforms can cost over $100 million (c. £40 million).

C Special supply ships keep up a constant shuttle service with material from the shore to the offshore well sites.

D Cables from a surface vessel guide equipment down to an underwater wellhead assembly on the ocean floor.

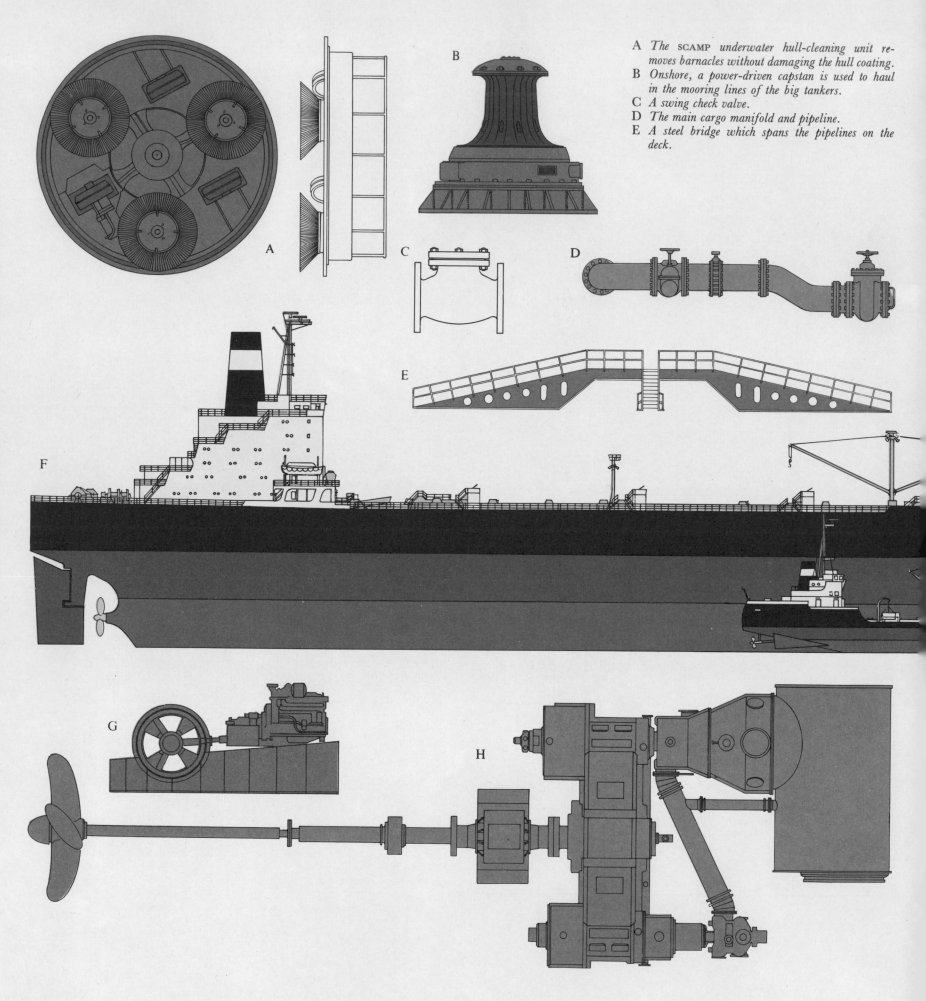

A *The* SCAMP *underwater hull-cleaning unit removes barnacles without damaging the hull coating.*
B *Onshore, a power-driven capstan is used to haul in the mooring lines of the big tankers.*
C *A swing check valve.*
D *The main cargo manifold and pipeline.*
E *A steel bridge which spans the pipelines on the deck.*

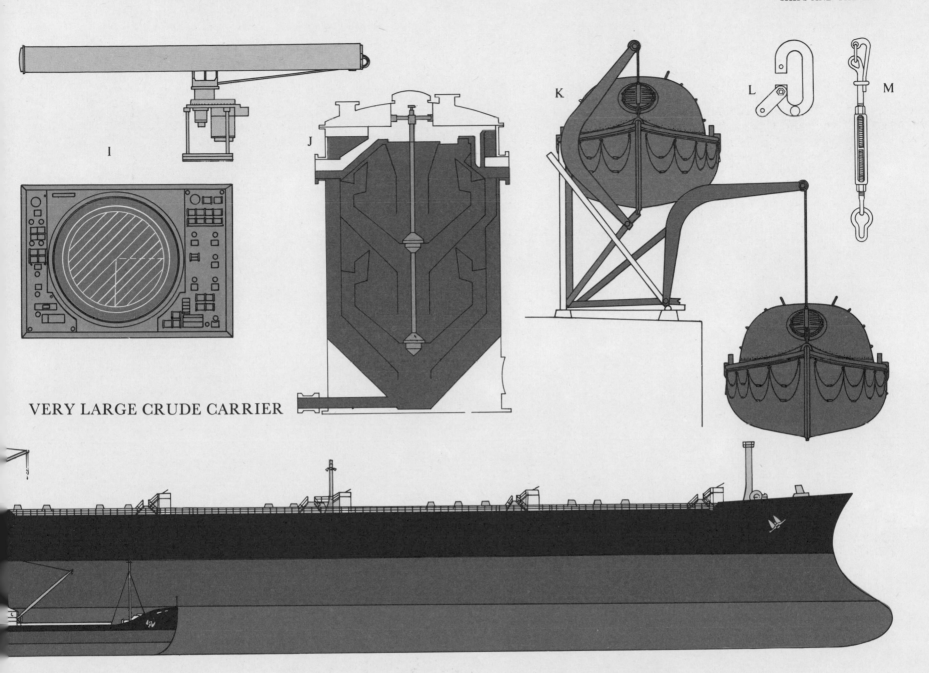

VERY LARGE CRUDE CARRIER

F *The* ESSO CALEDONIA, *253,000 dwt, is a VLCC.*
G *A diesel-powered side thruster with reversible pro-*
   peller placed in a tunnel through the width of the
   bow or stern permits greater manoeuvrability.
H *The main engine and propeller of a steam*
   turbine-driven tanker.
I *Radar scanner and anti-collision radar screen.*
J *An oil-water separator recovers oil from tank-wash*
   water.
K *Lifeboat davits in stowed and embarcation positions.*
L *A forged steel shackle link.*
M *A turnbuckle with a quick-release hook.*
N *A lifeboat fall which is used to raise and lower*
   the boats.
O *A double-ended mooring winch.*

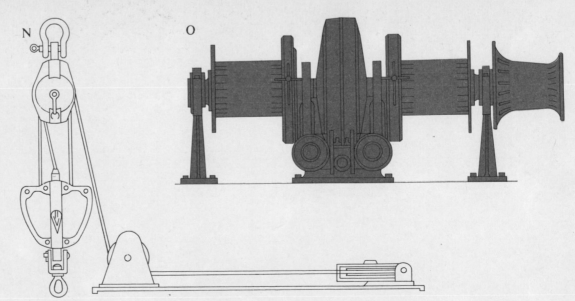

LOADING AND UNLOADING OIL

A Coupler on the cargo transfer arm attaches to a tanker's cargo manifold.

B The cargo transfer arm connects a tanker's cargo manifold (left) and the dock (right) for loading and unloading.

C A cargo hook.

D A gate valve of the type used on cargo pipelines.

E The IOTTA valve disperses gases that escape during loading.

F A tanker pumps oil into the base of a single anchor mooring leg through the floating hose, and thence to the shore via the underwater pipeline.

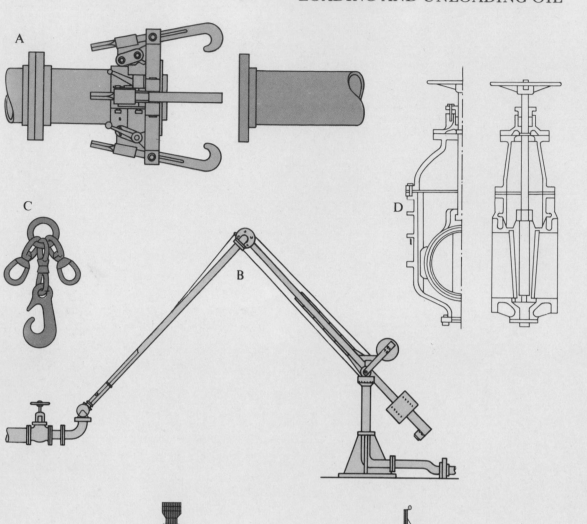

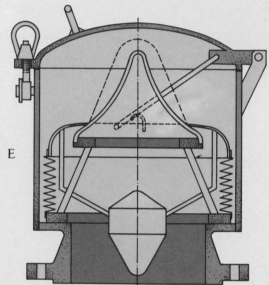

A DE ZEVEN PROVINCIEN, *1953, whose building was delayed because of the Second World War.*

NOVEMBER 18, DECEMBER 17, 1953

The two Dutch cruisers DE RUYTER and DE ZEVEN PROVINCIEN are delivered. They were laid down in 1939, and launched in 1944 and 1950 respectively. These must be two of the longest building periods recorded.

1954

The world's first nuclear-powered submarine, the NAUTILUS, enters service with the U.S. Navy. The atomic reactor alone cost £25,000,000 of a total cost of £40,000,000. Her radius of action is 41,000 miles (75,900 km), her depth of dive 720 foot (219.5 m), and her speed 21 knots. She has a crew of 101.

1955

The SOUTHERN CROSS, owned by Shaw, Savill & Albion, is the first British passenger liner with engines aft. Built for a round-the-world passenger service via New Zealand, she has no cargo space.

JULY 26, 1956

Italia Line's ANDREA DORIA, outward bound from Genoa to New York, is some 45 miles (83.3 km) off Nantucket when, in the early morning mist, she is sliced into by the Swedish America Line's STOCKHOLM. Eleven hours after the collision, the ANDREA DORIA, which was struck on the starboard side just aft of the bridge, sinks. The United Fruit Line's CAPE ANN and the French Line's ILE DE FRANCE are quickly on the spot, and all but 45 out of a total of 1,706 are saved.

1957

The world's first nuclear-powered ice-breaker is the Russian LENIN. She is designed to work in ice up to 6 foot (1.8 m) thick. Refuelling is necessary only once a year.

1957

The American Seatrain Lines, which started to carry railway container vans in 1928, introduces the detachable 35-foot (10.7 m) Seamobile container, made from fibre-glass and reinforced with a steel frame. It can be loaded directly onto a railway flat or lorry. Later, 350 aluminium containers are built and the type soon becomes standard.

1957

The American Grace Line convert their C2 cargo vessels SANTA ELIANA and SANTA LEONOR for the carriage of 476 seventeen-foot (5.2 m) long 'Seatrainers', each with a capacity of 900 cubic foot (25.5 m³). These two vessels provide a weekly service from Port Newark, United States, to Caracas, Venezuela.

1957

Sea-Land Service Inc. of New Jersey is the first major container ship operator. The company begins by converting C2 ships, the first three being AZALEA CITY, GATEWAY CITY, and FAIRLAND. Later, tankers are converted, which can carry almost twice as many containers as the earlier ships. The custom-built container ship has yet to come, but the demand is clearly there.

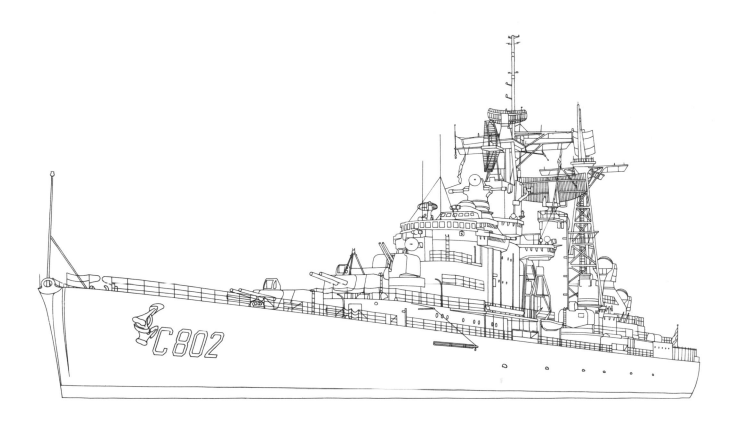

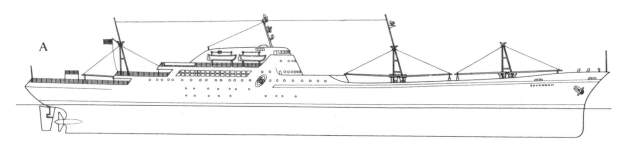

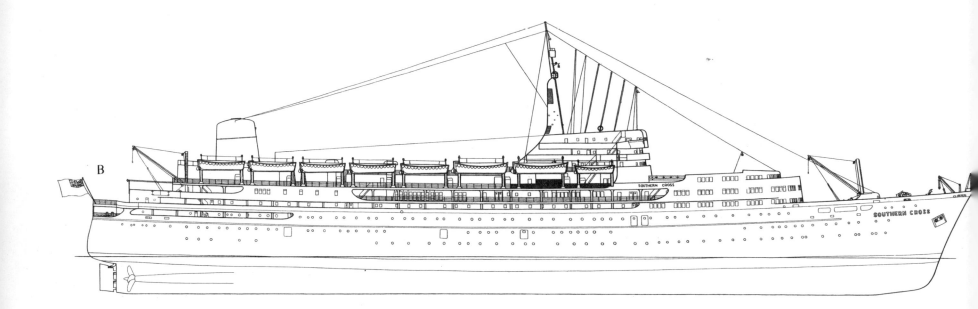

A SAVANNAH, *1959.*
B SOUTHERN CROSS, *built for round-the-world cruises in 1954.*
C TRITON, *1958.*
D GEORGE WASHINGTON, *1959.*
E NAUTILUS, *1954.*
F VOIMA, *an ice breaker built by Wärtsilä for the Finnish Government, 1955. She was the first ice breaker to have two bow propellers.*

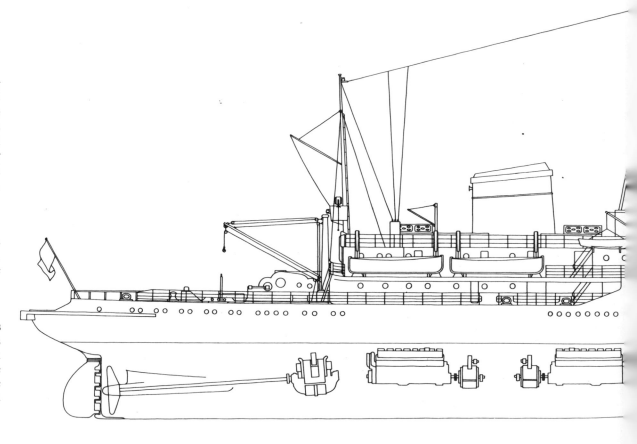

1957
The first specially constructed off-shore drilling rig tender is built for Booth Leasings Corporation in the United States, and is named the HOWARD B. COLE JR. Previously, rig tenders were built from modified tugs or converted barges. The HOWARD B. COLE JR. has her engines aft. However, it soon becomes the trend to build the whole superstructure well forward, thus leaving a long, clear deck aft.

1958
The PRINCESS SOPHIE is built for the Niarchos interests by the Bethlehem Steel Corporation. She is the largest tanker yet built, and the largest ship to be built in the United States.

1958
The Japanese Navy begins to reconstruct its forces. No vessel larger than a destroyer is planned. The first vessels are transferred from the U.S. Navy. New ships are built under the terms of the U.S. Military Aid Programme and are based on American designs, although they are built in Japan.

C

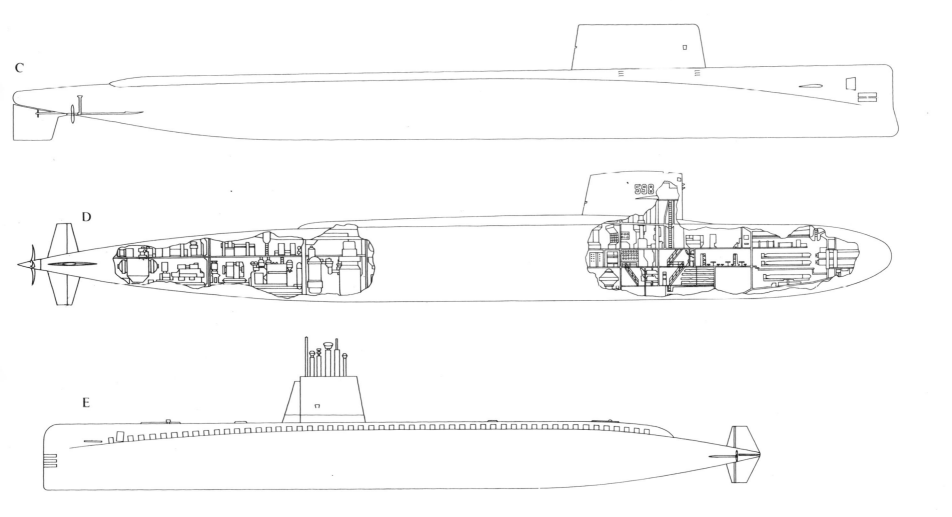

D

E

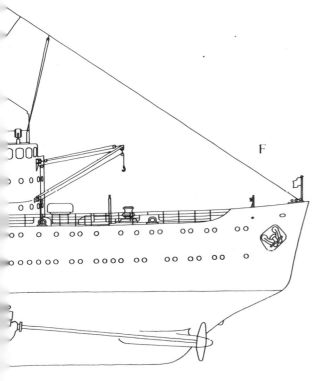

F

JANUARY 1958

The German Navy is re-established with the help of the United States and Great Britain. Six American destroyers are loaned for five years, and are numbered Z1 to Z6. Five British frigates are transferred and given famous names: HIPPER, SCHARNHORST, SCHEER, GRAF SPEE, and GNEISENAU.

AUGUST 3, 1958

The U.S. nuclear submarine NAUTILUS reaches the North Pole under the ice.

1959

The U.S. Maritime Administration's SAVANNAH is launched, the world's first commercial atomic-powered ship. Steam produced by nuclear reactors drives a double reduction-geared turbine to one screw. No funnel is necessary in such a ship. Sixty passengers could be carried. After trials and various commercial voyages, she was laid up.

1959

The first nuclear submarine built for the Russian Navy is launched. She is the LENINSKY KOMSOMOL.

1959

The Royal Mail Line have three sister ships built for the River Plate route, the AMAZON, the ARAGON, and the ARLANZA. They have bridge and passenger accommodation split by a hatch to enable all unloading berths to be used simultaneously.

JANUARY 1959

The Danish ship HANS HEDTOFT, on her maiden voyage on the Denmark-Greenland service, hits an iceberg off Greenland and is never seen again.

JANUARY 31, 1959

National Bulk Carriers' UNIVERSE APOLLO is commissioned into service. At 104,520 tons deadweight, she is the largest ship in the world to date.

APRIL 15, 1959

The U.S.S. SKIPJACK is commissioned. She is

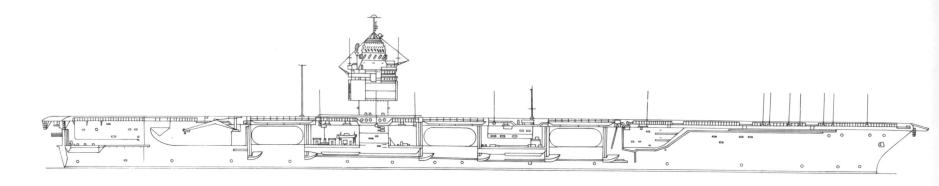

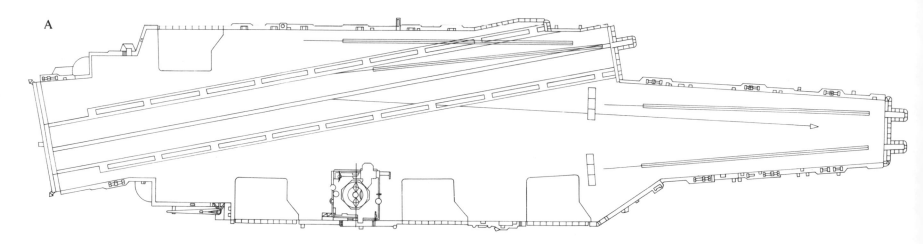

the first nuclear submarine with the tear-drop-shaped high-speed hull.

NOVEMBER 10, 1959
The U.S.S. TRITON is the longest submarine built to date. She is 447.5 foot (136.4 m) long.

DECEMBER 30, 1959
The U.S.S. GEORGE WASHINGTON is the first submarine to be armed with Polaris missiles. She has two 112-man crews, 'blue' and 'gold', each doing alternative patrols.

1960
The TRITON becomes the first submarine to circumnavigate the world under water, a distance of 41,300 miles (76,488 km) in eighty-three days at an average speed of eighteen knots. Off the Falkland Islands, her conning tower broke surface so that a sick sailor could be taken off.

1960
The JAMES LYKES, built for Lykes Brothers of New Orleans, is the first American flag dry-cargo ship to be built since the war.

JULY 20, 1960
The GEORGE WASHINGTON, off Cape Canaveral,

Florida, is the first vessel to fire Polaris missiles whilst lying on the sea bed. She is also the first submarine to have her nuclear reactor refuelled, after having sailed 100,000 miles (185,200 km) in four and a half years.

1961
The CAP SAN NICHOLAS is built for the Hamburg South America Line. She is the most markedly streamlined cargo vessel to date.

1961
The SOVIETSKAYA ROSSIA is the largest whaling factory ship built yet. She is also the largest Russian merchant ship.

1961
The P. & O. Line's CANBERRA is the biggest ship built for the Australian service, and the largest ship with engines aft.

1961
The American aircraft carrier ENTERPRISE is the largest warship yet built. She is 1,123 foot (342.3 m) long, 257 foot (78.3 m) wide, and weighs 89,600 tons full load. She has four propellers, which are driven by four steam turbines powered by eight nuclear reactors. Her crew consists of 3,100 sailors and 2,400 airmen.

A *The nuclear-powered aircraft carrier* ENTERPRISE, *1961.*

MODERN PASSENGER SHIPS

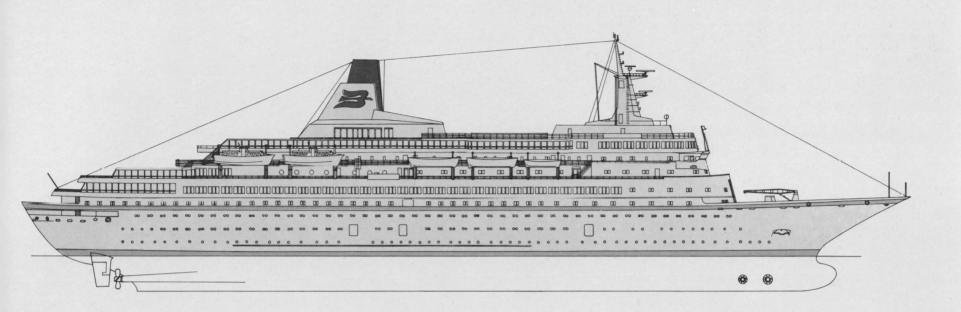

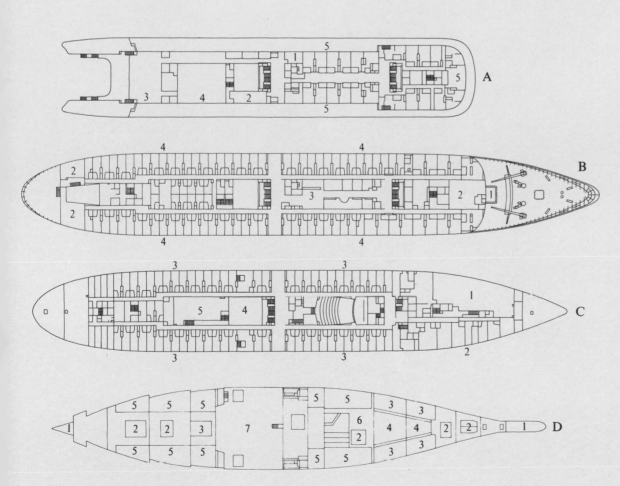

ROYAL VIKING STAR

Cruiser built in 1972 for Det Bergenske Damp-
skibsselskab Star Cruises by Wärtsilä in Finland.
She has a speed of 21.5 knots.

A *Promenade deck.*
1 *Library*
2 *Card room*
3 *Bar*
4 *Club room*
5 *De luxe cabins and suites*
B *Atlantic deck.*
1 *Crew's swimming pool*
2 *Crew's day rooms*
3 *Reception and shopping area*
4 *Cabins*
C *Mediterranean deck.*
1 *Crew's mess*
2 *Hospital area*
3 *Cabins*
4 *Main engine casing*
5 *Air conditioning plant*
D *Tank top.*
1 *Water ballast*
2 *Sewage tanks*
3 *Fresh water tanks*
4 *Potable water tanks*
5 *Fuel oil tanks*
6 *Pump room*
7 *Main engine room*

TOR BRITANNIA

A One of the largest car-ferries in the world, TOR BRITANNIA went into service on the North Sea in June, 1975, between Gothenburg, Felixstowe, and Amsterdam. She has a maximum speed of 26 knots, with a service speed of 24.5 knots. Her crew numbers 140, and she can take 1,230 passengers and 420 cars. Her builders were Flender Werft of Lübeck, West Germany.

1 Bow thrusters
2 Navigation deck
3 Sundecks
4 Cabins
5 Sauna
6 Shopping centre
7 Swimming pool
8 Casino
9 Machine room
10 Restaurants
11 Main engines, which consist of four Pielstick 12PC3V engines with a total of 4,600 horse power
12 Stabilizers
13 Upper car deck
14 Lower car deck
15 Stern ramp
16 Night club
17 Bar
B Side and plan elevations.

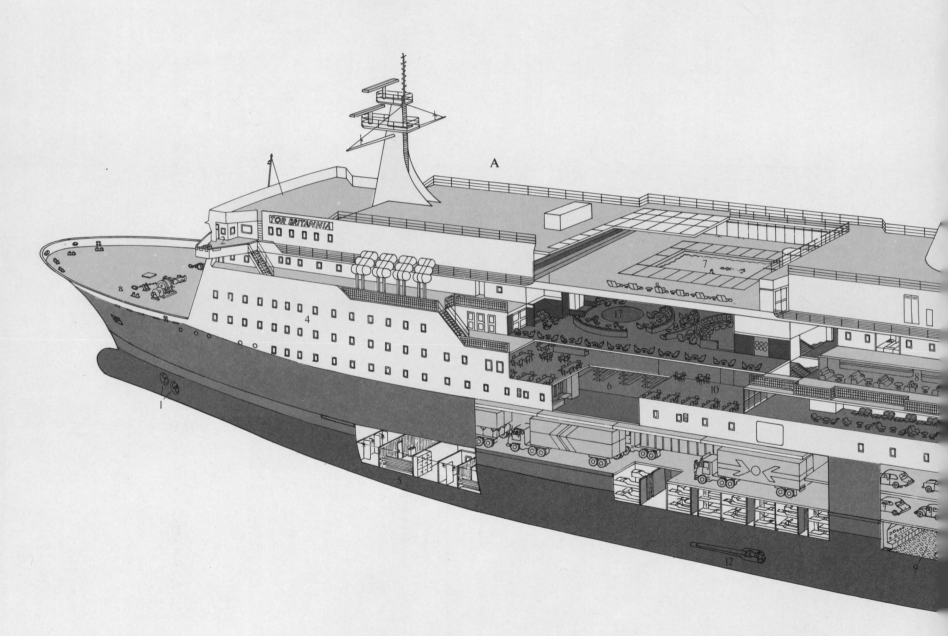

TOR LINE

B

TOR BRITANNIA
Göteborg

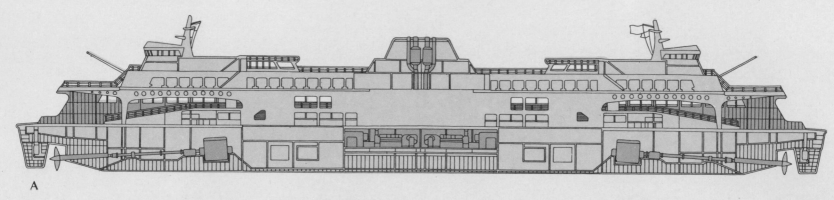

A

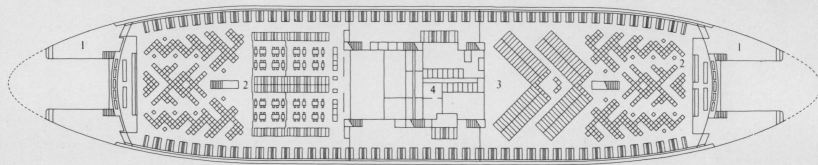

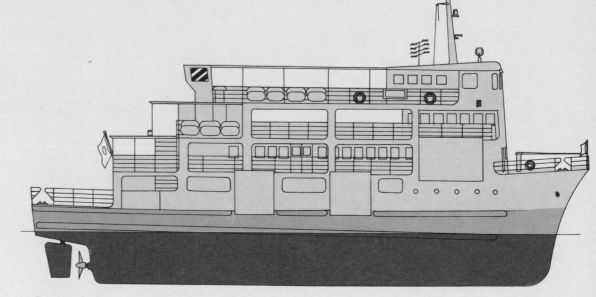

A SPOKANE, *an American double-ender ferry, 1974.*
She is used on short return trips, and does not need
to turn around. The vessel is intended for inter-
island service in sheltered waters.

1 *Passenger embarcation areas*
2 *Passenger lounges*
3 *Cafeteria*
4 *Galley*

B AJISAI *is a Japanese catamaran passenger ferry*
capable of carrying 1,508 passengers. She traffics
the Nagasaki-Koyaki Island-Taka Island route
and has a service speed of 12.3 knots.

1 *Plan of the upper deck*

B

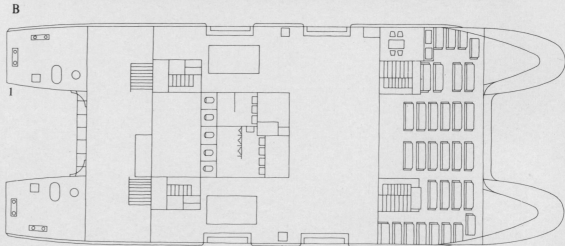

A FRANCE, *1962.*

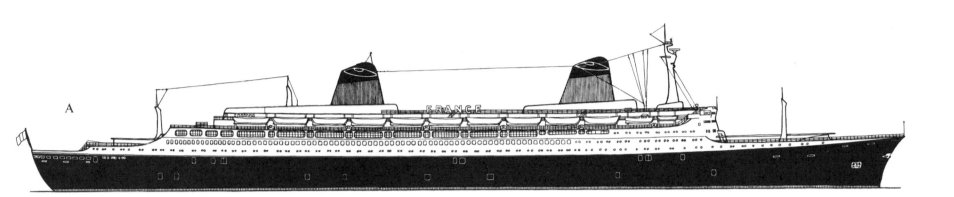

A

FRANCE

SEPTEMBER 9, 1961
The first ever nuclear-powered surface warship, the U.S.S. LONG BEACH, is commissioned. She is also the first warship to have guided missiles as her main armament.

1962
The longest passenger ship in the world is built. She is the French Line's FRANCE. Built at Penhoet St. Nazaire, she is the last transatlantic liner in the Grand Tradition, a tradition that was started by Cunard's MAURETANIA in 1907.

The FRANCE, which cost £30,000,000 to build, is 1,035 foot (315.5 m) long, and 66,300 tons gross. She has a service speed of 31 knots, and can accommodate 2,044 passengers.

1962
The PRESIDENT LINCOLN and the PRESIDENT TYLER are the first cargo liners to be built for container carriage. Only one hold was specifically adapted to carry six tiers of containers that would accommodate 108 units. Another 18 units could be carried on deck. The hold was served by an unloading gantry. These vessels, built for the American President Line, represent an intermediate stage in the development of the container ship.

1962
The world's largest tanker to date is built for the Niarchos Group's Manhattan Tankers. She is the MANHATTAN, 106,500 tons deadweight. She is 940 foot (286.5 m) long by 132 foot (40.2 m) wide, and her gross tonnage is 65,740. Later on, she is fitted with ice-breaker bows, and tried on northern Alaska's oil-fields.

APRIL 17, 1963
The DREADNOUGHT, Britain's first nuclear submarine, is commissioned. The hull is British-built, and the reactors are American.

DECEMBER 23, 1964
The Greek ship LAKONIA, ex-JOHAN VAN OLDEN-BARNEVELDT, catches fire whilst cruising off Madeira with 1,028 aboard. One hundred and thirty-two people perish.

1965
The British Yukon Navigation Co.'s FRANK H. BROWN is the first ship to be designed totally for container carriage. She is 7,600 tons gross and operates from Vancouver to Skagway, carrying 260 containers.

1965
The Union Castle Line's GOOD HOPE CASTLE and SOUTHAMPTON CASTLE are built, the fastest cargo liners to date. At 22½ knots, they are designed to maintain the same speed in service as the fastest passenger liners.

1967
Atlantic Container Lines' ATLANTIC SAGA, ATLANTIC SONG, ATLANTIC SPAN, and ATLANTIC STAR are the first examples of the modern container ship. Their main features are that they have no handling gear, but, instead, side loading doors and a stern ramp.

Each of these ships has a capacity of 525 twenty-foot (6.1 m) containers, and a full cargo of cars, loaded by the stern ramp.

1967
Russia's largest research ship, the KOSMONAUT VLADIMIR KOMAROV, is built. She is the converted cargo ship GENICHESK, and is used to study the higher layers of the atmosphere in the tropical Atlantic zones.

MARCH 18, 1967
The TORREY CANYON, one of the new breed of 'super-tankers', becomes the largest ship to be wrecked when she drives onto the Seven Sisters Reef, off south-west England, ripping a 650-foot (198.1 m) long hole in her hull. This causes the first major oil pollution problem since the introduction of V.L.C.C.s—Very Large Crude Carriers—over 100,000 tons. The TORREY CANYON was fully laden with 117,000 tons of oil. Her wreck was bombed and set on fire in order to burn up as much oil as possible. But many miles of coastline were polluted.

JUNE 1967

The Six Day War between Israel and her Arab neighbours causes the closing of the Suez Canal. Fourteen ships are trapped in the Bitter Lakes, and one in Lake Timsah. They remain there until the canal is finally cleared.

JANUARY 23, 1968

The U.S. Navy ship PUEBLO, under Lieutenant-Commander Bucher, is captured by the North Koreans, who accuse her of spying.

MAY 1968

The OTTO HAHN becomes East Germany's first, and the world's third, nuclear-powered surface ship.

JULY 16, 1968

India purchases four Russian 'F' class submarines. The first to be commissioned is the KALVARI.

AUGUST 24, 1968

UNIVERSE IRELAND, the first of six sisters built for the National Bulk Carriers, is completed. At 149,609 tons gross, she is the world's then largest ship.

1969

The Italian Navy's first guided-missile helicopter cruiser, the VITTORIO VENETO, enters service. She is armed with Terrier missiles, and has a flight deck for nine torpedo-carrying helicopters.

1969

The KHIAN CAPTAIN is built for the Freedom Maritime Corporation, Greece, and is the first replacement vessel for the ubiquitous Liberty ship, which was the largest class of standard vessel from the Second World War.

1969

The world's first LASH (Lighter Aboard SHip) vessel, the ACADIA FOREST, is built for the Torrey Mosvold Line, Norway. She carries seventy-three lighters of 370 tons capacity. These are loaded and unloaded over the stern by a 510-ton gantry crane.

MAY 2, 1969

The Cunard Line's QUEEN ELIZABETH II commences her maiden voyage.

1971

LE REDOUTABLE is commissioned. She is the first French nuclear-powered submarine.

1971

There are six liners built this year, all of them for cruising. They are the NORDIC PRINCE, the SONG OF NORWAY, and the SUN VIKING for the Royal Caribbean Cruise Lines, Norway; the SEA VENTURE for Norwegian Cruising A/S; and the CUNARD ADVENTURER and the CUNARD AMBASSADOR for Cunard.

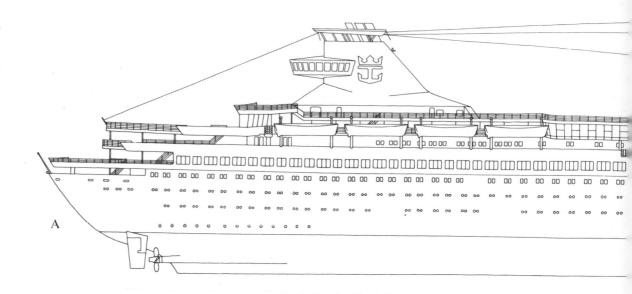

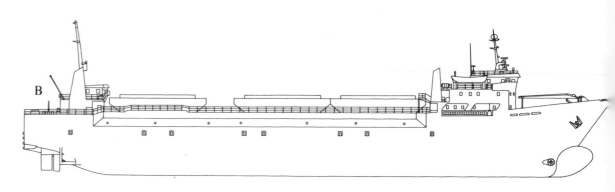

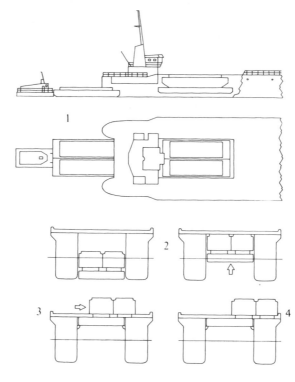

1971

Scarsdale Shipping Co.'s EUROLINER is the world's first gas-turbine container ship. She is also the fastest ship of her kind, having a speed of 25 knots. EUROLINER is operated by Seatrain International.

AUGUST 6, 1971

Tokyo Tanker Co.'s NISSEKI MARU becomes, at 372,400 tons deadweight (186,500 tons gross), the largest ship in the world to date. She took only ten months to build in No. 2 Dock at the Kure Shipyard. She is 1,142 foot (348.1 m) long by 179 foot (54.6 m) wide.

DECEMBER 1971

During the war between India and Pakistan, four neutral merchant ships are lost.

1972

The Trio Line is set up by three companies, H.A.P.A.G.-Lloyd of Germany, Ben Line of Britain, and the Japanese Nippon Yusen, to operate a direct Europe—Far East container service. N.Y.K.'s KAMAKURA MARU inaugurates the service. Her capacity is 1,838 containers, and her average speed is 25.5 knots.

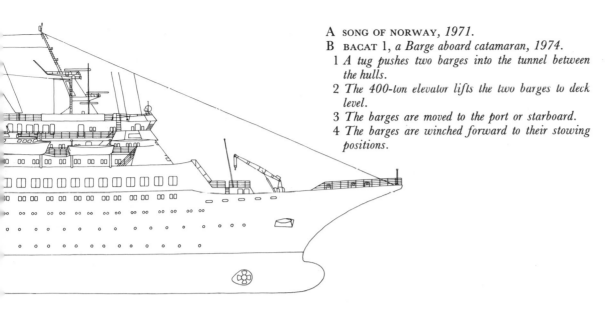

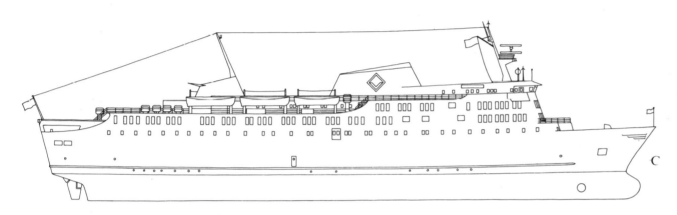

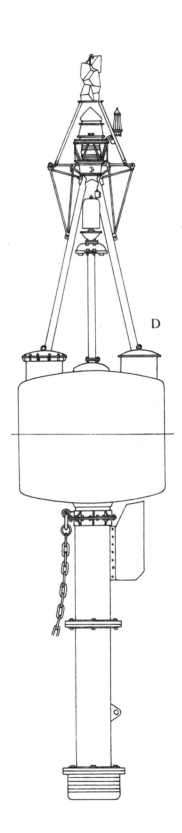

A SONG OF NORWAY, *1971.*
B BACAT 1, *a Barge aboard catamaran, 1974.*
  1 *A tug pushes two barges into the tunnel between the hulls.*
  2 *The 400-ton elevator lifts the two barges to deck level.*
  3 *The barges are moved to the port or starboard.*
  4 *The barges are winched forward to their stowing positions.*

C VIKING 5, *a roro ferry built in Germany, 1974, for the Stockholm-Helsinki route.*
D *A modern light buoy.*

JANUARY 9, 1972

SEAWISE UNIVERSITY is burnt out in Hong Kong harbour. She is the ex-Cunard Line's QUEEN ELIZABETH, which had been reconstructed at a cost of £11,000,000.

1973

The BENALDER becomes the largest container ship to date. She carries 73,596 tons deadweight, and is capable of over 30 knots. She is 947 foot (288.6 m) long by 106 foot (32.3 m) wide and can carry 2,687 twenty-foot (6.1 m) containers.

1973

The SVEALAND is built for the Broström Line. At 282,450 tons deadweight, this oil-ore carrier is the world's largest dry cargo ship to date.

1974

Globtik Tankers receive delivery of the world's largest ship to date, the GLOBTIK LONDON. Built at the Kure Shipyards in Japan, she carries 483,939 tons deadweight, and has a cargo capacity of 20,518,015 cubic foot (581,000 m³). She is 1,220 foot (371.8 m) long by 173 foot (57.9 m) in the beam. Her crew numbers only thirty-eight.

1974

The Brazilian Navy's guided missile destroyer NITHEROI is launched. Built by Vosper Thorny-croft at Southampton, England, she is the first of six ships ordered by the Brazilian Navy in September 1970 for a total order amount of £100,000,000. The last of the ships is due to be delivered in 1979.

1974

Work begins on clearing the Suez Canal, which has been blocked since the Six Day War. British, French and American naval groups start the dangerous task of removing all the explosive devices left there.

JUNE 5, 1975

The Suez Canal, finally cleared of wrecks and explosives, is re-opened for traffic. Over 600,000 explosive devices of all kinds have been removed at a cost of about £130,000,000 ($300,000,000). The voyage from the Persian Gulf to, for instance, the port of Rotterdam is thus cut from twenty-eight to eighteen days.

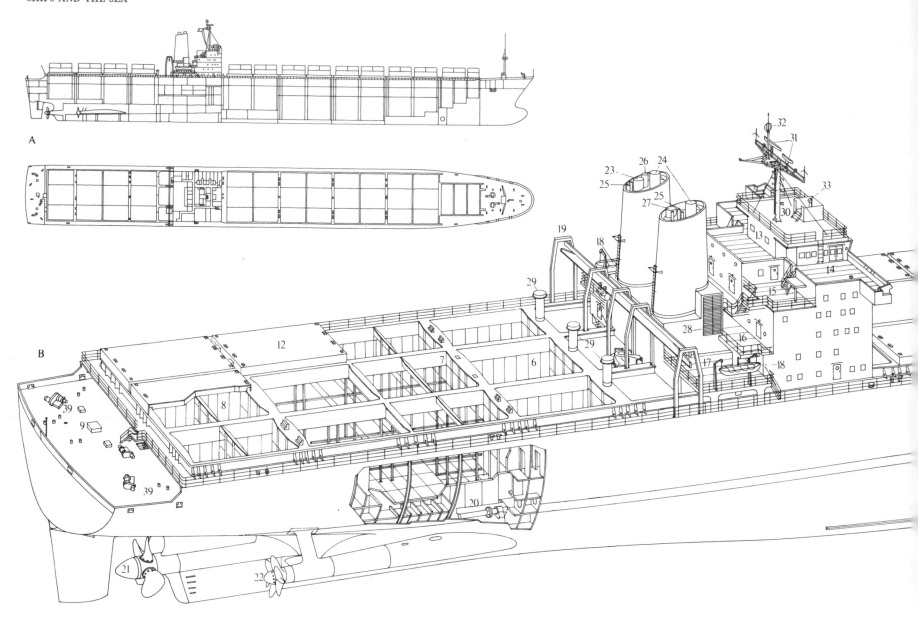

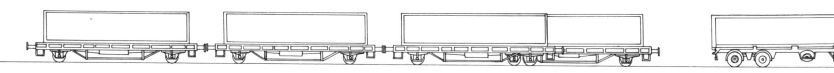

SELANDIA

A triple-screw container ship for the East Asiatic Co.

A *Side and plan views showing how the containers are packed.*

B *A sectioned drawing of the vessel.*

1-8 *Holds*
 9 *Mooring deck*
10 *Main transverse bulkhead*
11 *Water ballast tanks*
12 *Hatch covers*
13 *Wheel house*
14 *Navigating bridge deck*

15 *Captain's deck*
16 *Officers' deck*
17 *Boat deck*
18 *Motor lifeboats*
19 *Service gantry crane*
20 *Centre propeller shaft*
21 *Four-bladed centre propeller*
22 *Six-bladed wing propeller*
23 *Centre engine exhaust*
24 *Wing engine exhausts*
25 *Auxiliary engine exhausts*
26 *Oil-fired boiler uptake*
27 *Sludge burner uptake*

28 *Engine room ventilation*
29 *Hold ventilators*
30 *Radar mast*
31 *Radar scanners*
32 *Hinged D.F. aerial*
33 *Magnetic compass*
34 *Bow thruster propeller*
35 *Stabilizer*
36 *Bilge keel*
37 *Foremast*
38 *Combined winch/windlass*
39 *Mooring winches*
40 *Portable derrick*

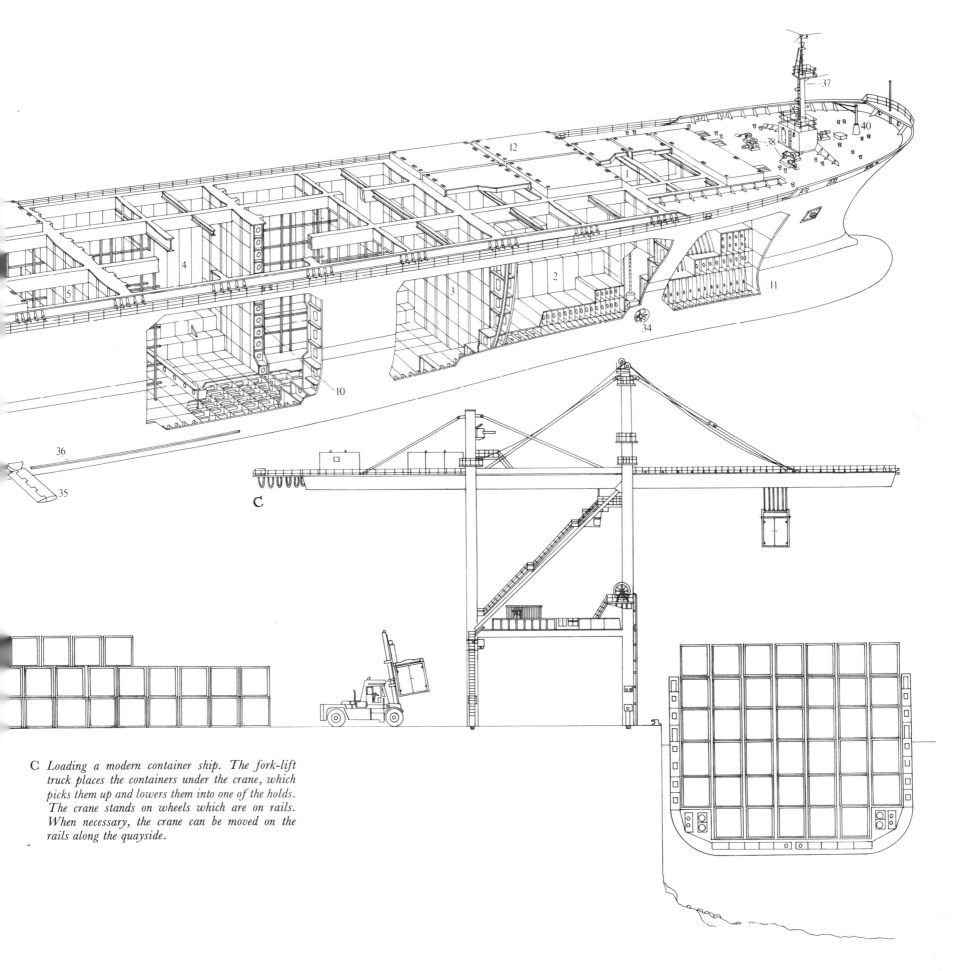

C *Loading a modern container ship. The fork-lift truck places the containers under the crane, which picks them up and lowers them into one of the holds. The crane stands on wheels which are on rails. When necessary, the crane can be moved on the rails along the quayside.*

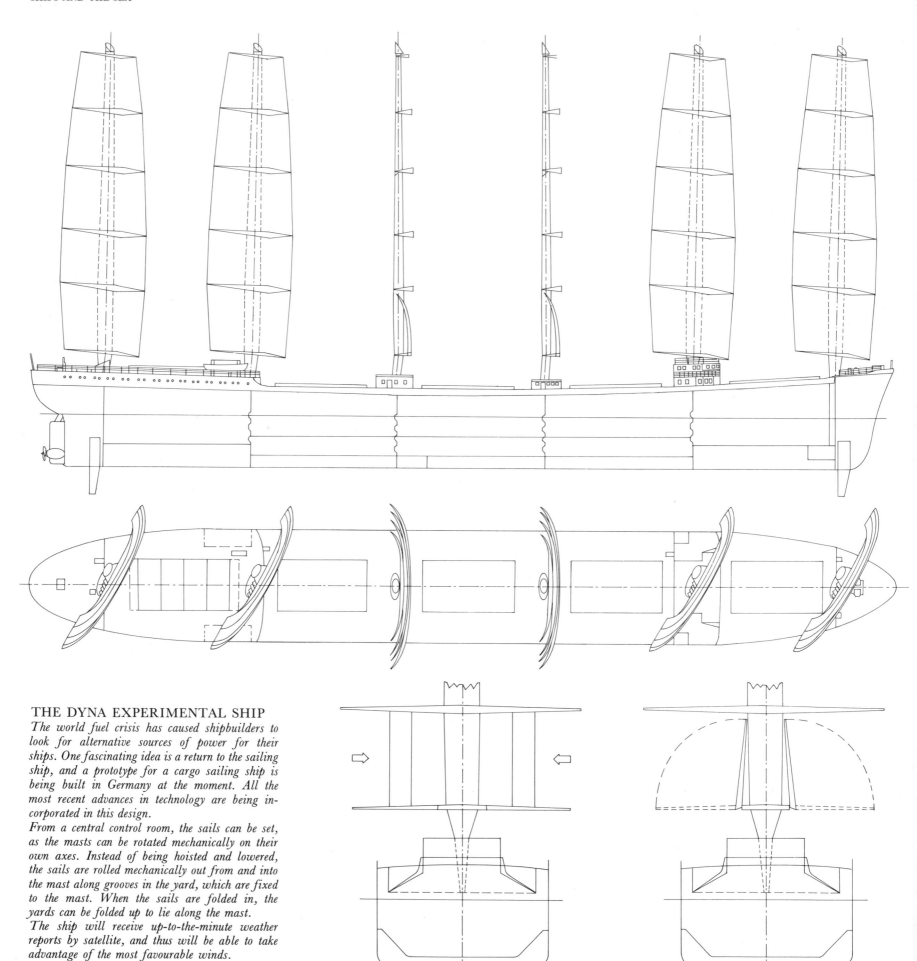

THE DYNA EXPERIMENTAL SHIP

The world fuel crisis has caused shipbuilders to look for alternative sources of power for their ships. One fascinating idea is a return to the sailing ship, and a prototype for a cargo sailing ship is being built in Germany at the moment. All the most recent advances in technology are being incorporated in this design.

From a central control room, the sails can be set, as the masts can be rotated mechanically on their own axes. Instead of being hoisted and lowered, the sails are rolled mechanically out from and into the mast along grooves in the yard, which are fixed to the mast. When the sails are folded in, the yards can be folded up to lie along the mast.

The ship will receive up-to-the-minute weather reports by satellite, and thus will be able to take advantage of the most favourable winds.

BIBLIOGRAPHY

ABELL, SIR WESTCOTT. *The Shipwright's Trade*, Cambridge 1948

ALBOLDT, E. *Die Tragödie der alten deutschen Marine*, Berlin 1928

ANDERSON, R. C. *Rigging of Ships 1600-1720*, London 1927
—*Oared Fighting Ships*, London 1962

ASHLEY, CLIFFORD W. *The Ashley Book of Knots*, New York 1944

BAKER, W. A. *The Development of Wooden Ship Construction*, Quincy, Massachusetts 1955
—*The Engine Powered Vessel*, New York 1965

BARFOD, JØRGEN H. *Orlogsflåden på Niels Juels Tid. 1648-1699*, København 1963

BASS, GEORGE F. (ed.) *A History of Seafaring*, London 1972

BATTINE, R. *Method of Building and Rigging Ships of War*, London 1684

BAXTER, JAMES PHINNEY. *The Introduction of the Ironclad Warship*, University of Harvard n.d.

BERGSTRÖM, C. A. *Fartygsmaskiner*, Stockholm 1934

BLANCKLEY, T. R. *The Naval Expositer*, London 1750

BONWICK, GEORGE J. *Seamanship Handbook*, Liverpool 1952

BOWEN, FRANK C. *A Century of Atlantic Travel, 1830-1930*, Boston 1930
—*Mail and Passenger Steamships*, London 1928

BRAGADIN, M. *Che ha fatto la Marina?*, Milano 1955

BRANCH, W. J. V. and BROOK-WILLIAMS, E. *A Short History of Navigation*, Annapolis 1942

BRIN, B. *La nostra Marina Militare*, Roma 1881

BRØGGER, A. W. and SHETELIG, H. *The Viking Ships*, 2nd ed. Oslo 1951

BROWNE, DOUGLAS G. *The Floating Bulwark. The Story of the Fighting Ship 1514-1942*, London 1963

BUCHANAN, LAMONT. *Ships of Steam*, New York 1956

BUCKNELL, RIXON. *Boat Trains & Channel Packets*, London 1957

BUGLER, ARTHUR. *H. M. S. Victory*, London 1966

CASSON, LIONEL. *The Ancient Mariners*, London 1959
—*Illustrated History of Ships and Boats*, New York 1964
—*Scheepvaart in de oudheid*, Utrecht 1964

CHAPELLE, HOWARD I. *The Baltimore Clipper, Its Origin and Development*, Salem, Massachusetts 1930
—*The History of the American Sailing Ships*, New York 1935
—*The History of the American Sailing Navy*, New York 1949
—*The Pioneer Steamship Savannah: A Study for a scale Model*, Washington 1961
—*The Search for Speed under Sail, 1700-1855*, New York 1967

CHAPMAN, F. H. AF. *Architectura Navalis Mercatoria*, Stockholm 1768

CHARNOCK, J. *History of Marine Architecture*, London 1800-02

CHASSELOUP-LAUBAT, M. DE. *Les Marines de guerre modernes*, Paris 1903

CHATTERTON, E. KEBLE. *Steamships and their Story*, Toronto and Melbourne 1910

CLERC RAMPAL, GEORGE. *La Marine française pendant la grande guerre 1914-1918*, Paris 1919

COOPER, JAMES FENIMORE. *The History of the Navy*, Philadelphia 1847

COWBURN, PHILIP. *The Warship in History*, London 1966

CROUCH, H. F. *Nuclear Ship Propulsion*, Cambridge 1960

DAYTON, F. E. *Steamboat Days*, New York 1939

DEACON, G. E. R. (ed.). *Seas, Maps and Men*, New York 1962

DEGENKOLV, H. *Oplysninger vedrørende Den Danske Flaade i sidste Aarhundrede*, København 1906

DI GIAMBERARDINO, OSCAR. *L'arte della guerra sul mare*, Roma 1938

DODMAN, FRANK E. *The Observer's Book of Ships*, London 1961

DOLBY, JAMES. *The Steel Navy—A History in Silhouette 1860—1963*, London 1965

DUGAN, JAMES. *The Great Iron Ship*, New York 1953

EIDEM, O. and LUTKEN, O. *Vor Somagts Historie*, København 1905

ELIAS, J. E. *Schetsen uit de geschiedenis van ons Zeewezen*, 's-Gravenhage 1916-30

ENGSTRÖM, IVAR A. *Lärobok i skeppsbyggeri*, Stockholm 1924

ESKEW, G. L. *The Pageant of the Packets*, New York 1929

ESPAGNAC DU RAVAY. *Vingt ans de Politique navale 1919-1939*, Paris-Grenoble 1941

EVERS, F. J. H. *Oorlogsschepen*, Amsterdam 1902

EVERS, HEINRICH. *Kriegsschiffbau*, Berlin 1943

FAHEY, JAMES C. *The Ships and Aircraft of the U. S. Fleet*, New York, etc., 1939-65

FALCONER, W. *Universal Dictionary of the Marine*, London 1769 & 1815

FERNANDEZ-DURO, CESAREO. *Armada Espanola*, Madrid 1903

FINCHAM, J. *History of Naval Architecture*, London 1851

FLEXNER, J. T. *Steamboats Come True*, New York 1944

FORSHELL, HANS. *Minan i sjökriget*, Stockholm 1959

FRY, HENRY. *The History of North Atlantic Steam Navigation*, New York 1896

GELDER, M. J. DE. *Elementair overzicht van bouw der hedendaagsche oorlogsschepen*, Amsterdam 1897

GIBBS, C. R. VERNON. *Passenger Liners of the Western Ocean*, London 1952
—*British Passenger Liners of the Five Oceans*, London 1963

GIORGERINI, G. and NANI, A. *Le Marine Militari nel Mondo*, Milano 1961
—*Le Navi di Linea Italiane*, Roma 1961
—*Gli Incrociatori Italiani*, Roma 1964

GRÖNER, ERICH. *Die deutschen Kriegsschiffe 1815-1945*, München 1966-67

HAMBLETON, F. C. *Famous Paddle Steamers*, London 1948

HARDY, A. C. *Havsfiske i hela världen*, Malmö 1947
—*Modern Marine Engineering. Vol. II*, London 1948
—*The Book of The Ship*, London 1948

HEDDERWICK, P. *Treatise on Marine Architecture*, Edinburgh 1830

HOLMES, G. C. V. *Ancient and Modern Ships*, London 1910

HUTCHINSON, W. *Treatise of Naval Architecture*, Liverpool 1794

JONGE, J. C. DE. *Geschiedenis van het Nederlandsche Zeewezen*, Harlem 1858-62

JOUAN, RENÉ. *Historie de la Marine Francaise* (2 volumes), Paris 1932

KERCHOVE, RENÉ DE. *International Maritime Dictionary*, New York 1948

KNOX, DUDLEY W. *A History of the United States Navy* (revised), New York, 1948

KVARNING, LARS ÅKE. *Wasa*, Stockholm 1968

LACOUR GAYET, G. *La Marine militaire de la France pendant le règne de Louis XV*, Paris 1905
—*La Marine militaire de la France pendant le règne de Louis XVI*, Paris 1909

LANDSTRÖM, B. *The Ship*, Stockholm and London 1961

LANE, F. C. *Venetian Ships and Shipbuilding of the Renaissance*, Baltimore 1934

LA ROËRIE, G. and VIVIELLE, J. *Navires et Marins (de la rame à l'hélice)*, Paris 1930

LAUBEUF, MAXIME and STROH, HENRI. *Sous-marins*, Paris 1923

LAUGHTON, L. G. C. *Old Ship Figureheads and Sterns*, London and New York 1925

LAWSON, W. *Pacific Steamers*, Glasgow 1927

LE FLEMING, H. M. *Warships of World War I*, London 1961

LE MASSON, HENRI. *Historie du torpilleur en France 1872-1940*, Paris 1967
—*La Marine de guerre moderne (porte-avions, sous-marins, escorteurs)*, Paris 1950

LENTON, H. T. and COLLEDGE, J. J. *Warships of World War II*, London 1964

LEWIS, MICHAEL. *The Navy of Britain*, London 1948
—*Armada Guns*, London 1961

LINDSAY, W. S. *History of Merchant Shipping and Ancient Commerce*, London 1876

LINDSTRÖM, CLAES. *Sjöfartens historia*, Stockholm 1951

LISLE, B. O. *Tanker Technique 1700-1936*, London 1936

LOIR, MAURICE. *La Marine francaise*, Paris 1893

LUBBOCK, BASIL. *The Western Ocean Packets*, Glasgow 1925
—*The Last of the Windjammers*, Glasgow 1927
—*Barbow's Journal 1659-1703*, London 1934

MACBRIDE, ROBERT. *Civil War Ironclads*, Philadelphia 1962

MACINTYRE, DONALD and BATHE, B. W. *Man-of-War*, New York 1969

MAHAN, A. T. *The Influence of Sea Power upon History, 1660-1783*, New York 1962

MANNING, T. D. and WALKER, C. F. *British Warship Names*, London 1959

HARRISON MATTHEWS, L. *The Whale*, London 1968

MIDDENDORF, F. *Bemastung und Takelung der Schiffe*, Leipzig 1903

MOLLI, G. *La Marina Antica e Moderna*, Genève 1906

MOORE, A. H. *Sailing Ships of War 1800-1860*, London and New York 1926

MORDAL, JACQUES. *25 Siècles de guerre sur mer*, Paris 1959

MORRISON, J. H. *History of American Steam Navigation*, New York 1903

MUNCHING, L. L. VON. *Oorlogsschepen van vandaag*, Amsterdam 1949
—*Moderne Oorlogsschepen*, Alkmaar 1962
—*Vliegkampschepen*, Alkmaar 1964

MURRAY, ANDREW. *The Theory and Practice of Shipbuilding*, Edinburgh 1861
—*Ship-building in Iron and Wood*, Edinburgh 1863

NILSSON, N. G. and ÅSBRINK, G. *Sveriges sjöfart*, Stockholm 1921

OPPENHEIM, M. *Administration of the Royal Navy, 1509-1660*, London 1896

PAASCH, H. *From Keel to Truck*, Antwerpen 1885
—*Marine Encyklopedia*, Antwerpen 1885

PARIS, EDMOND. *Souvenirs de Marine* (6 volumes), Paris 1882-1908

PARKER, H. and BOWEN, F. C. *Mail and Passenger Steamships of the 19th Century*, London 1928

PESCE, G. -L. *La Navigation sousmarine*, Paris 1912

POTTER, EDWARD B. (ed.). *The United States and World Sea Power*, Eaglewood Cliffs, New York 1955

PREBLE, G. H. *Origin and Development of Steam Navigation*, Philadelphia 1895

RADCLIFFE, WILLIAM. *Fishing from the Earliest Time*, London 1921

RANDACCIO, CARLO. *Storia Navale Antica e Moderna*, Roma 1891

REED, E. J. *Transactions of the Institution of Naval Architects*, London 1860

RITTMEYER, R. *Seekriege und Seekriegswesen in ihrer weltgeschichtlichen Entwicklung*, Berlin 1907-11

RONCIÈRE, CHARLES DE LA. *Historie de la Marine française*, Paris 1898-1932

RONCIÈRE, CHARLES DE LA and CLERC RAMPAL, GEORGE. *Histoire de la Marine française*, Paris 1935

ROOIJ, G. DE. *Practical Shipbuilding*, Haarlem 1961

ROSSELL, H. E. *Types of Naval Ships*, London 1945

RÅLAMB, ÅKE CLASSON. *Skeps Byggerij eller adelig öfnings tionde tom*, Stockholm 1691

RÖDING, J. H. *Allgemeines Worterbuch der Marine*, Hamburg 1798

SALAUN, H. *La Marine française 1871-1932*, Paris 1934

SAVANT, JEAN. *Historie de la Marine*, Paris 1964

SCHOERNER, G. *Regalskeppet*, Stockholm 1964

SLOAN, EDWARD W. *Benjamin Franklin Isherwood, Naval Engineer*, Annapolis, Maryland 1965

SMITH, EDGAR C. *A short History of Naval and Marine Engineering*, Cambridge 1938

SPRATT, H. P. *Outline History of Transatlantic Steam Navigation*, London 1950
—*Merchant Steamers and Motorships*, London 1949
—*Marine Engineering*, London 1953
—*The Birth of the Steamboat*, London 1958

STANTON, SAMUEL W. *American Steam Vessels*, New York 1895

STEEL, D. *Elements and Practice of Rigging and Seamanship*, London 1794
—*Naval Architecture*, London 1804

STENZEL, A. *Seekriegsgeschichte in ihren wichtigsten Abschnitten mit Berücksichtigung der Seetaktik*, Hannover and Leipzig 1907-11

STEVENS, J. R. *Ole Time Ships*, Toronto 1949

SUTHERLAND, W. *Shipbuilding Unveiled*, London 1717

SWANN, LEONARD A. *John Roach, Maritime Entrepreneur*, Annapolis Maryland 1965

Svenska Flottans Historia (publ. by AB Allhems Förlag), Malmö 1942-45

SVENSSON, SAM. *Segel genom sekler*, London 1961

THOMAZI, A. *Napoléon et ses Marins*, Paris 1950

THROCKMORTON, PETER. *Shipwrecks and Archeology*, Boston 1970

TRE TRYCKARE. *The Lore of Ships*, Göteborg 1963

TUTE, WARREN. *Atlantic Conquest*, Toronto 1962

TYLER, D. B. *Steam Conquers the Atlantic*, New York 1939

UGGLA, C. L. *Afhandling uti skeppsbyggeri till navigationsskolornas tjenst*, Göteborg 1856

UNDERHILL, HAROLD A. *Masting and Rigging the Clipper Ships and Ocean Carrier*, Glasgow 1946

VAN NOUHUYS, J. *De eerste Nederlandsche Transatlantic Stoomvaart in 1827 van zr MS Stoompakket Curacao*—Vol. L III Werken der Linschotenvereeniging

VREUGDENHIL, A. *Koningen, Scheepsbouwers en Zeevaarders*, Amsterdam 1951

WATTS, ANTHONY J. *Japanese Warships of World War II*, London 1966

SHIP INDEX

238

GENERAL INDEX